Objective-C® Programming

FOR

DUMMIES®

Objective-C® Programming

FOR

DUMMIES®

by Neal Goldstein and Karl G. Kowalski

WILEY

John Wiley & Sons, Inc.

Objective-C® Programming For Dummies®

Published courtesy of EMC Corporation by
John Wiley & Sons, Inc.
111 River Street
Hoboken, NJ 07030-5774

www.wiley.com

WILEY

About the Authors

Neal Goldstein is a recognized leader in making state-of-the-art and cutting-edge technologies practical for commercial and enterprise development. He was one of the first technologists to work with commercial developers at firms such as Apple Computer, Lucasfilm, and Microsoft to develop commercial applications using object-based programming technologies. He was a pioneer in moving that approach into the corporate world for developers at Liberty Mutual Insurance, USWest (now Verizon), National Car Rental, EDS, and Continental Airlines, showing them how object-oriented programming could solve enterprise-wide problems. His book (with Jeff Alger) on object-oriented development, *Developing Object-Oriented Software for the Macintosh* (Addison Wesley, 1992), introduced the idea of scenarios and patterns to developers. He was an early advocate of the Microsoft .NET framework, and he successfully introduced it into many enterprises, including Charles Schwab. He was one of the earliest developers of Service Oriented Architecture (SOA), and as Senior Vice President of Advanced Technology and the Chief Architect at Charles Schwab, he built an integrated SOA solution that spanned the enterprise, from desktop PCs to servers to complex network mainframes. (He holds four patents as a result.) As one of IBM's largest customers, he introduced the folks at IBM to SOA at the enterprise level and encouraged them to head in that direction.

Since the release of the iPhone SDK in March 2008, he has been focusing on mobile applications. He has had eight applications in the App Store. These include a series of Travel Photo Guides (developed with his partners at mobileforlytwo), and a Digital Field Guides series (http://lp.wileypub.com/DestinationDFGiPhoneApp), developed in partnership with John Wiley & Sons. He also has a free app called Expense Diary that allows you to keep track of things like expenses, mileage, and time by adding them to your calendar.

He has developed mobile strategies for a number of businesses, ranging from National Cinemedia to the American Automobile Association (AAA). His strategies focus on Mobile 2.0 — integrating mobile across the enterprise, creating a consistent user experience across devices and applications in an application ecosystem, and developing a user experience architecture that both leverages — and is constrained by — the device. He has spent the last three years working with mobile device users and developers to determine what makes mobile devices so appealing, what users want from an application on a phone or tablet, and what makes an app compelling. These efforts have resulted in the Application Ecosystem model for mobile applications and an underlying Model Application Controller Architecture based on web services that has become a key element in his client work and his books.

In his copious spare time, he also teaches introductory and advanced classes on iPhone and iPad development (for clients as well as some public classes) and does expert witness work.

Along with those apps and his consulting, he has written several books on iPhone programming, *iPhone Application Development For Dummies* (multiple editions) (Wiley), *Objective-C For Dummies* (Wiley), and he co-authored (with Tony Bove) *iPad Application Development For Dummies* (including multiple editions) (Wiley) and *iPhone Application Development All-in-One For Dummies* (Wiley). He's also the primary author (with Jon Manning and Paris Buttfield-Addison) of *iPhone & iPad Game Development For Dummies*.

Karl Kowalski has traveled the world of computers and software development for far longer than he's willing to admit. He has written programs for airplanes, robots, games, and even particle accelerators, and he has developed software on platforms ranging from desktop computers to mainframes all the way down to smartphones. He is also the author of *Mac Application Development For Dummies* (John Wiley & Sons, Inc., 2011). He lives near Boston and works for RSA, The Security Division of EMC, where he develops security solutions for mobile platforms such as iPhone and BlackBerry, and desktop operating systems such as Windows and Mac OS X. In his spare time, he develops software for smartphones as part of a startup, BlazingApps. And if there are any spare seconds in the day, he does some voice-over work for one of his favorite journals, *The Objective Standard*.

Dedication

To my friends and family, and especially my children Sarah and Evan and my wife, Linda. She deserves special recognition for her support and patience and for maintaining her (and my) sense of humor. Without her support I never would have been able to write 12 books in 3.5 years. Thank you so much.

This is for you
As day follows night
The tunnel ends in the light
Finally time to play

— Neal Goldstein

To my incredible family: Connie, Stanley, Lee Anne, David, Rosemarie, Joseph, Candi, Reeseling the Nieceling, and Mason — thank you for all your love and support.

— Karl Kowalski

Author's Acknowledgments

Acquisitions Editor Kyle Looper for extending the vision of this book and keeping this project on track. Thanks to Project Editor Charlotte Kughen for guiding us through the process and keeping everything on track and Copy Editor John Edwards for helping us make things clear. Tech Editor Jesse Feiler kept us on our toes, and his comments made this a better book. Great job, team, and I deeply appreciate all of your work.

Thanks again to my agent Carole Jelen for her continued work and support in putting and keeping these projects together.

— *Neal Goldstein*

Publisher's Acknowledgments

We're proud of this book; please send us your comments at http://dummies.custhelp.com. For other comments, please contact our Customer Care Department within the U.S. at 877-762-2974, outside the U.S. at 317-572-3993, or fax 317-572-4002.

Some of the people who helped bring this book to market include the following:

Acquisitions and Editorial

Project Editor: Charlotte Kughen,
The Wordsmithery LLC

Senior Acquisitions Editor: Kyle Looper

Copy Editor: John Edwards

Technical Editor: Jesse Feiler

Editorial Manager: Jodi Jensen

Editorial Assistant: Leslie Saxman

Sr. Editorial Assistant: Cherie Case

Cover Photo: © John Shepherd/iStockphoto.com

Cartoons: Rich Tennant
(www.the5thwave.com)

Composition Services

Project Coordinator: Katherine Crocker

Layout and Graphics: Joyce Haughey,
Julie Trippetti

Proofreaders: Lauren Mandelbaum,
Bonnie Mikkelson

Indexer: BIM Indexing & Proofreading Services

Publishing and Editorial for Technology Dummies

    Richard Swadley, Vice President and Executive Group Publisher

    Andy Cummings, Vice President and Publisher

    Mary Bednarek, Executive Acquisitions Director

    Mary C. Corder, Editorial Director

Publishing for Consumer Dummies

    Kathleen Nebenhaus, Vice President and Executive Publisher

Composition Services

    Debbie Stailey, Director of Composition Services

Contents at a Glance

Table of Contents

Introduction

When the folks at John Wiley & Sons approached me about writing *Objective-C Programming For Dummies,* I thought long and hard about it. Within 480 pages, I wanted to be sure that I could explain to someone with no programming experience how to actually create useful programs.

So I started to think about what makes programming so difficult.

It isn't the concept of how programs work, which I cover easily in Part I. And it isn't really the language itself (or the instruction set — I cover that in Chapter 4). It isn't even the user interface — all that code needed to open and close windows, process menus and the mouse and user touches, draw graphics, and play audio and video (did I leave anything out?). No, while all that used to be really hard, now it's made much easier by using the frameworks available with Mac OS X and iOS.

What is really hard, after you understand the language and framework, is how you structure your program — how you actually go about taking your idea for an application and turning it into a robust Objective-C application.

Finding out how to use the tools is (relatively) easy; knowing how to use them to create a useful application is the real challenge.

So, besides explaining the instruction set and everything else involved with coding, what I do along the way is explain the other things you need to know (things like application architecture and design) — those things that will make it possible for you, when you are done with this book, to go out and start developing your first application. Nothing less.

So instead of a book that only shows you *how* to use all the features (instructions and frameworks) available to you, I decided to write a book that shows you both *how* and *why.* I do that by having you start to develop an application in Chapter 5 (after I go over the instruction set) and add to that same application until you end up with it running on both the iPhone and Mac in Chapters 17 and 18. Granted, this application isn't the most exciting one in the world, but it gives you the opportunity to use every feature of Objective-C that you'll need to know to go out and build your own killer app. What's more, you build the application incrementally, just as a professional develops a commercial application. Occasionally, you will enter some code only to delete it later, which may seem annoying at times. However, you will get a flavor for how you'll work when you are out on your own.

And while some development will be annoying and tedious, in general it is fun. So go enjoy yourself while you're finding out about Objective-C. I know I do.

About This Book

Objective-C Programming For Dummies is a beginner's guide to developing applications for both iOS devices and the Mac. You don't need any programming experience to get started. I expect you to come as a blank slate, ready to be filled with useful information and new ways to do things. In some ways, the less you know, the easier it will be for you because you won't have any preconceived notions about programming.

This book distills the hundreds (or even thousands) of pages of Apple documentation, not to mention my own development experience, into only what's necessary to start you developing real applications. I explain not only the language, but also along the way, I explicitly talk about object-oriented principles and how doing things in a certain way (that is, following those principles) leads to more extensible and enhanceable programs, which you will discover is the holy grail of programming.

Conventions Used in This Book

This book guides you through the process of building applications by using Objective-C.

Code examples in this book appear in a monospaced font so that they stand out a bit better. This means that the code you see will look like this:

```
NSLog(@"I am an Objective-C statement.");
```

Objective-C is based on C, which (I want to remind you) *is* case sensitive, so please enter the code that appears in this book *exactly* as it appears in the text. I also use the standard Objective-C naming conventions — for example, class names always start with a capital letter, and the names of methods and instance variables always start with a lowercase letter.

All URLs in this book appear in a monospaced font as well:

```
www.dummies.com
```

If you're ever uncertain about anything in the code, you can always look at the source code at the website associated with this book: www.dummies.com/go/objcprogrammingfd. And from time to time, I provide updates for the code and post other things you might find useful on my website, www.nealgoldstein.com.

Foolish Assumptions

To find out how to program in Objective-C for Mac OS X or iOS, you need a Macintosh computer with the latest version of the Mac OS on it. You also need to download the Software Development Kit (SDK). You don't have to become a registered Apple Developer to do that, but registering with Apple gives you access to all the information Apple provides for understanding Objective-C, iOS, and Mac OS X. I show you how to do both in Chapter 2 (don't worry; it doesn't cost a cent).

I assume that you don't have any programming knowledge but that you have at least a passing acquaintance with some of the ideas, and more important, a desire to know how to program. In general, the code is easy and straightforward (the book isn't written to dazzle you with fancy coding techniques).

I also assume that you're familiar with the Mac and/or iPhone and that you are comfortable doing all the things you have to do on the Mac to run applications, including using the Finder to cruise the file system to see what's there.

How This Book Is Organized

Objective-C Programming For Dummies has five main parts.

Part 1: Getting to the Starting Line

Part I introduces you to the world of application development. You find out how programs work and what you have to do to take an idea and turn it into a computer program. I explain the tools that are available to you and describe how to use them, and I lead you through downloading the Software Development Kit (SDK), which includes Xcode (Apple's development environment for the OS X and iOS operating systems). You get up and running on your first application, which gives you a taste for what words like *compiling* and *building* mean. You also find out how to become a registered Apple Developer, both for the Mac and the iPhone (and if you are an iPhone developer, what you are required to do to distribute your applications through Apple's App Store).

Part II: Speaking the Language of Objective-C

As with any other skill, you have to pay your dues, and that means understanding the instruction set of the language and knowing how to use some of the languagelike features made available to you in the frameworks. You start by building an application that you will add to as you discover more and more about Objective-C.

Think of this as getting down the vocabulary of a new language, but without the pain and all that memorization.

Part III: Walking the Object-Oriented Walk

After you understand the basic instruction set and the other Objective-C and framework features, it's time to put those instructions together to create a program. In this part, I focus on the right way to structure your program — what's known as the *program architecture.* Having the right architecture results in a program that not only works but also can be extended to add new functionality easily. And not only that, it enables you to easily track down and fix those pesky bugs that make their home in everyone's programs. I also show you how to deal with the mundane, but necessary, plumbing issues such as memory management and object initialization.

Whereas Part II is about getting down the vocabulary, Part III is about using the vocabulary to create sentences and paragraphs and even entire books.

Part IV: Moving from Language to Application

With an architecture in place, you can begin to add more and more functionality to your program. You start to work with data and discover some of the tricks that framework developers use to make their frameworks so extensible.

After you have your application doing what you want it to do, you need to take all that functionality and make it available to the user. So, in this part, I show you how your application fits into the user SDK-supplied frameworks that do all the user interface heavy lifting on Mac OS X and iOS. And because you design the application the right way from the start, you'll be able to plug it into the user interface with minimal effort. You just do some building of the user interface in Interface Builder (part of the SDK), add a few lines of code, and you are there. No sweat, no bother. And yes, because you did it the right way from the start, the same application code will run on both the Mac and iOS devices (using the frameworks for Mac OS X and iOS).

Part V: The Part of Tens

Part V consists of voices from the trenches. I also show you some tips on debugging (yes, your application will, upon occasion, have bugs) that might shorten those late, into-the-night debugging sessions that are (unfortunately) part and parcel of being a developer. Although they may not always be fun, solved bugs are often a great source of conversation among developers. I also offer some tips about approaching application development that will lead to good health and happiness as a developer.

Icons Used in This Book

When you see this icon, you can be sure that the code available at this book's website applies to the current example. You can find the code for all projects in this book at www.dummies.com/go/objcprogrammingfd — perfect for those who don't feel like typing the code.

This icon indicates a useful pointer that you shouldn't skip.

This icon represents a friendly reminder. It describes a vital point that you should keep in mind while proceeding through a particular section of the chapter.

This icon signifies that the accompanying explanation might be informative (dare I say, interesting), but it isn't essential to understanding Objective-C application development. Feel free to skip past these tidbits if you like (though skipping while trying to absorb the main concepts may be tricky).

This icon alerts you to potential problems that you may encounter along the way. Read and obey these bits of experience to avoid trouble.

Objective-C Programming For Dummies

On the Web

I've uploaded all the code for the projects in this book to the website at www.dummies.com/go/objcprogrammingfd. You'll find folders for each chapter starting with Chapter 4. In each of these chapter folders is a folder that contains the Xcode project that provides the starting point for that chapter. So for Chapter 4, for example, the folder is labeled `Chapter 4 Start Here`.

Also in the chapter folder is a folder that contains the final version of the project for each chapter (except for Chapter 4 where it isn't applicable). Some chapters also have intermediate versions of the project; so, in Chapter 5, for example, the folders are Chapter 5 A, Chapter 5 B, and so on. I explain what is in each in the corresponding chapter.

Where to Go from Here

Occasionally, we have updates to our technology books. If this book does have technical updates, they will be posted at `www.dummies.com/go/objcprogrammingfdupdates`.

Part I
Getting to the Starting Line

In this part . . .

So you've decided you want to learn to program. You may have a good idea for a Mac or iPhone application and realize that the first thing you need to do is find out how to program in Objective-C. And although you may have a vague idea about it, you know you're going to have to learn exactly what programming is and what's required to create an application.

In this part, I help you understand what you need to know to get started. First of all, how do applications even work? How do you translate your ideas into a computer language that tells the computer what you want it to do, and then how does it take those instructions and actually do them? What is all this complier and framework stuff, and what exactly is object-oriented programming?

You find out what makes a good application and what you can do to make yours a good one. Finally, so you can get free development software from Apple, I take you through the process of registering as an Apple developer. I explain how you can download the Software Development Kit (SDK), and even how to build your first program.

Chapter 1

Computer Programming Exposed!

· ·

· ·

*L*ooking at it from the outside, computer programming can appear complicated and a bit mysterious. But once I let you in on a few of the secrets, you'll realize that when you write a computer program, whether it is a small program that's just a few lines or one that is tens or even hundreds of thousands of lines, you are generally doing the same thing:

1. **Getting input — from a keyboard or touch screen, or even something stored on your computer.**

   The input might be instructions to the program itself — for example, to display the web page `https://developer.apple.com`, to print a document such as Chapter 1, to process data like "Enter your Apple ID and Password" when you log on to the Mac Dev Center (the browser is just another program), or even to process a list of credit card transactions stored on a computer.

2. **Doing something based on, or with, the input.**

   Your browser may go on the Internet and access the page corresponding to `https://developer.apple.com`, or your word processing program may display a Print dialog box and print the chapter (at least that is what mine does). Based on your input, the program may also go out and use data it has stored or even has access to over the Internet. For example, when you enter your Apple ID and password, eventually a computer accesses a database to see whether your Apple ID and password are both valid and, if so, allows you access to the site and displays the site for you.

3. **Displaying the results of your adroitness on a monitor (or storing it away for future use).**

Computers are no doubt engineering marvels. But what will make you a good programmer is not your understanding of all that wizardry. No, what will make you a good programmer is taking the time to really understand the world of the user, and what you can do with a computer to make things better. For example, when I travel, I often zone out on the fact that even though it looks like Monopoly money, foreign currency actually does amount to something in dollars. I could use a computer to keep track of my budget and convert foreign currency into dollars. Writing a program simply involves detailing the steps the computer needs to follow (in a language the computer understands — but I'll get to that). You know, something like

Subtract the amount he just spent from the amount he started with.

or

Multiply the amount in foreign currency times the exchange rate.

Is it hard? No, not really. It can be pedestrian, but even more often, it is fun.

Why a Computer Program Is Like a Recipe

At its heart (yes, it does have one), computer programming is actually not that alien to most people. If you don't believe me, take the following programming test. Now, don't peek ahead for the answer. Okay?

The Never-Fail Programming Test:

Write down the recipe for making a peanut butter and jelly sandwich.

Answer:

If what you wrote down looks anything like

```
Recipe: Peanut Butter and Jelly Sandwich
  Ingredients
    Peanut Butter
    Jelly
    2 slices of bread
  Directions
    Place the two slices of bread close to each other.
    Spread peanut butter on one slice of bread.
    Spread jelly on the other slice of bread.
    Put one slice of bread on top of the other.
```

you're ready to go.

Although this example may seem overly simple, it generally illustrates what programming is all about. When you write a program in Objective-C, all you are doing is providing a set of instructions for the computer to follow. The preceding example is not perfect, but actually it is much closer to illustrating how Objective-C programming works than you might think. So, considering the peanut butter and jelly sandwich example, here is how you get your lunch made (if you are lucky enough to have a chef):

1. **Give your chef the recipe.**

2. **He or she gets the ingredients together and then follows the instructions on what to do with the ingredients.**

   Voilà, you have a peanut butter and jelly sandwich.

Figure 1-1 shows how a computer program works, using the peanut butter and jelly sandwich example.

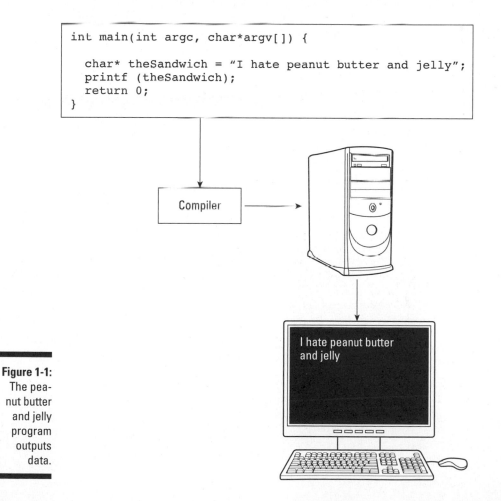

```
int main(int argc, char*argv[]) {

   char* theSandwich = "I hate peanut butter and jelly";
   printf (theSandwich);
   return 0;
}
```

Compiler

I hate peanut butter and jelly

Figure 1-1:
The peanut butter and jelly program outputs data.

This is what you do to get that output:

1. **You write instructions for the computer to follow.**

   Unfortunately, the computer can't speak English, or read for that matter, so you use something called a *compiler* to take the instructions you write in the Objective-C language and translate them into something the computer can understand.

2. **You provide data for the computer to use.**

   In this case, you write, "I hate peanut butter and jelly," and then the computer follows the instructions you have given it on what to do with that data.

   Voilà, you see "I hate peanut butter and jelly" displayed on your computer screen.

Fundamentally, programs manipulate numbers and text, and all things considered, a computer program has only two parts: *variables* (and other structures), which "hold" data, and *instructions,* which perform operations on that data.

Examining a simple computer program

Is there really any difference between a chef reading a recipe to create a peanut butter and jelly sandwich and a computer following some instructions to display something on a monitor? Quite frankly, no.

Here is the simple Objective-C program that displays I hate peanut butter and jelly on the computer screen:

```
int main(int argc, char *argv[]) {

  char* theSandwich = "I hate peanut butter and jelly";

  printf (theSandwich);
  return 0;
}
```

This program shows you how to display a line of text on your computer screen. The best way to understand programming code is to take it apart line by line:

```
int main(int argc, char *argv[]) {
```

Ignore the first line; it's not important now. It just provides your program with some information it can use. I explain exactly what that line means in the next few chapters.

```
char* theSandwich = "I hate peanut butter and jelly";
```

theSandwich is what is known as a *variable*. The best way to think of it for now is as a bucket that holds some kind of data (I get more precise in Chapter 4). char* tells you what kind of variable it is. In this case, theSandwich is a bunch of characters (text) known as a *string* (technically a string is more than that, but for now, that description is good enough for our purposes). I hate peanut butter and jelly is the data that the variable contains.

```
printf (theSandwich);
```

printf is an instruction (called an *operation*) that tells the computer to display whatever data is in the theSandwich bucket.

```
    return 0;
}
```

You can also safely ignore the last two lines for the time being.

Figure 1-2 shows the similarities between the program and the recipe for making a sandwich.

Figure 1-2:
A computer program can be compared to a peanut butter and jelly sandwich recipe.

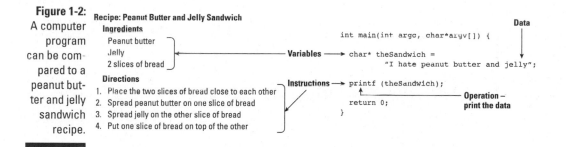

You can think of the following ingredients as variables that represent the data. For example, peanut butter is the name you give to pureed peanuts (and whatever else is in peanut butter), jelly is the name you give to some fruit that's been processed and put in a jar, and so on.

```
Peanut butter
Jelly
2 slices of bread
```

Similarly

```
Place the two slices of bread close to each other.
Spread peanut butter on one slice of bread.
Spread jelly on the other slice of bread.
Put one slice of bread on top of the other.
```

are simply instructions on how to take the ingredients and make a sandwich. `Spread peanut butter on one slice of bread` is the instruction. Actually, spreading the peanut butter is the operation you are performing on the pureed peanuts being referenced by the `peanut butter` variable.

Understanding How Computer Languages Work

While conceptually it is pretty easy to understand computer programming — all you are doing is giving the computer a set of instructions and some data on which to perform those instructions — one of the challenges, as I mention previously, is that it's not that easy to tell a computer what to do.

Computers don't speak English, although computer scientists have been working on that for years (think of trying to do that as the Computer Scientist Full Employment Act). A computer actually has its own language made up of 1s and 0s. For that matter, Objective-C is not something a computer can understand either, but it is a language that can be turned into those 1s and 0s by using a *compiler.* A compiler is nothing more than a program that translates Objective-C instructions into computer code.

Creating a computer program

To create a computer program by using a computer language, follow these steps (see Figure 1-3):

1. **Decide what you want the computer to do.**

   You can have the computer write a line of text on the monitor or create an online multiplayer game that will take two years to complete. It really doesn't matter.

2. **Break the task you want the computer to complete into a series of modules that contain the instructions the computer follows to do what you want, and then provide the data it needs to do that.**

   The series of modules is often referred to as your *application architecture.* The data you provide to the computer can be some text, graphics, where the hidden treasure is, or the euro-U.S. dollar exchange rate.

3. **Run the instructions through the compiler.**

   A compiler is actually just another program, albeit one that uses your instructions as data for its instructions on how to turn Objective-C into computer code.

4. **Link the result to other precompiled modules.**

   As you will see, the code you write is a relatively small part of what makes up your program. The rest is made up of all the plumbing you need to run the program, open and close windows, and do all that user interface stuff. Fortunately, that code is provided for you in a form that is easy to attach (link) to your program. A linker program takes your code, identifies all the things it needs, collects all pieces (from the disk), and combines them into the executable program you see in your applications or utilities folder.

5. **Store that output somewhere.**

   You usually store the output on a hard drive, but it can be anything the computer can access, like punch cards.

6. **Run the program.**

   When you want to run the program (say, the user double-clicks the program icon), the operating system (Mac OS X, for example, which is also just another program) gets the program from where it's stored and loads it into memory, and then the CPU (central processing unit) executes the instructions.

Running a computer program

Just as you don't need to be a weatherman to know which way the wind blows, you don't need to be an engineer who understands the intimate details of a computer to write a world-class application.

Most people don't find it that difficult to learn to drive a car. Although you don't have to know everything about internal combustion engines, fuel injection, drivetrains and transmissions, you do need to know a little bit about how a car works. That means you need to know how to start it, make it go forward, make it go backward, make it stop (generally a very valuable piece of information), make it turn left or right, and so on.

In the same way, you do need to know *a little bit* about how computers work to have what you do to write a computer program make sense.

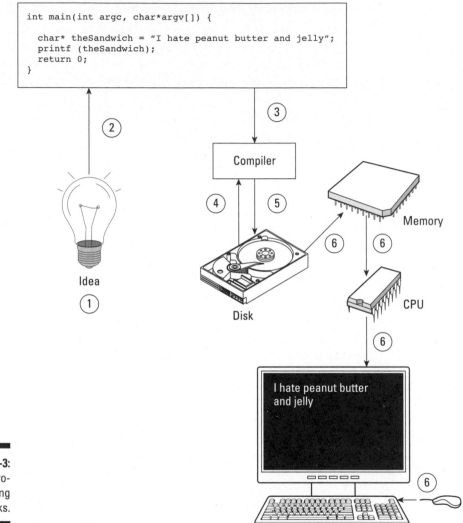

```
int main(int argc, char*argv[]) {

    char* theSandwich = "I hate peanut butter and jelly";
    printf (theSandwich);
    return 0;
}
```

Figure 1-3:
How pro-
gramming
works.

When you run a computer program, the computer does its primary work
in a part of the machine you cannot see, the central processing unit (CPU),
which executes the program instructions that are loaded into the computer's
memory. (This is a fast, temporary form of storage that is in one of those
chips you see when you look inside a computer, as opposed to persistent
storage such as a disk drive, which is slower and offers permanent storage.)
It requests the data it needs from memory, processes it, and writes new data
back to memory millions of times every second.

But if the data is all in memory, the CPU needs to be able to find a particular instruction or piece of data. How does it do that?

The location in memory for each instruction and each piece of data is identified by an *address,* like the mailboxes in the post office or an apartment house you see in Figure 1-4 (and notice that the first address for a mailbox in your computer is always 0). But these are very small mailboxes that can hold only one piece of information at a time, referred to as a *byte.* So for all practical purposes, you can think of the smallest division of memory as a byte, with each byte being able to be addressed on its own. The good news is that if you need more mailboxes, they are yours for the taking. So if you get more than one letter a day, the number of mailboxes assigned to you will increase to hold all the letters you need them to.

A byte represents 8 *bi*nary *dig*its, also known as *bits.* Most of the time, you'll use all 8 bits as a group, which could be the number 119 or the letter Z. You can also write code to access the individual bits independently, so those 8 bits could represent 8 flags that are either true (equal to 1) or false (equal to 0). I cover bytes in detail in Chapter 4.

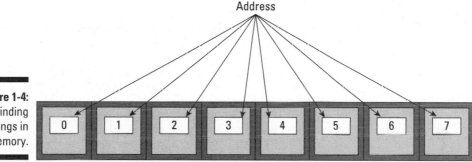

Figure 1-4: Finding things in memory.

What Is Objective-C, Anyway?

Objective-C is an object-oriented programming language, which means that it was created to support a certain style of programming. Yes, I know it is hard to believe, but even things like programming have different styles, in fact a lot of them, although the two heavyweights are object-oriented and procedural. Unless you're a dyed-in-the-wool member of a particular camp, it is really unnecessary to get into that discussion here (or probably ever). But you will, I promise, intimately understand what object-oriented programming is by the time you're done with this book, and you'll probably wonder why anyone would ever want to program in any other way.

But it takes more than a language to write a program; it takes a village. So who lives in the Objective-C village? Most object-oriented development environments consist of several parts:

- ✔ An object-oriented programming language
- ✔ A runtime environment
- ✔ A framework or library of objects and functions
- ✔ A suite of development tools

This is where, for many people, things start to cloud up. You may be saying, "You mean I have to master more than the language, and what is all this stuff about runtime environment and frameworks and libraries?" The answer is yes; but not to worry. I take you slowly through each part. The following sections cover each part of the Objective-C development environment.

Understanding programming languages

When you write a program, you write it as series of *statements*. Some of these statements are about data. You may allocate areas of memory to use for data in your program, as well as describe how data is structured. Other statements are really instructions for the computer to do something.

Here is an example of an Objective-C statement that adds together *b* and *c* and assigns the result to *a* (and you thought you'd never use all that algebra you picked up in school):

```
a = b + c;
```

Statements like these use operators (like + or –) or tell *modules* (functions or objects) to do something to, or with, the data. For now, think of functions or objects as simply a packaged series of statements that perform a task. It might help to think of operators and modules as words you use to create sentences (the statements) that tell the computer what to do. Chapters 4, 5, 6, and 7 cover operators, functions, objects, and modules in detail.

When most people want to learn how to program, they usually focus on the language. I want to program in C++, for example. Or C++ is a real dog; give me Java any day. People really do become passionate about languages, and believe me, it is best to keep out of the way when an unstoppable force meets an immovable object.

What you really should keep in mind, unless computer science is your life, is that what you want to master is how to create applications. What makes that easy or difficult is not just the language, but the application development tools available to you as well.

If you want to develop iOS and Mac OS X applications, Objective-C is the language you need to take full advantage of everything both platforms have to offer. Objective-C is the dominant programming language used by developers on both platforms, and Apple stands behind it.

Running your program in a runtime environment

One of the features of Objective-C is its runtime system. This is one of those things that gets linked into your program in Step 4 in the section "Creating a computer program," earlier in this chapter. It acts as a kind of operating system (like the Mac OS or iOS) for an individual Objective-C program. It is this runtime system that is responsible for making some of the very powerful features of Objective-C work.

Objective-C's runtime environment also makes it possible to use tools like Interface Builder (I explain Interface Builder in Chapters 17 and 18) to create user interfaces with a minimum of work (I'm all for that, and after you find out about Interface Builder, you will be, too).

Using frameworks and libraries

The framework you will use is called *Cocoa*. It came along with Objective-C when Apple acquired NeXT in 1996 (when it was called NeXTSTEP). I have worked in many development environments in my life, and Objective-C and Cocoa are hands down my favorites.

Cocoa enables you to write applications for Mac OS X, and a version of it enables you to write applications for iOS devices, such as the iPhone, iPad, and iPod. If the operating system does the heavy lifting vis-à-vis the hardware, the framework provides all the stuff you need to make your application an application. It provides support for windows and other user-interface items as well as many of the other things that are needed in most applications. When you use Cocoa to develop your application, all you need to do is add the application's specific functionality — the content as well as the controls and views that enable the user to access and use that content — to the Cocoa framework.

Framework or library?

What is the difference between a library and a framework? A library is a set of reusable functions or data structures that are yours to use. A framework, on the other hand, has an architecture or programming model that requires an application to be designed (divided into modules) in a certain way (application architecture) to use it. I like to think that whereas *you use a library, a framework uses you.*

Now, two excellent books explain the use of frameworks on the Mac and iPhone. One is *Mac Application Development For Dummies,* by Karl Kowalski. The other is *iPhone Application Development For Dummies,* 4th Edition, by Neal Goldstein (both published by John Wiley & Sons, Inc.).

Your suite of development tools

The main development tool you will use is Xcode. I explain Xcode in Chapter 2, and you use it throughout this book. In addition, when it's time to add a user-interface front end to your application, you'll make use of a tool within Xcode called Interface Builder. I talk a little about Interface Builder in Chapters 17 and 18, but again, pick up copies of *iPhone Application Development For Dummies* and *Mac Application Development For Dummies* to really understand the frameworks.

Using Xcode 4.4

You will use the Xcode 4.4 developer tools package that is available at the Mac App Store. This version of Xcode requires Mac OS X 10.7.3 (Lion) or later, and it is a major improvement over previous versions of Xcode.

Using Objective-C Version 2.0

You will find out about Version 2.0 of the Objective-C language, which was released with Mac OS X 10.5, and yes, you should care. I provide you examples of some of the very useful features of Objective-C 2.0, such as declared properties, fast enumeration, and Automatic Reference Counting, which greatly simplify memory management. All these features are available in the latest versions of Mac OS X and iOS. If possible, I'll also indicate some work-arounds if you need to write applications that run under earlier versions of the OS, but in general, writing applications that run under earlier versions of the OS will be up to you.

Chapter 2

Creating Your First Program

● ●

In This Chapter

▶ Becoming familiar with the Software Development Kit

▶ Setting up your first project

▶ Building and running your first program

▶ Getting up and running with the Xcode Development Environment

▶ Becoming familiar with the Xcode text editor

▶ Getting help with Xcode

● ●

*I*n Chapter 1, I provide some of the background context you need to know to write computer programs, and I complete that discussion in Chapter 3. Although you still need to know more to write *good* programs, it's time for a break. In this chapter, you get a taste of what programming is all about.

But before you do that, you need to go through some administrative matters, such as downloading the Software Development Kit (SDK) that you use to write programs.

Getting Started with the Software Development Kit

Everything you need to program in Objective-C for the Mac or iOS devices is included in something known as a *Software Development Kit,* or *SDK.* It contains Xcode (and some tools), frameworks and libraries, and iOS, Mac OS X, and Xcode documentation — in short, everything you need to develop applications for the Mac and iOS devices. After you have it installed on your computer, you are ready to begin developing that killer app you have been thinking of.

To register or not to register

When this book was originally published, the Mac App Store had not yet made its splash. Now, Xcode 4.4 is available for free from the App Store on your Macintosh. You still need to provide your Apple ID to download Xcode, but you no longer need to register with Apple as a developer. However, as a registered Apple Developer, you will be able to access a great deal more information through the Apple Developer website. And you will need to be a registered Apple Developer to load your apps onto iPhones and iPads, and to submit your apps to either the iOS App Store or the Mac App Store. You definitely have benefits to becoming an officially registered, card-carrying Apple Developer, but you can also just dip your toes into the waters of development to master Objective-C.

This book is designed to teach you how to use Objective-C to write both Mac OS X and iOS applications. I try to alternate which comes first in each discussion (just to be fair). Deciding which platform you want to develop for is a decision only you can make. Fortunately, the two are not mutually exclusive when it comes to the SDK.

To download the SDK, though, you need to register with Apple, so I take you through the process.

Downloading Xcode

It's now time to download Xcode, which contains everything you need to develop for iOS (which you do in Chapter 17) and Mac OS X (which you do in Chapter 18), or even both.

To get the complete set of tools to start mastering Objective-C, follow these steps:

1. **Go back to the iOS Dev Center, and under Resources for iOS 5, click Downloads (shown in Figure 2-1).**

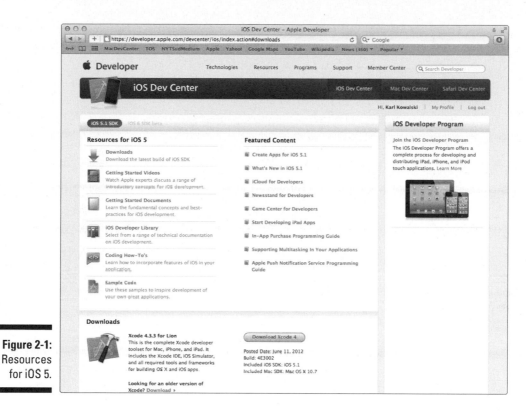

Figure 2-1:
Resources
for iOS 5.

This step takes you to the bottom of the page, where you can choose the
download you want (see Figure 2-2).

Figure 2-2:
Choose a
download.

2. Click Download Xcode 4.

You are taken to the Xcode 4 page, as shown in Figure 2-3. Apple now provides Xcode through the App Store on your Macintosh, and that's where you need to go next to download Xcode.

Figure 2-3:
Xcode 4 is
downloaded
through the
App Store.

3. **Click View in Mac App Store.**

   The App Store app launches and shows you Xcode 4 (see Figure 2-4).

Figure 2-4:
Xcode available for free in the Mac App Store.

4. **Click the Free button and then click Install App.**

   The App Store downloads and installs Xcode for you.

5. **Follow the instructions, and in no time, you'll have Xcode installed and ready to code.**

As I said, Apple continually updates the look and feel of its website, so the pages may look different when you see them, and the site's functionality may be slightly different.

You can also download Xcode 4 by launching App Store on your Macintosh and searching for Xcode. There's only one, made by Apple, and it's free.

Creating Your Xcode Project

To develop a Mac OS X or iPhone application, you work on an *Xcode project.* Here's how to start your foray into Xcode:

1. **Launch Xcode.**

   After you have installed Xcode, it's easy to launch. By default, Xcode was downloaded to /Applications, where you can find and launch it.

   Because you use Xcode a lot, you can also drag the icon for the Xcode application onto the Dock so that you can launch it from there.

   When you first launch Xcode, you see the Welcome screen shown in Figure 2-5. It has some links that you can explore on your own. You may want to leave this screen up to make it easier to get to those links, but I usually close it. If you don't want to be bothered with the Welcome screen in the future, deselect the Show This Window When Xcode Launches check box. You can always show it again by selecting Welcome to Xcode from the Window menu.

Figure 2-5: Xcode welcomes you.

2. **Start the New Project Assistant by choosing File⇨New Project to create a new project.**

   You can also just press Shift+⌘+N.

   Either way, you see the New Project window, which looks something like Figure 2-6, depending on the kind of project you created previously.

   The New Project window is where you get to choose what kind of project you want to create. Note that the leftmost pane has two sections: one for iOS and the other for Mac OS X.

3. **In the New Project window, click Application under the Mac OS X heading.**

   The main pane of the New Project window refreshes, revealing several choices, as shown in Figure 2-7. Each of these choices is actually a template that, when chosen, generates some code to get you started. You can then enter your own code into the template, build your application, and then generate output in the Debugger Console window (don't worry; I get to that very soon).

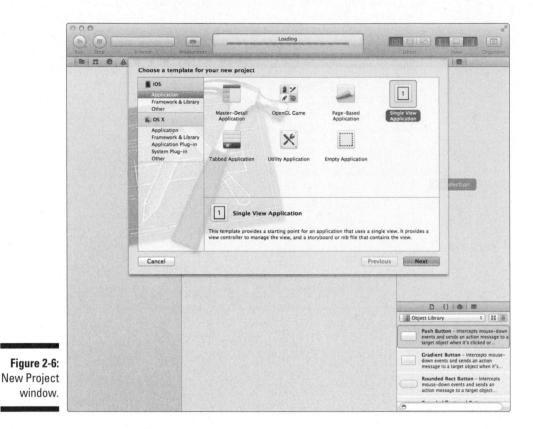

Figure 2-6:
New Project
window.

4. **Select Command Line Tool in the upper-right corner, as shown in Figure 2-7.**

Note that when you select a template, a brief description of the template displays underneath the main pane. Quite a few templates are available for both the iPhone and Mac OS X. You don't need any of the others until Chapters 17 and 18, but you may want to click around just to get a feel for what is available. Just be sure to click back to Application under the Mac OS X heading and select Command Line Tool when you're done exploring.

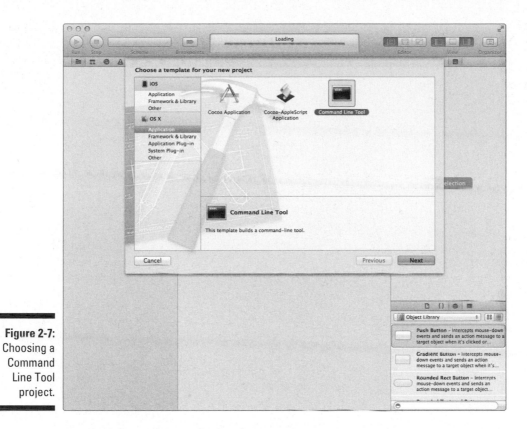

Figure 2-7:
Choosing a
Command
Line Tool
project.

5. **Click Next. Xcode displays the project options, as shown in Figure 2-8. Enter a name for your application in the Product Name field and a value for the Company Identifier. Select Foundation from the Type drop-down menu, and leave the other options at their default values.**

   I named this application First Program, and I suggest you do the same if you're following along with me. For the Company Identifier field, Apple suggests that you use a reverse-domain name as I have done. The Organization Name will be your company name, if you have one, but I just used my name. This project is a Foundation type of project because it will use code from Apple's Foundation libraries — the basic package of Objective-C code that you find out about in this book, up until Chapters 17 and 18. The checkbox at the bottom — Use Automatic Reference Counting — controls an important memory management feature, which I cover in Chapter 13.

Choose options for your new project:

Product Name | First Program
Organization Name | Karl Kowalski
Company Identifier | com.karlgkowalski
Bundle Identifier | com.karlgkowalski.First-Program
Type | Foundation
☑ Use Automatic Reference Counting

Cancel   Previous   Next

Figure 2-8:
Choose
project
options.

6. **Click Next and choose a location to save the project (the Desktop or any folder works just fine). Deselect the Source Control: Create Local Git Repository for This Project check box and then click Create.**

Git is a software control management (SCM) system that keeps track of changes in the code and saves multiple versions of each file on your hard drive. You can use Git as a local repository — thus the Create Local Git Repository for This Project option — or you can install a Git server on a remote machine to share files among team members. Git is beyond the scope of this book — but if you want to find out more about it, check out the Xcode 4 User Guide (choose Help➪Xcode User Guide).

After you click Create, Xcode creates the project and opens the Workspace window for the project, as shown in Figure 2-9. Your

Workspace window may look slightly different — for instance, if you've used Xcode before and modified your preferences for fonts and colors — but it should still look very similar to Figure 2-9.

Xcode remembers your choices for your next project.

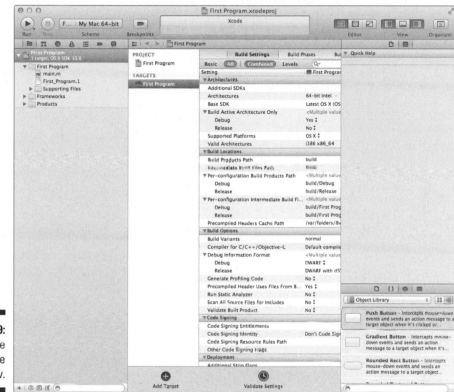

Figure 2-9:
The Xcode
Workspace
window.

Exploring your project

To develop an Objective-C application, you have to work within the context of an Xcode project. It turns out that you do most of your work on projects by using a Workspace window very much like the one shown in Figure 2-10. This is the primary interface for developing your application; it displays and organizes your source files and the other resources needed to build your application.

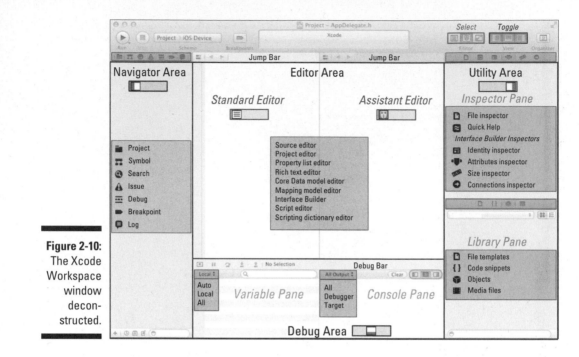

Figure 2-10: The Xcode Workspace window deconstructed.

The Workspace window consists of

- ✔ Workspace areas
- ✔ The toolbar
- ✔ An optional tab bar

The following sections describe each of these elements — the heart of Xcode.

Workspace areas

The Workspace is divided into four *areas,* as follows:

- ✔ Editor area (always shown)
- ✔ Navigator area
- ✔ Utility area
- ✔ Debug area

You can configure the Workspace area in a number of ways. Right off the bat, you can choose to hide and/or show various areas in various combinations. (Note that the Editor area is always present.) The Debug and Utility areas are already configured with panes, but in the Debug area, you can select the pane configuration.

Editor area (always present)

The Editor area is always present. If you want, you can show or hide various "editors" contained within the Editor area; you do so using the Editor selector, the group of buttons in the toolbar you can see in Figure 2-11.

Figure 2-11:
The Editor selector.

The term *editor* here is really a misnomer, even though that's the term used in the documentation. The "editors" you can select in the Editor area are really editor area *configurations,* within which you use the *content* editors available to you. (See the section "Editor area content editors," later in this chapter, for more on this distinction.)

The editors (configurations) you have available are as follows:

✔ **Standard editor:** The button for this Editor area configuration is on the left side of the Editor selector. The Standard editor displays a single pane for editing and is always shown.

✔ **Assistant editor:** Select this Editor area (configuration), using the center button. This displays an additional pane in the Editor area, with a content editor in each. The Assistant editor is most helpful when editing interface files with Interface Builder, and I explain this in greater detail in Chapters 17 and 18.

✔ **Version editor:** Open this editor using the right button on the Editor selector. This enables you to compare two different versions of files that you have saved in repositories. (Repositories and the Version editor are beyond the scope of this book.)

I explain the tasks you can perform within these areas later.

Additional areas to view as needed

You use the View selector (see Figure 2-12) to toggle between showing and hiding any of the optional areas. By *optional,* I mean that you can open and close these areas as needed. These areas are as follows:

Figure 2-12:
The View
selector.

✔ **Navigator area** (left button): No further configuration is possible (you don't divide this area into other views).

✔ **Debug area** (center button): Displays various panes depending on what you need to see (the Console pane, which displays debugging information or program output, for example, or the Variables pane, which displays your program's variables and their values); you change panes by using the Debug area scope bar, as shown in Figure 2-13.

Figure 2-13:
The Debug
area
scope bar.

The Debug area scope bar toggles from one to another of the following:

- *Variables pane only* (left button)
- *Both Variables and Console panes* (center button)
- *Console pane only* (right button)

✔ **Utility area** (right button): Is further configured with two panes (either can be expanded to hide the other):

- *Inspector pane*
- *Library pane*

I explain what you see in each of those panes when I explain the Utility area section, later in the chapter.

When you hover your mouse pointer over a toolbar button, a tooltip describes its function.

Displaying an area's content

Each area displays certain content, and each area has its own way of displaying its content:

- **The Navigator area** has navigators.
- **The Editor area** has content editors.
- **The Utility area** has

    - *Quick Help* or *Inspectors* in the Inspector/Quick Help pane
    - *Libraries* in the Library pane

- **The Debug area** has

    - *Debugger variables* in the Variables pane
    - *Debugger output* in the Console pane

The following sections tell you about these areas in more detail.

Navigator area navigators

The Navigator area contains a host of navigators that organize the tasks and components you use within your Xcode project. You use a Navigator selector bar to select the navigator you need. Figure 2-14 shows the various navigators you can choose from, and the following bullet list explains what each navigator does:

Figure 2-14:
The
Navigator
selector.

- **Project navigator:** Here's where you manage all the files in your project. You can add files, delete files, and even organize your files by placing them into groups. Selecting a file in the Project navigator launches the appropriate editor in the Editor area.

- **Symbol navigator:** Lets you zero in on a particular *symbol* — an element such as a variable, method, or function name — in your project. Selecting a symbol highlights it in the editor.

- **Search navigator:** Finds any string within your projects and frameworks.

✔ **Issue navigator:** Displays issues such as diagnostics, warnings, and errors that arise when you're coding and building your project.

✔ **Debug navigator:** Displays the *call stack* — information about what method has called what method — during program execution.

✔ **Breakpoint navigator:** Manages and edits the *breakpoints* — markers you add to your code that stop program execution at a certain point in your program — in your project or Workspace.

✔ **Log navigator:** Examines the logs that Xcode generates when you run and debug your application.

Editor area content editors

The Editor area has a number of editors that you use to edit specific content. Content editors are context based, meaning that the selection you make in a Navigator or Editor *jump bar* — the toolbar that appears at the top of each Editor area pane and is used to navigate through the files and symbols in your project — determines the Content editor. The following bullet list names each Content editor and outlines the tasks associated with each one (note that not all tasks are applicable to iOS application development):

✔ **Source editor:** Write and edit your source code; set, enable, or disable breakpoints; and control program execution.

✔ **Project editor:** View and edit settings such as build options, target architectures, and code signing.

✔ **Interface Builder:** Graphically create and edit user interface files. Interface Builder is the editor you use to create the visual interface of your applications, so I won't go into too much detail on it at this point. You find more about Interface Builder in Chapters 17 and 18.

✔ **Property list editor:** View and edit various types of small, highly structured property lists (plists). (You'll use one for some of your program's data.)

✔ **Rich text editor:** View and edit rich text (`.rtf`) files, much as you would with Text Edit.

✔ **Core Data model editor:** Implement or modify a Core Data model. (The use of Core Data is beyond the scope of this book.)

✔ **Mapping model editor:** Graphically create and edit a mapping between an old Core Data store and a new one. (Similarly, the use of the Mapping model editor is beyond the scope of this book.)

✔ **Script editor:** Create and edit AppleScript script files.

✔ **Scripting dictionary editor:** Create and edit the scripting definition (`.sdef`) file — used by AppleScript — for your application.

✔ **Viewer:** Display files for which no editor exists (some audio, video, and graphics files, for example) using the same Quick Look facility used by the Finder.

Utility area

The Utility area has two panes: the Inspector pane and the Library pane. Both of these panes are for editing the visual interface of your apps, which I cover in Chapters 17 and 18.

Debug area

The Debug area is where you try to track down the bugs in your code and squash them. A selection in the Debug area scope bar (refer to Figure 2-13) determines the information the debugger displays:

- ✔ **Variables Pane Only:** Left button
- ✔ **Both Variables and Console Panes:** Center button
- ✔ **Console Pane Only:** Right button

The pop-up menu in the Variables Pane scope bar lets you display

- ✔ **Auto:** Display recently accessed variables.
- ✔ **Local:** Display local variables.
- ✔ **All:** Display all variables and registers.

The pop-up menu in the Console Pane scope bar lets you display

- ✔ **All Output:** Target and debugger output
- ✔ **Debugger Output:** Debugger output only
- ✔ **Target Output:** Target output only

You can also find other controls and filters for what is displayed; explore them on your own.

Xcode has extensive contextual help articles that you can view by Control-clicking in the Workspace window in the context that you need help on.

The toolbar and Tab bar

The *toolbar* (see Figure 2-15) includes Workspace-level tools for managing and running *schemes* (instructions on how to build your application), viewing the progress of (executing) tasks, and configuring the Workspace window. That's a lot of tools, so to keep things straight, it's best to think of the toolbar as actually having three parts: a flow control part, an activity viewer part, and a workspace configuration part.

Flow controls are for defining, choosing, running, and stopping projects. A *scheme* defines characteristics such as build targets, build configurations, and the executable environment for which the product will be built.

The Flow controls are as follows:

✔ **Run button:** Clicking the Run button builds and runs the targets. (A *target,* in this context, is the product you want to build, as well as the instructions for building that product from a set of files in a project or Workspace for the currently selected scheme.) Pressing and holding the mouse button opens a menu (which is also available on the Product menu) that enables you to run, test, profile, or analyze your application.

✔ **Stop button:** Terminates your executing application in either the Simulator or the device.

✔ **Scheme menu:** Lets you select the scheme and build destination to use.

✔ **Breakpoints button:** Activates or deactivates all breakpoints.

The activity viewer part of the toolbar shows the progress of tasks currently executing. This viewer displays status messages, build progress, and other information about your project. Click the Issues icon in the activity viewer area to open the Issue navigator (explained earlier in this chapter, in the section "Navigator area navigators").

You use the final part of the toolbar — the workspace configuration part — to configure the Xcode Workspace window to suit your needs. You can use these controls to select an editor type, show or hide optional view areas, and open the Organizer window. (See the section "Displaying an area's content," earlier in this chapter, for more on your choices here.)

The Tab bar is great for keeping track of where you've been and what you might want to go back to. Note, however, that showing the Tab bar is optional. If you decide that the Tab bar is something you just can't do without, choose View⇨Show Tab Bar. You can reorder tabs, close them individually, or drag them out of the bar to create a new window.

If you lose the toolbar (or Tab bar), you can always add it back to any window by selecting View⇨Show Toolbar (or View⇨Show Tab Bar). The View menu also allows you to configure the Workspace window.

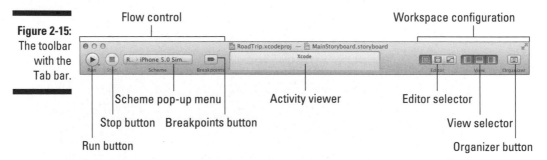

Figure 2-15: The toolbar with the Tab bar.

Flow control

Workspace configuration

Scheme pop-up menu

Activity viewer

Editor selector

Stop button   Breakpoints button

View selector

Run button

Organizer button

The First Program Project

When your project is launched in Xcode, the Navigator area appears on the left side of the Workspace window. If this is the first project you've created, the following options are selected for you by default:

✔ The Utility and Debug areas are hidden.

✔ The Navigator area is shown, with the Project navigator selected by default in the Navigator selector.

✔ The project (First Program, in this case) is selected in the Project navigator.

And as a result, the Project editor displays the First Program project information in the Standard editor.

Long story short: When you launch your First Program project in Xcode, what you see in the editor is the project information of the First Program project.

 When I refer to (or ask you to select) the *First Program project in the Project navigator*, I am referring to the First Program project that you see selected in Figure 2-8.

The Project editor

Having your First Program project selected in the Navigator area's Project navigator (refer to Figure 2-8) sets a couple of balls rolling. In the first column of the Project editor, under the Project heading, you see the project itself. (It turns out that a workspace can actually have more than one project, but you won't be doing that in this book.) A bit below the Project heading, you see the Targets heading. (Yes, there's room for more than one target here as well.) Any project you create defines the default build settings for all the targets in that particular project. (Note that each target can also specify its own build settings, which could potentially override the project build settings.)

A *target* is really just the *app* (the product you are building) and includes the information that Xcode requires to build the product from a set of files in a project or workspace — stuff like the build settings and build phases that you can see and edit in the Xcode Project editor. A target inherits the build settings for the project, but you can override one or more of them by specifying different settings at the target level. You can have one active target at a time, with the Xcode scheme (My Mac 64-bit, for example) specifying the target.

The Project editor shows tabs across the top; clicking these tabs opens panes that enable you to examine and change project settings. The default settings will work for your needs for the example code in this book. The tabs for the Project settings are as follows:

✔ **Info:** The Info tab contains basic information used by Xcode when building the code within the project. Figure 2-16 shows what Xcode displays for First Program.

✔ **Build Settings:** Most developers can get by with the default build settings, but if you have special requirements — ones that require anything from tweaking a setting or two to creating an entirely new build configuration — you'll take care of them on this tab. Figure 2-17 shows the beginning of the Build Settings for the First Program project (you find over a hundred different settings).

The tabs for the target settings include the Build Settings tab, which shows the same information as the Build Settings tab for the Project settings, as well as two others: Build Phases and Build Rules. You will use the default settings for these tabs for the examples in this book.

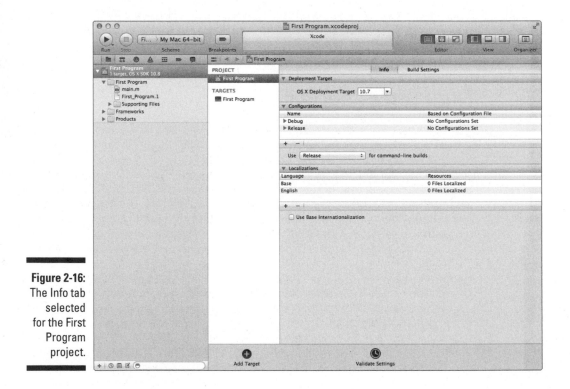

Figure 2-16:
The Info tab selected for the First Program project.

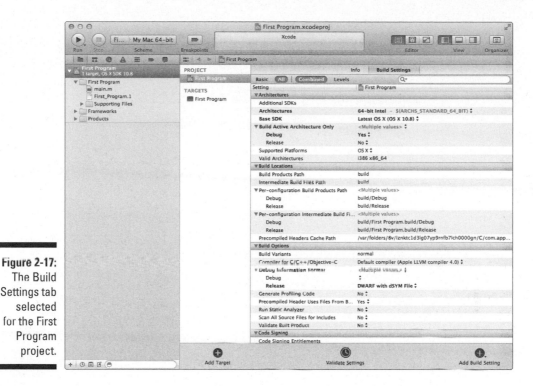

Figure 2-17:
The Build
Settings tab
selected
for the First
Program
project.

When a filename appears in red, this means that Xcode can't find the underlying physical file. And because you've never compiled the First Program app, it makes sense that the `First Program.app` file (the app itself) is missing.

The Project navigator

After your project is created, the Xcode workspace displays the Project navigator. I cover the important points of the Project navigator here, because you'll be using it a lot in the coding examples in the rest of the book.

Xcode has a lot of context-based help. Whenever you're curious about what something does, try Control-clicking in an area, and you'll likely find a menu with a Help selection. In Figure 2-18, for example, I Control-clicked in the Project navigator to bring up a shortcut menu from which I can choose the Project Navigator Help menu.

Figure 2-18:
Project
navigator
help.

The Navigator area is an optional area on the left side of the Workspace window where you can load different navigators — including the Project navigator — with the help of the Navigator selector. To hide or show the Navigator area, click the left View selector button on the Workspace toolbar, as shown in Figure 2-19.

Figure 2-19:
The View
selector
buttons
on the
Workspace
toolbar.

The Navigator area includes the Navigator selector bar, the Content area, and the Filter bar. It can also include other features specific to the selected navigator.

The Project navigator enables you to do things like add, delete, group, and otherwise manage files in your project or to choose a file to view or edit in the Editor area. In Figure 2-20, for example, you can see that I decided to open all the disclosure triangles so that the Project navigator displays all the files in the project. Only two are shown in First Program, because I created a command-line application — more complex app templates, such as for iOS or Mac OS X apps, come with more stuff.

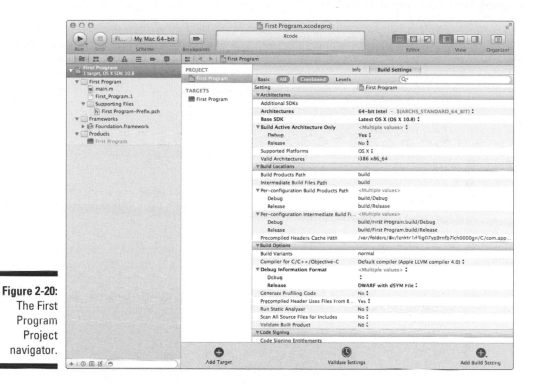

Figure 2-20:
The First Program Project navigator.

The *Filter bar* enables you to restrict the content that's displayed — such as recently edited files, unsaved files, or filenames.

For this simple command-line application, three folders are in the Project navigator:

✔ **First Program** contains two files and a folder. The first file is a source code module — main.m — and the second is a text file called First_ Program.1. main.m contains the source code for the command-line application, and First_Program.1 is the file used by the UNIX operating system to generate the online manual for using the application, otherwise known as the man page. The folder Supporting Files contains one file — First Program-Prefix.pch. This file is called a precompiled header. I talk about header files in Chapter 6. For now, all you need to know is that precompiling them significantly reduces the amount of time it takes to build your application.

Xcode uses the .m extension to indicate that the Objective-C compiler will process a file that holds Objective-C code. (Filenames ending in .c are handled by the C compiler, and .cpp files are the province of the C++ compiler — yes, you actually get all of those with Xcode as well.)

✔ **Frameworks** are code libraries that contain a good deal of what you would normally have to write yourself to create a functioning program — including things you need to display text in the Debugger Console. (I know, you don't know what that is, but I explain that in the next section.) By choosing the Foundation Command Line Tool template, you let Xcode know that it should add the Foundation.framework to your project because it expects that you need what's in the Foundation framework in a Foundation Command Line Tool.

Note: You use only this framework for now. Later, you use other frameworks when you start building iOS and Mac OS X applications.

✔ **Products** is the *compiled application*. It contains First Program. At the moment, this file is listed in red because the file cannot be found (which makes sense, because you haven't compiled the project yet).

You may notice that some items in the Project navigator look like folders, but you'll soon discover that they often don't act like folders. If you just happen to open the First Program folder on your Mac — outside of the Xcode context — you won't see all the "folders" that appear in the Xcode window. That's because those folders are simply groupings that help organize and find what you're looking for.

When you have numerous files, creating subgroups within the Classes group and/or Resources group, or even new groups, helps you find things. You create subgroups (or even new groups) by choosing New Project⇨New Group. You then can select a file and drag it to a new group or subgroup. I show you that in more detail in Chapter 6.

Building and Running Your Application

As I mention earlier, the Xcode toolbar (see Figure 2-21) is where you do things like run your application. I spell out the process a bit more here.

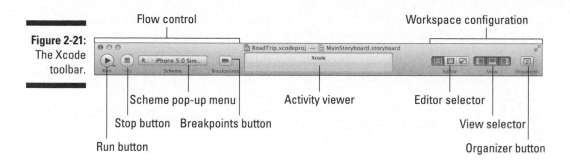

Figure 2-21:
The Xcode
toolbar.

The Flow controls are for defining, choosing, running, and stopping projects.
They consist of the following:

✔ **Run button:** Clicking the Run button builds and runs the *targets* — a
target is a product to build and the instructions for building the product
from a set of files in a project or workspace for the currently selected
scheme. Pressing and holding the mouse button opens a menu — also
available on the Product menu — that enables you to run, test, profile,
or analyze your application.

Holding various modifier keys while clicking the Run button enables you
to select these other run options:

> *Control key:* Run without building.

> *Shift key:* Build without running.

> *Option key:* Edit the scheme and run.

✔ **Stop button:** Terminates your (executing) application in the Simulator or
the device.

✔ **Scheme menu:** A *scheme* defines characteristics such as build targets,
build configurations, and the executable environment for the product
to be built. The *scheme menu* enables you to select which scheme and
which build destination you want to use. (I describe schemes in greater
detail in the next section of this chapter.)

✔ **Breakpoints button:** Activates or deactivates all breakpoints. The
Breakpoints button turns breakpoints on and off. (A *breakpoint* tells
Xcode to stop execution at a point in the code — I explain breakpoints
more fully in Chapter 8.)

The *Activity viewer* shows the progress of tasks currently executing by displaying status messages, build progress, and other information about your

project. For example, when you're building your project, Xcode updates the Activity viewer to show where you are in the process — and whether the process completed successfully. If an Issues icon appears in the Activity viewer, click it to open the Issues navigator and look there for messages about your project. (None exist yet in Figure 2-20, so you won't see an Issues icon there.)

The *Workspace configuration* includes the Editor and View controls, as well as the Organizer window button.

Building an app

Building an app in Xcode means compiling all the source code files in the project. It's really exciting (well, I exaggerate a bit) to see what you get when you build and run a project that you created from a template. Building and running an app is relatively simple; just follow these steps:

1. **In the Flow Controls section of the toolbar, choose a scheme from the Scheme pop-up menu.**

   A *scheme* tells Xcode the purpose of the built product. The schemes in the Scheme pop-up menu specify which targets (actual products) to build, what build configuration to use when building them, which debugger to use when testing them, and which executable to launch when running them on the device or Simulator. For this simple command-line application, you only see one scheme: My Mac 64-bit.

2. **Choose Product⇨Run to build and run the application.**

   You can also click the Run button in the upper-left corner of the Workspace window. The Activity viewer (shown previously in Figure 2-21) tells you all about the build progress, flags any build errors (such as compiler errors) or warnings, and (oh, yeah) tells you whether the build was successful.

   Figure 2-22 shows the results of a successful build and run.

You may have noticed that not very much happened when you ran the app — Xcode's Activity viewer tells you it finished running First Program, but how do you know? In the lower-right corner of the display is the *Console* pane, as mentioned earlier and visible in Figure 2-22.

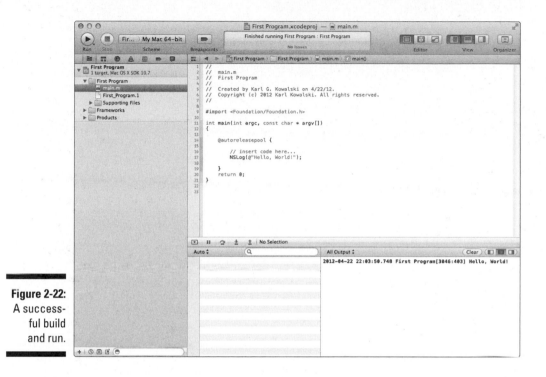

Now that you have your first working program, I'm ready to explain to you how it all happened.

All that stuff in main.m

You can see the code that Xcode writes for you when it creates your Project by looking at the contents of the main.m file.

In the Project navigator, click the main.m item under the First Program folder. The Standard editor will display the contents.

The Objective-C code you just built and ran is shown in Listing 2-1. It displayed `Hello World!` in the Console pane and connected you with generations of

C programmers who have created and run this as their first application. Over the next few chapters, I dissect each and very element in this program, but for now, the real point is to get you comfortable with Xcode and the compiler, although I point out a few highlights.

Listing 2-1:   Your First Program

```
#import <Foundation/Foundation.h>

int main (int argc, const char * argv[]) {
  @autoreleasepool {

    // insert code here...
    NSLog(@"Hello, World!");
  }
  return 0;
}
```

The first line you see tells the compiler to include the Foundation.h header file of the Foundation framework:

```
#import <Foundation/Foundation.h>
```

The Foundation framework provides plumbing features such as data storage, text and strings, dates and times, object creation, disposal persistence, and common Internet protocols — none of which you have a clue about at this point. But rest assured that you will not only understand but also appreciate them by the time you are done with this book. The Foundation framework provides commonly used functionality that is not part of the Objective-C language that you use hand in hand with Objective-C when you code your application. After all, it makes sense not to have to redo all the common things that programmers need (like display text in the Debugger Console) in every program.

The way a program accesses the framework is through *headers,* and I explain those mechanics in Chapter 6.

The next line in the listing begins the main function:

```
int main (int argc, const char * argv[])
```

As I explain in Chapter 1, a *function* is a collection of instructions all neatly packaged together to perform a task. main is the mother of all functions and is the place where all Objective-C programs start their execution — the instructions contained within main are always the first ones to be executed in Objective-C programs. All Objective-C programs have one. When you start to work with the frameworks, however, you really won't be aware of this because all the startup stuff is handled within the framework. But for now, this is where you start.

The word `main` is followed in the code by

```
(int argc, const char * argv[])
```

These are function arguments, which I cover in Chapters 5 and 7. Ignore them for now.

Before `main`, you also see another term, `int`. A function can return data to its caller. For example, the function `howOldAreYou` returns the age as an `int`, which, as you discover in Chapter 4, is the Objective-C official term for a whole number.

Right after the function arguments, you can find the body of the `main` function enclosed in curly braces (`{}`). What the function does when it is executed is contained within these braces. The first *statement*

```
@autoreleasepool {
```

has to do with memory allocation and management, which you don't need to know about until Chapter 13. This statement encloses the remaining code statements in another set of curly braces.

Now, explore the statement

```
NSLog(@"Hello, World!");
```

All it does is display (or print, if you like) `Hello World!` on the Debugger Console. To start with, `NSLog` is a function, just like `main`. Inside of it is a *string* (a variable that stores more than a single nonnumeric character is known as a *string*):

```
@"Hello, World!"
```

The @ sign before the quotation mark tells the compiler that this is not a C string. It is actually a Cocoa object called an `NSString` that has a number of features, including the ability to covert a "numeric" string (like `"42"`) to its numeric value (42) that you can use in a computation and to compare itself to another string. I explain more about this object later, but you use it now as an introduction to how you use strings in Objective-C.

`NSLog` is really used to log an error message, not as an application's output function. That's why the output is to the Debugger Console. But because Debugger Console is so convenient, you use it to display the program's output until you put on a user interface in Chapters 17 and 18 (and lots of people, myself included, use it during development as a way to output program information that is not part of the user interface).

Note that what is displayed in the Debugger Console when you build and run your program is this:

```
2012-04-22 22:03:50.748 First Program[3046:403] Hello,
         World!
```

2012-04-22 22:03:50.748 First Program[3046:403] is a time stamp and process ID that tells you when and from where the output string originated. It's not important here, and I won't include it when I show you output — that means from now on, I show the preceding output as

```
Hello, World!
```

As I explain various features of Objective-C, you use this NSLog quite a bit to see for yourself how things work, and I expect you will become rather fond of it. It is, as I mention earlier, part of the Foundation framework, which was automatically included when you used the Foundation Command Line Tool template. If you don't believe me, try leaving it out and see what happens.

The last line of the program is the return statement that ends the execution of main and finishes the program:

```
return (0);
```

The zero value returned says that our program completed successfully (remember earlier I explained that functions can return data; here is an example). As you see in Chapter 5, this is the way return statements work in Objective-C.

Congratulations, again! You've just written, compiled, run, and deconstructed your first Objective-C program.

Customizing Xcode to Your Liking

Xcode has options galore, many of which won't make any sense until you have quite a bit of programming experience, but a few are worth thinking about now. So I go through how you can set preferences in Xcode:

1. **With Xcode open, choose Xcode⇨Preferences.**

2. **Click the Behaviors tab at the top of the Preferences window to show the Behaviors pane.**

   The Xcode Preferences window refreshes to show the Behaviors pane.

The right side of the pane shows the Events pane (the check marks indicate events for which settings are set), whereas the left side shows the possible actions for an event.

3. **Select Run Generates Output in the left column and then choose the Show, Hide, or If No Output Hide option from the Debug area pop-up menu to the left of the debugger in the right pane.**

   This step controls what appears while you run your app. By default, you'll find that the check box for showing the debugger in the Debug area is selected. (See Chapter 8 for more about debugging.)

4. **Select other options from the left column (perhaps Build Starts, Build Generates New Issues, Build Succeeds, or Build Fails) and experiment with the options available.**

   You can link an event with playing a sound (something I like to do) or have an event trigger the Xcode icon bouncing up and down in the Dock. You can change many options in the Behaviors pane — too many to cover in this chapter! But take a look through them and experiment — they can make your life much easier.

   Figure 2-23 shows the behaviors I have chosen if the run pauses. (By *pause,* I mean the run hits, say, a breakpoint; I cover breakpoints in Chapter 8.) I like to have a sound inform me in case I'm busy daydreaming (submarine seems like the appropriate sound to play here).

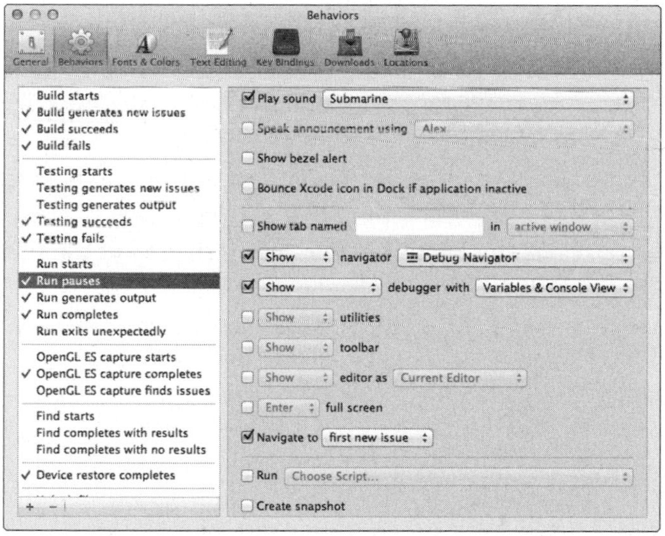

Figure 2-23:
Setting
behaviors.

Figure 2-24 shows the behaviors I have chosen if a build fails. I like to use a sound for this occurrence as well. I also want to have the Issue navigator display. (See Chapter 8 for more about the value and use of the Issue navigator.) I also want it to navigate to the first new issue.

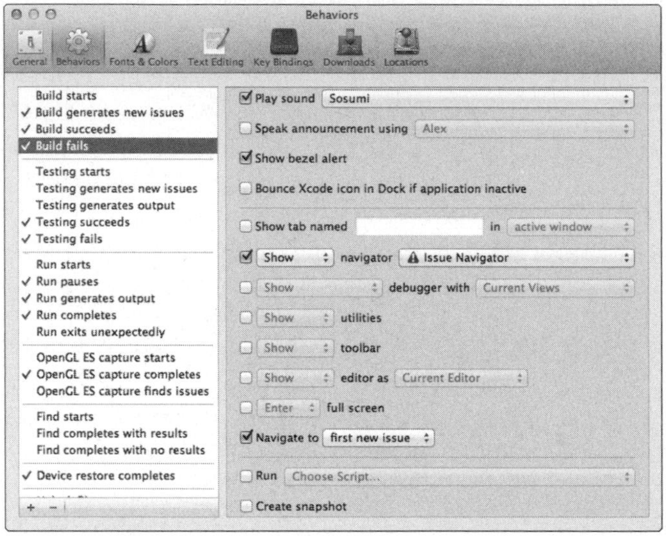

Figure 2-24:
Choosing
a behavior
for when a
build fails.

5. **Click the Downloads tab at the top of the Preferences window and then select Documentation in the segmented control.**

6. **Select the Check for and Install Updates Automatically check box and then click the Check and Install Now button.**

   This step ensures that the documentation remains up to date and enables you to load and access other documentation.

7. **(Optional) Click the Fonts & Colors tab at the top of the Preferences window and use the options to change your workspace theme.**

   When I get bored, I sometimes change the theme to Midnight to get a black background.

8. **(Optional) Click the Text Editing tab at the top of the Preferences window and set your text-editing preferences.**

   I set the Indent width to 2 in the Indentation settings to get as much code on a line as possible.

9. **Click the red Close button in the upper-left corner of the window to close the Xcode Preferences window.**

Getting to Know the Xcode Text Editor

The main tool that you use to write code for an iOS or Mac OS application is the Xcode Text Editor. The Text Editor has a lot of great features, such as these:

✓ **Code Sense:** As you type code, you can have the Editor help out by inserting text that completes the name of whatever Xcode thinks you're going to enter.

Using Code Sense can be really useful, especially if you are like me and forget exactly what the arguments are for a function. When Code Sense is active (it is by default), Xcode uses the text you typed, as well as the context within which you typed it, to provide suggestions for completing what it thinks you're *going to* type. You can accept suggestions by pressing Tab or Return. You may also display a list of completions by pressing Escape.

Try typing **NSL** in the Editor view and see what happens.

✓ **Code folding:** With code folding, you can collapse code that you're not working on and display only the code that requires your attention. You do this by clicking in the column to the left of the code you want to hide.

✓ **The Text Editor navigation bar (see Figure 2-25):** This navigation bar provides you with an easy way to navigate through the files in your project. These are shown in Figure 2-25. I explain more about them as you use them:

  • *Related Files Menu button:* Clicking this button displays a menu from which you can select files that Xcode considers to be related to the file you're currently editing.

  • *Back and Forward buttons:* You can use these buttons to cycle through the different files you've viewed in the editor during your work.

  • *Project hierarchy buttons:* When you select a file from the Project navigator for display in the Text Editor, the Project path to the file is displayed in the navigation bar. For instance, if you select `main.m`, you will see `First Program` (the Project), followed by `First Program` (the folder within the Project), followed by `main.m`, and finally followed by `No Selection`. This last item is the function that contains the cursor — if you click anywhere within the curly braces following the `main` function, you will see the last item change to `main()`.

✓ **Launching a file in a separate window:** Double-click the filename in the Project navigator to launch the file in a new window. This enables you folks with big monitors, or multiple monitors, to look at more than one file at a time.

Figure 2-25:
The Text
Editor navi-
gation bar.

Go back

Project hierarchy

Go forward

If you have any questions about what something does, just position the mouse pointer above the button and a tooltip explains it.

If you have never programmed before, some of this information may not make sense right away. But it makes sense as you do more coding while going through this book. I suggest that you come back to this section and the next two sections as you go through Chapter 6.

Accessing Documentation

Like many developers, you may find yourself wanting to dig deeper when it comes to a particular bit of code. That's when you really appreciate Xcode's Quick Help, header file access, documentation window, Help menu, and Find tools. With these tools, you can quickly access the documentation for a particular class, method, or property.

For example, what if you had a burning desire to find out more about NSLog?

Quick Help

Quick Help is an unobtrusive window that provides the documentation for a single symbol. It pops up inline, although you can use Quick Help as a symbol inspector (which stays open) by moving the window after it opens. You can also customize the display in Documentation preferences in Xcode preferences.

To get Quick Help for a symbol, press the Option key and click the symbol in the Text Editor (in this case, NSLog; see Figure 2-26).

Figure 2-26:
Getting
Quick Help.

> **NSLog**
>
> Name: NSLog
> Declaration: void NSLog (NSString *format, ...);
> Availability: Mac OS X (10.0 and later)
> Abstract: Logs an error message to the Apple System Log facility.
> Declared In: NSObjCRuntime.h
> Reference: Foundation Functions Reference

The header file for a symbol

Headers are a big deal in code because they're the place where you find the class declaration, which includes all its instance variables and method declarations. (You find out about classes and headers in Chapter 6). To get the header file for a symbol, press ⌘ and click the symbol in the Text Editor (for example, see Figure 2-27, where I pressed ⌘ and then clicked `NSLog`).

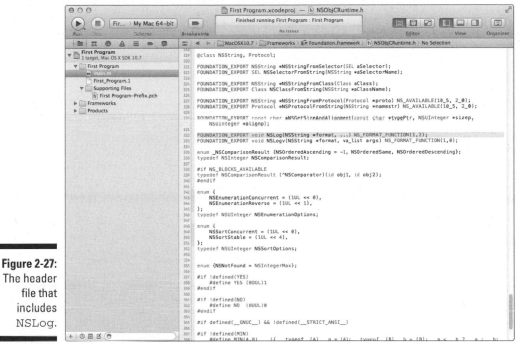

Figure 2-27:
The header file that includes `NSLog`.

This works for your classes as well.

Accessing Quick Help

You can quickly get summary information about any item in your source code by following this procedure:

1. **Click the Hide or Show Utilities view button to display the Utilities view.**

2. **Click the Show Quick Help inspector to display the Quick Help available for selections in the Text Editor.**

3. **Select** `NSLog` **in the Text Editor.**

   You should see the Quick Help display, as shown in Figure 2-28. Clicking the links within the Quick Help brings you more information by using the Documentation panel of the Organizer window, as shown in Figure 2-29.

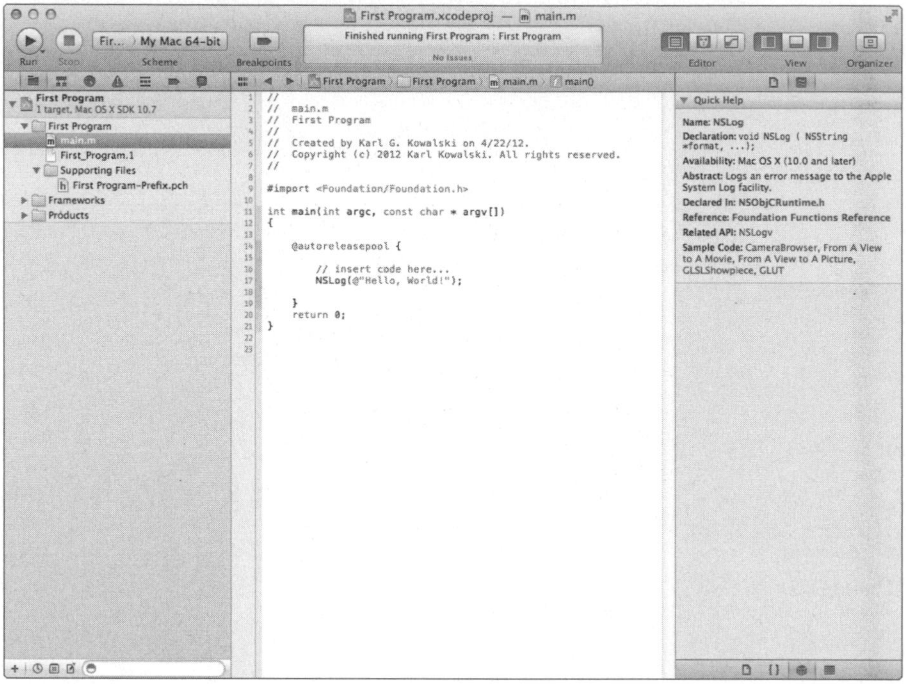

Figure 2-28:
Quick Help
for `NSLog`.

Help menu

The Help menu search field also lets you search Xcode documentation, as well as open the Documentation window and Quick Help.

You can also right-click a symbol and get a pop-up menu that gives you similar options to what you see in the Help menu. This is shown in Figure 2-30.

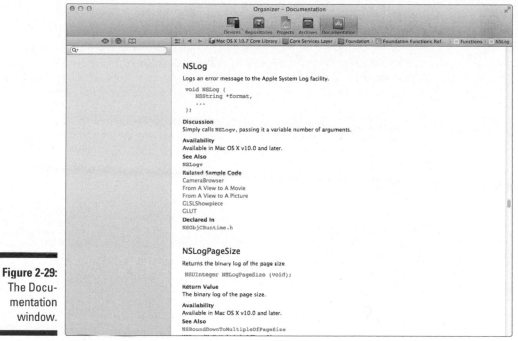

Figure 2-29:
The Docu-
mentation
window.

Cut
Copy
Paste

Find Selected Text in Workspace...

Show Issue
Jump to Definition

Structure   ▶

Discard Changes...

Refactor   ▶

Open in Assistant Editor
Reveal in Project Navigator
Reveal in Symbol Navigator
Show in Finder

Continue to Here

Figure 2-30:
Right-click
NSLog.

Speech   ▶

Source Editor Help   ▶

Add to iTunes as a Spoken Track

Find

Xcode can also help you find things in your own project. The submenu you access by choosing Edit➪Find provides several options for finding text in your own project. Choosing Edit➪Find➪Find or pressing ⌘+F searches in the file in the Editor window. It opens a Find toolbar to help you navigate.

You can also use Find to go through your whole project by choosing Edit➪Find➪Find in Project or by pressing ⌘+Shift+F. I pressed ⌘+Shift+F, which opens the Search navigator, as shown in Figure 2-31. I typed **NSLog** and then in the drop-down menu, I selected In Project.

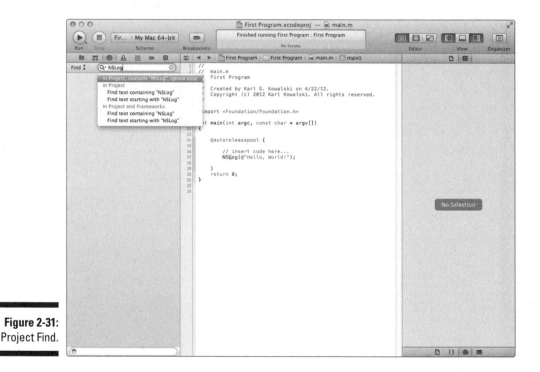

Figure 2-31:
Project Find.

You can see the results shown in Figure 2-32. I selected NSLog(@"Hello, World!"); in the top pane, and the file it's in opened in the bottom pane.

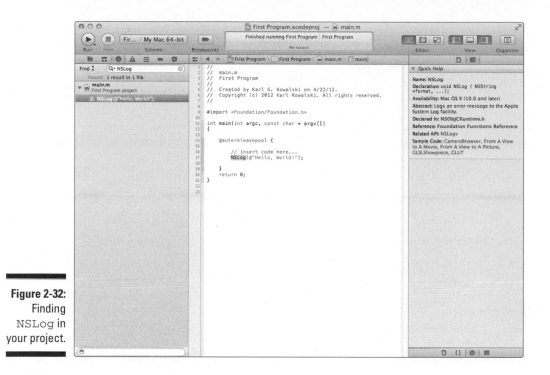

Figure 2-32:
Finding
`NSLog` in
your project.

If you've had some programming experience, you may also realize that you
have a lot of options as far as the compiler is concerned. You have a great
deal of control over the warnings the compiler gives you, as well as the option
to turn warnings into errors so that they don't slip by you (it happens to the
best of us). So take a look at Figure 2-32. If you select First Program at the top
of the Project navigator, you display the project information. If you click the
Build Settings tab and scroll all the way down (as I did in Figure 2-33) to Apple
LLVM compiler 4.0 – Warning Policies, you can see the start of many options
to customize those warnings to your heart's content. (You may have to click
the disclosure triangle for Apple LLVM compiler 4.0 – Warning Policies.) You
can even tell Xcode to always treat warnings as errors by setting the Treat
Warnings as Errors drop menu to Yes.

Figure 2-33:
Build con-
figuration.

On the Web

The website URL that accompanies this book has a folder for each chapter, starting with Chapter 4. Each of these folders has another folder that contains the Xcode project that provides the starting point for each chapter — labeled (cleverly enough) Chapter *XX* Start Here.

That same chapter folder has a folder that contains the final version of the project for each chapter labeled Example *XX* (except for Chapters 4 and 8, where a final version isn't applicable) or, in those chapters with more than one exercise, you see the exercises are labeled Example *XX* A, Example *XX* B, and so on. I explain what is in each of the folders in the appropriate chapter.

If you want to work with anything from the website, you have to download it to your Mac (or to any other folder) to be able to build the project.

Working with the Examples

My experience, both personally and in teaching, is that the more you type — that is, the more code you actually write — the more you discover and the faster you discover it.

You work on a single application starting in Chapter 5 that finally ends up as an application for both the iOS and Mac OS X. This application illustrates all the things you need to know to program in Objective-C. I help you build it step by step, much like a developer creates a "real" application. At times, you enter some code only to delete it later. Go with the flow. A method is behind all of this, one that has been developed to get you going as quickly as possible and to know as much as you need to, without being overwhelmed. More important, you see not only how to do something but also why you should do it that way.

The best way to work through this book is to complete Chapter 4, and then follow along with me and add to that project as you go from chapter to chapter (and create the new project along the way). If you are not the linear sort, or you want a fresh, up-to-date copy of the project, you can always use the Start Here copy from the website for each chapter. I do think adding to what you have already done is better and more in tune with how you (and other developers) really work — often two steps forward and a quarter step back.

Finally, experiment as much as you can. Don't always take my word for it; test things out, see what happens when you change something, and play with it until you really understand how something works. That's how I learned Objective-C, and I'm sure it will work for you as well.

Chapter 3

The Object in Objective-C

*I*n Chapter 2, you get your first taste of programming (all right, enough with the food), and throughout the next 15 chapters, I show you everything you need to know to write computer programs. Although you may think that's pretty cool, you shouldn't be satisfied with that alone. Your goal shouldn't be to simply be able to write programs by using Objective-C; your goal should be to write *good* programs by using Objective-C.

So what makes a good program? Well, a blinding flash of the obvious answer is one that meets the needs of the user. While that is true, it is only part of the answer. What also makes a program good is how easy it is to make changes to it.

I want to use the example I give you in Chapter 1 — a computer program that tracks my expenses when I travel. It keeps track of my budget and converts foreign currency charges into dollars.

As I develop this program, I am going to have to make changes to it for three reasons.

▶ **I'll want to add new functionality.** For example, starting out, the program will work with cash and credit card transactions. I'll get that up and running, and then eventually I'll want to be able to add ATM transactions, and also track my hotel and plane reservations. I will want to be able to do this without having to completely rewrite the program. In fact, I would like to be able to add a new feature without changing anything at all in the existing program and have that feature transparently incorporated into the program. The term for this is *extensible,* and that means adding functionality to an existing program or module.

✔ **I'll want to improve or change functionality.** To start with, I'm willing to enter the exchange rate by hand. Eventually, I'll want the program to go out and find the current exchange rate for me. Again, I want to be able to do this without having to make any changes in the program except to code the new functionality. The term for this is *enhanceable*. And that means changing the way existing functionality works.

✔ **I'll want to fix bugs.** It's hard to believe, but bugs will show up. I want to be able to fix them, without breaking something else.

One of the problems with changing things is that often a little change in one part of your program can have a disastrous effect on the rest of it. Most of us have had a similar experience when upgrading a program or the OS. I remember a fellow programmer once lamenting, "but I only changed one line of code," after making changes to a program and then putting it into production (without taking it through the entire testing process) — only to have it take down an entire mainframe complex.

To minimize the side effects of "only changing one line of code" requires that you divide your programs into *modules* so that a change you make in one module won't have an effect on the rest of your code. I refer to this as *transparency*.

A *module* is simply a self-contained, or independent, unit that can be combined with other units to get the job done. Modules are the solution to a rather knotty problem — even a simple program can run into hundreds of lines of instructions, and you need a way to break them into parts to make them understandable. But more important, you want to use modules because they make programs easier to modify, which, as you see you invariably need to do.

Not All Modules Are Created Equal

The idea of dividing your program into modules is as old as programming itself, and you know how old that is. The programming style (or *paradigm*) I mention in Chapter 1 dictates the way you do that.

You need to be concerned with two paradigms at this point, although with more experience, you'll probably explore others.

Functions (or things like that), and groups of functions, have historically been the basis of modularization. This way of dividing things into modules is used in the programming style or paradigm known as *procedural programming*. Going back to the example I started with — a program that helps me track my expenses — you will find functions like *spend dollars* or *charge foreign currency,* which will operate on *transaction* and *budget data.*

In the twenty-first century, however, the procedural paradigm has pretty much been supplanted, at least for commercial applications, by *object-oriented programming.* In Objective-C (and other object-oriented languages) objects (and as you will see, their corresponding classes) are the way a program is divided. In an object-oriented program, you will find *transaction objects* and *budget objects.*

For years, the arguments raged about which was the better way, procedural or object-oriented, with each side pointing out the limitations in the other's approach. This is not the place to relive it. It will serve no value because (a) for all practical purposes, the debate has been settled in favor of object-oriented programming for commercial applications (except for a few fanatics), and (b) because you are mastering Objective-C, which is an object-oriented language. You experience for yourself the differences in Chapters 5 and 6.

But to give you some perspective, you can think of objects in an *object-oriented program* as working as a team necessary to reach a goal. Functions in a *procedural program* are more like the command and control structure of a large corporation (think GM) or the army. Which is more flexible?

So, I'll get on with understanding objects.

Understanding How Objects Behave

An object-oriented program consists of a network of interconnected objects, essentially modules that call upon each other to solve a part of the puzzle. The objects work like a team. Each object has a specific role to play in the overall design of the program and is able to communicate with other objects. Objects communicate requests to other objects to do something by using *messages.*

Object-oriented programmers (including yours truly) think about objects as actors and talk about them that way. Objects have responsibilities. You *ask* them to do things, they *decide* what to do, and they *behave* in a certain way. You do this even with objects like sandwiches. You could, for example, tell a sandwich in an object-oriented program to go cut itself in half (ouch!) or tell a shape to draw itself.

It's this resemblance to real things that gives objects much of their power and appeal. You can use them not only to represent things in the real world — a person, an airplane reservation, a credit card transaction — but also to represent things in a computer, such as a window, button, or slider.

Inventing Objective-C

Brad Cox (a computer scientist among other things) invented Objective-C in the early 1980s. He took SmallTalk — one of the favorite object-oriented programming languages at the time — and used it as a basis to add extensions to the (non-object-oriented) standard ANSI C language to make it object-oriented.

ANSI C is the standard published by the American National Standards Institute (ANSI) for the C programming language. Having a standard means that no if, ands, or buts exist about what an instruction does — and it does the same thing no matter what computer, operating system, or compiler you are using.

Objective-C got its big break when it was chosen for the NeXTSTEP development environment, which eventually became the development system you use today on the Mac to develop applications for the Mac and iOS devices.

But what gives object-oriented programming its power is that the way objects are defined and the way they interact with each other make it relatively easy to accomplish the goals of extensibility and enhanceability — that is, achieve the transparency that is the hallmark of a good program. This is accomplished by using two features in object-oriented programming languages:

- ✔ *Encapsulation* **is about celebrating your object's ignorance about how things work in the objects they use.** My wife has no idea how a computer works but can effectively browse the Internet, create documents, and receive and send e-mail. Most people who can successfully drive cars have no idea of how the engine works. I'll refer to this as the I-don't-care-and-please-don't-tell-me approach.

  Encapsulation makes it possible for me to change how an object carries out its responsibilities or behaves (enhanceability) and to add new responsibilities to an object (extensibility) without having to disturb the existing code that uses those objects. One of the primary things that objects encapsulate is their data, and although this probably evokes a big yawn now, you will realize why this is important in Chapter 5. It also makes it possible, as you will see in Chapter 11, to even transparently add new objects.

- ✔ *Polymorphism* **is about cultivating more of the same.** When I get dressed in the morning, I throw on a pair of jeans and a black T-shirt. For me at least, one black T-shirt is as good as another, whether it comes from Nieman Marcus or Costco. Your objects shouldn't have to care about how one object is different from another as long as the object does what the requesting object needs it to do. I'll refer to this as the more-of-the-same approach.

  This feature in object-oriented languages makes it possible to add new objects of the same type and have your program handle them without making any changes to the code that uses them. For example, I can create a program that processes cash and credit card transactions, and then sometime later I can add an ATM transaction and have the program process that new kind of transaction without having to make any changes to the processing logic.

With respect to all the new ideas I have thrown at you, this is usually the hardest concept for most people to grasp right away (the name *polymorphism* doesn't help), although everyone gets it after seeing it in action. I give you a good example later in this chapter and cover it extensively in Chapter 11. I promise you that when you use it in your program, you'll wonder why you thought it was so hard in the first place.

Seeing the Concepts in Action

Reading about concepts can keep me entertained for only a short time, a very short time, before I need some concrete examples. I want to tell you a story about how encapsulation and polymorphism became real for me.

Encapsulation

I lived (briefly) in Minneapolis, Minnesota, where it can be not just cold, but *really* cold. During that time, I invented a device (in my head at least) called the uPhone — which was a hand-held device (it looked something like Figure 3-1) that enabled me to start my car and turn on the heater before I left the house in the morning.

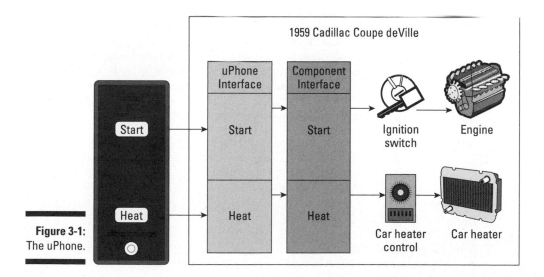

Figure 3-1: The uPhone.

I happily used my uPhone until one day my mechanic found a new heater for me that worked much more quickly and used a lot less gas. I was a bit concerned, but he told me not to worry; it was plug-compatible with my old heater — it had the same controls. All he had to do was just plug it in. Surprisingly (to me not to him), when he installed it, my uPhone application still worked in the same way. You can see that in Figure 3-2.

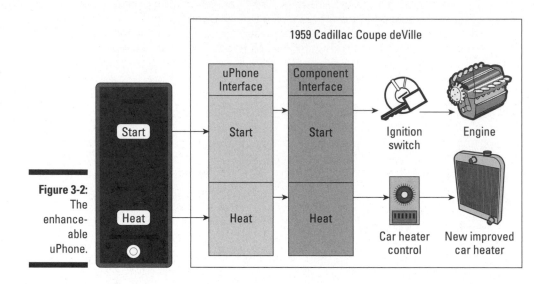

Figure 3-2:
The
enhance-
able
uPhone.

The reason that worked, as you can see in Figure 3-2, was that my application (including the uPhone, uPhone interface, and component interface) knew nothing about heaters. All the application really cared about was the heater switch (car heater control). As long as that stayed the same, everything worked. Had I not used the uPhone and component interfaces, but had instead modified the heater so the uPhone actually interacted with the heater components, I would have had a more difficult job on my hands.

To make your programs enhanceable, you want to depend on the implementation details as little as possible. As I mention previously, the programming term for this I-don't-care-and-please-don't-tell-me approach is *encapsulation*.

What you are doing is hiding *how* things are being done from *what* is being done. In a program, that means hiding the internal mechanisms and data structures of a software component behind a defined interface in such a way that users of the component (other pieces of software) only need to know what the component does and do not have to make themselves dependent on the details of how the component does what it promises to do. This means the following:

✔ The internal mechanisms of a module can be improved without having to make any changes in any of the modules that use it.

✔ The component is protected from user meddling (like me trying to rewire a heater).

✔ Things are less complex because the interdependencies between modules have been reduced as much as possible.

This is the way that modules, or objects, should work in an object-oriented program. You want the objects to limit their knowledge of other objects to what those objects can do — like turn on and off. That way, if you change something, you don't have to go digging through a zillion lines of code to figure out whether any code in your program is depending on something being done in a particular way and then changing that dependent code to work with the new way it will be done. Ignorance is bliss — for the programmer, that is.

Polymorphism

After my device worked so well for me, my wife decided she wanted one, too. The problem is she had a different kind of car with a different heater control, and my old component interface wouldn't work. Well, this time I did have to make some changes, but all I had to do was change the component interface to the heater. I kept the uPhone interface the same, which also meant no changes to the uPhone, as shown in Figure 3-3.

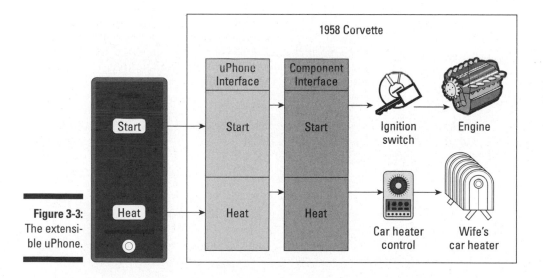

Figure 3-3: The extensible uPhone.

What you are looking for is a situation in which the requestor doesn't even care who receives the message, as long as it can get what it wants.

So the uPhone doesn't care whether it is sending the heat message to a 1959 Cadillac, a 1958 Corvette, or even an SSC Ultimate Aero TT, as long as it can respond to the message.

This capability of different objects to respond, each in its own way, to identical messages is called *polymorphism*.

Whereas encapsulation enables you to ignore how things are done, polymorphism enables you to escape the specific details of differences between objects that do the same thing in different ways. In the real world, if you can drive a Chevy, you can drive a Caddy or any other car, as long as the controls are more or less the same. It is not that a 1959 Cadillac and a 1958 Corvette are the same; if they were, what would be the point? What is important is that they are different, but you can go about using them in the same way.

I used to travel a lot and rent lots of cars. Can you imagine if I had to spend two hours being trained every time I rented a different car? In a program, different objects might perform the same methods in different ways — if I spend cash, a cash transaction object will subtract that amount from my budget. If I use my credit card, a credit card transaction will first have to convert the amount in foreign currency that I charged to dollars and then subtract it from the budget.

Reusable Code

When people talk about object-oriented programming, they tend to talk about two things. The first is all that cool encapsulation and polymorphism stuff, which makes it easy to modify programs. Then they talk about reuse, and that you can create reusable objects that save time and money. Years ago, you always heard talk about object stores, where you could buy objects that would do what you needed them to do.

Will this book teach you how to write reusable code? Well, it depends on what you mean by *reusable*. If you really think about it, when you enhance or extend your program, what you are doing is *reusing* the existing code to essentially create a "new" program. And in that respect, the answer is yes.

As you will see, the best models for reusability are found in the frameworks you'll use to develop applications for the iPhone and Mac. You reuse the frameworks by adding your own application functionality to the framework that already includes the code that can display windows and controls and menus — the whole kit and caboodle of the user interface, and then some.

I explain some of the things that the framework designers did to make reusing their frameworks as easy as it is. You'll find that when you use those same principles and techniques in your programs, you will have taken a giant step forward in enabling the kind of reusability you need to make your programs enhanceable and extensible.

Part II
Speaking the Language of Objective-C

The 5th Wave   By Rich Tennant

"We're here to clean the code."

In this part . . .

Now that you have the tools downloaded, it's time to start programming. I help you do that in this part by first covering most of the Objective-C instruction set, which you need to get started. Think of the instruction set as the words that Objective-C understands, along with some rules about how you are allowed to combine them into sentences.

I also show you the language features that enable you to create industrial-strength applications. This is what makes your application suitable for commercial distribution. I also get you up to speed using some prepackaged functionality (frameworks) that helps make your programming tasks easier.

You get the rundown on the vocabulary of a new language, but as you will find out, it's a lot easier than learning to speak Sanskrit, for example.

Chapter 4

Language and Programming Basics

As I mention in Chapter 3, Objective-C is a set of extensions to standard ANSI C. This means that at some point (that is, this chapter), you'll have to sit down and understand the basics of the C instruction set, along with some less-than-inspiring examples and detailed explanations on the basics of the language — kind of like mastering the alphabet. I know that all this can be tedious and excruciatingly boring, although when you're just starting out, you don't have any other way (we all have to pay our dues at some point). But after you are done with this chapter, you will switch to finding out about Objective-C by developing a "real world" application, which I promise is (for the most part) much more interesting. So hang in there.

It All Comes Down to Your Statements

At the end of the day, it's all about the instructions you give the computer. Those instructions are called *statements*. You can easily recognize a statement because it ends with a semicolon, as shown here:

```
NSLog(@"This is a statement");
```

You find a number of different kinds of statements. In this chapter, I show you two of them:

- ✔ **Declarations** of a variable allow space for data. They look something like this:

  ```
  int aNumber;
  ```

  Declarations are used to allocate areas in memory where you can store data.

- ✔ **Instructions,** or "do this, please." They usually look like the following:

  ```
  a= b + c;
  NSLog(@"Yo Stella");
  ```

  Instructions can consist of the following:

  Operators, which are symbols that represent operations. For example the +, shown in the preceding example, is an arithmetic operator. I cover operators in this chapter.

  Functions, which are groups of statements. NSLog, printf, and main are examples of a function. I cover functions in Chapter 5.

  Objects, which group together methods (similar to a function) and data. I cover objects in Chapters 6 and 7.

You also find other kinds of statements. One kind you'll be using describes how data is structured (see Chapter 5 for more on data structures). Another kind of statement has to do with the language itself, such as typedef, which I cover in Chapter 5. You also find control statements, such as the if statement, which I start explaining later in this chapter in the section "Making Logical Decisions in Your Code." I finish that explanation, along with loops, in Chapter 9.

Your program will also have other lines of code. These lines will consist of things like compiler directives such as

```
@implementation
```

as well as preprocessor directives (the preprocessor is used by the compiler before compilation to expand macros, which are brief abbreviations for longer constructs) such as

```
#include
```

I explain compiler and preprocessor directives as you need to use them.

Computer languages are really like all other languages in that they have *syntax* and *semantics.* Because the compiler will be happy to give you *syntax errors,* and some things you will read will use the term *semantics,* I explain what each means.

Syntax

Syntax refers to the ways that symbols may be combined to create well-formed statements in a given language. Think of all the grammar you had to master in school, and you have a good idea of what syntax is. Syntax errors are what the compiler gives you when it can't understand the code you have written.

Semantics

But even though your code may be syntactically (grammatically) correct, it still may be meaningless. For example, Noam Chomsky's

> *Colorless green ideas sleep furiously*

is syntactically correct but has no meaning (at least to most of us). *Semantics* is about meaning, and it describes the behavior of a computer when executing a program in the language. It describes what you get as the result of an operation:

```
a = b + c;
```

For example, a = b + c means that the value of b is added to the value of c, without modifying either of their values, and the result is assigned to a. The previous value for a is gone and replaced with the new value. (I bet you never thought high school algebra would come in this handy.)

Semantics also describes the results of a series of operations or statements as well. For example, a function named computeZimbabweanValue (I explain what functions are in Chapter 5) computes the number of Zimbabwean dollars you can get for one U.S. dollar at the current exchange rate.

You have semantic errors when the program doesn't do what you expect it to do.

Understanding How Variables Work

The memory in a computer is organized in *bytes*. A byte is the minimum amount of memory that you can address. A byte can store a relatively small amount of data — one single character or a small integer (generally an integer between 0 and 255). But the computer actually groups bytes together to create and manipulate more complex data, such as integers and floating-point numbers.

Variables are nothing more than convenient names that refer to a specific piece of data, such as a number, that is stored in memory.

To use a variable in Objective-C, you must first *declare* it by specifying which *data type* you want it to be and give it a name — called an *identifier* — and, optionally, an initial value. Here is an Objective-C statement (that is, a line of code) where the type of the variable is specified, along with a name and an initial value:

```
int anInteger = 42;
```

Data types

When you ask some memory to store data, the compiler has to know what kind of data you want to store. The compiler needs to know that to determine how much memory you need and how that variable can be used (how to do math with it is one example). The kind of data you are requesting memory for is called a *data type,* and this concept will become important because not only can you use what are known as *built-in* types, which I explain in this section, but you can also create your own types, which I explain in Chapters 5 and 6.

While the minimum amount of memory that your computer can manage is 1 byte, the data types you will be working with will range from that 1 byte up to 8 bytes (or more for your own types or some of the types defined in the frameworks you will be using).

Table 4-1 shows the basic data types.

Table 4-1	Basic Data Types		
Type	*What It Is*	*Example*	*Size, bytes*
char	A character	N or g	1
int	An integer — a whole number	42, –42, 1234	4
float	Single-precision floating-point number	1.99999	4
double	Double-precision floating-point number	1.9999999999	8

Figure 4-1 illustrates an example of the amount of memory allocated to a char and an int, respectively. Each numbered box represents one byte, with each number representing the unique position of that byte in memory.

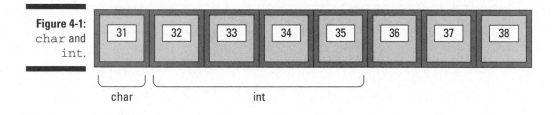

Figure 4-1:
char and int.

char   int

You also find a number of variations on the int, which are shown in Table 4-2.

Table 4-2	Additional Types Based on int		
Type	*What It Is*	*Example*	*Size, bytes*
short	A short integer	42, –42, 1234	2
long	A double short	42, –42, 1234	4
long long	A double long	4398046511104, –2251799813685248	8

You also find types like BOOL, void, and id, which I explain as you need to use them.

With the exception of both the float and the double, each of the types can be *signed* or *unsigned*. If you don't specify *signed* or *unsigned,* the compiler will assume signed.

If you don't specify a type, the compiler will assume you want an int. For example, you can use signed and unsigned to mean a signed int and unsigned int, respectively.

Note that

```
signed anInteger = 42;
```

is the same as

```
int anInteger = 42;
```

If it's a kind of int, the largest value a data type can hold depends on its size and whether it is signed or unsigned, as shown in Table 4-3.

Table 4-3	Signed and Unsigned Data Types
Size, bytes	*Range*
1	signed: −128 to 127
	unsigned: 0 to 255
2	signed: −32768 to 32767
	unsigned: 0 to 65535
4	signed: −2147483648 to 2147483647
	unsigned: 0 to 4294967295
8	signed: −9,223,372,036,854,775,808 to 9,223,372,036,854,775,807
	unsigned: 0 to18,446,744,073,709,551,615

For floating-point numbers, such as float or double, you should think instead in terms of *significant digits*. For a float, the number of significant digits is 7 or 8, and for a double, the number of significant digits is 15 or 16.

Identifier

As I said, when you declare a variable in Objective-C, not only do you specify the data type, but you also give it a name — called an *identifier* — that you can use to refer to the variable. Consider the declaration I started with:

```
int anInteger = 42;
```

In this case, the name or identifier is anInteger. I can then use anInteger whenever I want to refer to the variable.

You do have to follow some rules when it comes to the identifier:

✔ **Use only letters from the alphabet.** For your purposes, even though you have other choices, name your identifiers by using one or more of the 26 letters of the alphabet.

✔ **Use uppercase to help readability.** Start by using lowercase, but as I did with anInteger, if it helps readability and describes the variable better, use uppercase inside the name. Be sure to give your variables a name that describes them so that your code is more readable.

✔ **Avoid using words used by Apple or Objective-C.** Also be aware that names cannot match any of the words used by Apple (in the frameworks) or Objective-C. I include a list of reserved words at the end of this chapter, but don't worry, if you make a mistake, the compiler will let you know. Naming is generally not one of the major challenges in programming (easy for me to say), and after a while, you get the hang of it.

✔ **Pay attention to uppercase and lowercase.** And, oh yes, this is very important: The Objective-C language is a *case-sensitive* language. That means that an identifier written in uppercase letters is not equivalent to another one with the same name but written in lowercase letters. Thus, for example, the `Karl` variable is not the same as the `KARL` variable or the `karL` variable. These are three different variable identifiers.

Initialization

In a declaration, not only do you specify a type and a name, but you also *may* specify an initial value — as in the declaration

```
int anInteger = 42;
```

Take a look at the equal sign; it's not what you may think. Most people recognize the equal sign by, oh, about first grade, but the equal sign here is a little more than that. In fact, the equal sign is an *operator,* more specifically the *assignment operator.* It is an instruction that tells the computer to set that portion of memory that I am calling `anInteger` to the value of `42`.

Specifying an initial value is called *initialization,* and it's not required. For example,

```
int anInteger;
```

works just fine. Memory will be reserved, but you can't count on what the value will be. Of course, sometimes you don't care, such as when you are going to use that variable to hold the result of a subsequent operation.

I could also declare two variables by doing the following:

```
int anInteger1, anInteger2;
```

In this case, I reserved space for two `int`s: `anInteger1` and `anInteger2`.

Finally, note the semicolon at the end of the statement. A semicolon is required at the end of every statement. Because an *instruction* can span multiple lines, the semicolon is the way to tell the compiler that you are done with your instruction.

To summarize, the *declaration* I have been explaining is a request for memory to hold a data type of `int` that I can refer to using the name `anInteger`, which has an initial value of `42`, as illustrated in Figure 4-2. The memory location 32 is for illustrative purposes only. But I will return and use this example again when I discuss pointers later in this chapter in the section "Accessing Data with Pointers."

Figure 4-2:
The `int` known as `anInteger`.

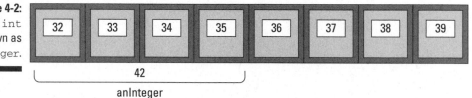

32   33   34   35   36   37   38   39

42

anInteger

Giving Instructions with Operators

Operators perform operations on (do things to) data, which enables you to actually do something with those pesky variables. As I explain in Chapter 1, operators are one of the basic building blocks that you'll work with.

In this chapter, I cover the operators you'll need to use. Quite a few operators are available to you, but if you made it through grammar school, most of them will be familiar.

Really learning how operators (and everything else) work in Objective-C

Before you start coding, I want to help you understand the best way to go through this chapter and the rest of the book. Entering the code is not meant to be a typing exercise. As you enter each line, you should be thinking about what will happen as a result of that line of code being executed. Then after you build the project, you should look to see whether you were correct in your expectation. If you were, great; you can continue. If not, you should reread the explanation until you are sure that you understand it. In most of this chapter (with a few exceptions), this issue won't be a problem. At times, however, the results of executing your code are not so obvious, or you may not be sure that you completely understood what you just read. I encourage you (I'll actually do a bit of nagging as well) to write code that uses what I am explaining, even if I do not have you do it in a formal exercise, to make sure that you understand it.

In fact, one of the themes running through this book is code, code, code. My experience, both personally and in teaching, is that the more you type (that is, the more code you actually write), the more you understand and the faster you understand it. (I know I have said this before, but just in case you thought I wasn't serious about it, I say it again.)

Using arithmetic operators

Using the lowly (or lovely, depending on your perspective) `int`, I look at the various operations you can perform.

In Chapter 2, you created a project called First Program. You can continue to use that project in this chapter, or you can copy it (to your desktop, for example) from the website that accompanies this book. You can find it in the Chapter 4 Start Here folder in the Chapter 4 folder.

To use that project to start writing code, follow these steps:

1. **Go to the Xcode Project Window, and in the Project Navigator pane, click the triangle next to First Program to expand the folder.**

2. **From the First Program folder, select** `First Program.m` **— this contains the** `main` **function.**

   The contents of the file appear in the main display pane of the Xcode editor.

3. **Look for the following lines of code:**

   ```
   #import <Foundation/Foundation.h>

   int main (int argc, const char * argv[]) {

     @autoreleasepool {

     // insert code here...
     NSLog(@"Hello, World!");

     }
     return 0;
   }
   ```

In some cases in the book, you see statements on two lines. I have to do that to fit the code on the page; you should use only one line where you can. This is especially important for strings, which will give you an error if they are on two lines, unless you tell the compiler that's what you want to do. I show you a way to have a single string span multiple lines in the section "Using Constants," later in this chapter.

4. **Delete bold, italic, underlined code (you won't need the memory management features).**

```
#import <Foundation/Foundation.h>

int main (int argc, const char * argv[]) {

  @autoreleasepool {

  // insert code here...
  NSLog(@"Hello, World!");

  }
  return 0;
}
```

Your editor window should look like what is shown in Figure 4-3.

I will be using this format for the balance of this chapter. So when I tell you to start with an *empty* `main` *function,* this is what I mean.

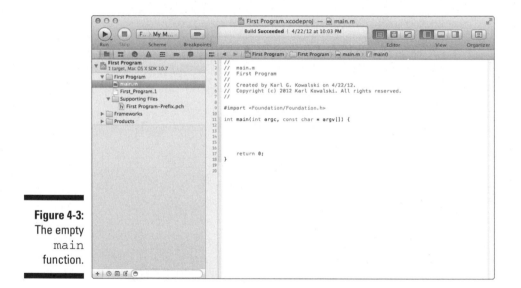

Figure 4-3:
The empty
`main`
function.

5. **Type the following lines of code after the first brace and before the** `return 0;` **statement:**

```
int a;
int b;
int c;

a = 1;
b = 2;
c=a+b;
```

```
NSLog (@" a + b = %i", c);
NSLog (@" a + b = %i",a + b);
NSLog (@" a still = %i", a);
NSLog (@" b still = %i", b);
```

When you're done typing, your code should look exactly like what is shown in Figure 4-4.

Remember, I said that variables should be descriptive, except sometimes, and this is one of those times. You'll also use single-letter variables such as *i* and *n* in things like loops (I cover loops in Chapter 9).

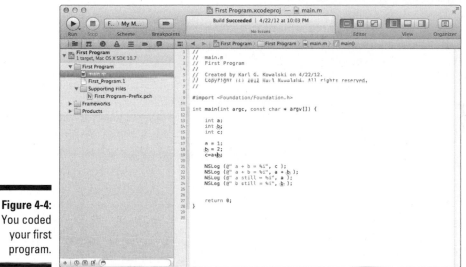

Figure 4-4:
You coded
your first
program.

As I said, the point of these exercises is to make sure that you understand what I am explaining. As you enter the code, you should be thinking about what the results of each line of code will be, and then build the program and use the output to confirm your understanding. To do that, I want to review what you just did:

1. You declared three variables, a, b, and c (they are not initialized, so you don't know what their value is):

```
int a;
int b;
int c;
```

2. You assigned values to a and b:

```
a = 1;
b = 2;
```

As I mention earlier, assignment is an operator that tells the computer to set the area of memory represented by a to 1 and the area represented by b to 2.

3. You added a and b and then assigned (placed) the result in c:

```
c=a+b;
```

In doing that, you just used another arithmetic operator, the *addition operator* (the assignment operator was the first one). You can use five arithmetic operators, as shown in the following list:

- +: Addition

- –: Subtraction

- *: Multiplication

- /: Division

- %: Modulo

In a programming language, a + b is an *expression*. An expression is a combination of variables, operators (and functions and messages, which I explain in Chapters 5 and 6, respectively) that can have a value. Computing that value is called *evaluating* the expression.

Although perhaps not obvious, a number like 42 or a variable like a are also considered expressions because both have a value.

In the statement c=a+b, no spaces are placed between the c and the =, or between any of the other identifiers or operators. Generally, spaces are not needed if the compiler can tell what you mean (although feel free to use them for readability, as I will). In this case, the compiler can recognize the operators, so spaces are not necessary.

4. You displayed the results:

```
NSLog (@" a + b = %i", c);
```

NSLog enables you to display in the Debugger Console (see Chapter 2 for more on displaying in the Debugger Console).

In the NSString (again, refer to Chapter 2 if this is unfamiliar), you use a % character as a placeholder for a value, and the character that follows it indicates the kind of value it is. This is called a *string format specifier*. So, in the expression

```
(@" a + b = %i", c)
```

%i is a string format specifier, and it says replace me with the value of what you see after the closing ", in this case c, and display c as an integer (i). As you can see, you follow the string you want to display with a comma and then a list of what you want to have replaced in the same order as they are specified in the string.

The string format specifiers supported are the format specifiers defined for the ANSI C function `printf()` plus %@ for any object. Here are some of the string format specifiers:

- %i: Signed 32-bit integer (`int`)
- %u: Unsigned 32-bit integer (`unsigned int`)
- %f: 64-bit floating-point number (`double`)

You can find all the string format specifiers by entering **string format specifiers** in the Search ADC field on the Mac or iPhone Dev Center websites, and then selecting the document String Programming Guide for Cocoa: String Format Specifiers.

5. You did a computation in the NSLog function and displayed the results:

```
NSLog (@" a + b = %i",a + b);
```

Even though you did a computation in the NSLog function, a + b, the value of the variables used as *operands* or *arguments* (such as a and b) did not change when using the arithmetic operators you have been using. To ensure that you understood that, you displayed a and b to make sure that they were both still the same:

```
NSLog (@" a still = %i", a);
NSLog (@" b still = %i", b);
```

This is a good example of what you should do to make sure that you understand how something works — display the result of a line of code. In this case, you want to make sure that you understand what does happen to the variables a and b after the expression (@" a + b = %i",a + b) is evaluated.

However, as you will see shortly, some operators do change the value of their operands, and I will be sure to point them out when you get to them.

With that review finished, you are ready to build and run the application. To do that, just click the Run button in the Project Window toolbar. The status bar in the Project window tells you all about build progress, build errors such as compiler errors, or warnings — and (oh, yeah) whether the build was successful.

Your results should look like what is shown Figure 4-5. If you changed your Xcode preferences in Chapter 2, the Debugger Console will display automatically. Otherwise, you will have to open it yourself by clicking the Hide or Show the Debug Area View button or pressing Shift+⌘+C.

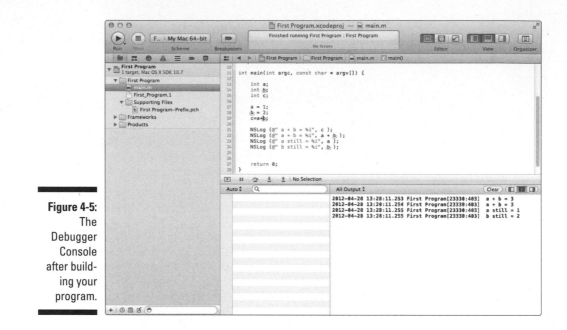

Figure 4-5:
The
Debugger
Console
after build-
ing your
program.

Now that you have gone through coding your first real program, I want to
show you some things about the other arithmetic operators.

Start with an empty `main` function (delete the code that you typed) and do
the following:

1. **Type the following lines of code between the first curly brace and the**
`return 0;` **statement:**

```
int a;
int b;
int c;

a = 2;
b = 3;

c = a % b;
NSLog (@" a %% b = %i", c);
c = b % a;
NSLog (@" b %% a = %i", c);
c = a % a;
NSLog (@" a %% a = %i", c);
c = a + b;
NSLog (@" a + b = %i", c);
c = b + a;
NSLog (@" b + a = %i", c);
c = a - b;
```

```
NSLog (@" a - b = %i", c);
c = b - a;
NSLog (@" b - a = %i", c);
c = a * b;
NSLog (@" a * b = %i", c);
c = a * b + 5 ;
NSLog (@" a * b + 5 = %i", c);
c = a * (b + 5);
NSLog (@" a * (b + 5) = %i", c);
c = (a * b) + 5;
NSLog (@" (a * b) + 5 = %i", c);
c = b * a;
NSLog (@" b * a = %i", c);
c = a / b;
NSLog (@" a / b = %i", c);
c = b / a;
NSLog (@" b / a = %i", c);
```

Writing code to make sure that you understand the arithmetic operators should be old hat to you by now, and perhaps a little boring; you may be thinking, "This is arithmetic!" Well, that's true, but some things are not so obvious when you do arithmetic on the computer. Take a look at some of the code you just entered, where the result of its execution may surprise you.

For example, an operator you probably haven't used that much (if ever) is % — the *modulus operator*. It is not what it appears to be, a percentage calculation. The result of the % operator is the remainder from the integer division of the first operand by the second (if the value of the second operand is 0, the behavior of % is undefined).

```
c = a % b;
NSLog (@" a %% b = %i", c);
```

results in

```
a % b = 2
```

and

```
c = b % a;
NSLog (@" b %% a = %i", c);
```

results in

```
b % a = 1
```

and finally

```
c = a % a;
NSLog (@" a %% a = %i", c);
```

results in

```
a % a = 0
```

So, as you can see, a divided by b, which is 2 divided by 3, gives you a remainder of 2. Similarly, 3 % 2 gives you a remainder of 1. However, 2 divided by 2 has no remainder, so the modulus is 0. Try a few other values for a and b and compile the code to see what happens.

The modulus operator can come in handy at times (you can use it to tell whether a number is even or odd, or whether it's a multiple of another number, for example), but it only works with integers. Notice that the NSLog statement that displays the results has two %s. That's because the % is also a control character, as you just saw (it tells the NSLog function that what follows is formatting information), so if you want to display a %, you have to use %%.

Look at the following statements:

```
c = a + b;
NSLog (@" a + b = %i", c);
c = b + a;
NSLog (@" b + a = %i", c);
c = a * b;
NSLog (@" a * b = %i", c);
c = b * a;
NSLog (@" b * a = %i", c ):
```

As you would expect, the order of operands using the arithmetic operators + and * doesn't matter, although when you are programming, it's generally better not to make too many assumptions.

Next, take a look at the following:

```
a * b + 5 = 11
a * (b + 5) = 16
(a * b) + 5 = 11
```

If parentheses were a challenge for you in high school, here's a chance to redeem yourself. Parentheses, as used in the preceding code, determine the order in which operations are performed. In Objective-C, * and / take precedence over + and –, which means that the compiler, unless directed otherwise, will generate code that does multiplication and division before it does the addition and subtraction. That's why a * b (or 2*3) then + 5 = 11. By using parentheses, you can force the addition to be performed first: a * (b + 5) = 2 * (3 + 5) equals 16.

2. **Click the Run button on the Project Window toolbar to build and run the application.**

    From now on, I'll just ask you to do this, although you can always press ⌘+R, or choose Product⇨Run if you like.

Your results in the Debugger Console should look like

```
a % b = 2
b % a = 1
a % a = 0
a + b = 5
b + a = 5
a - b = -1
b - a = 1
a * b = 6
a * b + 5 = 11
a * (b + 5) = 16
(a * b) + 5 = 11
b * a = 6
a / b = 0
b / a = 1
```

Where you may have gotten unexpected results is when you predicted
a / b and b / a. Here's what you found:

```
a / b = 0;
b / a = 1;
```

Why does 2 divided by 3 equal 0, much less 3 divided by 2 equal only 1?
As I said earlier, ints are whole numbers. If you want a decimal, you
need to declare it that way, and that is what floats are about.

Back to variables — floats

Floats and doubles are the types you will use if you want to see decimal
places in the results of your arithmetic calculations:

1. **Delete the previous example and type the following into your project:**

```
float a;
float b;
float c;

a = 2;
b = 3;

NSLog (@" a + b = %i", a + b);
NSLog (@" a - b = %i", a - b);
NSLog (@" b - a = %i", b - a);
NSLog (@" a * b = %i", a * b);
NSLog (@" a * b + 5 = %i", a * b + 5);
NSLog (@" a / b = %i", a / b);
NSLog (@" b / a = %i", b / a);
```

I'm going to save you some typing by just doing the computation in the
function as I showed you earlier.

2. **Click the Run button on the Project Window toolbar to build and run the application.**

   You should see the following results (or similar) in the Debugger Console:

   ```
   a + b = 1649899712
   a - b = 0
   b - a = 0
   a * b = 0
   a * b + 5 = 5
   a / b = 0
   b / a = 0
   ```

Were you surprised? You got this result because I didn't have you change how the results were to be formatted in the NSLog statement (remember the String Format Specifiers in the first example). In the code you just entered, you are specifying that the result is an int (see the %i shown in bold in the following line):

```
NSLog (@" a * b + 5 = %i", a * b + 5);
```

The computer, just following your instructions, does what it is supposed to do with the int. I had you do this because this is a common error and a source of great confusion for many beginning programmers (see also some discussion of it in Chapter 19 in the debugging tip to create a "paper" trail).

Also notice the compiler warnings in Figure 4-6. The first warning might be useful if you realized that you actually meant to use a variable and didn't. Here it was just sloppiness on my part (actually I wanted to make the point). The remaining warnings are telling you that you're using a formatter for an int but the argument you're providing is a double.

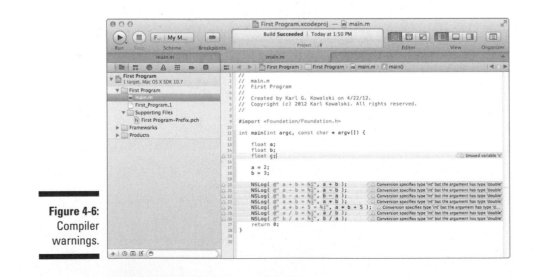

Figure 4-6:
Compiler
warnings.

To get the results of your calculation to display correctly, and to get rid of the annoying compiler warnings, do the following:

1. **Delete the previous example and this time type the following:**

```
float a;
float b;
//float c;

a = 2;
b = 3;

NSLog (@" a + b = %f", a + b);
NSLog (@" a - b = %f", a - b);
NSLog (@" b - a = %f", b - a );
NSLog (@" a * b = %f", a * b);
NSLog (@" a * b + 5 = %f", a * b + 5);
NSLog (@" a / b = %f", a / b);
NSLog (@" b / a = %f", b / a);
```

The String Format Specifier %f in an NSLog function tells the function to display a double — that is more or less the standard on the Mac for a floating point. The difference is that a float that will have only 7 or 8 significant digits, whereas a double will have 15 or 16.

Although you won't see comments in the examples I will be taking you through (because I describe what is happening in detail in the text), it is important that you use them in your own code. To have the compiler treat something as a comment, you use two forward slashes:

```
//float c;
```

Anything to the right of a // is a comment, even if it is on the same line as an instruction or declaration or anything else (it also turns green in Xcode), as in the following line:

```
double a = 4.2; //This is treated as a comment
```

You can also comment out large blocks by starting with /* and ending the block with */. Be careful; these blocks can't be nested. If you try to compile the following code, the even more stuff line will not be treated as a comment. Go try that on your own. You'll see that even more stuff will not turn green, and you'll get a compiler error when you build it:

```
/* some stuff
/* some more stuff */
even more stuff */
```

Extensively commenting your code is critical. Use real explanations about what something does, as well as why you wrote the code the way you did. What and why you did something may not be obvious, not only to someone else who reads your code but even to you a few days later.

2. **Click the Run button on the Project Window toolbar to build and run the application.**

You should see the following results in the Debugger Console:

```
a + b = 5.000000
a - b = -1.000000
b - a = 1.000000
a * b = 6.000000
a * b + 5 = 11.000000
a / b = 0.666667
b / a = 1.500000
```

This time you get what you expect.

Floating-point numbers can be expressed in the following ways:

```
double a = 4.2;
double b = 4.2e1;
double c = 4.2e-1;
```

The following code will display a, b, and c:

```
NSLog (@" a = %f, b = %f, c = %f",a , b, c);
```

What you get is

```
a = 4.200000, b = 42.000000, c = 0.420000
```

If you want to specify the significant digits you want to be displayed, all you have to use are a decimal point and a number between the % and the f — %.2f, as in the following:

```
NSLog (@"a = %.2f, b = %.2f, c = %.2f",a ,b, c);
```

This displays

```
a = 4.20, b = 42.00, c = 0.42
```

Bitwise operators

On the computer, your data is actually stored as 1s and 0s, which corresponds to something called a *bit*. In fact, the basic computations you do are in something called *binary arithmetic*.

I'm going to leave binary arithmetic as an exercise for you, the reader. Although I find it fascinating, you probably don't, and it is not usually necessary for most programmers to know. If you need to understand it, understand it when you need to; that's what I always say.

If you do understand it, however, several operators are available to you that work on the bit level. Table 4-4 describes these bitwise operators.

Table 4-4	Bitwise Operators
Operator	*What It Does*
&	Bitwise AND
|	Bitwise Inclusive OR
^	Bitwise Exclusive OR
~	Unary complement (bit inversion)
<<	Shift Left
>>	Shift Right

Compound assignment operators

I love this feature. It enables you to compute and assign a value to a variable. Table 4-5 describes the compound assignment operators.

Table 4-5	Compound Assignment Operators
Operator	*What It Does*
+=	Addition
-=	Subtraction
*=	Multiplication
/=	Division
%=	Modulo
&=	Bitwise AND
|=	Bitwise Inclusive OR
^=	Bitwise Exclusive OR
<<=	Shift Left
>>=	Shift Right

To make sure that you understand how the compound assignment operators work, you should code a few examples:

1. **Start with an empty** `main` **function and enter the following code:**

```
int a;
int b;
//float c;

a = 2;
b = 3;

NSLog (@" a += b = %i", a += b);
NSLog (@" a now = %i", a );
a = 2;
NSLog (@" a -= b = %i", a -= b);
a = 2;
NSLog (@" a *= b = %i", a *= b);
a = 2;
NSLog (@" b /= a = %i", b /= a);
b = 3;
NSLog (@" b %%= a = %i", b %= a);
b = 3;
NSLog (@" a *= b + 2 = %i", a *= b + 2);
```

I previously make the point that the arithmetic operators did not affect the value of their operands. The compound assignment operators do change the value of the first operand, however (assignment in the operator name does give you a hint). You use a compound assignment operator to modify the value of a variable by performing an operation on the value currently stored in that variable. For example,

```
a += b
```

says that you want to take the value of b, add it to a, and store the result in a. This is the equivalent to

```
a = a + b;
```

The results here are what you would expect, but I want to call your attention to the last statement:

```
NSLog (@" a *= b + 2 = %i", a *= b + 2);
```

The compound assignment treats whatever is on the right side of the assignment operator as if it were in parentheses. That means that a `*=` b + 2 is equivalent to a = a * (b + 2) and not a = a * b + 2.

2. **Click the Run button on the Project Window toolbar to build and run the application.**

You should see the following in the Debugger Console:

```
a += b = 5
a now = 5
a -= b = -1
```

```
a *= b = 6
b /= a = 1
b %= a = 1
a *= b + 2 = 10
```

Anything to avoid typing; that's my motto. As you saw, a set of compound assignment operators also allow you to use the bitwise operators.

Increment and decrement operators

These operators are also some of my favorites because they provide another way to avoid typing. They are called the *increment operator* (++) and the *decrement operator* (--). They increase or reduce by 1 the value stored in a variable. They are equivalent to +=1 and to -=1, respectively. They can be a little tricky to use, however.

When used on a pointer, the increment and decrement operators increment and decrement a pointer by the size of the object being referenced. I introduce you to pointers in the section "Accessing Data with Pointers," later in this chapter.

To discover the increment and decrement operator subtleties that are important for you to understand, you should code the following example. Before you look at the output, see whether you can predict what it will be:

1. **Start with an empty** main **function and enter the following code:**

```
int a;
int b;

a = 2;
b = 3;
NSLog (@" a++ = %i", a++);
NSLog (@" a now = %i", a );
a = 2;
NSLog (@" ++a = %i", ++a);
NSLog (@" a now = %i", a );
a = 2;
NSLog (@" a-- = %i", a--);
NSLog (@" a now = %i", a );
a = 2;
NSLog (@" --a = %i", --a);
NSLog (@" a now = %i", a );
```

You see a difference depending on whether you put the ++ before or after the variable. Where you place the operator determines when the operation is performed. Sometimes you don't care, but in other situations, when the operation is performed may be important.

When it is a *suffix,* as in a++, the value stored in a is increased *after* the expression a++ = %i is evaluated. When the ++ is a *prefix,* as in ++a, the value of a is increased *before* the expression ++a = %i is evaluated. Notice the difference:

```
NSLog (@" a++ = %i", a++);
```

In this case, the a replaces the %i in the string and displays 2. After that, a is incremented:

```
NSLog (@" a now = %i", a );
```

And as you will see, it becomes 3.

In this next series of statements, a is assigned back to 2, but in this case, a is incremented before it replaces the %i in the string, and as a result displays 3:

```
a = 2;
NSLog (@" ++a = %i", ++a);
```

As I said, sometimes when the operation occurs doesn't matter, but when it does, it really does.

2. **Click the Run button on the Project Window toolbar to build and run the application.**

   The output in the Debugger Console should look like the following (remember, after every operator, you reset a to 2):

```
a++ = 2
a now = 3
++a = 3
a now = 3
a-- = 2
a now = 1
--a = 1
a now = 1
```

Comma operator

The comma operator (,) enables you to use two or more expressions where only one expression is expected. It evaluates the first operand (usually an expression) and then discards the results. It then evaluates the second operand and returns that value. Obviously, the only time you'll want to use this is when the evaluation of the first operand changes something in the second operand.

For example, the code

```
int a;
int b;

a = (b = 3, b + 2);

NSLog (@" a = (b = 3, b + 2) = %i", a);
NSLog (@" b = %i", b );
```

produces the output

```
a = (b = 3, b + 2) = 5
b = 3
```

The comma operator, in the expression (b = 3, b + 2) will first evaluate b = 3, resulting in the value of b becoming 3. The second operand is then evaluated, adding 2 to b, which results in the comma operator returning 5. Finally a is assigned that result, or 5. So, at the end, variable a will contain the value 5, whereas variable b will contain the value 3.

Cast operator

The cast operator (()) enables you to convert one type to another:

```
int i;
float f = 42.9;
i = (int)f;
```

The preceding code converts the float number 42.9 to an integer value (42); the remainder is lost. Here, the cast operator was (int).

As you'll see, this is something you will become familiar with when you start working with objects and classes (for example, you'll use it to tell Objective-C what the argument types are in messages you send to objects).

sizeof operator

If you are curious about how much memory variables really use (and don't necessarily distrust me, but like to prove things for yourself), you can use the sizeof operator to determine sizes.

You can discover for yourself how much memory a variable uses by doing the following:

1. **Start with an empty** `main` **function and enter the following code:**

As I have said previously, in some cases in the book, you'll see statements on two lines. I have to do that to fit the code on the page; you should use only one line where you can. This is especially important for strings, which will give you an error if they are on two lines, unless you tell the compiler that's what you want to do. This is especially relevant in the following code. As I said, I show you a way to have a single string on multiple lines in the section "Using Constants," later in this chapter.

```
// %lu tells the compiler to expect an unsigned long
NSLog(@" A char = %lu bytes", sizeof(char));
NSLog(@" An unsigned char = %lu bytes",
                             sizeof(unsigned char));
NSLog(@" A short = %lu bytes", sizeof(short));
NSLog(@" An unsigned short =
                 %lu bytes", sizeof(unsigned short));
NSLog(@" An int = %lu bytes", sizeof(int));
NSLog(@" An unsigned int =
                 %lu bytes", sizeof(unsigned int));
NSLog(@" A long = %lu bytes", sizeof(long));
NSLog(@" An unsigned long  =
                 %lu bytes", sizeof(unsigned long));
NSLog(@" A long long = %lu bytes", sizeof(long long));
NSLog(@" An unsigned long long = %lu bytes",
                           sizeof(unsigned long long));
NSLog(@" A float = %lu bytes", sizeof(float));
NSLog(@" A double = %lu bytes", sizeof(double));
//There is no unsigned float or double
```

2. **Click the Run button on the Project Window toolbar to build and run the application.**

You will soon find the following in the Debugger Console:

```
A char = 1 bytes
An unsigned char = 1 bytes
A short = 2 bytes
An unsigned short = 2 bytes
An int = 4 bytes
An unsigned int = 4 bytes
A long = 8 bytes
An unsigned long = 8 bytes
A long long = 8 bytes
An unsigned long long = 8 bytes
A float = 4 bytes
A double = 8 bytes
```

If you aren't deadly bored by now, all the more power to you. I am pretty much done with the real boring part (at least as compared to the more interesting things you discover starting in the next chapter), so hang in there.

It's time to move on to the last two operators you need to know before you get going on a real application in Chapter 5 — the logical and relational operators. This upcoming section also includes a brief discussion of the `if` statement, which enables you to make some logical decisions in your code. (I cover a few more ways to make decisions in your code in Chapter 9.) Now is when things start to get interesting — well, at least I think so.

Making Logical Decisions in Your Code

When you are programming, you may need to make some decisions within your code. If the user just clicked a button, does that mean I should play Pink Floyd's "The Wall" or a selection from Barry Manilow's greatest hits? A number of control structures are available that enable you to make these kinds of decisions. In the following sections, I cover one, the `if` statement. (I cover the balance in Chapter 9; it's amazing how far you can actually get without ever making a decision.)

In general, control structures use *relational* and *equality operators* to compare variables. The result is a Boolean value that is either YES or NO, or `true` or `false`. To start, I will explain what a Boolean type is.

Boolean types

A *Boolean type* is a variable whose value is either `true` or `false`. In Objective-C, you are lucky; you actually have two Boolean types. Objective-C provides a type, BOOL, that can have the values YES and NO (corresponding to `true` and `false`, respectively). In C, you find a Boolean data type, `bool`, that can take on the values `true` and `false`. (You would normally use the Objective-C version when writing Objective-C code.) Unfortunately, they do not always behave the same way. (A historic Mac OS type `Boolean` exists that you shouldn't use.)

The BOOL type in Objective-C is actually a `typedef` (you find out about `typedef`s in Chapter 5):

```
typedef signed char BOOL;
```

And because the type of BOOL is actually char, it does not behave in the same way as a bool in C (I'll leave exactly why as an exercise for you).

Sometimes programmers actually assign a value to the BOOL, and that can get you into trouble. To avoid that problem, assign only YES or NO to an Objective-C BOOL.

Several operators return a Boolean type, and I give you a list of them shortly. Of course, determining whether something is true or false is kind of pointless, unless you can do something based on that information, and that is where the if statement comes into play.

Take a look at how if statements, logical and equality operators, and Boolean types work to enable you to implement logic into your program:

1. **Start with an empty** main **function and enter the following code:**

```
int a = 5;
int b = 6;

if (a == b) NSLog(@" a is equal to b");
if (a != b) NSLog(@" a is not equal to b");
if (a > b) NSLog(@" a is greater than b");
if (a < b) NSLog(@" a is less than b");
if (a >= b)
        NSLog(@" a is greater than or equal to b");
if (a <= b) NSLog(@" a is less than or equal to b");

if (!(a == b)) NSLog(@ " a is NOT (equal to b)");
if ((a == b) || (a =-- b)) NSLog(@" a is equal to b,
                            or a is equal to --b");
if ((a <= b) && (a < ++ b)) NSLog(@" a is less than or
            equal to b, and a is less than ++b");

if (a == b) NSLog(@" a is equal to b");

if (a == b) {
  NSLog(@" a equal to b");
}
else {
  NSLog (@" a is not equal to b");
}

BOOL z = (a == b);
if (!z) NSLog(@" a is NOT (equal to b)");
BOOL y = (a > b);
if (y != YES) NSLog(@" a is NOT (greater than b)");
```

2. Click the Run button on the Project Window toolbar to build and run the application.

You see the following in the Debugger Console:

```
a is not equal to b
a is less than b
a is less than or equal to b
a is NOT (equal to b)
a is equal to b, or a is equal to --b
a is less than or equal to b, and a is less than ++b
a is not equal to b
a is NOT (equal to b)
a is NOT (greater than b)
```

Now go through it in detail:

The first line of code

```
if (a == b) NSLog(@" a is equal to b");
```

simply says if a is equal to b, execute the NSLog statement. If not, do nothing. This is what happened — nothing. (Remember, == is the equality operator — the two equal signs are not misprints.)

The if keyword is used to execute a statement or block (I explain what a block is momentarily) only if a condition is true. Its form is

```
if (condition) statement
```

condition is an expression that is evaluated. If the result of the valuation is true, statement is executed. If it is false, statement is ignored, and the program chugs merrily along.

The next statement

```
if (a != b) NSLog(@" a is not equal to b");
```

says that if a is not equal to b (!= is the not equal operator), execute the NSLog function, which is what happens as you can see:

```
a is not equal to b
```

The code continues chugging along, exercising each relational and logical operator in turn until something else interesting pops up:

```
if (a == b) NSLog(@" a is equal to b");
else NSLog (@" a is not equal to b");
```

Previously, if the evaluation of a compare were false, the execution bypassed the next statement and continued. In this case, the else says, if it's not true, do this instead. In this example, the code in one of those two statements will be executed based on the compare:

```
if (condition) statement1; else statement2;
```

The `if else` structures can be concatenated as well. For example:

```
if (x > 0) doThis;
else if (x < 0) doThat;
else takeABreak;
```

As you can imagine, these can get pretty complicated, and in Chapter 9, I show you a way to get the same result by using other, more obvious means.

Then you see the `if else` statements looking a little different:

```
if (a == b) {
   NSLog(@" a equal to b");
}
else {
   NSLog (@" a is not equal to b");
}
```

In this case, you can see that the NSLog statement is in braces, which defines a *block*. A block is a group of statements enclosed in braces: { }:

```
{ statement1; statement2; statement3; }
```

If you want to execute only one statement as the result of the `if` or `else`, you don't *need* a block. But you can choose to use a block, as you just saw. A block is required, however, whenever you want to execute more than one statement as a result of an `if` or `else`.

Finally, the lines of code

```
BOOL z = (a == b);
if (!z) NSLog(@" a is NOT (equal to b)");
BOOL y = (a > b);
if (y != YES) NSLog(@" a is NOT (greater than b)");
```

show you that the result of a compare can be assigned to a Boolean variable.

In this case, z is a BOOL, to which you assign the result of the comparison (a == b). You then use that result (remember, it is either YES or NO) in the `if` statement (!z).

I leave it as an exercise for you to study the results of these operations. Admittedly, they do make more sense in context, and you will have an opportunity to use them later in the book.

Pay real attention to the equality operator — *two* equal signs. It is all too easy to use only one by mistake. If you do, rather than make a compare, you do an assignment.

Apple introduced an enhancement to the Objective-C language that makes some types of programming tasks easier, such as supplying code to be executed when a particular event occurs. This feature is also known as a "block," but is different from the concept of the same name described here.

Relational and equality operators

In the section on Boolean types, you used a number of operators that enabled you to compare two expressions. They allowed you to determine, for example, whether two expressions were equal, or if one was greater than the other. When you use one of these operators, the result is the Boolean value, as you saw in the previous section.

You used the following relational and equality operators, described in Table 4-6, in the preceding examples.

Table 4-6	Relational and Equality Operators
Operator	*What It Does*
==	Equal to
!−	Not equal to
>	Greater than
<	Less than
>=	Greater than or equal to
<=	Less than or equal to

Logical operators

Logical operators are similar to the relational operators in that they return Boolean values. In this case, rather than comparing two *expressions,* you are comparing the results of two *comparisons* (except for the NOT operator). Table 4-7 describes the logical operators.

Table 4-7	Logical Operators
Operator	*What It Does*
!	NOT
&&	Logical AND
||	Logical OR

! (NOT) evaluates a single expression and returns the opposite Boolean value. For example, !(a < b) returns NO if a is less than b and YES if a is greater than or equal to b.

&& (logical AND) evaluates two expressions and returns YES when both expressions result in YES. For example, (a < b) && (a < c) returns YES when a is less than both b *and* c. Otherwise, it returns NO.

|| (logical OR) evaluates two expressions and returns YES when either one or both expressions result in YES. For example, (a < b) && (a < c) returns YES when X is less than either b *or* c. It returns NO when a is greater than or equal to both b and c.

Conditional operator

The conditional operator (?) evaluates an expression and enables you to do one thing if an expression is true and another if it is false:

```
condition ? result1 : result2;
```

If condition is true, the expression will execute result1; if it is not true, the expression will execute result2.

For example:

```
int a = 5;
int b = 6;

(a == b) ? NSLog(@" a is equal to b"):
                      NSLog(@" a is not equal to b") ;
(a != b) ? NSLog(@" a is NOT equal to b"):
                      NSLog(@" a is equal to b");
```

If you were to build this code, you would find

```
a is not equal to b
a is NOT equal to b
```

Looks familiar, doesn't it?

Accessing Data with Pointers

As I explain earlier, memory in your computer can be imagined as a series of mailboxes, each one the smallest size (a byte) that a computer manages. These mailboxes are numbered sequentially, so to get the next address, you add 1 to the current address. Things are located in memory by these addresses.

For example, take the following declaration:

```
int anInteger = 42;
```

Assume that `anInteger` (with the value 42) is located at *memory address 32*, as shown earlier in Figure 4-2. In other words, memory address 32, which I have named `anInteger`, contains the value 42. With me so far?

Until now, variable names have held some kind of value, an `int` or `float` for example, as you just saw with `anInteger`. But they also can hold a pointer, which is an address in memory.

Now look at this declaration:

```
int *anIntPointer = &anInteger
```

The first part of that declaration declares a variable named `anIntPointer`. The * tells the compiler that this type is a *pointer to an int*, rather than an *int*. The & (reference) operator tells the compiler that you want the `intPointer` initialized with the *address* of `anInteger`, the variable you declared earlier. In other words, `intPointer` will have the memory address of `anInteger`. Because I told you that the memory address `anInteger` was located at 32, `anIntPointer` will hold the value 32.

Think about it this way. The address of Apple Computer's main building is Apple Computer, Inc., 1 Infinite Loop, Cupertino, CA 95014. The address is the location of — a pointer to — a building, and the physical building is what's at that address. Similarly, `anIntPointer` is the location of — address of — an integer, and `anInteger` is what's at that address.

To go from the pointer `anIntPointer`, which contains the address of `anInteger`, to the actual value of `anInteger`, you use the dereference operator (*) — this is called *dereferencing* a pointer:

```
#import <Foundation/Foundation.h>

int main (int argc, const char * argv[]) {

  int anInteger = 42;
  int *anIntPointer = &anInteger;

  NSLog (@"anInteger = %i", anInteger);
```

```
    NSLog (@"*anIntPointer = %i",  *anIntPointer);

    return 0;
}
```

This results in

```
anInteger = 42
*anIntPointer = 42
```

As you can see, dereferencing the pointer (*anIntPointer) enables you to access the value store in the address of anInteger.

Another operator can also be used to deference a pointer. The arrow operator (->) is used only with pointers to objects (as well as structs). I show you how to use the arrow operator, as well as explain more about pointers, in Chapter 5.

You will use pointers extensively when you start working with objects, and it will become a lot clearer as you work with pointers in this context. As you'll find out, it won't be particularly difficult to get the hang of it.

But if you were to study C, you would find that pointers are a significant part of the language, and you would discover something called *pointer arithmetic*. This, in part, comes from C's roots as a system programming language. Most of you will never need to do pointer arithmetic, but just in case, you're not on your own. *C For Dummies,* 2nd Edition, by Dan Gookin (published by John Wiley & Sons, Inc.) can offer some insight.

Using Constants

Constants, as you might expect, are expressions that have a fixed value. You had some experience with them when you did the following:

```
int a = 5;
a = 5;
```

When you code a = 5, you are using a *literal*.

Literals are not just numbers, however. The following expression is called a string literal:

```
@"Hello World";
```

You have used string literals quite a bit already, and you will continue to use them throughout the rest of this book. But what if you want to include a double quote (") in the string literal itself? (A problem also exists with *special characters* such as newline or tab, which you won't be using.) To include a double quote, all you have to do is place a backslash (\) in front of the " (or any other special character) you want to use. For example:

> \ ' will display as a single quote (').
>
> \ " will display as a double quote (").
>
> \ \ will display as a backslash (\).

As I have been warning you (more than once), string literals need to be on a single line of code. However, you can extend string literals to more than a single line of code by putting a backslash sign (\) at the end of each unfinished line:

```
@"string expressed on \
two lines"
```

You can express any character by using its numerical ASCII code by writing a backslash character (\) followed by the ASCII code as an octal (for example, \23 or \40) or hexadecimal number (for example, \x20 or \x4A).

The problem with literals, however, is that tracking down and changing their values can be very difficult. Other kinds of constants can provide a better way to include a constant in your programs.

Declared constants (const)

With the const prefix, you can declare constants of a specific type in the same way as you do with a variable:

```
const int aConstInt = 42;
const float aConstFloat = 42.00;
```

Here, aConstInt and aConstFloat are two typed constants. They are treated just like regular variables except that their values cannot be modified after they have been declared and initialized (obviously, you have to initialize them). const variables have the benefit that the Objective-C compiler enforces their usage just as if they were regular variables; for instance, when using a const variable as a parameter passed into a function, the compiler warns you if its type is different from what is expected. Using const variables enables you to use the same value in multiple places, and so you only have to change it where it's defined should you decide its value needs to change.

Defined constants (#define)

Defined constants are a better solution to your need for certainty, although they are best placed in a single file where you can easily find all of them. But because I haven't explained how to use more than one file in your program, (although it is coming up in Chapter 6), I just go through the mechanics of creating them.

`#define` enables you to define names for the constants you use:

```
#define identifier value
```

For example, you can define two new constants: `aDefineInt` and `aDefineFloat` by doing the following:

```
#define aDefineInt 42
#define aDefineFloat 42.00
```

After you have defined `aDefineInt` and `aDefineFloat`, you can use them throughout your code as you would a literal or declared constant.

`#define` is a preprocessor directive of the kind I mention at the start of this chapter in the section "It All Comes Down to Your Statements." Whenever the preprocessor encounters `#defines` (`aDefineInt` and `aDefineFloat`, for example), it replace them with the values you specified (`42` and `42.00`, respectively).

The `#define` is not an Objective-C statement, so it doesn't need a semicolon. If you put one in, it becomes part of the `#define`.

I'll write some code where you will use constants, float declarations, and the backslash escape code (which will allow you to define a string on two lines):

1. **Start with an empty** `main` **function and enter the following code:**

```
#define aDefineInt 42
#define aDefineFloat 42.00
#define aDefineFloat2 .4200e2
#define aDefineFloat3 4200.00e-2

  const int aConstInt = 42;
  const float aConstFloat = 42.00;
  const float aConstFloat2 = .42000e2;
  const float aConstFloat3 =4200.00e-2;


  NSLog(@" aDefineInt = %i",aDefineInt);
  NSLog(@" aDefineFloat = %.2f",aDefineFloat);
  NSLog(@" aDefineFloat2 = %.2f",aDefineFloat2);
  NSLog(@" aDefineFloat3 = %.2f",aDefineFloat3);
```

```
    NSLog(@" aConstInt = %i",aConstInt);
    NSLog(@" aConstFloat = %.2f",aConstFloat);
    NSLog(@" aConstFloat2 = %.2f",aConstFloat2);
    NSLog(@" aConstFloat3 = %.2f",aConstFloat3);

    NSLog(@" A \"\\backslash with double quotes\" \
on two lines");
```

2. **Click the Run button on the Project Window toolbar to build and run the application.**

   You should see the following in the Debugger Console:

```
aDefineInt = 42
aDefineFloat = 42.00
aDefineFloat2 = 42.00
aDefineFloat3 = 42.00
aConstInt = 42
aConstFloat = 42.00
aConstFloat2 = 42.00
aConstFloat3 = 42.00
A "\backslash with double quotes" on two lines
```

Knowing the Objective-C Reserved Words

As I mention, your names or identifiers cannot match any keyword of the Objective-C language. Some of those reserved keywords are as follows:

asm	double	int	static
auto	else	long	struct
bool	enum	new	switch
BOOL	extern	nil	true
break	false	Nil	typedef
case	float	NO	union
char	for	register	unsigned
Class	goto	return	void
const	id	SEL	volatile
continue	if	short	wchar_t
default	IMP	signed	while
do	inline	sizeof	YES

The best way to tell whether a name or identifier you want to use is a reserved word is whether it changes color in the editor. If it does, it is either a keyword or is being used somewhere in your program.

In addition, prefixes are used extensively. Cocoa prefixes all its function, constant, and type names with "NS." So don't prefix any of your own variables or function names with NS — doing so can cause a great deal of confusion. At a minimum, the reader will assume that it is a Cocoa function, as opposed to being your code. At worst, the name is already being used, and you'll get a compiler error. (Actually, I'm not sure which is worse.)

Congratulations

Congratulations! You've gotten through the most tedious part of understanding a computer language.

Some of the things I didn't cover in this chapter are certain kinds of control structures, like `switch` statements, and things called loops, which allow you to repeat a block of statements while a condition is true or until a condition is met. I will show you those, I promise, when you are going to need to use them in Chapter 9.

Chapter 5

Functions and Data Structures

. . . .

In This Chapter

▶ Looking at an application

▶ Creating data structures

▶ Working with defined data types

▶ Collecting statements into functions

▶ Understanding function prototypes

▶ Knowing what happens when you want to extend the functionality of a program

. . . .

*A*s I mention in Chapter 1, discovering how to program in Objective-C involves more than the instruction set and data types you read about in the last chapter. In fact, you've received a considerable amount of the instruction set covered by now. So it's time to get on with the more interesting aspects of the language, the ones you'll need to know to create the kinds of applications you are probably interested in.

One of the most important features of Objective-C is its support for object-oriented programming. Although Objective-C is about objects, before I take you there in Chapter 6, I introduce you to two features of C that are important to understand along the way — data structures and functions. Data structures and functions are fundamental parts of the language, and understanding them will make it easier for you to understand what objects are really about.

Thinking about an Application

In Chapter 1, I mention that when I travel, I often zone out on that fact that even though it looks like Monopoly money, foreign currency actually does amount to something in dollars. I said it would be helpful if I could use a computer to let me know when I charged something on a credit card in a foreign currency, how much that was in dollars. It would also be helpful if I could use that same program to generally keep track of my spending (I do tend to get carried away when I am on vacation) against a budget I set at the beginning of a trip. Although this is not the most exciting application (a classic understatement if I've ever made one), it is actually perfect for my purposes — to show you how to develop applications by using Objective-C. It will enable me to explain all the Objective-C you'll need to know to write *any* kind of application — even a cool game or something that uses audio and video. (Of course, you'll still have to master the *specifics* of how to use the graphics and sound on the Mac or iPhone.)

The application you are about to start developing will help me manage my budget when I travel by allowing me to track my spending in dollars. This will enable me to avoid the rather embarrassing situation of ending up with only three dollars left for four days in Venice.

Of course, doing this is something you really don't even need a computer to do; a computer just makes it easier and faster (and provides the example application I need to show you Objective-C). In fact, my father, who was an accountant, did the same thing I'm planning to do with a pencil and paper whenever he and my mom went to Europe. I use what he did as a basis for how my application needs to work.

To manage his budget, he used the form you see in Figure 5-1. Whenever he changed dollars into euros, he put that amount in the dollars column and subtracted it from the balance. Whenever he charged something on a credit card, he took the amount in foreign currency, multiplied it times the exchange rate to get the dollar amount, and then subtracted that amount from the dollar balance. (He was an accountant after all.)

Date	Amount in euros	Exchange rate	Amount in dollars	Balance in dollars

Figure 5-1: Tracking your expenses.

Fortunately, today with my laptop or mobile device, I am free to harness the power of hundreds, if not thousands, of dollars worth of modern computer technology to do the same thing my dad did with pencil and paper.

At this point, you have actually seen enough Objective-C to begin creating the *model* for this application (also sometimes called the *content engine*). The model is part of a design pattern known as Model-View-Controller (MVC) that you will use to develop applications, using the Cocoa framework. The model contains the application-specific logic for your application — in this case, how to track expenses and apply them to a budget. I explain MVC in detail in Chapter 11.

For the majority of this book, I show you how to use what you have already mastered about Objective-C, and the additional features that make it so powerful (objects, for example), to add more and more functionality to the model. Then in Chapters 17 and 18, you'll create simple user interfaces for the iPhone and Mac and see how easily it all fits together.

Enough discussion — time to code!

You begin a new Xcode project by following these steps:

1. **Launch Xcode.**

   I have you create a new project here. You can do that, or you can skip Steps 2 through 6 and start with the project in the Chapter 5 Start Here folder, which is in the Chapter 5 folder at the website (you'll have to move it to your desktop).

   If you want to work with anything from the website, you must drag it onto your desktop (or into any other folder) to be able to build the project.

2. **Start the New Project Assistant by choosing File⇨New Project to create a new project.**

3. **In the New Project window, click Application under the Mac OS X heading.**

4. **Select Command Line Tool from the choices displayed; then click Next.**

5. **Enter the name in the Product Name field, and select Foundation from the Type drop-down menu; then click Next.**

   Xcode then displays a standard save sheet.

6. **Choose a Save location (the desktop works just fine) and then click Save.**

   After you click Save, Xcode creates the project and opens the project window — which should look like what is shown Figure 5-2.

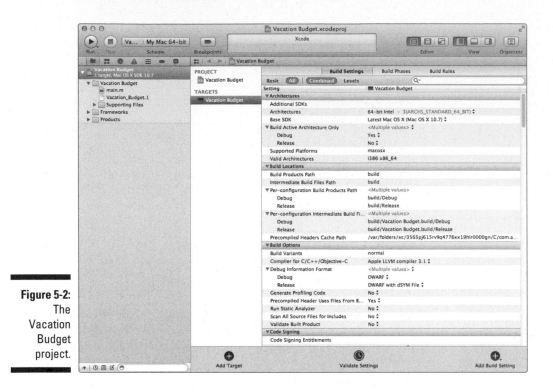

Figure 5-2:
The
Vacation
Budget
project.

You'll work in the `main.m` file for the balance of this chapter.

7. Start with an empty `main` function.

I cover this in Chapter 4. You need to delete all the statements in `main` except for `return 0;` so that you end up with a `main` function that looks like this:

```
#import <Foundation/Foundation.h>

int main (int argc, const char * argv[]) {

  return 0;
}
```

8. Add the code in bold between the first brace and the `return 0` statement.

In some cases (like the following one), you'll see statements on two lines in the book. I have to do that to fit the code on the page; you should simply use one line where you can.

```
#import <Foundation/Foundation.h>

int main (int argc, const char * argv[]) {

    float   exchangeRate = 1.2500;
    double budget = 1000.00;
    double euroTransaction;

    budget -= 100;

    NSLog(@"Converting 100 US dollars into euros leaves
                                   $%.2f", budget);
    euroTransaction = 100*exchangeRate;
    budget -= euroTransaction;
    NSLog(@"Charging 100 euros leaves $%.2f", budget);

    return 0;
}
```

9. **Click the Run button on the Project Window toolbar.**

    In Chapter 4, I gave you other options — press ⌘+R or choose
    Product⇨Run to build and run the application. In this chapter, and from
    now on, I only tell you to click the button, but feel free to use the key-
    board shortcut or the menu option if you prefer.

10. **If necessary, open the Xcode Console, which displays your program's
    output, by pressing Shift+⌘+C.**

Your output should look like the following. (***Note:*** I removed the time stamp
and process ID that tells you when and where the output string originated,
and I do that for the balance of this chapter and book.)

```
Converting 100 US dollars into euros leaves $900.00
Charging 100 euros leaves $775.00
```

This code is pretty simple. For a cash transaction — that is, when I am converting my dollars into euros, or actually paying in dollars — you simply
subtract 100 from the budget by using the compound assignment subtraction
operator to simulate a straight foreign exchange transaction:

```
budget -= 100;
```

For a charge transaction, you convert the number of euros you are charging
into dollars and store that amount as a euroTransaction:

```
euroTransaction = 100*exchangeRate;
```

Then you subtract that amount from the budget to simulate a charge transaction:

```
budget -= euroTransaction;
```

You can find the completed project at the website in the Example 5A folder, which is in the Chapter 5 folder.

Defining and Declaring Data Structures

The budget-tracking system covered in the preceding section gives you a starting point for writing a program that does something more or less useful. In this section, I cover *data structures,* which are data elements grouped together under one name, and show you how to use them in your program.

You can declare the built-in data types as variables. But what about those situations when the data you need to work with, or on, is really more than one variable — it is a logical collection of variables that hang out together because they have some relationship to each other. For example, the data I used in the preceding example is all related to each other and provides the data needed for this whole idea of budgeting:

```
float    exchangeRate;
double budget;
double euroTransaction;
```

Another example is an address book, where you would want all the information about a person grouped in a single entity. You can easily do that by using a data structure (`struct`). Data structures are defined in Objective-C, using the following syntax:

```
struct structName {

  type member1Name;
  type member2Name;
  ...
};
```

A `struct` tells the compiler that this is a data structure. `structName` is a name for the *structure type* — when you define a `struct`, you are actually defining a new data type that can be used just like the built-in types such as `int` and `double`. Within the braces { } is a list of the variables that are included in this `struct`, which are called *members,* each one specified with a type and a valid identifier as its name. And, yes, structures can have other structures as members, although a structure can't be a member of itself.

Variables included in a `struct` are called *members*.

Just as I do with any other variable, I have to declare a `struct` when I use it:

```
struct structName structVariable1, structVariable2 ... ;
```

When you *declare* a structure, the compiler reserves enough memory to hold the data, just as it does for the built-in types (for example, 4 bytes for an `int`), although here the compiler has to figure out how much to reserve by adding up all the requirements for each of the types that will be in the structure.

In the preceding example, `structVariable1` and `structVariable2` are the variables' names (identifiers) for the structures I declared. Because I have two declarations, memory is reserved for each. (As I mention in Chapter 4, you can declare more than one variable of the same type in one statement.)

What you are going to do now is group `exchangeRate`, `budget`, and `euroTransaction` into a `struct` named `budget` and then use the `budget` `struct` in your program.

If you have been following along with me, I extend what you just did in the first example. If you want to start from a clean copy of the project from where you left off, you can use the project found in the Example 5A folder found in the Chapter 5 folder.

To improve your code to take advantage of a `struct`, follow these steps:

1. **Return to your project and add the following code in bold, right after the first line** `#import <Foundation/Foundation.h>` **to** main.m.

   ```
   #import <Foundation/Foundation.h>

   struct budget {
     float   exchangeRate;
     double budget;
     double euroTransaction;
   };
   ```

   This code defines the `struct` `budget` that contains the three variables I referred to earlier, `exchangeRate`, `budget`, and `euroTransaction`.

2. **Delete the code you previously entered in the** main **function and enter the code (in bold) as shown here:**

```
#import <Foundation/Foundation.h>

struct budget {
  float exchangeRate;
  double budget;
  double euroTransaction;
};
int main (int argc, const char * argv[]) {

  struct budget vacationBudget;

  vacationBudget.exchangeRate = 1.2500;
  vacationBudget.budget = 1000.00;

  vacationBudget.budget -= 100;
  NSLog(@"Converting 100 US dollars into euros leaves
                   $%.2f", vacationBudget.budget);
  vacationBudget.euroTransaction =
                   100*vacationBudget.exchangeRate;
  vacationBudget.budget -=
                   vacationBudget.euroTransaction;
  NSLog(@"Charging 100 euros leaves $%.2f",
                   vacationBudget.budget);


  return 0;
}
```

3. **Click the Run button on the Project Window toolbar to build and run the application.**

   Your output in the Debugger Console should look like this:

   ```
   Converting 100 US dollars into euros leaves $900.00
   Charging 100 euros leaves $775.00
   ```

   You can find the completed project at the website in the Example 5B folder, which is in the Chapter 5 folder.

The code in the preceding numbered list is not all that different from the program you coded in the preceding section, with a couple of exceptions.

You define a `struct` that you named `budget` (you did that outside the `main` function, which makes the definition usable by any function in the file `main.m`, as you will see). You then declare a `struct budget` (which allocates some memory for its variables), named `europe`, just as you would declare any other variable.

As you can see, Objective-C treats this data structure (or `struct`) exactly as it does its built-in types. Or at least, almost the same, because the type is `struct budget`, as opposed to simply `budget`. (I show you how you can omit the `struct` next.)

It is important to understand the difference between the *structure type name* and a *variable* of this (structure) type. You can declare as many variables (for example, `europe` and even `england`) as you like of this structure type (`struct budget`), just as you can `int`s, `float`s, `double`s, and so on.

After you have declared the variable of that structure type, you can operate directly on its members. To do that, you use the dot operator, a (`.`), inserted between the structure type variable's name (identifier) and the member name. For example:

```
vacationBudget.budget = 1000.00;
vacationBudget.budget -= 100;
```

Using Defined Data Types

When you define a `struct`, you are creating a new data type, but it can be a bit awkward to use. Every time I use it I have to use

```
struct budget someBudget;
```

Because I hate having to type more than absolutely necessary, I'm going to show you a way to avoid using `struct` in a declaration. This also makes a `struct` look more like a built-in data type. All you need to do is use the keyword `typedef` (this is another example of a statement in Objective-C that describes how data is structured):

```
typedef type typeName;
```

Here, `type` is a built-in type, or one that you created by using a `struct` (`struct budget`, for example), and `typeName` is the name for the new type you are defining. For example:

```
typedef struct budget budget;
```

You can also create a new type name for a built-in type:

```
typedef int theTypeAlsoKnownAsInt;
```

You could then use that type name rather than `int` in the following:

```
theTypeAlsoKnownAsInt anInt;
```

To define the `budget typedef` in my program, all I have to do is add one line of code (in bold):

```
struct budget {
 float   exchangeRate;
 double budget;
 double euroTransaction;
 };

 typedef struct budget budget;
```

Now you can use the new type — budget — just like any of the built-in types (no struct required). For example:

```
 budget vacationBudget;
```

To make things even easier, you can *define a struct and a typedef* in one fell swoop. This is then followed by the declaration of the variable of that type:

```
typedef struct {
   float   exchangeRate;
   double budget;
   double euroTransaction;
} budget;

budget vacationBudget;
```

This is more consistent with the way that you need to think about classes and objects, and the way I have you do it in your program.

You need to be aware of the two-step process I explain first because you may see it done that way in some of the framework header files. It enables you to *define a struct and declare a variable of that type* in one fell swoop, which is then followed by the typedef:

```
struct budget {
   float   exchangeRate;
   double budget;
   double euroTransaction;
} vacationBudget;

typedef struct budget budget;
```

typedef does not actually create different types — it only creates a new name for whatever you specify. As far as the compiler is concerned, when it sees budget, it just understands budget to be struct budget.

As you will see, you will no longer have to use struct when you declare a variable of type budget. And just as before, with struct budget, when you declare a variable as type budget, you are reserving memory for it.

Now it's time to update your code to use typedef:

1. **Delete what you entered previously so that** `main.m` **looks like this:**

```
#import <Foundation/Foundation.h>

int main (int argc, const char * argv[]) {


   return 0;
}
```

2. **Add the following code in bold, right after the first line,** `#import`
   `<Foundation/Foundation.h>`:

```
#import <Foundation/Foundation.h>

typedef struct {
  float   exchangeRate;
  double budget;
  double euroTransaction;
} budget;
```

This defines the `struct budget` that contains the three variables I refer
to earlier: `exchangeRate`, `budget`, and `euroTransaction`. It also
does the necessary `typedef`.

3. **Enter the rest of the code shown in bold:**

```
#import <Foundation/Foundation.h>

typedef struct {
  float exchangeRate;
  double budget;
  double euroTransaction;
} budget;


int main (int argc, const char * argv[]) {

  budget vacationBudget;

  vacationBudget.exchangeRate = 1.2500;
  vacationBudget.budget = 1000.00;

  vacationBudget.budget -= 100;
  NSLog(@"Converting 100 US dollars into euros leaves
                   $%.2f", vacationBudget.budget);
  vacationBudget.euroTransaction =
                   100*vacationBudget.exchangeRate;
  vacationBudget.budget -=
                   vacationBudget.euroTransaction;
  NSLog(@"Charging 100 euros leaves $%.2f",
                        vacationBudget.budget);


  return 0;
}
```

4. **Click the Run button on the Project Window toolbar to build and run the application.**

Your output in the Xcode Debugger Console should look like this:

```
Converting 100 US dollars into euros leaves $900.00
Charging 100 euros leaves $775.00
```

You can find the completed project at the website in the Example 5C folder, which is in the Chapter 5 folder.

Writing Functions

In this section, you collect the statements previously coded in main that display the results of a transaction into functions that do the same thing. One of the advantages of using a module like a function is that after you check that this set of statements works, you don't have to worry about that function anymore.

The set of statements called a *function* has a *name,* and you can *call* that set of statements by this name to have its code executed. This concept of using functions is as fundamental to programming as any of the instructions in Chapter 4. It is so fundamental, in fact, that you can never hide from functions — it is in a function, main, after all, where you have been doing all your work so far. The main function is required in your program because when you run your application, main is where execution of the code starts.

Take a look at the example of main again:

```
int main (int argc, const char * argv[]) {

  NSLog(@"Hello, World!");

  return 0;
}
```

You see a return type (int), a name (main), some arguments inside parentheses, and then some instructions inside braces ({}). This structure is the basic structure of a function. Now you will see how to create your very own function. I explain the main function a bit more in Chapter 7.

For now, you'll modify the program you just wrote to use functions. You start by adding code to main, something that is old hat to you by now, and then you move the code you wrote into a function.

If you have been following along with me, I extend what you just did in the preceding example. If you want to start from a clean copy of the project where you left off, you can use the project found in the Example 5C folder, which is in the Chapter 5 folder.

Follow these steps to start using functions in your program:

1. **Start with the code you already have and add the following code in bold, right after the line** } budget.

```
typedef struct {
float exchangeRate;
double budget;
double euroTransaction;
} budget;

budget vacationBudget;
```

You've now declared the variable vacationBudget outside of the main function, and in a way that makes it accessible to other functions, such as the ones you are about to create. I explain why you need to do this, which is known as *variable scoping,* in the next section.

2. **You now add some functions. Right after the line**

```
budget vacationBudget;
```

add the following lines of code:

```
void spendDollars (double dollars) {

  vacationBudget.budget  = dollars;
}

void chargeEuros (double euros) {

  vacationBudget.euroTransaction =
                euros*vacationBudget.exchangeRate;
  vacationBudget.budget -=
                vacationBudget.euroTransaction;
}
```

You probably notice that all you did was move the line of code

```
vacationBudget.budget -= dollars;
```

from main to the new function spendDollars, and the lines of code

```
vacationBudget.euroTransaction =
                euros*vacationBudget.exchangeRate;
vacationBudget.budget -=
                vacationBudget.euroTransaction;
```

from main to the new function chargeEuros.

3. **In the** `main` **function, delete the commented bold, italic, underlined code, and add the code in bold:**

```
//budget vacationBudget;

  vacationBudget.exchangeRate = 1.2500;
  vacationBudget.budget = 1000.00;
  double numberDollars = 100;
  double numberEuros = 100;

//vacationBudget.budget -= 100;
  spendDollars(numberDollars);
//NSLog(@"Converting 100 US dollars into euros leaves
                    $%.2f", vacationBudget.budget);
  NSLog(@"Converting %.2f US dollars into euros leaves
        $%.2f", numberDollars, vacationBudget.budget);
//vacationBudget.euroTransaction =
                    100*vacationBudget.exchangeRate;
//vacationBudget.budget =
                    vacationBudget.euroTransaction;
  chargeEuros(numberEuros);
//NSLog(@"Charging 100 euros leaves $%.2f",
                    vacationBudget.budget);
  NSLog(@"Charging  %.2f euros leaves $%.2f",
            numberEuros, vacationBudget.budget);
```

As you can see, you deleted the line of code

```
budget vacationBudget;
```

because you declared it in Step 2.

You declared two new variables:

```
double numberDollars = 100;
double numberEuros = 100;
```

These represent individual *transactions* (and you will have more, of course), and I use these variables as the function arguments.

You replaced the code

```
vacationBudget.budget -= 100;
```

with

```
spendDollars(numberDollars);
```

which calls the function `spendDollars`, passing it the number of dollars (`numberDollars`) I just spent, as an argument.

And, similarly, you replaced the code

```
vacationBudget.euroTransaction =
                100 *vacationBudget.exchangeRate;
vacationBudget.budget -=
                vacationBudget.euroTransaction;
```

with

```
chargeEuros(numberEuros);
```

which calls the function `chargeEuros` to update my budget to take into account what I just charged on my credit card in euros.

You also replaced the two `NSLog` statements

```
NSLog(@"Converting 100 US dollars into euros leaves
                    $%.2f", vacationBudget.budget);
NSLog(@"Charging 100 euros leaves $%.2f",
                             vacationBudget.budget);
```

with

```
NSLog(@"Converting %.2f US dollars into euros leaves
        $%.2f", numberDollars, vacationBudget.budget);
NSLog(@"Charging  %.2f euros leaves $%.2f",
        numberEuros, vacationBudget.budget);
```

to display the variable that contains the amount being spent.

Your code should look like Listing 5-1.

Listing 5-1:   Moving Instructions into Functions

```
#import <Foundation/Foundation.h>

typedef   struct {
  float  exchangeRate;
  double budget;
  double euroTransaction;
} budget;

  budget vacationBudget;


void spendDollars (double dollars) {

  vacationBudget.budget -= dollars;
}

void chargeEuros (double euros) {

  vacationBudget.euroTransaction =
                    euros*vacationBudget.exchangeRate;
  vacationBudget.budget -= vacationBudget.euroTransaction;
}

int main (int argc, const char * argv[]) {

  vacationBudget.exchangeRate = 1.2500;
  vacationBudget.budget = 1000.00;
```

(continued)

Listing 5-1 *(continued)*

```
    double numberDollars = 100;
    double numberEuros = 100;

    spendDollars(numberDollars);
    NSLog(@"Converting %.2f US dollars into euros leaves
            $%.2f", numberDollars, vacationBudget.budget);
    chargeEuros(numberEuros);
    NSLog(@"Charging  %.2f euros leaves $%.2f", numberEuros,
                                      vacationBudget.budget);

    return 0;
}
```

4. **Click the Run button on the Project Window toolbar to build and run the application.**

   Your output in the Debugger Console should look like this:

   ```
   Converting 100 US dollars into euros leaves $900.00
   Charging 100 euros leaves $775.00
   ```

You can find the completed project at the website in the Example 5D folder, which is in the Chapter 5 folder.

What you have done here is simply move things around. You haven't changed functionality.

At this point, the amount of code is trivial, so why you would want to move code into functions may not be compellingly obvious. But humor me: One of the universal laws of programming is that things can get very complex very quickly, and functions (as modules), as I explain in Chapter 3, will make your life easier.

Now, take a moment to examine what you did here.

When you entered the lines of code

```
void spendDollars (double dollars) {

  vacationBudget.budget -= dollars;
}
```

you *declared* a function spendDollars.

Notice that all you actually did to create the function body was cut and paste the original code that was in the main function into the new function body. You did something called *factoring* your code. You changed the way things are organized in your program without changing its (observable) behavior. As you develop applications, you'll find yourself doing that a lot to improve code readability, simplify code structure, make it consistent with the principles of object-oriented programming that improve maintainability and extensibility, and so on.

To be more precise, which is important when working with computers, a function looks like this:

```
returnType functionName(functionArgument1, ...) {

  statements;
  return expression;
}
```

Let me explain what each of the pieces are:

- ✔ *returnType* is the data type of the data returned by the function. Every function *can* return something when it is finished. The function might return something like the cost of one euro in U.S. dollars or a status indicator, such as 0, that tells you the function successfully completed what you asked it to do. In fact, that's what you have been doing when you end your programs with `return 0` in `main`.

  The return value is optional. If you want to declare a function that does not return a value, as you did in the function `spendDollars`, use the data type of `void`. If you leave out the return type, the compiler will assume that the return type is `int` and annoy you with warnings.

- ✔ *functionName* is the, well, name of the function; it is how you will *call* it. This is what you did when you replaced the line of code

  ```
  vacationBudget.budget -= 100;
  ```

  with

  ```
  spendDollars(numberDollars);;
  ```

  This is known as *calling* the function. You told the compiler that you want to execute the lines of code you gathered under the function name `spendDollars`.

- ✔ *functionArguments* (as many as needed or none) are enclosed in the parentheses after the function name. These can be built-in types or even your own data types. Each argument consists of a data type specifier followed by an identifier, like all the variable declarations you did in Chapter 4. This allows you to pass data to the function when it is called. The arguments, if more than one exist, are separated by commas.

  The arguments, like the return value, are optional. The function declaration

  ```
  void spendDollars (double dollars) {
  ```

  has one argument. If no arguments existed, you could declare it as

```
void spendNoDollars (void) {
```

or

```
void spendNoDollars () {
```

You could simply leave out the `void` in the argument list, and the compiler, when no arguments exist, assumes `void`. (This is as opposed to when you leave out the return type, in which case the compiler assumes an `int`.)

Just as you have been doing in the `main` function, you could have also declared variables inside the functions you code. These are called *local variables:*

```
float aLocalVaraible = 1.2643;
```

When you declare a local variable and the function is called, memory is allocated for that variable and initialized if necessary.

For example, in Step 7 in the section "Thinking about an Application," earlier in this chapter, you declared the following local variables in `main`:

```
float   exchangeRate = 1.2500;
double budget = 1000.00;
double euroTransaction;
```

Execution begins at the open brace and continues through to the return statement. If the return type is `void`, the return statement is optional. If it isn't present, execution returns to the calling function at the closing brace.

The format for calling a function includes specifying its name and enclosing its arguments in parentheses. Even if no arguments exist, you need the parentheses anyway. For that reason, the call to `spendNoDollars` is

```
spendNoDollars();
```

This is how the compiler knows that this call is a call to a function and not the identifier of a variable or some other statement. The following call would generate admonishments from the compiler:

```
spendNoDollars;
```

All the various parts of a function are illustrated in Figure 5-3.

Getting back to `spendDollars`: You created a new function with one argument and no return type. Also notice the general format for the name is lowercase.

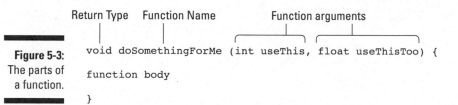

Figure 5-3: The parts of a function.

```
Return Type   Function Name        Function arguments

void doSomethingForMe (int useThis, float useThisToo) {

function body

}
```

In main, you call the function spendDollars with the variable number Dollars (which is a double) as the argument. This corresponds to the double dollars argument in the spendDollars function declaration.

At the point at which the function is called from within main, the control is lost by main and passed to the function spendDollars.

The argument is treated exactly the same way that other local variable declarations are treated. That is, when you call the function

```
void spendDollars (double dollars) {

  vacationBudget.budget -= dollars;
}
```

you are actually declaring a local variable double dollars that is initialized when the function is called with the value that you passed in as the argument. The only difference between double dollars and something like

```
float numberDollars = 100;
```

is that the variable dollars sits in the declaration, separated by commas, rather than in the body of the function.

You need to understand another thing. When you call the function

```
spendDollars(numberDollars);
```

the dollars function argument is a *copy* of numberDollars.

If you modify dollars in the spendDollars function, it will not affect numberDollars in main. That is because when a function is called, the arguments are *copies* of the variables you use as the arguments.

Within the function spendDollars, you could also further assign these arguments to local variables if you wanted to; but in this function, you just use the argument to subtract the amount from the budget.

The closing brace, }, terminates the function spendDollars and returns the control back to the function that called it in the first place (in this case, main), and the program continues chugging along from the same point at which it made the function call.

You also can have a return statement in the function. For example, if you want to also return the value of the euro charge transaction to main, you can declare and implement the function in this way:

```
double returnDollarsSpent (double euros) {

  vacationBudget.euroTransaction =
                        euros*vacationBudget.exchangeRate;
  vacationBudget.budget -= vacationBudget.euroTransaction;
  return vacationBudget.euroTransaction;
}
```

And the statement

```
    return vacationBudget.euroTransaction;
```

returns control to main. You can see the relationship between how a similar function is called and its various parts in Figure 5-4.

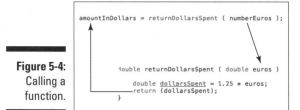

Figure 5-4:
Calling a
function.

At this point, go back to main and look at it again:

```
int main (int argc, const char * argv[])
```

main is nothing more than a function with two arguments — int argc and const char * argv[] — that returns an int. (**Note:** The second argument is an array, which I explain in Chapter 7.)

Scope of variables

Although I haven't gotten into classes and encapsulation yet (which I explain a little in Chapter 3), you do need to realize that variables are not accessible from every nook and cranny in your program. In the preceding examples, variables are accessible only within the function in which they are declared (that is, within the braces). This is also referred to as *scoped* to the function.

There is actually a little more to it than that. You can have braces (which define a block) within a function, in which case variables are scoped within that code block. A code block is a group of statements grouped together in a block enclosed in braces: { }, as shown here:

```
{ statement1;
  statement2;
  statement3; }
```

(You see examples of blocks in Chapter 4, where I explain if statements, and you see a lot more of them in Chapter 9, where I explain more about loops and control structures.)

That means that earlier in the main function

```
int main (int argc, const char * argv[]) {

budget vacationBudget;
```

the variable budget was accessible only to instructions within the main function.

So if you move the code in main

```
vacationBudget.budget -= dollars
```

into the function spendDollars, you won't have access to vacationBudget. budget any longer.

You may want to try this yourself.

To be able to access vacationBudget from any function, you have to make it *global,* by moving *both* its definition (the struct statement) and subsequent declaration (budget vacationBudget;) to the *file scope* (that is, in the file but not within any particular function). That's what happened when you did the following:

```
#import <Foundation/Foundation.h>

typedef struct {
  float exchangeRate;
  double budget;
  double euroTransaction;
} budget;

  budget vacationBudget;
```

Well, in general, this does violate some of the basic ideas of encapsulation I mention in Chapter 3. That being said, in a few limited occasions, you do need variables accessible to all functions, although this is really not one of them. In Chapter 6, using objects enables me to get rid of this global reference.

Actually, the issues of scoping, especially global scoping, are more complex than this. Fortunately, global scoping is something you won't have to be too concerned about until your programs become very complex, and you can find out about it at your leisure.

Variable scoping is all nicely illustrated in Figure 5-5.

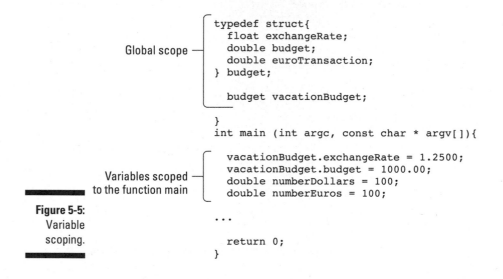

Figure 5-5: Variable scoping.

```
                 ┌  typedef struct{
                 │    float exchangeRate;
Global scope ─── │    double budget;
                 │    double euroTransaction;
                 │  } budget;
                 │
                 └    budget vacationBudget;

                    }
                    int main (int argc, const char * argv[]){
                 ┌  vacationBudget.exchangeRate = 1.2500;
Variables scoped │  vacationBudget.budget = 1000.00;
to the function main │ double numberDollars = 100;
                 └  double numberEuros = 100;

                    ...

                       return 0;
                    }
```

Unions

Unions allow the same portion of memory to be accessed by using different variable names and as (potentially) different types. I explain a little about them because you may come across them in other people's code, but I won't get into the topic too deeply because you are not likely to use them yourself.

While a `union` looks a lot like a `struct`, it is very different:

```
union theBudget {
  double budget;
  long long amountIWantToSpend;
} europeUnion;
```

Both `budget` and `amountIWantToSpend` *occupy the same physical space in memory.* This is illustrated in Figure 5-6. Its size is one of the largest elements in the declaration. Because both of them are referring to the same location in memory, the modification of one is the same as modifying both — you cannot store different values in them independent of each other. Using unions in this way is of value when you need to conserve space.

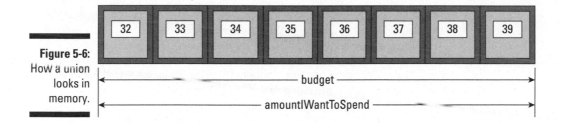

Figure 5-6:
How a union
looks in
memory.

Here is something else you might see:

```
struct theBudget {
   double budget;
   union {
      double euros;
      double pounds;
   };
};
```

Using a union enables you to access the same variable, using two different names. Although this is an amusing novelty, it actually violates some of the basic principles of encapsulation that I discuss in Chapter 3.

Once again, I remind you that in a union, the members euros and pounds occupy the same physical space. This means that modifying the value of one is identical to modifying the value of the other.

Enumerations (enum)

Enumerations enable you to create new data types in a similar way that you did earlier with the struct:

```
typedef enum {
   value1,
   value2,
   value3,
} enumerationName;
```

For example, you could create a new type of variable called currency to store the various currencies you might use in your program with the following declaration:

```
typedef enum {dollar, euro, pound} currency;
```

The "mechanics" of an `enum` actually work the same way as a `struct`, so the alternative ways of defining and declaring a `struct` apply to an `enum` as well.

Enumerations are actually `int`s. If you don't specify it, the integer value of the first value (`dollar`) will be 0. If you display the value of `dollar`, you get 0, the value of the `euro` will be 1, and the `pound` will be 2. You can also specify an integer value for any of the constant values that your enumerated type can take. If the constant value that follows it is not given an integer value, it is assigned the value of the previous one plus 1. For example:

```
typedef enum {dollar=1, euro, pound} currency;
```

In this case, `dollar` will be 1, `euro` 2, and `pound` 3.

The possible values that variables of this new type `currency` may take are the new constant values included within braces. For example, after the currency enumeration is declared, the following works:

```
currency aCurrency = dollar;
aCurrency = pound;
```

Declaring Function Prototypes

Up until now, you have had to *define* your functions (provide the code for the function) before they were called. You may have wondered about the order I had you enter code, or even experimented with the order and found yourself chastised by the compiler.

With a *function prototype,* you inform the compiler that it will eventually see a *definition* of the function — so trust me, and let me use it before you get to it. As a result, the compiler will let you use it before it is defined, but if you double-cross the compiler, it won't be a happy camper, and neither will you.

To declare a function prototype, all you do is this:

```
void spendDollars (double dollars);
```

Doing so means that you can move the definition — the implementation of the code — of `spendDollars` to after `main`. The value of this will become obvious in the next chapter.

If you have been following along with me, I extend what you just did in the previous example. If you want to start from a clean copy of the project where you left off, you can use the project found in the Example 5D folder, which is in the Chapter 5 folder.

You're now going to modify `main.m` to use function prototypes by following these steps:

1. **Start with the code you already have, add the function prototypes in bold, and move the function definitions for** spendDollars **and** chargeEuros **to after** main, **as I have done in Listing 5-2.**

Listing 5-2:   Function Prototypes

```
#import <Foundation/Foundation.h>

typedef struct {
  float   exchangeRate;
  double budget;
  double euroTransaction;
} budget;

budget vacationBudget;

void spendDollars (double dollars);
void chargeEuros (double euros);

int main (int argc, const char * argv[]) {

  vacationBudget.exchangeRate = 1.2500;
  vacationBudget.budget = 1000.00;
  double numberDollars = 100;
  double numberEuros = 100;

  spendDollars(numberDollars);
  NSLog(@"Converting %.2f US dollars into euros leaves
          $%.2f", numberDollars, vacationBudget.budget);
  chargeEuros(numberEuros);
  NSLog(@"Charging %.2f euros leaves $%.2f", numberEuros,
          vacationBudget.budget);

  return 0;
}

void spendDollars (double dollars) {

  vacationBudget.budget -= dollars;
}

void chargeEuros (double euros) {

  vacationBudget.euroTransaction =
                    euros*vacationBudget.exchangeRate;
  vacationBudget.budget -= vacationBudget.euroTransaction;
}
```

2. **Click the Run button on the Project Window toolbar to build and run the application.**

   Your output in the Debugger Console should look like this:

   ```
   Converting 100 US dollars into euros leaves $900.00
   Charging 100 euros leaves $775.00
   ```

You can find the completed project at the website in the Example 5E folder, which is in the Chapter 5 folder.

Extending the Functionality of a Program

Because I am flying all the way to Europe from San Francisco, I decided that I might as well visit London. To me, there's nothing like a spring shower with the wind blowing hard enough to make the rain go sideways. But before I go, I am going to have to make some additions to my program.

Obviously, the first thing that I will need to do is create a new budget for my trip to England. Doing that is pretty easy:

```
budget vacationBudgetEngland;
```

I need this new budget because England has a different currency — and a different exchange rate — than Europe, and I want to keep the two budgets separate. I'll also change the name of the old budget, vacationBudget, to vacation-BudgetEurope to make things clearer. You can see that in Listing 5-3.

The problem I face, though, is how do I update the vacationBudgetEngland variable? Right now, with a single budget, I updated the vacationBudget from each of the functions. But if I have two budgets, vacationBudgetEurope and vacationBudgetEngland, I need a way to let the function know which budget it should update.

One way would be to have a set of functions for each country. I could create spendDollarsInEurope and spendDollarsInEngland functions (and corresponding chargeForeignCurrencyEurope and chargeForeign-CurrencyEngland functions that would convert euros and pounds into dollars, respectively), and each one them would update the corresponding budget. For example:

```
void spendDollarsInEurope (double dollars) {
  vacationBudgetEurope.budget -= dollars;
}

void spendDollarsInEngland (double dollars) {
  vacationBudgetEngland.budget -= dollars;
}
```

Somehow this doesn't work for me. Adding new functions for each country I want to visit would not only be a lot of work, but it also seems like a waste, because, as you can see, they all are basically the same function — just operating on a different budget.

And as you can imagine, adding more countries requires coding and testing new functions and would quickly get out of hand. Remember, you want to make your programs easy to extend and enhance.

The alternative, which is the more sane approach, would be to pass to the function the budget variable it should operate on as an additional argument. So if I am spending dollars in Europe, I pass in the vacationBudgetEurope. If I am spending dollars in England, I pass in the vacationBudgetEngland.

That way, the functions will operate on the right data.

The mechanics of doing that are not quite that straightforward. While, as I said earlier, I can pass a struct as an argument to a function, that is not going to get me what I want. For example, if I changed the spendDollars function to take a budget as an argument

```
void spendDollars (budget theBudget, double dollars) {
  theBudget.budget -= dollars;
}
```

and I called it and then displayed the results (numberDollarsInEuroland is a new variable I declared that is initialized with the amount of a dollar transaction in Europe)

```
spendDollars(vacationBudgetEurope,
                    numberDollarsInEuroland);
NSLog(@"Converting %.2f US dollars into euros leaves
                    $%.2f", numberDollarsInEuroland,
                    vacationBudgetEurope.budget);
```

I would find

```
Converting 100.00 US dollars into euros leaves $1000.00
```

Whoops! This is because, as I also say earlier, when you pass in a variable as an argument in a function, it is *copied*. For a function to modify a member in a budget variable, you have to use a pointer to the budget variable as the argument. The function could then operate on the member (variable) directly.

To do that, I will change the spendDollars function to take a pointer to a budget as an argument and use that pointer to access and modify a member:

```
void spendDollars (budget *theBudget, double dollars) {
  theBudget->budget -= dollars;
}
```

I could then call it and display the results:

```
spendDollars(&vacationBudgetEurope,
                          numberDollarsInEuroland);
NSLog(@"Converting %.2f US dollars into euros leaves
                    $%.2f", numberDollarsInEuroland,
                    vacationBudgetEurope.budget);
```

The results will be

```
Converting 100.00 US dollars into euros leaves $900.00
```

Although I cover pointers in Chapter 4, I didn't really explain how to use them in this way, so I'll do that now.

Think of vacationBudgetEurope as a safety deposit box full of money. Up until now, the function withdrew money at will. When I use a pointer, instead of passing it the contents of the box, the function is passed the address of the box. That is what the &vacationBudgetEurope is in the function call:

```
spendDollars(&vacationBudgetEurope,
                          numberDollarsInEuroland);
```

&vacationBudgetEurope is the address of the vacationBudgetEurope variable.

Then in the spendDollars function itself, instead of taking money out of the box directly, the function first finds the box by using the address. That is accomplished in the spendDollars function by using the arrow operator. The arrow operator tells the compiler I want to operate on the contents of an address:

```
void spendDollars(budget* theBudget, double dollars) {

   theBudget->budget -= dollars;
}
```

The arrow operator is a dereference operator that is used with pointers to structs (and to objects as well) with members that enable you to access a member of an object to which you have a reference (address). What you are doing is called *dereferencing* a pointer.

Although for structs and objects, the arrow is commonly used, I could also have accessed the budget variable in the way I show you in Chapter 4:

```
(*theBudget).budget -= dollars;
```

Passing on the pointer to the appropriate `budget` makes adding a trip to England pretty straightforward. I need to declare and initialize the variables necessary for my new England excursion:

```
budget vacationBudgetEngland;
   vacationBudgetEngland.exchangeRate = 1.5000;
   vacationBudgetEngland.budget = 2000.00;
   double numberDollarsInPoundland = 100;
   double numberPounds = 100;
```

And I need to modify the code to simulate the transactions:

```
spendDollars(&vacationBudgetEngland,
        numberDollarsInPoundland);
NSLog(@"Converting %.2f US dollars into pounds
        leaves $%.2f", numberDollarsInPoundland,
        vacationBudgetEngland.budget);
chargeForeignCurrency(&vacationBudgetEngland,
        numberPounds);
NSLog(@"Charging %.2f pounds leaves $%.2f",
        numberPounds, vacationBudgetEngland.budget);
```

I also need to change the `spendDollars` and `chargeForeignCurrency` functions as I just described, to use the pointer to the `vacationBudget Europe` and `vacationBudgetEngland` variables:

```
void spendDollars(budget* theBudget, double dollars) {

   theBudget-> budget -= dollars;
}

void chargeForeignCurrency(budget* theBudget, double
        foreignCurrency) {

   theBudget->exchangeTransaction =
        foreignCurrency*theBudget->exchangeRate;
   theBudget->budget -= theBudget->exchangeTransaction;
}
```

I also change a few names, from `vacationBudget` to `europeVacation Budget` as I mention, and the `struct` member name from `euroTransaction` to `transaction`. That, of course, requires changing the code that used those names as well.

Well, it's back to work. In Listing 5-3, I boldfaced the changes.

If you have been following along with me, I extend what you just did in the preceding example. If you want to start from a clean copy of the project where you left off, you can use the project found in the Example 5E folder, which is in the Chapter 5 folder.

In the `main` function, delete the commented bold, italic, underlined code and add the code in bold shown in Listing 5-3.

Listing 5-3: Adding More Functionality

```
#import <Foundation/Foundation.h>

typedef struct {
  float exchangeRate;
  double budget;
//double euroTransaction;
  double exchangeTransaction;
} budget;

//budget vacationBudget;
budget vacationBudgetEurope;
budget vacationBudgetEngland;

//void spendDollars (double dollars);
//void chargeEuros (double euros);
void spendDollars(budget* theBudget, double dollars);
void chargeForeignCurrency(budget* theBudget,
                                double foreignCurrency);

int main (int argc, const char * argv[]) {

//vacationBudget.exchangeRate = 1.2500;
  vacationBudgetEurope.exchangeRate = 1.2500;
//vacationBudget.budget = 1000.00;
  vacationBudgetEurope.budget = 1000.00;
//double numberDollars = 100;
  double numberDollarsInEuroland = 100;
  double numberEuros = 100;

  vacationBudgetEngland.exchangeRate = 1.5000;
  vacationBudgetEngland.budget = 2000.00;
  double numberDollarsInPoundland = 100;
  double numberPounds = 100;


//spendDollars(numberDollars);
  spendDollars(&vacationBudgetEurope,
                              numberDollarsInEuroland);
//NSLog(@"Converting %.2f US dollars into euros leaves
          $%.2f", numberDollars, vacationBudget.budget);
  NSLog(@"Converting %.2f US dollars into euros leaves
                  $%.2f", numberDollarsInEuroland,
                          vacationBudgetEurope.budget);
//chargeEuros(numberEuros);
  chargeForeignCurrency (&vacationBudgetEurope,
                                    numberEuros);
```

```
//NSLog(@"Charging  %.2f euros leaves $%.2f", numberEuros,
          vacationBudget.budget);

  NSLog(@"Charging %.2f euros leaves $%.2f", numberEuros,
                              vacationBudgetEurope.budget);
  spendDollars(&vacationBudgetEngland,
                            numberDollarsInPoundland);
  NSLog(@"Converting %.2f US dollars into pounds leaves
                        $%.2f", numberDollarsInPoundland,
                            vacationBudgetEngland.budget);
  chargeForeignCurrency(&vacationBudgetEngland,
                                        numberPounds);
  NSLog(@"Charging %.2f pounds leaves $%.2f",
          numberPounds, vacationBudgetEngland.budget);


  return 0;

}
//void spendDollars (double dollars) {

//   vacationBudget.budget -= dollars;
//}

void spendDollars(budget* theBudget, double dollars) {

  theBudget->budget -= dollars;
}


//void chargeEuros (double euros) {

//   vacationBudget.euroTransaction = euros*vacationBudget.
          exchangeRate;
//   vacationBudget.budget -= vacationBudget.
          euroTransaction;
//}

void chargeForeignCurrency(budget* theBudget, double
          foreignCurrency) {

  theBudget->exchangeTransaction =
          foreignCurrency*theBudget->exchangeRate;
  theBudget->budget -= theBudget ->exchangeTransaction;
}
```

Your output in the Debugger Console should look like this:

```
Converting 100.00 US dollars into euros leaves $900.00
Charging 100.00 euros leaves $775.00
Converting 100.00 US dollars into pounds leaves $1900.00
Charging 100.00 pounds leaves $1750.00
```

You can find the completed project at the website in the Example 5F folder, which is in the Chapter 5 folder.

Thinking about Extensibility and Enhanceability

Although making the changes you just made does make it easier to add new countries (all you need to do is declare another budget for New Zealand, for example, and call the spendDollars and chargeForeignCurrency functions as needed), this approach is fraught with danger.

For example, one problem with this kind of module design is that the data itself is accessible to all functions, and an errant function could think it was updating vacationBudgetEngland. Because of a typing or copy-and-paste error (easily done on my part), it could end up updating vacationBudget Europe instead.

Perhaps you think that this is one of those theoretical issues that won't usually happen if you're doing your job right. Well, when I was doing the code for this example, I actually did that — I typed vacationBudgetEurope when I meant to type vacationBudgetEngland.

But more important, if you ever want to change the struct, you have to go out and find all the functions that used it and change them. For example, what if I decided I wanted to change the budget member so that it continued to hold the starting budget, and I wanted to add a new variable whatsLeft to let me know what my remaining balance was? In this program, that's not a problem because I only have to change two functions. But in a more complex program, I could have functions all over the place that are using budget that I would have to find and change.

In addition, this program is not very extensible. If you wanted to have a different kind of budget for New Zealand, for example, one where you tracked your wool purchases, you would either have to add that to all the countries you visited (even though you didn't use it anywhere except New Zealand) or you would have to create a special struct for New Zealand and rewrite the spendDollars and spendForeignCurrency functions to use the new struct. If you then needed to go back to make a change to the original struct for any reason, you would have to remember to change both structs and all the functions that used them.

Changes like this happen all the time, because as you can see so far, factoring (or moving things around) and adding functionality are a way of life in the programming biz.

Objects (and classes) provide the solution to both of these problems.

The first problem, the global accessibility of data and the global effect of modifying the structure of the data, is solved by packaging data with functions that own them into something called an *object*. Objects enable you to implement encapsulation — as I explain in Chapter 3. This is the world of Objective-C's object-oriented extensions to C, and you explore objects in Chapter 6.

Using objects can also help with the second problem. In Chapter 3, I explain polymorphism, which enables me to add new "more of the same" functionality to my program without affecting the existing code. In Chapter 10, I show you how Objective-C makes that possible by using a mechanism called inheritance.

Chapter 6

Adding a Little More Class to Your Program

*T*his chapter covers objects and classes and messages, and the difference between a program based on functions and global data and one based on objects. I show you quite a bit about the mechanics of using objects and classes in your program.

I also introduce you to some basic ideas about encapsulation. Encapsulation involves more than simply hiding instance variables behind the object's wall, as you see as you read this chapter and the rest of this book.

I also explain and illustrate some of the advantages of using objects, but to be frank, I only scratch the surface when it comes to that. As you continue through this book, I illustrate, and you discover on your own, many more.

Grasping Objects and Their Classes

In Chapter 5, I show you what you have to do to make your program easier to extend. You created two functions, spendDollars: and chargeForeign-Currency:, that used a pointer to a budget variable. You could then pass in the pointer to vacationBudgetEurope or vacationBudgetEngland depending on where you were (Europe or England), and the function would operate on the data for that country.

The program architecture you created looked like the following (I'm going to omit the `main` function and the function implementations for the time being):

```
typedef struct {

  float exchangeRate;
  double budget;
  double exchangeTransaction;
} budget;

void spendDollars (budget *theBudget, double dollars);
void chargeForeignCurrency (budget *theBudget,
                                    double foreignCurrency);
```

The problem with that, as I point out, is that if I wanted to change the `struct`, I would have to go out and find all the functions that used it and change them. In a program this small that would be simple (only two functions exist after all), but in a more complex program, functions all over the place could be using the budget `struct`.

This is one of the problems that object-oriented programming solves through *encapsulation*.

Moving from Functions and Global Data to Objects and Classes

As you might guess, object-oriented programs are built around *objects* — no surprises here. An object packages data with the particular operations that can use or affect that data. A class that provides the same functionality as the `budget struct` and the functions that use it looks like this:

```
@interface

Budget : NSObject {

  float   exchangeRate;
  double budget;
  double exchangeTransaction;
}

- (void) spendDollars: (double) dollars ;
- (void) chargeForeignCurrency: (double) foreignCurrency;

@end
```

If you look carefully, you can see that I have taken (for the most part) the elements in the `budget` struct and the function prototypes and moved them into a *class* called `Budget` (ignore some of the details such as @interface and @end).

A class definition is like a structure definition in that it defines the data elements (which are called *instance variables*) that become part of every instance. But a class expands the idea of a data structure — containing both data and functions rather than just data. Functions, however, become *methods* that both specify and implement the behavior of a class.

This class definition is a template for an *object*; it declares the instance variables that become part of every object of that class and the methods that all objects of the class can use.

Whereas a *class* is a structure that represents an object's type — just like a `struct` did in Chapter 5 — an *object* is something that exists in a computer's memory. An object is an instantiation (big computer science word here) of a class. In more down-to-earth terms, a class is a type (just as a `budget` or an `int` is), and an object is like a variable.

When I use the word *class,* I am talking about code that you write, and when I use the word *object,* I am talking about behavior at runtime.

In Chapter 5, you declared a `struct` of type `budget` and then declared two variables of the type `budget`:

```
budget vacationBudgetEurope;
budget vacationBudgetEngland;
```

When you use a class, you do something similar:

```
Budget *europeBudget = [Budget new];
Budget *englandBudget = [Budget new];
```

Each instance of a class (object) has memory allocated for its own set of instance variables, which store values particular to the instance.

When you create an object from a class, you are essentially creating a `struct` out there in memory land that holds its instance variables. But although every object has its own instance variables, all objects of that class share a single set of methods. How a method knows which object's instance variables to use is an interesting story, and one I tell you shortly.

Operations (or functions) are known as the object's *methods;* the data they affect are its *instance variables.* In essence, an object bundles a data structure (instance variables) and a group of functions (methods) into a self-contained programming unit. You then ask an object to do something for you, such as subtract the amount you just spent from your budget, by sending it a *message.*

When an object receives a message, it then executes the code in the appropriate method.

This encapsulation solves the problem of the widespread impact that changing a data structure may have. Only an object's methods that are packaged with the data can access or modify that data, although an object can, and often does, make its data available to other objects through its methods.

While on the surface, it may appear that I am just changing some terminology — methods for functions, instance variables for struct members, and messages for function calls — essentially, this is a very different approach.

One more thing — in Objective-C, classes have two parts:

- ✔ An *interface* that *declares* the methods and instance variables of the class and names its superclass (don't worry, I explain all that)
- ✔ An *implementation* that actually *defines* the class — the code that implements its methods

These two parts are almost always split between two files (although you can have more), but to make things easier, I postpone doing that until later, in the section "Spreading the Wealth across Files."

Creating the Interface

You begin your journey through object-oriented wonderland with the interface. The interface in the object-oriented world is the public commitment to the behavior you can count on from an object.

I want to start with a new project. Chapter 2 explains how to do this in detail, so if you need more information, refer to that chapter.

Here's what you need to do to start making use of objects in a program:

1. **Launch Xcode.**

   I have you create a new project here. You can do that or you can skip Steps 2 through 6 and start with the project in the Chapter 6 Start Here folder, in the Chapter 6 folder at the website.

2. **Select File⇨New⇨Project to create a new project.**

3. **In the New Project window, click Application under the OS X heading.**

4. **Select Command Line Tool from the choices displayed. Then click Next.**

5. **Enter the name** Budget Object **in the Product Name field, select Foundation from the Type drop-down menu, and select the check box Use Automatic Reference Counting; then click Next.**

   Xcode displays a standard Save sheet.

6. **Choose a Save location (the desktop works just fine) and then click Save.**

   After you click Save, Xcode creates the project and opens the project window. For more information on the project window, see Chapter 2.

7. **Start with an empty** main **function.**

   I cover this in Chapter 4. You need to delete all the statements in main except for return 0; so that you end up with a main function that looks like this:

   ```
   #import <Foundation/Foundation.h>

   int main (int argc, const char * argv[]) {

      return 0;
   }
   ```

Declaring the class interface

The purpose of the class interface is to give users of a class the information they need to work with the class. The declaration of a class interface begins with the compiler directive @interface and ends with the directive @end. (All Objective-C compiler directives begin with @.) You can see this here:

```
@interface ClassName : ItsSuperclass {
   instance variable declarations
}
method declarations
@end
```

In the interface, you specify the following:

✔ The class's name and *superclass:*

   ```
   @interface ClassName : ItsSuperclass {
   ```

   A class can be based on another class called its superclass, and it inherits all the methods and instance variables of that class. I explain all about inheritance in Chapter 10. For now just follow along.

✔ The class's *instance variables*. Instance variables correspond to the members (variable declarations) in a `struct`.

✔ The class's *methods*. Methods correspond to the function prototypes discussed in Chapter 5.

For example, here is the interface for the `Budget` class:

```
@interface Budget : NSObject  {

  float   exchangeRate;
  double budget;
  double exchangeTransaction;
}

- (void) createBudget: (double) aBudget
              withExchangeRate: (float) anExchangeRate;
- (void) spendDollars: (double) dollars ;
- (void) chargeForeignCurrency: (double) foreignCurrency;
@end
```

By convention, class names begin with an uppercase letter (such as `Budget`); the class's instance variables and methods typically begin with a lowercase letter (such as `exchangeRate:` and `spendDollars:`).

Four parts to the interface exist, and I have you enter them in the empty `main` file over the next four sections. The parts appear in this order:

1. The `@interface` compiler directive and first line
2. The instance variables
3. The methods
4. The `@end` compiler directive

Enter the @interface compiler directive and first line

Enter the following code right after the first line, `#import <Foundation/Foundation.h>`, and before `main`:

```
@interface Budget : NSObject {
```

`@interface` tells the compiler that you are declaring a new class. You also see Xcode automatically adding `@end` to balance the `@interface` for you.

`Budget : NSObject` declares the new class name and links it to its superclass.

In this case, `Budget` is the name of the new class. This is exactly the same (well, close) as declaring the `struct` (see Chapter 5).

`: NSObject` on the `@interface` line tells the compiler that the `Budget` class is a *subclass* or a "child" of the `NSObject` class. As I explain, `Budget` will inherit all the methods and instance variables of `NSObject`. This means that for all practical purposes, even though you don't see them in your class declaration, `Budget` includes all the instance variables and all the methods that are in `NSObject`.

Because `Budget` inherits from `NSObject`, it has all the functionality that an Objective-C object needs at runtime.

Xcode will try to help you as you enter the text in this chapter. For instance, when you start to type `@interface`, Xcode will display a pop-up window with suggestions for what it thinks you're trying to do, as you can see in Figure 6-1. The instructions in this chapter assume that you've ignored Xcode's recommendations and are just typing things in as shown. However, as you become more familiar with programming in Objective-C, you will find that Xcode is really very helpful for stepping in and assisting you with most of the boring pieces of programming so that you can concentrate on the important stuff. You can modify Xcode's code completion behavior in the Xcode preferences, on the Text Editing tab.

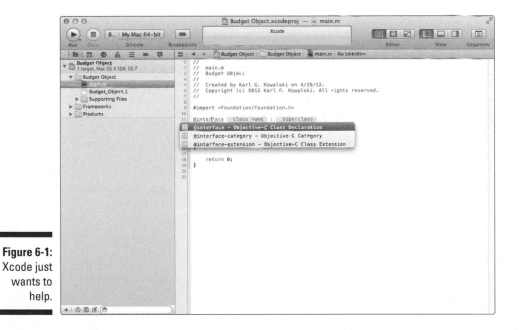

Figure 6-1: Xcode just wants to help.

Enter the instance variables

After starting to declare a new class, you tell the compiler about the various pieces of data — the instance variables and methods.

Type the following lines of code on the line after `@interface Budget : NSObject {`:

```
float   exchangeRate;
double  budget;
double  exchangeTransaction;
}
```

`exchangeRate`, `budget`, and `exchangeTransaction` are the *instance variables* for objects of the class `Budget`.

The reason they are called instance variables is that when you create an object of class `Budget`, you are creating an *instance* of the class, which means that for each class object you create, you allocate some amount of memory for its variables (just as you do for the `struct`) — instance variables are often shortened to *ivars*. Notice that the instance variables correspond to the ones used in the `struct`:

- ✔ `exchangeRate` is the current, well, exchange rate — the number of dollars it will cost me to get one euro, or one pound, for example.
- ✔ `budget` holds the amount of dollars I have left to spend in a given country.
- ✔ `exchangeTransaction` is the amount in U.S. dollars of a foreign currency transaction.

Objective-C is case-sensitive. In the preceding code, `Budget` and `budget` are not the same thing — `Budget` is a class and `budget` is a variable.

Because you declared `budget`, `exchangeRate`, and `exchangeTransaction` in the class definition, every time a `Budget` object is created, it includes these three instance variables. So, every object of class `Budget` has its own `budget`, `exchangeRate`, and `exchangeTransaction`. The closing brace tells the compiler that you're done specifying the instance variables for `Budget`.

Enter the methods

Type the following lines of code on the line after the closing brace (`}`):

```
- (void) createBudget: (double) aBudget
               withExchangeRate: (float) anExchangeRate;
- (void) spendDollars: (double) dollars;
- (void) chargeForeignCurrency: (double) foreignCurrency;
```

In Objective-C, these lines of code are called *method declarations*. They make public the behavior that the Budget has implemented — that is, this is what the object of class Budget can do.

Method declarations are functionally similar to the function prototypes you declared in the last chapter, although they look a lot different. So let me explain methods.

I start with spendDollars: (I get to createBudget:withExchangeRate: soon):

```
- (void) spendDollars: (double) dollars;
```

The leading dash signals that this is the declaration for an Objective-C method. That's one way you can distinguish a method declaration from a function prototype, which has no leading dash.

Following the dash is the return type for the method, enclosed in parentheses. Methods can return the same types as functions, including standard types (int, float, and char), as well as references to other objects (an object reference is similar to the pointer to the struct that you used in Chapter 5).

spendDollars: is a method that takes a single argument of type double. Notice that instead of the parentheses used in a function to indicate arguments, methods use a :. Also notice that the colon is part of the method name, as you saw when I referred to the spendDollars: method earlier. Finally, a method that takes no arguments has no : as part of its name.

Another difference between a function and method declaration is that in a method declaration, both the *return type* and the *argument type* are enclosed in parentheses. This is the standard syntax for casting one type to a another (you can refer to Chapter 4, where I explain the cast operator, if you like).

Although this method doesn't return a value, it could, just like any function does, and in the same way:

```
return someValue;
```

For all practical purposes, chargeForeignCurrency is the same:

```
- (void) chargeForeignCurrency: (double) foreignCurrency;
```

Finally, you've come to the mind-numbing part — createBudget: withExchangeRate:

```
- (void) createBudget: (double) aBudget
        withExchangeRate: (float) anExchangeRate;
```

`createBudget:withExchangeRate:` is a method that initializes the values — the `budget` and `exchangeRate` — for an object that is the budget for a particular country. In Chapter 5, you did that in `main` by assigning those values to the members in the `budget struct`. For example:

```
vacationBudgetEurope.exchangeRate = 1.2500;
vacationBudgetEurope.budget = 1000.00;
...
vacationBudgetEngland.exchangeRate = 1.5000;
vacationBudgetEngland.budget = 2000.00;
```

But because (as I explain later in this chapter in the section "Scoping instance variables") you don't have access to the instance variables in a `Budget` object (repeat *encapsulation* three times and click your heels), you need to create a method to assign initial values to the instance variables. Initialization is an important part of Objective-C, and I explain it in detail in Chapter 12.

Although you might be able to guess that the method takes two arguments, the syntax of the declaration is probably not something you are familiar with (talk about a classic understatement):

```
- (void) createBudget: (double) aBudget
          withExchangeRate: (float) anExchangeRate;
```

When you have more than one argument, the arguments are declared within the method name after the colon. What makes it interesting is that the additional arguments after the first have a name. In fact, the real method name is `createBudget:withExchangeRate:`.

Although this may appear to be confusing, operationally it is no different than a function. For example, inside your methods, you access the arguments by using the identifier, just as you did in the functions you used in Chapter 5. In this case, the identifiers are `aBudget` and `anExchangeRate`.

Argument names are one of the major differences between a method and a function.

Argument names make it easier to understand the messages in your code. `createBudget:withExchangeRate:` does have a nice ring to it. When you create your own methods, name them in the same way I just did — making them closer to sentences. This way of naming methods makes it much easier to match arguments with what they are used for. This solves one of the problems that you can run across when using functions in your code — you can't tell, when reading the code, what each of the arguments in a function call is for without looking at the function.

This does take some getting used to, but after you do, you will like it a lot.

If a method takes an argument, it has one or more colons, corresponding to the number of arguments. If it takes no arguments, it has no colons. If you are not going to specify the full name, you add the number of colons corresponding to the number of arguments to the name. For example, `createBudget:withExchangeRate:` indicates that it takes two arguments.

Because `createBudget:withExchangeRate:` won't be returning anything, I use `void` to indicate that no return value exists.

Enter the @end compiler directive
Type **@end**.

This tells the compiler that you have finished the `Budget` interface declaration.

The interface is done! It's the complete interface for the `Budget` class. Now, anyone using this object knows that this class has three methods that can create a new budget, spend dollars, and charge something in a foreign currency. While he or she could also see that three instance variables exist, that should be of no concern unless he or she is going to modify that class.

Scoping instance variables

As you saw in Chapter 5, instance variables are scoped to (accessible within) the code block they're in. This can be a function, a code block within a function, or in this case, a class. It is this built-in scoping mechanism that allows an object to hide its data. But to provide flexibility, when it comes to a class (here come the Objective-C extensions to C again), you can actually explicitly set the scope to three different levels through the use of a compiler directive:

- `@private`: The instance variable is accessible only within the class that declares it.
- `@protected`: The instance variable is accessible within the class that declares it and within classes that inherit it. This is the default if you don't specify anything.
- `@public`: The instance variable is accessible everywhere.

There's also another approach you can use to achieve the same result of using `@private` to deny access to a class's data, through the use of *categories*. I explain categories in Chapter 16, and cover this aspect in that chapter.

Don't use @public! If you do — go directly to jail, do not pass Go, and do not collect $200. If you have to ask why, reread the first part of this chapter, the last part of the previous chapter, and Chapter 3.

Another level also exists: @package: On 64-bit machines, an instance variable acts like @public inside the framework that defines the class, but like @private outside. I mention it because you may see it in some of the Cocoa header files, but it's beyond the scope of this book.

What you have just done implements one of the fundamental concepts in object-oriented programming — *encapsulation*. Data and functions are now both members of the object. You no longer use sets of global variables or structs that you pass from one function to another as arguments. Instead, you use objects that have their own data *and* functions as members.

Now that you have the interface done, it's time to write the code that makes this class actually do something.

The Implementation — Coding the Methods

The @interface directive, which I discuss earlier in this chapter, declares a class's interface. This is where another developer (or even you) can go to understand the class's capabilities and behavior. But it's here in the implementation that the real work is described and done.

Just as with the interface, I break the implementation down into a number of steps and explain what you are doing as you go along. Here are the steps:

1. Add the implementation compiler directive.

2. Define the createBudget: method.

3. Define the rest of the methods.

Adding the implementation compiler directive

Type the following line of code after the @end statement into main.m and before main:

```
@implementation Budget
```

@implementation (like @interface) is a compiler directive that says you're about to present the code that implements a class. The name of the class appears after @implementation. Here is where you code the definitions of the individual methods. (Here, order is unimportant — the methods don't have to appear in the same order as they do in the @interface.) Once again, Xcode adds @end to be helpful and save you some typing.

In fact, you can add methods in an @implementation that have not been declared in the @interface. In other languages, these might be considered private methods. Not so in Objective-C, which doesn't have private methods — those you add to the implementation that are not in the interface are still accessible to other objects.

Defining the createBudget: method

Type the following lines of code after @implementation Budget:

```
- (void) createBudget: (double) aBudget
         withExchangeRate: (float) anExchangeRate {
  exchangeRate = anExchangeRate;
  budget = aBudget;
}
```

This is your brand-spanking-new initialization function. The first line of the definition of createBudget:withExchangeRate: looks a lot like the declaration in the @interface section (one would hope), except that rather than a semicolon at the end, you find a brace. Notice that you have an argument named aBudget and an instance variable budget. If you had named that argument budget, the compiler would have needed to decide which one you meant when you tried to access the budget variable. You will find that the compiler will tell you in no uncertain terms that it was going to hide the instance variable from your method code. I mutilated my beautiful code to illustrate that in Figure 6-2.

You want to use a name like aBudget in the method declaration because it tells the reader exactly what the argument is for. In general, though, as you will see, I don't want the user to know that this is initializing an instance variable. I explain why, and more about encapsulation, in Chapter 14 when I explain properties.

The body of the method, as you might expect, contains these instructions:

```
exchangeRate = anExchangeRate;
budget = aBudget;
```

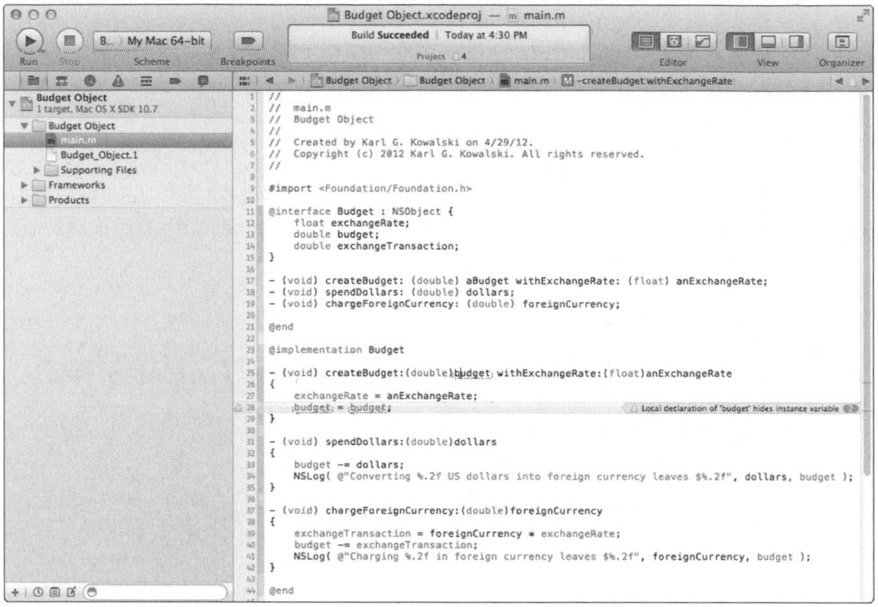

Figure 6-2:
The
compiler's
revenge.

As I explain earlier, in the program you coded in Chapter 5, you did this initialization in `main`:

```
vacationBudgetEurope.exchangeRate = 1.2500;
vacationBudgetEurope.budget = 1000.00;
vacationBudgetEngland.exchangeRate = 1.5000;
vacationBudgetEngland.budget = 2000.00;
```

But now that you are an official object-oriented programmer, you don't want to assign the value to the variables in this way for a couple of reasons. First, you made those instance variables protected (by default), so you can't access them. But even if you could, you wouldn't want to because it violates the principle of encapsulation.

Defining the rest of the methods

Enter the following lines of code after the `createBudget:withExchangeRate:` method:

```
- (void) spendDollars: (double) dollars {

  budget -= dollars;
  NSLog(@"Converting %.2f US dollars into foreign currency
                       leaves $%.2f", dollars, budget);
}

- (void) chargeForeignCurrency: (double)
                                   foreignCurrency {

  exchangeTransaction = foreignCurrency*exchangeRate;
  budget -= exchangeTransaction;
  NSLog(@"Charging %.2f in foreign currency leaves $%.2f",
                     foreignCurrency, budget);
}
```

Because of the size of this book's pages, occasionally I have to break up some really long lines of code. You can see this in the two NSLog statements in the code above. If you enter the lines of code exactly as they are shown above, with the line break between foreign currency and leaves $%.2f in the first NSLog statement, the Debug Console will include the line break in its output. This happens because all the text between double-quotes (") is presumed to be one contiguous piece, and this includes spaces and line breaks. To avoid this situation, you should keep quoted text strings all on the same line.

Both of these methods are almost identical to the previous functions you used. I also moved the NSLog statements from main into the methods because it enables me to track the methods as they are invoked.

You are not using these NSLog statements for any other reason than to be able to follow what is going on in the program, so don't be too concerned with what is being displayed. I add a real user interface in Chapters 17 and 18.

Exploring the Program Logic

Now that you have declared your objects, it's about time to do something with them. Although it seems as though I've been working backward, which is true, it's time to get to the real meat (or tofu, if you prefer) of the program. Just remember, I have been working backward because in programming, and in life, and in cooking (and in painting), most of the work is in the preparation. After you have everything ready, the execution should be easy, and as you will see, it is.

Note: You are still working in the `main.m` file. If you need to, scroll down to find the `main` function. It should look like the following:

```
#import <Foundation/Foundation.h>

int main (int argc, const char * argv[]) {


    return 0;
}
```

Coding the functionality in the main function

I now take you through coding the `main` function. I break this down into a series of steps:

1. Declaring the local variables

2. Instantiating an object

3. Sending messages to your objects

4. Adding the code for England

Declaring the local variables

The first thing you do in your program is to declare some local variables, just as you did in Chapter 5.

Type the following lines of code into `main` after the first brace and before the `return 0;` statement:

```
double numberDollarsInEuroland = 100;
double numberEuros = 100;
double numberDollarsInPoundland = 100;
double numberPounds = 100;
```

Xcode displays a warning indicator — a yellow triangle — to the left of the lines you just entered and also in the Activity viewer. Don't panic! Xcode is letting you know that these variables are being initialized but Xcode hasn't seen them get used — yet. These warnings vanish after you enter more code later in this section.

Instantiating an object

The next thing you do is instantiate an object.

Type the following line of code after the variables you just declared:

```
Budget  *europeBudget = [Budget new];
```

Congratulations! You have instantiated (created) your first object, and you have sent it a message.

To create a new object, you send the new message to the class you are interested in. Messaging is an important part of working with objects in Objective-C, and it is very different than the function calls that you have been working with.

To start with, the syntax of sending a message is

```
[receiver message : arguments];
```

The receiver of a message can be either an *object* or a *class.* One of the more interesting features of Objective-C is that you can send messages to a class. If you haven't done object-oriented programming before, sending messages to a class probably means nothing to you. But if are coming from something like C++, it is very interesting. Class methods enable you to implement behavior that is not object specific, but is applicable to an entire class.

The methods defined for an object are called *instance methods,* and the ones defined for a class are called *class methods.* Although I mention class methods in this book, you won't be using them. I only refer to them when it is important to distinguish them from instance methods and where you really need to know about them — in Chapter 13, for example.

The line of code you entered

```
Budget *europeBudget = [Budget new];
```

sends the new message to the Budget class. The new method (inherited from NSObject) does two things, in this order:

1. Allocates memory for the object to hold its instance variables.

2. Sends the new object an init message.

   The default init method will (more or less) initialize its instance variables to 0. This works fine for the time being. Initialization, as boring as it sounds, is, however, a very important part of working with objects. In Chapters 12 and 13, I go into detail about initialization and show you how to write a proper init method for your objects.

At runtime, a class object for each class is created — one that knows how to build new objects belonging to the class.

What is important here is that what is returned is a *pointer* to the memory that has been allocated to hold this object's instance variables. This is similar to what you did in Chapter 5, where you created a pointer to each of the budget structs you declared. I explain more about memory allocation in Chapter 13. (If you are a little fuzzy on pointers, refer to Chapter 4.)

Sending messages to your objects

Enter the following lines of code after Budget *europeBudget = [Budget new];:

```
[europeBudget createBudget:
              1000.00 withExchangeRate:1.2500];
[europeBudget spendDollars:numberDollarsInEuroland];
[europeBudget chargeForeignCurrency:numberEuros];
```

You have sent three messages to the europeBudget *object* that you just instantiated. Take a look at the first message:

```
[europeBudget  createBudget:1000.00
                      withExchangeRate:1.2500];
```

Using the europeBudget pointer to the object, you are sending it the createBudget:withExchangeRate: message with 1000.00 and 1.2500 as arguments. As I explain, the net result is the same as the initialization of the members in the structs that you did in the main function.

Instead, you use this method to initialize the object with a budget and an exchange rate. As you'll see, the initialization I've done here is pretty rudimentary, especially compared to what you'll be doing in a few chapters, but it gets the job done for now.

After initialization, the next message you send to the europeBudget object tells it how much you just spent in dollars (it has an argument number DollarsInEuroland just as the function did):

```
[europeBudget spendDollars:numberDollarsInEuroland];
```

And the third message reports a credit card transaction:

```
[europeBudget chargeForeignCurrency:numberEuros];
```

The question that occurred to me when I first learned about object-oriented programming was how did the europeBudget method code (of which only a single copy exists) get to the object's *ivars* (instance variables), which are sitting some place in memory?

The answer is very clever. When you send a message in Objective-C, a hidden argument called `self`, a pointer to the object's instance variables, is passed to the receiving object. For example, in the code

```
[europeBudget spendDollars:numberDollarsInEuroland];
```

the method passes `europeBudget` as its `self` argument. Whereas the code you wrote in the method `chargeForeignCurrency:` looks like

```
NSLog(@"Converting %.2f US dollars into foreign currency
                    leaves $%.2f", dollars, budget);
```

what the compiler is really doing is modifying your code so that it conceptually looks like this:

```
NSLog(@"Converting %.2f US dollars into foreign currency
            leaves $%.2f", dollars, self->budget);
```

This should look familiar. This is what you did in Chapter 5 to access the `struct` members. The `->` is the arrow operator. It is used only with pointers to objects (as well as `struct`s). See Chapter 4 to refresh your memory about pointers.

As you create objects, you get a new pointer for each one, and when you send a message to a particular object, the pointer associated with that object becomes the `self` argument.

Adding the code for England

First you need to create the `Budget` object for England. (I wouldn't fancy being in England with no money to spend after all.) Then you will be able to send it a message as well.

Type the following lines of code, before the `return 0;` statement to finish `main`:

```
Budget   *englandBudget = [Budget new];


[englandBudget  createBudget:2000.00
                            withExchangeRate:1.5000];
[englandBudget spendDollars:numberDollarsInPoundland];
[englandBudget chargeForeignCurrency:numberPounds];
```

You just wrote a program that implements one of the fundamental concepts in object-oriented programming — encapsulation. The data and the operations on that data are now encapsulated within the `Budget` object.

You no longer use sets of global variables or `struct`s that you pass from one function to another as arguments. Instead, you have objects that have their own data and functions embedded as members. (I know that I have said this before, but it is worth repeating.)

Building and running the application

To build and run the application, click the Run button on the Workspace window toolbar.

Your output in the Debugger Console should look like the following:

```
Converting 100.00 US dollars into foreign currency leaves
        $900.00
Charging 100.00 in foreign currency leaves $775.00
Converting 100.00 US dollars into foreign currency leaves
        $1900.00
Charging 100.00 in foreign currency leaves $1750.00
```

You can find the completed project at the website in the Example 6A folder, which can be found in the Chapter 6 folder.

Extending the program

In Chapter 4, I raise two concerns about being able to extend my program. The first one, the vulnerability that you face when all your functions have access to all the data, and are dependent on that data's structure, is mostly solved by encapsulating the data in an object. The data becomes an internal implementation detail; all the users of that data outside the object know about is the behavior it can expect from an object.

But what if another object needs to know the amount left in your budget for England, for example? This requires that you add a method that provides that information. Notice I said information, not the instance variable. It becomes the responsibility of an object to supply the budget information to any object that needs it. It does not mean, however, that an instance variable has to hold that information. That makes it possible to change how you represent that data, and also makes it possible to change what instance variables you choose for the object. In the preceding chapter, I brought up the problems that I would run into if I wanted to change the struct that the functions used. Making that change now, using classes and objects in the way you should, would have no effect on the objects that were using that information!

So although its internal data structure is part of the class interface, in reality, an object's functionality should be defined only by its methods. As a user of a class, you shouldn't count on a one-to-one correspondence between a method that returns some data and an instance variable. Some methods might return information not stored in instance variables, and some instance variables might have data that will never see the light of day outside the object.

This allows your classes to evolve over time (remember Chapter 3, where I spoke about the inevitability of change). As long as messages are the way you interact with a class, changes to the instance variables really don't affect its interface and the other objects that use this class — and that's the point.

But what about my second concern — what if I want a new kind of budget or want to tailor my Budget object to New Zealand to keep track of my sheep purchases? Do I have to take the old object, copy and paste it, and add the new features — thus creating a new object that I have to maintain in parallel with the existing Budget object?

As you might expect, the answer is, "Of course not!" But to find out exactly how to do that, you have to wait until Chapter 10 when I talk about inheritance.

In addition, you will do even more to make your program even more extensible, which you discover in Chapter 11.

Spreading the Wealth across Files

So far, everything you have done has been added to a single source file. All your projects have created one file, main.m, where you wrote all your code. While this works for what you have been doing thus far, it won't scale when you start to develop your own applications. As your program gets larger, scrolling through a single file becomes more difficult. (Other issues, which are beyond the scope of this book, should not concern you for a while.) But a well-thought-out solution exists for that problem that just about everyone uses.

When I write even the simplest programs for iOS or Mac OS, I divide things into multiple files.

As you've seen, the source code for Objective-C classes is divided into two parts. One part is the interface, which provides the public view of the class.

The `@interface` directive contains all the information necessary for someone to use the class.

The other part of a class's source is the implementation. The `@implementation` directive contains the method definitions.

Because of the natural split in the definition of a class into interface and implementation, a class's code is often split into two files along the same lines. One part holds the interface components: the `@interface` directive for the class and any `enum`, `constants`, `#defines`, and so on. Because of Objective-C's C heritage, this typically goes into a header file, which has the same name as the class with an `.h` at the end. For example, the class `Budget` header file will be called `Budget.h`.

All the implementation details, such as the `@implementation` directive for the class, definitions of global variables, the method definitions (implementations), and so on, go into a file with the same name as the class and with an `.m` at the end. `Budget.m` will be the implementation file for your class.

I start by having you create a new *group* in the Project Navigator pane to hold the new files. A group (whose icon looks like a yellow folder) provides a way to organize the source files in your project. (For example, you can make one group for your user interface classes and another for your model classes to make your project easier to navigate.) When you set up groups, Xcode doesn't actually move any files or create any directories on your hard drive. The group relationship is just a lovely fantasy maintained by Xcode.

After that, you'll create the files themselves.

If you have been following along with me, I extend what you just did in the previous example. If you want to start with a clean copy of the project where you left off, you can use the project found in the Example 6A folder, which is in the Chapter 6 folder.

You will move the `Budget` class into its own file by following these steps:

1. **Click the Budget Object project icon and then choose File➪New➪ Group (see Figure 6-3).**

   You get a brand-spanking-new folder named New Group, already selected and waiting for you to type in the name you want.

2. **Type the name** Classes, **as I did in Figure 6-4.**

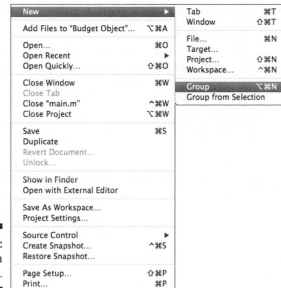

Figure 6-3:
Creating a
new folder.

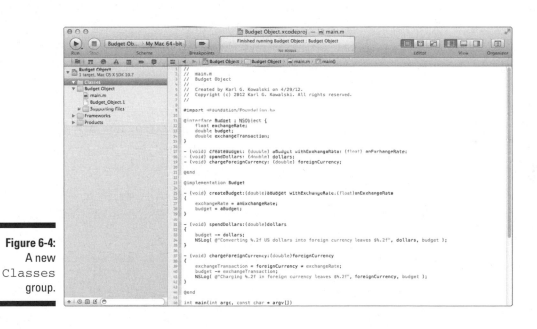

Figure 6-4:
A new
Classes
group.

3. Choose File➪New File (or press ⌘+N) to open the New File dialog.

Make sure that the `Classes` folder is still selected; Xcode puts new files into the selected folder.

4. In the leftmost column of the dialog, first select Cocoa under OS X, select the Objective-C class template in the upper-right pane as I did in Figure 6-5, and then click Next.

You see a new dialog asking for some more information.

Figure 6-5:
A Cocoa class template.

5. Enter Budget in the Class field and make sure that `NSObject` is selected in the drop menu, as I did in Figure 6-6, and then click Next.

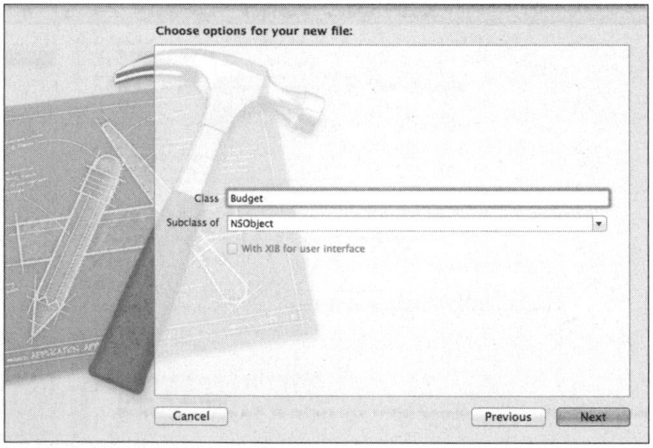

Figure 6-6:
Creating the `Budget` class.

6. **Choose a place to save the file (the default location is fine) and then click Create.**

   Xcode will then add the files to the project, as you can see in the window on the left side in Figure 6-7 (I deleted the comments at the start of the file that Xcode automatically puts in there). After you created the files, you can select or double-click them in the list to edit them. Xcode also includes some standard code, depending on the template, such as empty `@interface` and `@implementation` directives for you to fill in as well as `#import <Foundation/Foundation.h>`.

   I find it useful at this point to double-click `main.m` to open it in a new window, which is shown as the window on the right side in Figure 6-7.

   At this point, you have the files you need to separate the `Budget` interface (into `Budget.h`) and implementation (into `Budget.m`), as you can see in Figure 6-7.

7. **Select the interface code in** `main.m`**, as shown in Figure 6-7.**

8. **Make sure that** `Budget.h` **is displayed in the Editor view, as you can see in Figure 6-7, and select everything except the** `#import <Foundation/Foundation.h>`**, as shown in the figure.**

9. **Cut the interface (don't worry, you can always undo it if it doesn't work) from** `main.m` **and paste it into the** `Budget.h` **file, as shown in Figure 6-8.**

Figure 6-7:
Ready to cut and paste.

10. **Select the implementation code in** `main.m`**, as I did in Figure 6-9.**

11. **Select** `Budget.m` **in the Project navigator pane so that you can see it in the Editor view, as I did in Figure 6-9, and select everything except** `#import "Budget.h"`**, as I have in Figure 6-9.**

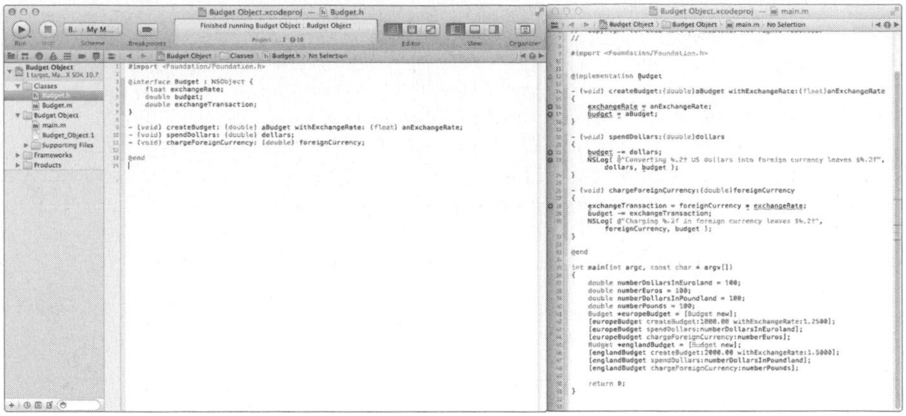

Figure 6-8:
Cut and
paste.

12. **Cut the implementation code in the** `Budget.m` **file and paste it into the** Budget.m **file.**

13. **Add a line of code to the** `main.m` **file, as shown in Figure 6-10:**

```
#import "Budget.h"
```

This imports the header file for the class, which makes the classes and methods accessible from `main`. This is standard procedure, which you'll end up doing in virtually every project you create. The compiler needs to know what is in the interface of any classes you refer to from `main` (or any of your other classes). So to keep the compiler happy, you add the `#import "Budget.h"` statement. Try commenting it out and see how the compiler responds.

Figure 6-9:
Ready to cut
and paste.

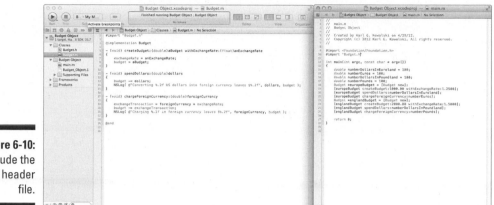

Figure 6-10:
Include the
new header
file.

14. **Click the Run button on the Project Window toolbar to build and run the application.**

    You should get a successful build, as I did in Figure 6-11.

If you look at the text editor jump bar (at the top of the Editor view), you can see a pair of triangles on the left side of the bar, pointing left and right. To the right of these you should see several items, which in Figure 6-11 are Budget Object, followed by Classes, and then Budget.m. If you click Budget.m, you will see a pop-up menu that allows you to select either Budget.m or Budget.h to display in the Editor view. You can quickly switch from the header, or interface file, to the implementation file, and vice versa. And clicking the Show the Assistant Editor button will split the Editor view to show you the header and implementation files next to each other. This enables you to look at the interface and the implementation files at the same time, or even the code for two different methods in the same or different classes. If you have any questions about what something does, just position the mouse pointer above the button and a tooltip will explain it.

You can find the completed project at the website in the Example 6B folder, which is in the Chapter 6 folder.

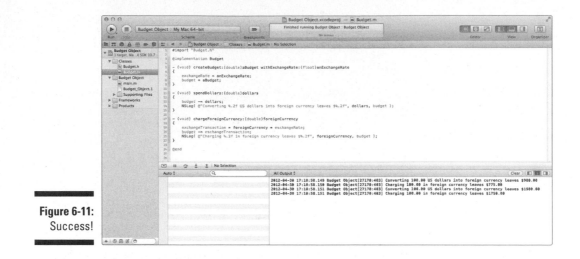

Figure 6-11:
Success!

Knowing the Naming Conventions

It is helpful to have some idea about how to name things to avoid having the compiler scream at you. Here are some areas you need to pay attention to:

✔ The names of files that contain Objective-C source code have the .m extension. Files that declare class and category (a category is used to extend a class; I explain that in Chapter 16) interfaces or that declare protocols (I explain that in Chapter 16 as well) have the .h extension typical of header files.

✔ Class, category, and protocol names generally begin with an uppercase letter; the names of methods and instance variables typically begin with a lowercase letter. The names of variables that hold instances also typically begin with lowercase letters.

✔ In Objective-C, identical names that serve different purposes are allowed:

• A class can declare methods with the same names as methods in other classes.

• A class can declare instance variables with the same names as variables in other classes.

• An instance method can have the same name as a class method.

• A method can have the same name as an instance variable.

• Method names beginning with _, a single underscore character, are reserved for use by Apple.

✔ However, class names are in the same name space as global variables and defined types. A program can't have a defined type with the same name as a class.

Using id and nil

As part of its extensions to C, Objective-C adds two built-in types that you will use.

id is a generic type that's used to refer to any kind of object regardless of class — id is defined as a pointer to an object data structure. All objects, regardless of their instance variables or methods, are of type id. You use id when I explain protocols in Chapter 16. For now, just keep this in mind.

Similarly, the keyword nil is defined as a null object, an id with a value of 0. You use it starting in Chapter 7.

id, nil, and the other basic types of Objective-C are defined in the header file objc/objc.h.

Chapter 7

Objects Objects Everywhere

. . . .

In This Chapter

▶ Turning numbers into objects

▶ Working with mutable arrays

▶ Using each object in an array in a message

▶ Getting to know C arrays

. . . .

*N*ow that you know how to create classes and send messages to your objects, I want to expand your ideas about what you can do with objects. In Chapter 6, what you did was create objects and then you sent messages from main to the objects you created. What you will soon find out is that your objects will be sending messages to other objects to assist them in carrying out their responsibilities as well. You also discover that you don't have to write all the objects you need to use in your program. The frameworks I mention in Chapter 1 supply many of them for you. So you not only create your own objects but also use the objects in Cocoa's Foundation classes that provide some of the "utility" functionality you need.

In this chapter, I introduce you to two of those objects. The first is NSNumber, one of the hundred or so classes in the Foundation Framework. All the data types I explain in Chapter 4 — signed or unsigned char, short int, int, long int, long long int, float, double, and BOOL — can be represented by using the NSNumber class.

The second will be NSMutableArray. Arrays are what you will use to manage lists of objects. Right now, you don't have that many objects to manage, but as you develop your application you'll begin to see how useful they can be. In this chapter, I show you how to take the NSNumber objects that you create and manage them by using an NSMutableArray.

Replacing Numbers with Objects

As you discover more about object-oriented programming and the Cocoa frameworks, you'll discover that virtually everything you'll work with will be an object. Many of these objects are things you would expect to be objects, such as windows and controls and so on, but some of them may surprise you.

One striking example of this is NSNumber, which enables you to represent the built-in numerical data types as objects.

Although some of the reasons framework designers think it is important to use things like NSNumber objects are based upon technical computer science issues that are beyond the scope of this book, others are eminently practical. One practical reason is that an NSMutableArray object can only hold a list of other objects, and so to store an array of integers you create an NSNumber for each one. You discover that later in this chapter when I introduce you to arrays, and in Chapter 15 when I explain about property lists and data storage.

Up until now, you have been using a variable of type double to represent a transaction — the amount in dollars you are converting into a foreign currency when you send the spendDollars: message:

```
double numberEuros = 100;
double numberPounds = 100;
```

In the spendDollars: method, you use the dollars argument, which is also a double:

```
- (void) spendDollars: (double) dollars {

budget -= dollars;
NSLog(@"Converting %.2f US dollars into foreign currency
        leaves $%.2f", dollars, budget);
}
```

To start with, I show you how you could use an NSNumber object rather than a double as an argument in the spendDollars: method. As I said, NSNumber objects enable you to create objects out of the basic number types you work with in Chapter 4 — int, long, float, double, and so on.

I do this only for the spendDollars: message and its arguments. This is actually only an intermediate step in evolving this program to one that uses the full-blown transaction objects discussed in Chapter 11.

You start by creating an NSNumber object.

In Chapter 5, you create the Budget object by sending it a new message like so:

```
Budget *europeBudget = [Budget new];
```

As I said earlier, the new message actually does two things. First, it allocates memory for your object, and then it calls the default init method, which initializes everything to 0. Although that works for your Budget object, it won't work for the NSNumber object because you want to initialize the NSNumber object with a value.

To create an NSNumber object from a value, all you have to do is create code like this:

```
NSNumber *europeDollarTransaction = @100.00;
```

The @ is a signal to the Objective-C compiler to do all the work needed to create an NSNumber object and initialize it with a double value of 100.00.

Versions of Xcode prior to version 4.4 required you to write code that involved sending messages to NSNumber objects. You may still see examples of the following in older code:

```
NSNumber *europeDollarTransaction =
                 [[NSNumber alloc] initWithDouble:100.00];
```

You can create NSNumber objects from all the primitive data types supported by Objective-C, as I show you in Chapter 4. For instance, you can create NSNumber objects as follows:

```
NSNumber* anInt = @65;
NSNumber* aChar = @'A';
NSNumber* aBOOL = @YES;
```

In addition to creating an NSNumber by using a known initial value, you can also create one from a variable whose value isn't known until your program is running. For instance, if a user provides a set of values — such as the amounts from all their purchases during their European vacation — and you want to create each one as a separate NSNumber, you could create a function to do that task as follows:

```
NSNumber* createNSNumberFromDouble( double aDouble )
{
    NSNumber* aNumber = @(aDouble);
    return (aNumber);
}
```

Although you create an NSNumber object by initializing it with a certain type, part of the power of NSNumber is that the type it is initialized with does not limit it. For example, to get the numeric value as a double (which you'll need to use in the spendDollars: method), you can send the NSNumber object the message

```
[dollars doubleValue]
```

But NSNumber can also return its value converted into almost any of the built-in types such as char, int, BOOL, or even an NSString (to refresh your memory, this is what you have been using in the NSLog statements to display something on the Debugger Console).

You could also have created an NSNumber by using something called a *factory method*:

```
NSNumber *europeDollarTransaction =
                    [NSNumber numberWithDouble:100.00];
```

This enables you to skip the new and init messages and let the class do it for you.

Revisiting the documentation

I can't possibly go through all the possibilities of every class with you, and that is why in Chapter 2 I show you how to access the documentation. Until now, you haven't used the documentation all that much because what you were doing didn't involve the Cocoa classes that you find in the documentation. But all that has changed, and now is a good time to review how to access the documentation for the various classes that you will use.

In Figure 7-1, I typed **NSNumber** into the Search field of the Organizer - Documentation window.

This brings up the NSNumber Class Reference in the Organizer - Documentation window. I clicked the rightmost button on the Documentation navigator bar to display a number of methods to create NSNumbers from quite a few types of inputs. You can see the hierarchical menu leading to the NSNumber method names in Figure 7-2.

For example:

```
initWithChar: (char) value;
initWithInt: (int) value;
initWithFloat: (float) value;
initWithBool: (BOOL) value;
```

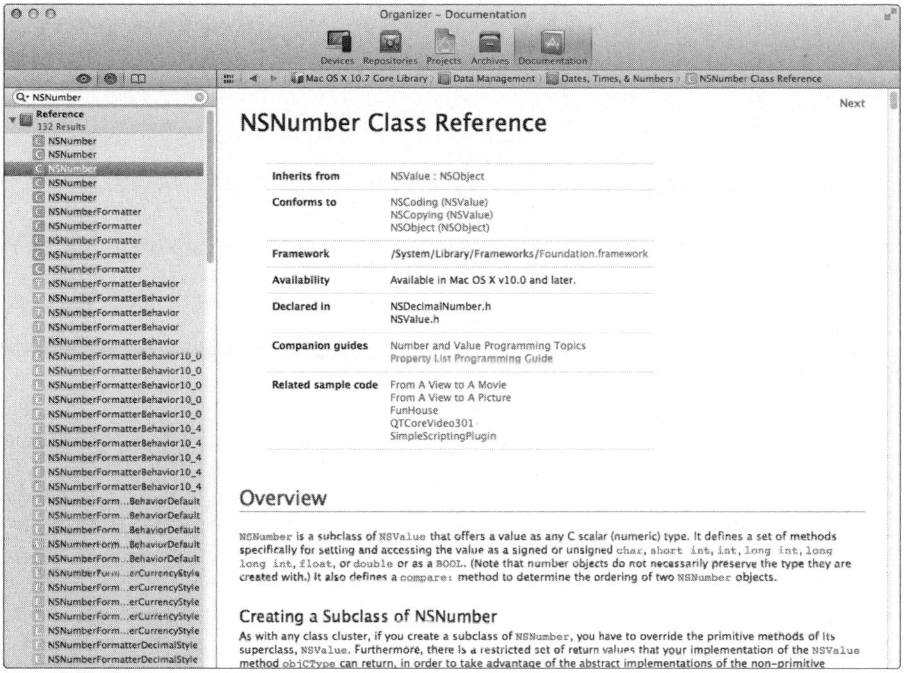

Figure 7-1:
Accessing
documenta-
tion.

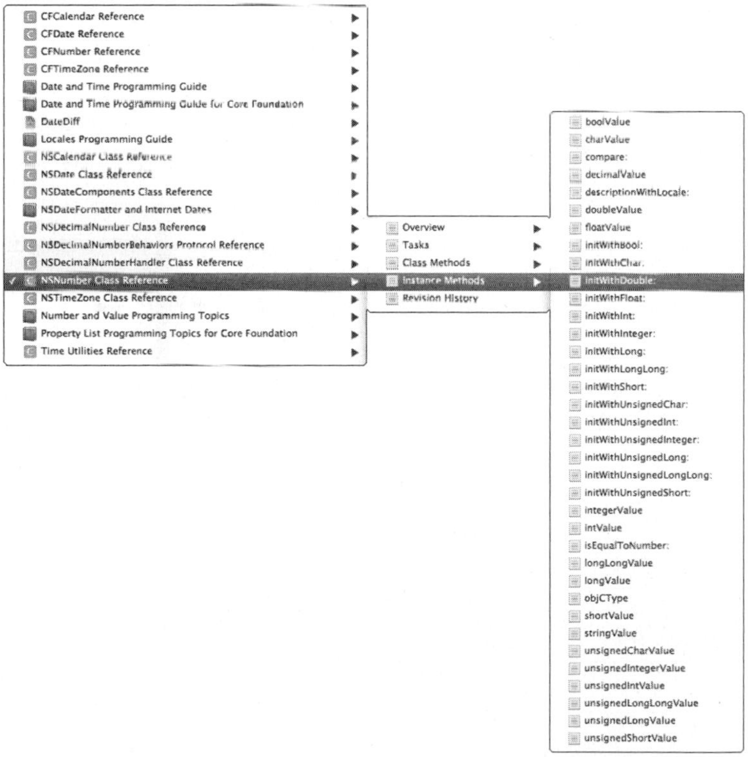

Figure 7-2:
NSNumber
methods.

TIP

As you become more comfortable with coding in Objective-C and using the framework objects, you'll find yourself exploring the APIs just to see what else a class can do.

Using an NSNumber as an argument

Although I'm not going to have you do any coding, I go through how you could use an NSNumber object rather than a double as an argument in the spendDollars: method, because it does illustrate some important things about using an NSNumber object. To replace the double with an NSNumber, you do the following:

1. **Modify the** spendDollars: **method in the** Budget **class to take an** NSNumber **object as an argument rather than a** double **as it does currently.**

2. **Modify** main **to create** NSNumber **objects and send the new and improved** spendDollars: **message (the one that has an** NSNumber **as the argument) to the** Budget **objects.**

Modifying Budget

To modify the Budget class, you need to do a couple of things.

First, you must replace the method declaration in the header with a new one that takes an NSNumber as an argument:

```
//- void) spendDollars: (double) dollars;
//- (void) spendDollars: (double) dollars;
- (void) spendDollars: (NSNumber*) dollars;
```

Of course, you also have to change the method implementation:

```
//(void) spendDollars: (double) dollars {

//  budget -= dollars;
//  NSLog(@"Converting %.2f US dollars into foreign
     currency leaves $%.2f", dollars, budget );
//}

- (void) spendDollars: (NSNumber*) dollars {

  budget -= [dollars doubleValue];
  NSLog(@"Converting %.2f US dollars into foreign
                  currency leaves $%.2f",
                  [dollars doubleValue], budget);
}
```

You deleted the previous implementation of spendDollars: and replaced it with one that has an NSNumber as an argument. But now, instead of simply subtracting the dollars amount from budget as you did previously

```
budget -= dollars;
```

you send the doubleValue message to the NSNumber object to get its value as a double:

```
budget -= [dollars doubleValue];
```

You also changed the NSLog statement in the same way, sending the message, doubleValue, to the NSNumber object to get the value as a double returned:

```
NSLog(@"Converting %.2f US dollars into foreign
   currency leaves $%.2f",[dollars doubleValue], budget);
```

As you work through the example, think about why you are deleting some code and what the code you are adding does.

Modifying main

To implement the new spendDollars: method, you need to make some changes to main. You start by deleting the variable numberDollarsInEuroland you were using to represent the dollar transactions. You replace it with an NSNumber object, which you created by using alloc and init and initialized with the same amounts that you used to initialize the variables you just deleted:

```
//double numberDollarsInEuroland = 100;
NSNumber *europeDollarTransaction = @100.00;
```

You then delete the old spendDollars: message and replace it with the new one that uses the NSNumber argument:

```
//[europeBudget spendDollars:numberDollarsInEuroland];
[europeBudget spendDollars:europeDollarTransaction];
```

Taking Advantage of Array Objects

Although using a number as an object is an interesting exercise in using objects (that is, replacing a double with an NSNumber), it doesn't really buy you anything. But it turns out that a similar use exists for an NSNumber object that can help you as you develop your program.

As you examine the program you have developed so far, you'll realize that as you add more and more transactions, the code is going to get a bit unwieldy.

Currently, for every transaction I create, I have to code a `spendDollars:` statement. For example, for every transaction where I spend dollars in Europe I need

```
[europeBudget spendDollars:numberDollarsInEuroland];
```

For example, if I want to process 50 transactions, I end up with

```
[europeBudget spendDollars:numberDollarsInEuroland1];
...
[europeBudget spendDollars:numberDollarsInEuroland50];
```

This is not a pretty picture.

Of course, this is not a problem unique to this application. In most applications, you'll find you need a way to be able to deal with large numbers of objects.

Often you may not even know how many transactions you are going to have. For example, you may be getting the transactions from a database or from a list of previously stored instructions, or user actions may determine how many transactions you will have — the user adds address book entries, for example, or enters transactions as they occur (bingo!).

But even if you did know how many transactions you were going to have, a long series of messages simply makes your program too confusing, prone to error, and hard to extend.

Because this is a common problem, you have a widely available solution — container classes.

Container classes

In object-oriented programming, a container class is a class that is capable of storing other objects. In Cocoa, several kinds are available, and I explain the two most widely used. One is a *dictionary,* which I cover in Chapter 15, and the other is an *array,* which you use in this chapter. You also continue to use this array in Chapter 9 and beyond, and in no time (or at least by the end of this book), using arrays will become second nature to you.

Two kinds of arrays are available to you in Cocoa. The first is an `NSMutableArray`, which enables you to add objects to the array as needed — that is, the amount of memory allocated to the class is dynamically adjusted as you add more objects. An NSMutableArray also enables you to remove or rearrange objects it contains.

Of course, you aren't really storing the object in an array any more than you stored an NSNumber object in the europeDollarTransaction variable when you created it:

```
NSNumber *europeDollarTransaction = @100.00;
```

In both cases, you are storing a pointer to the object.

The second kind of array is an NSArray, which enables you to store a fixed number of objects that are specified when you initialize the array. Because in this case you need the dynamic aspect of an NSMutableArray, I start my explanation there. I explain NSArrays later in this chapter, and you actually use an NSArray in Chapter 15.

NSMutableArray arrays (I just call them arrays from now on when what I have to say applies to both NSArray and NSMutableArray) are ordered collections that can contain any sort of object. The collection does not have to be made up of the same objects. So, you could have a number of Budget objects, for example, or Xyz objects mixed in, but they must be objects. One of the reasons for introducing you to NSNumbers, besides showing you how an object can use other objects, is that when you convert your transactions into NSNumbers, you make it possible to store them in an array.

As I've said, arrays can hold only objects. But sometimes you may, for example, want to put a placeholder in a mutable array and later replace it with the "real" object. You can use an NSNull object for this placeholder role.

The first step in being able to eliminate all those spendDollars: messages is to create an NSMutableArray of the NSNumber objects I use in the spendDollars: message:

```
NSMutableArray *europeTransactions =
                [[NSMutableArray alloc] initWithCapacity:1];
```

This allocates and initializes the mutable array. When you create a mutable array, you have to estimate the maximum size, which helps optimization. This is just a formality, and whatever you put here does not limit the eventual size. I use 1 to illustrate that; even though I specify 1, I can actually add two elements (or more) to the array.

To make things simpler, for the time being, I just create an array for the spendDollars: transactions in Europe. You see why in Chapter 9.

After I create a mutable array, I can start to add objects to it:

```
[europeTransactions addObject:europeDollarTransaction];
```

Technically (computer science–wise) what makes a collection an array is that you access its elements by using an index, and that index can be determined at runtime. You get an individual element from an array by sending the array the `objectAtIndex:` message, which returns the array element you requested. For example

```
[europeBudget spendDollars: [europeTransactions
    objectAtIndex:0]];
```

returns the first element in the `europeTransactions` array (remember the first element is 0) as an `NSNumber` and passes it to the `spendDollars:` method.

In your program, the index you will use is the relative position in the array, which starts at 0.

Depending on what you are doing with the array or how you are using it (arrays are very useful), `objectAtIndex:` is one of the main array methods that you use (although you won't be using it in this chapter — you see why shortly).

The other method you will use is `count`, which gives you the number of elements in the array.

Arrays have some other methods you might find useful, such as sorting the array, comparing two arrays, and creating a new array that contains the objects in an existing array. In addition, mutable arrays have methods that include inserting an object at a particular index, replacing an object, and removing an object.

But one of the most powerful things you can do with an array is to use each of the elements in an array as an argument in a message — which means that you won't have to code a `spendDollars:` message for each transaction. You can even send messages to all objects in the array, which will knock your socks off when you discover what you can do with that in Chapter 10.

Tiptoeing through an array

Objective-C 2.0 provides a language feature that enables you to enumerate over the contents of a collection. This is called *fast enumeration,* and it became available in Mac OS X 10.5 (Leopard) with version 2.0 of

Objective-C. As I mention, this book is based on Mac OS X 10.7 — and iOS 5.0 on the iPhone. (If you need to program for OS X 10.4, you need to use an NSEnumerator, which I leave as an exercise for you.) Fast Enumeration uses the for in feature (a variation on a for loop, which I explain in Chapter 9).

What enumeration effectively does is sequentially march though an array, starting at the first element and returning each element for you to do "something with." The "something with" you will want to do in this case is use that element as an argument in the spendDollars: message.

For example, this code marches through the array and sends the spendDollars: message by using each element in the array (an NSNumber "transaction"), eliminating the need for a separate line of code for each spendDollars: message statement sent for each transaction:

```
for (NSNumber *aTransaction in europeTransactions) {
   [europeBudget spendDollars: aTransaction];
}
```

Here's the way this works:

1. Take each entry (for) in the array (in europeTransactions) and copy it into the variable that you've declared (NSNumber * aTransaction).

2. Use it as an argument in the spendDollars: message ([europeBudget spendDollars: aTransaction]).

3. Continue until you run out of entries in the array.

The identifier aTransaction can be any name you choose. NSNumber is the type of the object in the array (or it can be id, although I won't get into that here).

You may also have noticed that [europeBudget spendDollars: aTransaction] is enclosed in braces. The braces signify a code block. (Code blocks are described in Chapter 4.)

To be more formal (I just put on a tie to write this), the construct you just used is called for in, and it looks like

```
for ( Type aVariable in expression ) { statements }
```

or

```
Type aVariable;
for ( aVariable in expression ) { statements }
```

where you fill in what is italicized. There is one catch, however — you are not permitted to change any of the elements during the iteration, which means that you can go through the array more than once without worry.

The `for in` loop is just one example of a control statement, the rest of which I explain in Chapter 9.

Adding mutable arrays

If you have been following along with me, I extend what you did in Chapter 6. If you want to start with a clean copy of the project from where you left off, you can use the project found in the Chapter 7 Start Here folder, which is in the Chapter 7 folder.

You can add an `NSMutableArray` to your program by following these steps:

1. **In the Files list (on the left side of the project window), click the tri-angles next to the Classes and Budget Object folders to expand them, as shown in Figure 7-3.**

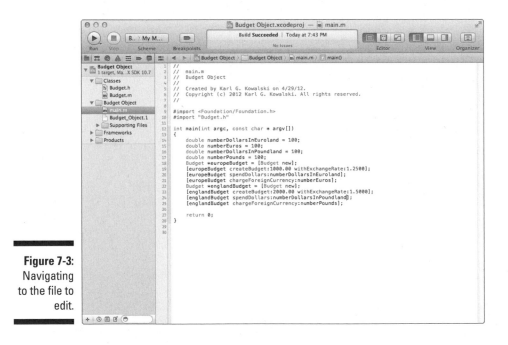

Figure 7-3:
Navigating to the file to edit.

2. **In the Budget Object folder, click** `main.m`, **shown in Figure 7-3, and you see that file ready for editing.**

   In this example, you work only in `main` in the `main.m` file.

   This is the way you navigate to the file you want to edit.

3. **Delete the bold, italic underlined code and then add the code in bold, as shown in Listing 7-1.**

Listing 7-1:   main in main.m

```
#import <Foundation/Foundation.h>
#import "Budget.h"

int main (int argc, const char * argv[]) {

//double numberDollarsInEuroland = 100;
  double numberEuros = 100;
  double numberDollarsInPoundland = 100;
  double numberPounds = 100;

  NSNumber *europeDollarTransaction = @100.00;
  NSNumber *europeDollarTransaction2 = @200.00;

  NSMutableArray *europeTransactions = [
               [NSMutableArray alloc] initWithCapacity:1];
  [europeTransactions addObject:europeDollarTransaction];
  [europeTransactions addObject:europeDollarTransaction2];

  Budget *europeBudget = [Budget new];
  [europeBudget createBudget:1000.00
          withExchangeRate:1.2500];
  //[europeBudget spendDollars:numberDollarsInEuroland];
  for (NSNumber *aTransaction in europeTransactions)  {
    [europeBudget spendDollars: aTransaction];
  }
  [europeBudget chargeForeignCurrency:numberEuros];

  Budget *englandBudget = [Budget new];
  [englandBudget createBudget:2000.00
          withExchangeRate:1.5000];
  [englandBudget spendDollars:numberDollarsInPoundland];
  [englandBudget chargeForeignCurrency:numberPounds];

  return 0;
}
```

4. Click the Run button on the Project Window toolbar to build and run the application.

Your output in the Debugger Console should look like this:

```
Converting 100.00 US dollars into foreign currency
        leaves $900.00
Converting 200.00 US dollars into foreign currency
        leaves $700.00
Charging 100.00 in foreign currency leaves $575.00
Converting 100.00 US dollars into foreign currency
        leaves $1900.00
Charging 100.00 in foreign currency leaves $1750.00
```

Let me explain what you did here. First, you added

```
NSMutableArray *europeTransactions = [[NSMutableArray
                        alloc] initWithCapacity:1];
```

This allocates and initializes the mutable array for you. As I said, when you create a mutable array, you have to estimate the maximum size, which helps optimization. This is just a formality, and whatever you put here does not limit the eventual size.

To make it (a little) more interesting, you created two NSNumber objects

```
NSNumber *europeDollarTransaction = @100.00;
NSNumber *europeDollarTransaction2 = @200.00;
```

and added both to the array

```
[europeTransactions addObject:europeDollarTransaction];
[europeTransactions addObject:europeDollarTransaction2];
```

The next thing you should notice is that you deleted

```
[europeBudget spendDollars:numberDollarsInEuroland];
```

Instead, you're going to go through the array and send a spendDollars: message for each object:

```
for (NSNumber *aTransaction in europeTransactions)  {
   [europeBudget spendDollars: aTransaction];
}
```

As I explain, this takes each entry (for) in the array (in europeTransactions) and copies it into the variable that you have declared (NSNumber * aTransaction). You then get the value as an NSNumber (aTransaction) and use it as an argument in the spendDollars: message until you run out of entries in the array. (aTransaction can be any name you choose.) NSNumber is the type of the object in the array (or it can be id).

You can find the completed project at the website in the Example 7 folder, which is in the Chapter 7 folder.

What you have accomplished here is that no matter how many cash transactions you create for Europe, you only need one spendDollars: message. Although that's pretty good, you ain't seen nothing yet. In Chapter 10, I show you how to extend that so that you need only one spend message for every transaction (both cash and charge and any other transaction you can come up with) statement for all the countries you visit.

As you may have noticed, I'm not quite out of the woods yet. I still have to declare a variable for each NSNumber object I'm adding to the array. Although this will disappear when you add the user interface in Chapters 17 and 18, it still is annoying. I show you how to eliminate all those variable declarations in Chapter 9.

Working with fixed arrays

Actually, NSMutableArray is a subclass (I explain that in Chapter 10) of NSArray, which manages a static array — after you have created it, you cannot add objects to it or remove objects from it. For example, if you create an array with a single NSNumber to represent a transaction, later you can't add to it another NSNumber object that represents another transaction. Although only allowing a single transaction may be good for your budget, it's not very flexible.

NSArrays give you less overhead at a cost of less flexibility. So if you don't need to be able to add and remove objects, NSArrays are the preferred choice. I show you when that makes sense, and how to use an NSArray, in Chapter 15. If you want to use an NSArray (and I suggest you experiment on your own), you have to initialize it with the objects that you want in it when you create it.

So rather than

```
NSMutableArray *europeTransactions =
          [[NSMutableArray alloc] initWithCapacity:1];
  [europeTransactions addObject:europeDollarTransaction];
```

you do the following:

```
NSArray *europeTransactions =
        [[NSArray alloc] initWithObjects:
        europeDollarTransaction, nil];
```

Even though I added only one object to the fixed array, `initWithObjects:` allows you to initialize the array with as many objects as you want, separating them with commas and terminating the list with `nil` as you can see.

Alternatively, you can create and initialize an `NSArray` as follows:

```
NSArray *europeTransactions = @[
        europeDollarTransaction ];
```

You can use the `for in` loop to access each element in an `NSArray`. In addition to this, you can also use the following code to access a specific element:

```
NSNumber* aTransaction = europeTransactions[0];
```

Using C Arrays

Arrays are also a part of the C language. Although most of the time you'll use array objects, you'll also find uses for C arrays, not to mention seeing them used in Apple documentation and code samples.

Arrays in C store elements just as an `NSArray` does (although they must be of the same type), and you can think about them as an ordered list as well.

That means, for example, that you can store five values of type `int` in an array without having to declare five different variables, each one with a different identifier.

To declare an array, use

```
double europeTransactionsArray [2];
```

Now you have an array with enough room for two `doubles`, effectively similar to the `NSMutableArray` you created earlier; but this one is of fixed size, just like an `NSArray`. It is really just like having a set of the same variable types, one right after another.

To access a specific element of the array, use

```
europeTransactionsArray[0] = 100.00;
```

This places 100.00 in the first element in an array (again, element 1 is at index 0).

You can also initialize arrays when you create them. For example

```
double europeTransactionsArray [2] = {100.00, 200.00};
```

creates a two-element array of `doubles`. You can access an element in the arrays as though it is a normal variable by doing the following:

```
transaction1 = europeTransactionsArray[0];
```

Expanding to multidimensional arrays

One useful aspect of arrays is multidimensional arrays. For example

```
int twoDArray[3][3] = {{1,2,3}, {4,5,6}, {7,8,9}};
```

declares and initializes an array that has two dimensions, like a tic-tac-toe board. You can make three-dimensional arrays, and even more.

Although no multidimensional array objects exist, in Objective C you could have an array of arrays that accomplish the same thing. Arrays of arrays are used extensively in Mac OS X and iOS programming, and you can find them used in some of the samples on their respective Dev Center sites.

The following code shows a two-dimensional array in C, and the way to simulate that two-dimensional array in Objective-C. No applause — I leave you to figure this out on your own:

```
int main() {

  int twoDArray[3][3] = {{1,2,3}, {4,5,6}, {7,8,9}};
  NSLog (@"twoDArray[2][2] is %i", twoDArray[2][2]);

  NSArray *array1 = @[ @1, @2, @3 ];
  NSArray *array2 = @[ @4, @5, @6 ];
  NSArray *array3 = @[ @7, @8, @9 ];

  NSArray *arrayOfArrays = @[ array1, array2, array3 ];
  NSLog (@"NSArray of NSArrays equivalent is
          %i", [[[arrayOfArrays objectAtIndex:2]
          objectAtIndex:2] intValue]);
}
```

The result is

```
twoDArray[2][2] is 9
NSArray of NSArrays equivalent is 9
```

Finishing up with the main function

Arrays can be passed as a parameter in C. To accept arrays as parameters, the only thing that you have to do when declaring the function is to specify that its argument is an array by using its identifier and a pair of void brackets [ ]. For example, the function

```
void someFunction (int arg[])
```

accepts a parameter that is an array of `int`s.

Now that you understand arrays, I can finally explain the argument list in the `main` function:

```
int main (int argc, const char * argv[]) {
```

The name of the variable `argc` stands for *argument count* and contains the number of arguments passed to the program. The name of the variable `argv` stands for *argument vector* and is a one-dimensional array of strings; that's what a `char*` is in C (but because you won't be using them, I won't be going any farther into C strings in this book).

This finally (and thankfully) closes the chapter on `main`.

Chapter 8

Using the Debugger

*N*ow that things have gotten a little more interesting, so will the errors.

Let's face it. You are always going to have errors. No matter how good you are, how much experience you have, how careful you are, or even how smart you are, they are a programming fact of life.

You'll come up against three kinds of errors. Each one has a unique personality and associated techniques for finding and correcting. Here is a list of the three types you'll find:

✓ Syntax errors

✓ Runtime errors

✓ Logic errors

The last two types, runtime and logic errors, are what are commonly referred to as "bugs."

Identifying the Usual Suspects

Although no exercise is in this chapter, you can follow along with me if you like by using the project in the Chapter 8 Start Here folder in the Chapter 8 folder at the website. Or, you can use the project that you used at the end of Chapter 7.

Catching syntax errors

As I mention earlier in this book, compilers take your source code and turn it into something that the computer understands. For that process to go smoothly, the source code you give the compiler has to be something it understands. All the operations and framework functionality I cover in Chapter 4 and continue to cover have to be coded in a certain way, and the compiler expects that you follow those rules (syntax). When you don't, it gets visibly annoyed. So when you type `New` rather than `new`, or the subtler `[Budget new}` rather than `[Budget new]`, the compiler suddenly has no idea what you're talking about and generates a syntax error. In Figure 8-1, you can see what happens when I accidentally delete the opening `{` after `int main(int argc, const char* argv[])` at line 13 — if you try this yourself, it may take a second or two to update the display.

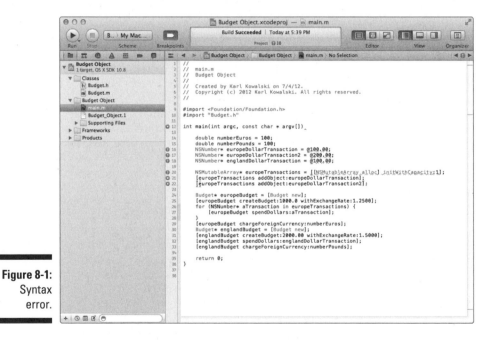

Figure 8-1:
Syntax
error.

It's generally better to ignore the subsequent errors after the first syntax error because they may be (and frequently are) a consequence of that first error. You can see that in Figure 8-1. In this case, because of the first error, the compiler is not expecting code execution statements such as `[NSNumber alloc]`, and you get the subsequent syntax errors as a result.

If you click the Show the Issue navigator on the navigator selector bar, you'll see the results of your compile in the navigator area in Figure 8-2 (select Product⇨Build to tell Xcode to try to build the error-prone project). If you click an error in the Issue navigator pane, the error message bubble animates so that you can find it in the Editor pane. In addition, double-clicking the error message in the top pane opens a new window and animates the error message in that window as well.

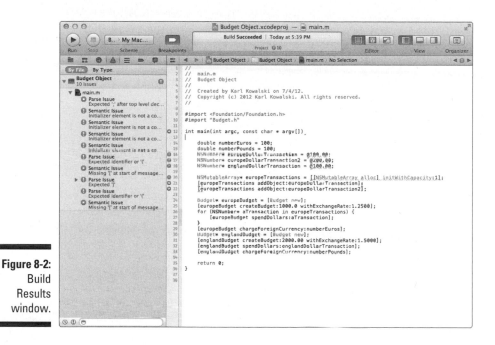

Figure 8-2:
Build
Results
window.

You may have noticed that my Editor area is now displaying line numbers. I did that by choosing Xcode⇨Preferences (as you do in Chapter 2), selecting Text Editing on the toolbar, and then selecting the Show Line Numbers check box.

Fortunately, syntax errors are the most obvious of errors out there — when you have one, your program won't compile, much less run, until the error is fixed. Many of the syntax errors are a result of typographical errors like those I just mentioned. Others occur when you try to pass the wrong argument type to a message or function. You can see an example in Figure 8-3 when I try to pass in a string rather than a double to the `createBudget:withExchangeRate:` method at line 31.

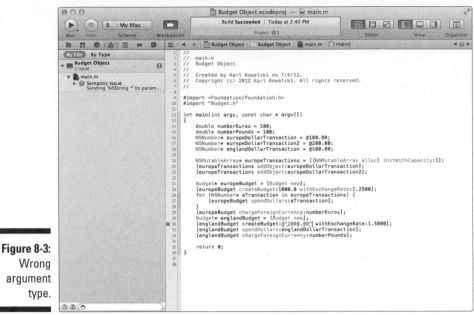

Figure 8-3:
Wrong
argument
type.

Fixing it with Live Issues and Fix-It

Xcode comes with built-in features to help you find and fix errors like these in your code. *Live Issues* is part of the Apple LLVM compiler, and it continuously evaluates your code in the background and alerts you to coding mistakes. Before this feature came along, you had to build your app first, and trust me, this new way saves lots of time and effort.

But not only is Live Issues happy to point out your mistakes, *Fix-it* will also offer (when it can) to fix the problem for you. Clicking the error displays the available Fix-its, such as correcting an assignment to a comparison, repairing a misspelled symbol, or appending a missing semicolon. With a single keyboard shortcut, you can instantly have the error repaired and you can continue coding. Fix-it marks syntax errors with a red underline or a caret at the position of the error and with a symbol in the gutter — the space to the left of the line numbers.

For example, in Figure 8-4, the semicolon is missing after the `NSNumber *englandDollarTransaction = @100.00` statement. (Notice the error indicator — the red circle with exclamation point — in the Activity viewer, your Go To place for showing status messages, build progress, and errors). Pressing Return will automatically fix this problem. This is a very useful feature and will cut down your debugging time significantly (especially if you actually use it).

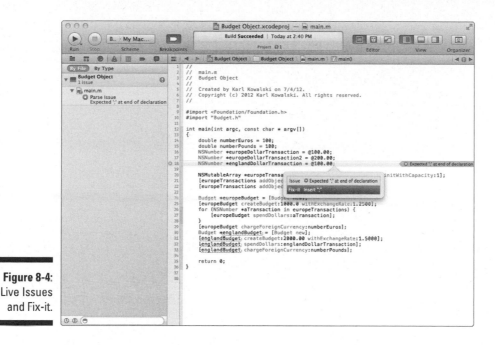

Figure 8-4:
Live Issues
and Fix-it.

Crashing with runtime errors

Runtime errors cause your program to stop executing — this is commonly known as a "crash." You are probably familiar with that happening to programs you are using, and it's quite annoying. But it's a little different when it happens to a program you have written. You can see the result of that at line 36 in Figure 8-5 for a Foundation Command Line Tool, although when you are running on a Mac as an application or on an iPhone simulator, or an iOS device itself, you get other kinds of messages. Don't worry; while a message may not tell you why, the fact that it is a runtime error is usually obvious.

Runtime errors can be created in all sorts of ways. However, you can rule out one way; at least it wasn't a syntax error (although it could be a warning that you ignored). You might have had data that you hadn't expected (a division-by-zero error, for example), or you had a problem with an argument you used in a message. Sometimes you even get some build warnings for these errors; sometimes you're blindsided by a crash. At other times, instead of crashing, the program may "hang" and become incommunicado.

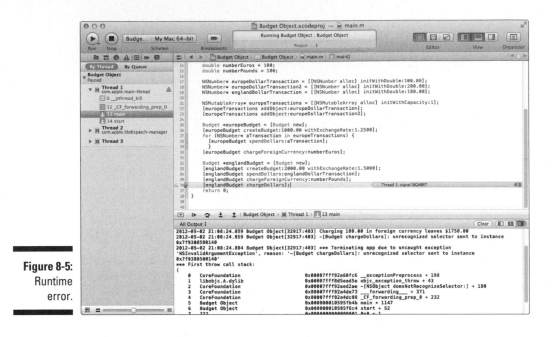

Figure 8-5:
Runtime
error.

Dealing with logic errors

When a program doesn't do what it is supposed to, people tend to blame the problem on the computer. "The computer gave me the wrong answer." Well, computers are actually blameless creatures; they do what they are told to do, and they do that with a vengeance. If you were to tell a computer to go jump off a cliff, it would. It does exactly, and I mean exactly, what you tell it to do — over and over and over again. When you have a logic error, the problem is not that the computer didn't do what you told it to; the problem is that it did. You just told it to do the wrong thing. Another possibility is that you may have forgotten to tell it to do something, like initialize an object for example. In Figure 8-6, everything looks fine — not a compiler error in sight (ignore the highlighted line for a second).

The problem is that the output looks a little screwy:

```
Converting 100.00 US dollars into foreign currency
        leaves $1100.00
Converting 200.00 US dollars into foreign currency
        leaves $1300.00
Charging 100.00 in foreign currency leaves $1175.00
Converting 100.00 US dollars into foreign currency
        leaves $2100.00
Charging 100.00 in foreign currency leaves $1950.00
```

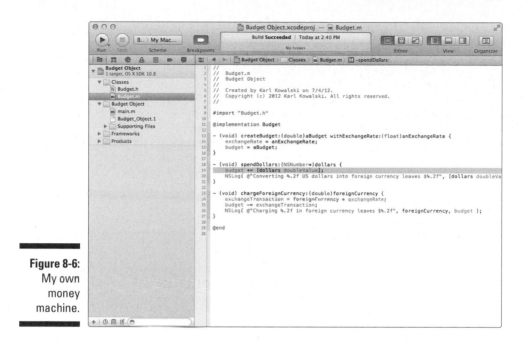

Figure 8-6:
My own
money
machine.

Think about this. I start with my $1,000 budget for Europe, and when I convert $100 (U.S. dollars) into foreign currency, I am left with $1,100. While this is a nice trick if you can do it, I doubt that is what really happened. (Somehow I don't think I have invented a perpetual balance-increasing machine.)

Looking at the code that computes the balance (highlighted in Figure 8-5 and in bold here),

```
- (void) spendDollars: (NSNumber*) dollars {
  budget += [dollars doubleValue];
  NSLog(@"Converting %.2f US dollars into foreign currency
        leaves $%.2f",[dollars doubleValue], budget);
}
```

you can see that instead of subtracting the transaction amount from the balance (-=), I added it (+=). Wishful thinking I suppose, but regardless of the cause, what I have here is a logic error.

Another type of error also more or less falls into the logic error category — "typos." This is when you send the wrong message to an object, or use the wrong instance variable, because the names are very similar and you simply mistype the message name or variable.

Because of the similarity of names, the error can be pretty hard to spot because the code, at first glance, seems "right."

All three of these errors — syntax, runtime, and logic — are the bane of a programmer's existence. But get used to it. Like death and taxes, they are something you can never escape. But what you can do is figure out how to deal with and dispatch them as quickly and efficiently as possible. To do that, you'll call upon one of the Xcode tools that comes with the SDK — the Debugger. Although the Debugger is no help with syntax errors, it is a veritable star when it comes to runtime errors and your trusty assistant when you need to hunt down logic errors.

Using the Debugger

In Figure 8-7, I deliberately created a situation that gives me a runtime error. (Intentionally creating a runtime error may seem a bit bizarre, but this is for teaching purposes.)

As you can see from the highlighted code — lines 26 and 27 — I am going to divide by 0. If I had done something like i/0, I would have gotten a compiler warning (which I could choose to ignore for teaching purposes). In this case, I fooled the compiler (it's generally not a good idea to try to fool the compiler; it really has your best interests at heart). So the compiler thinks everything is fine, but at runtime, the processor is chugging along, executing its instructions, only to result in the unexpected program halt you see in Figure 8-8.

In Figure 8-8 the Debug Console shows a warning with some text that looks like this: __NSCFNumber autoreleased with no pool in place. Don't panic — this is a result of using the NSNumber initializer I introduced in Chapter 7, combined with the use of Automatic Reference Counting and the removal of some code in main in Chapter 4, which involved the Objective-C directive @autoreleasepool. This warning has to do with memory management, something I explain in Chapter 13.

How can the Debugger help me determine the source of a runtime error like this one? The next section gives you the details.

You can see that in Xcode's Editor view in Figure 8-8, the offending instruction is highlighted and you see an arrow (you see it as green in Xcode) pointing to line 27 in the Editor view, and the error EXC_ARITHMETIC, listed on the right side. The Editor view has also changed, and the Xcode Debugger controllers are available to you in the Editor view. My Editor window automatically shows the Debug navigator, the Variables view, the Console view, and the Debug controllers bar whenever a program pauses, as I show you in Chapter 2. A crashing app is definitely a pause, so Xcode displays these views when it occurs.

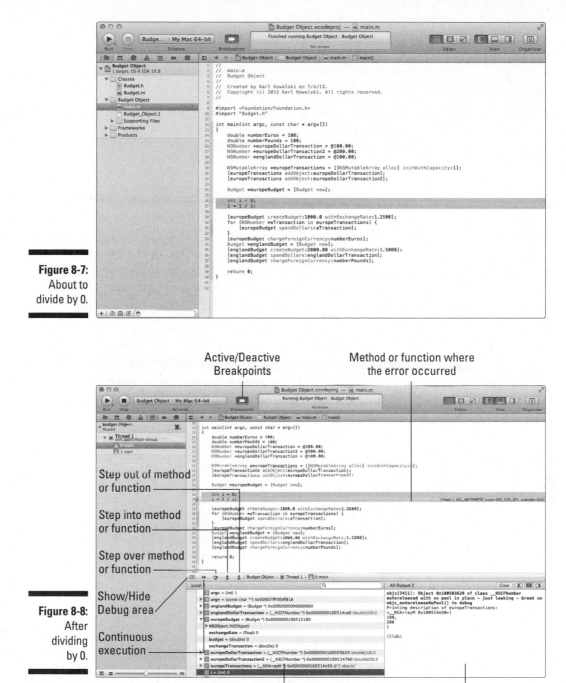

Figure 8-7:
About to
divide by 0.

Figure 8-8:
After
dividing
by 0.

Active/Deactive
Breakpoints

Method or function where
the error occurred

Step out of method
or function

Step into method
or function

Step over method
or function

Show/Hide
Debug area

Continuous
execution

Variables pane

Debug console

I explain most of these controls in the section "Using Breakpoints," later in this chapter.

If you have any questions about what something does, just position the mouse pointer above the icon and a tooltip explains it.

In the Debug navigator pane of Figure 8-8, you can see the *stack* — a trace of the objects and methods that got you to where you are now.

In this case, you are in `main`, which is where you started.

Stacks *can* be very useful in complex applications. They can help you understand the path you took to get where you are. If you are tracking down a logic error, for example, seeing the path of messages from one object to another can be really helpful, especially if you didn't expect the program to execute in that order.

Looking again at the Workspace window in Figure 8-8, you can see that the Editor view shows the source code and also highlights the instruction that caused the problem. In the left pane of the Debug area, you can see the program's variables. (I show you how that can be useful in the section "Using Breakpoints," later in this chapter.)

Examine the left pane of the Debug area. There you see a list of the program's variables. I selected Local from the drop-down menu in the upper left of the pane and clicked the disclosure triangles next to `europeTransactions` and `europeBudget`. These are what are known as *local* variables. These are the variables declared in methods and functions (such as `main`). In the next section, I also show you some instance variables.

As you debug a program error, the Variables pane is useful in a number of ways:

✔ **Checking values:** Because, in this case, I have a runtime error and the Debugger has pointed out the offending instruction, and because the offending instruction involves dividing by the variable i, it doesn't take a rocket scientist to figure out that perhaps you need to look at the value of that variable. In this case, you can see in the Variable list that the value is 0. At this point, I have at least tracked down the *immediate cause* of the problem — division by 0.

I say *immediate cause* because in some cases, although not here, I might wonder how it got set to 0. (I show you how to watch the value of a variable in the next section, where I explain how to set a breakpoint. But for now, just know that using a breakpoint can stop the execution of your program at any point, and you can look back and see how you got to that point.)

✔ **Checking objects:** Certain logic errors you may encounter are the result of what some people call a "feature" and others call a "design error" in Objective-C. Objective-C allows you to send a message to a nil object _without_ generating a runtime error.

As you can see in Figure 8-8, you have variables that contain pointers to objects. I clicked the disclosure triangle next to europeBudget. You can see the contents of europeBudget — the values of exchangeRate, budget, and exchangeTransaction — initialized and ready to go. The running code created this before my runtime error was executed, and messages to it were working fine. In addition, you can also see the value for englandBudget is 0x0.

If I were to send a message to englandBudget, it would go into the aether. So, when things don't happen the way I expect, one of the things I'm going to check is whether any of the object references I am using has 0x0 as its value. When you see 0x0 as the value of an object reference, you should assume that the object has not been allocated yet.

This can actually happen easily. You can forget to assign the object you created to a variable, or, as you see in Chapter 17, you can forget to make a connection in Interface Builder.

europeTransactions, which is my transaction array, shows that it contains two entries. Because there were two addObject: messages sent to europeTransactions before the Debugger halted the program, you can safely conclude that these two elements correspond to the values for the europeDollarTransaction and europeDollar-Transaction2 objects I created. If you want to get a closer look at the contents, right-click europeTransactions in the Variables pane and select Print Description of "europeTransactions" from the pop-up menu. You should see text in the Console pane that looks something like the following:

```
Printing description of europeTransactions:
<__NSArrayM 0x10a614cc0>(
100,
200
)
```

But what about logic errors? In fact, the Debugger can help there as well.

One of the ways to figure out why something happened is to be able to see what is going on in your program before you wander down a particular path to oblivion (which can help you figure out runtime errors as well). For that, the Debugger provides you with the ability to set breakpoints, which is the subject of the next section.

Using Breakpoints

A *breakpoint* is an instruction to the Debugger to pause execution at that instruction and wait for further instructions (no pun intended). If you have a logic error, a breakpoint can help by allowing you to step your way through your code (refer to the earlier section, "Dealing with logic errors"). By setting breakpoints at various places in your program, you can step through its execution, at the instruction level, to see exactly what it is doing. You can also examine the variables that the program is setting and using, which allows you to determine whether that is where the problem lies.

Returning to the logic error introduced in Figure 8-6, I'm going to set a breakpoint at the entry of the method I think is causing the problem — spend Dollars: — to see whether I can figure out what is going on. In Figure 8-9, I set a breakpoint simply by clicking in the far-left column of the Editor area — this column contains the line numbers, and is also called the *gutter*.

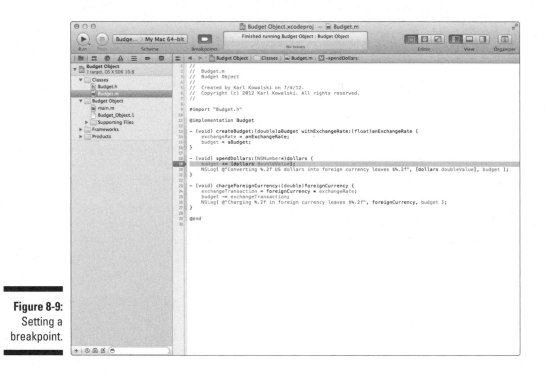

Figure 8-9:
Setting a
breakpoint.

In Figure 8-9, you can see that the Breakpoint button to the left of the Activity view has inverted. This lets you know that you have at least one breakpoint set. If you click that button, it temporarily turns off all breakpoints (if you think you fixed something and want to see how your program runs without all those pesky breakpoints).

When I build and run the program again (as you can see in the Editor window in Figure 8-10), the program has stopped executing right at the breakpoint I set.

You can see the source code around the breakpoint where the Debugger has halted in the Editor area. You can also see in the stack pane on the left that you went from main to [Budget spendDollars:]. In the Variables pane, you can see that I clicked the disclosure triangle next to the self variable. Under self are the object's instance variables. (I want to remind you, as I explain in Chapter 6, that self is the "hidden" argument in every message and is a pointer to the object's instance variables.) You can see that the exchangeRate is 1.25, as it should be, and budget is 1000, as you would expect before the first transaction. You can also see the dollars argument, which is the NSNumber object I created. If you had any local variables, you would have also seen them as you did in Figure 8-8.

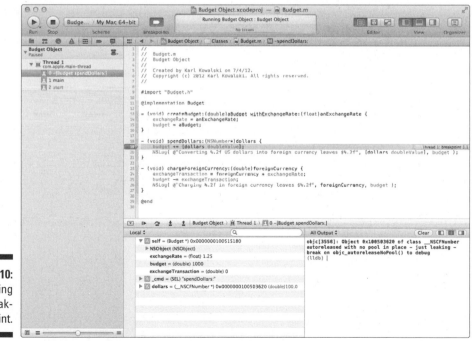

Figure 8-10:
Stopping at a break-point.

If I want to see how the budget variable gets changed (which is the result of the logic error), I can do two things. First, I can execute the program instruction by instruction, simply by clicking the Step Into button on the Debugger area toolbar. I can keep clicking that Step Into button at every instruction until I get to where I want to be (which, by the way, can be a long and winding road).

In this case, I execute budget += [dollars doubleValue]; and then go on to the next instruction, as you can see in Figure 8-11. budget has been changed to 1100, and the computer did exactly what I told it to do, which was to add rather than subtract the transaction amount.

The Debugger area gives you a number of other options for making your way through your program in addition to Step Into. For example, you could try one of the following:

✔ **Step Over** gives you the opportunity to skip over an instruction.

✔ **Step Out** takes you out of the current method.

✔ **Continue** tells the program to continue its execution.

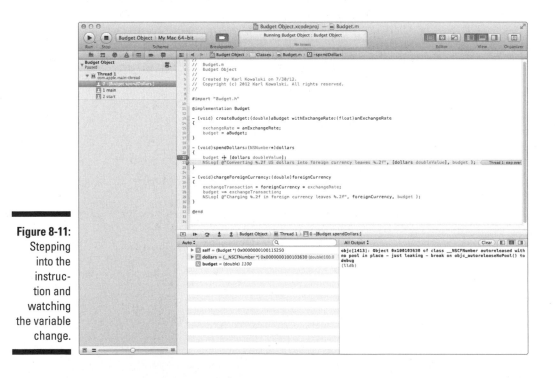

Figure 8-11: Stepping into the instruction and watching the variable change.

To get rid of the breakpoint, simply drag it off to the side. You can also right-click the breakpoint and choose Remove Breakpoint from the shortcut menu that appears.

If your app has stopped at a breakpoint, one other option you have is to restart. All you need to do is click the Run button again, and Xcode asks if you're certain that you want to terminate your app, as you can see in Figure 8-12.

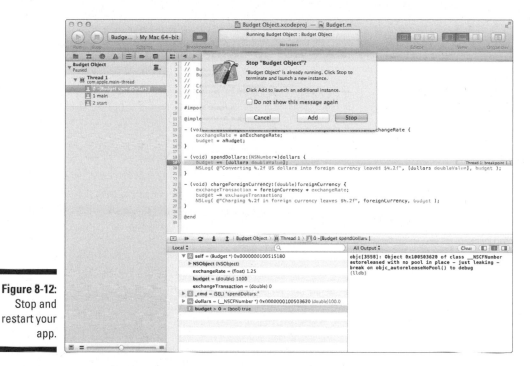

Figure 8-12:
Stop and restart your app.

Using the Static Analyzer

Xcode has an Analyze feature (the Static Analyzer) that analyzes your code.

The results show up like warnings and errors, with explanations of where and what the issue is. You can also see the flow of control of the (potential) problem. I say *potential* because the Static Analyzer can give you false positives.

In Figure 8-13, I chose Analyze from the Product menu (choose Product⇨ Analyze).

Figure 8-13:
Running
the Static
Analyzer.

The results, shown in the Editor window (Figure 8-14), show the potential problems in the code, both at line 27 (you need to click the number at the right side of the window to see both of the problems):

- ✔ Value stored in 'i' is never read. The analyzer can tell that I've assigned a new value to the variable i but that I never look at that value later on in the code.

- ✔ Division by zero. The analyzer knows that this is a bad thing, and is telling me that I should fix this.

Congratulations — you've now mastered the basics you need to find and fix the errors that always seem to appear in code. The more code you create, the more bugs you will see, and the more you will benefit from finding and fixing them.

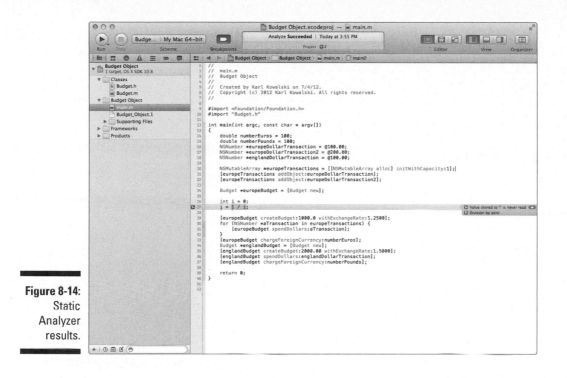

Figure 8-14:
Static
Analyzer
results.

Chapter 9

Using Control Statements and Loops

. . . .

In This Chapter

▶ Understanding how control statements and loops work

▶ Knowing when to use — and not use — `switch` statements

▶ Getting a handle on loop statements

▶ Building your application

▶ Using jump statements

. . . .

*I*n Chapter 7, I introduce you to `NSMutableArray`s to help you manage lists of objects. You see how you can use an array of objects and then iterate through the array, passing each object as an argument in a message. In Chapter 7, you use an array for only one transaction type, `spendDollars:` using one country's budget, `europeBudget`. If you want to extend that to `chargeForeignCurrency:`, you need another array. And if you want to extend that to use `englandBudget`, you need to add two additional arrays — one each for the `spendDollars:` and `chargeForeignCurrency:` messages.

This may seem pretty awkward, and it is. To manage my objects, what I really want is a single array that I can iterate through, one that holds all the different transaction types for all the countries I will be visiting.

And that's what you will be doing in this and the next chapter.

Along the way, I also complete your knowledge of the C functionality that is part of Objective-C — showing you how to use loops and control statements to determine the execution sequence of instructions.

Creating Transaction Objects

To start the journey to a single array that manages all my transactions for the countries I visit, I want to review how the program works currently.

I start by creating a dollar transaction for Europe

```
NSNumber *europeDollarTransaction = @100.00;
```

and then add it to the `europeTransactions` array. Currently, this array really can hold only dollar transactions, and Europe transactions to boot, because when I iterate through the array, I send the `spendDollars:` message to the `europeBudget` object:

```
for (NSNumber *aTransaction in europeTransactions)  {
  [europeBudget spendDollars: aTransaction];
}
```

The way this `for in` statement is coded poses two problems:

- I need to know what kind of transaction is in the array so that I can send the `Budget` object the right message. Currently, as I iterate through the array, I know that these are dollar transactions, and I send the `spend-Dollars:` message. To use an array to process credit card transactions, I have to create a new array and then send `europeBudget` the `charge-ForeignCurrency:` message like so:

  ```
  for (NSNumber *aTransaction in englandTransactions) {
    [englandBudget spendDollars: aTransaction];
  }
  ```

- I need to know what `Budget` to send the message to. As I iterate through the array, because I know that these are dollar transactions for Europe, I send the `spendDollars:` message to the `europeBudget:` object. To use an array to process England transactions, I must create a new array and then send `englandBudget` the `spendDollars:` message like so:

  ```
  for (NSNumber * aTransaction in englandTransactions) {
    [englandBudget spendDollars:
                          [aTransaction doubleValue]];
  }
  ```

As you can see, this can be quite problematic. I need an array for each transaction type and each country. This would require a bit of coding whenever I decided to add a new transaction or go to another country.

Not a rosy future is it? Kind of makes you want to stay home.

Managing all those objects

This particular situation is not unique — managing a list of similar objects is the kind of thing you'll need to do in many of your applications.

As you'll see, using the features available in an object-oriented programming language such as Objective-C enables you to manage all these objects in a single array. To do that, you'll use inheritance to create different *types* of transaction objects (you haven't seen this yet, but you will in the next chapter) and take advantage of polymorphism — one of the ways to create extensible programs that I speak about in Chapter 3.

But before I do that, I want to show you an interim "solution" to the multiplying array problem by using a C control statement called the *switch statement,* or switch. This solution will still require an array for each country, but you will be able to store both cash and credit card transactions in the same array.

To do that, you'll need to extend your NSNumber-based transaction object to store the kind of transaction it is (dollar or credit card). Then I'll show you how to use a switch statement in main to determine which "spend" message (spendDollars: or chargeForeignCurrency:) should be sent to the Budget and for what amount, based on the kind of transaction it is.

Adding the Transaction class

I start by having you change the current NSNumber-based transaction object from a wrapper (an object that is there mostly to turn something into an object) into a real Transaction object with its own instance variables and methods.

If you have been following along with me, I extend what you do in Chapter 7. If you want to start with a clean copy of the project from where you left off, you can use the project found at the website in the Chapter 9 Start Here folder, which is in the Chapter 9 folder.

I have you start by adding a new file to your project. (I explain how to do this in more detail in Chapter 6.) Follow these steps:

1. **Select the** Classes **folder in the Project navigator.**

   This tells Xcode to place the new file in the Classes folder.

2. **Choose File⇨New File (or press ⌘+N) to get the New File dialog.**

3. **In the leftmost column of the dialog, first select Cocoa under OS X; then select the Objective-C class template in the upper-right pane. Click Next.**

   You see a new screen asking for some more information.

4. **Enter** Transaction **in the Class field, and make sure that NSObject is selected in the subclass of the drop-down menu. Then click Next.**

   Xcode shows you the usual file-save screen. The default location works fine.

5. **Click Create.**

This is a good time to read Chapter 2 (the section "Getting to Know the Xcode Text Editor"). Many of the features I explain are now more relevant to you, especially the Counterpart button, which switches you from the header, or interface file (.h), to the implementation file (.m) and vice versa.

I find it useful at this point to double-click Transaction.h to open it in a new window.

To add the new Transaction class, you do three things:

1. Add the Transaction class interface.

2. Add the Transaction class implementation.

3. Update the Budget class.

Adding the Transaction class interface

Navigate to the Transaction.h file and add the code in bold, as shown in Listing 9-1. (I deleted, and will continue to delete, the comments inserted by Xcode at the beginning of the .h and .m files it creates — feel free to keep yours if you like.)

Listing 9-1:   The New Transaction Class Interface

```
#import <Foundation/Foundation.h>

typedef enum {cash, charge} transactionType;

@interface Transaction : NSObject
{
  transactionType type;
  NSNumber *amount;
}

- (void) createTransaction: (double) theAmount
```

```
                         ofType: (transactionType) aType;
- (NSNumber *) returnAmount;
- (transactionType) returnType;
@end
```

This `Transaction` class does what you need it to do — it stores both an amount and its type. To do that you did the following:

1. To know what kind of transaction it is, you created a new type, `transactionType`, by using a `typedef` (I explain `typedef`s in Chapter 5, so if you are a bit vague about what I am doing, you can refer to that chapter) and an instance variable `type`. You'll use *cash* for the dollar transaction and *charge* for the credit card ones:

   ```
   typedef enum {cash, charge} transactionType;
   transactionType type;
   ```

2. You added an instance variable `amount`, which is the value of the transaction.

3. You declared three new methods:

   ```
   - (void) createTransaction: (double) theAmount
                       ofType: (transactionType) aType;
   - (NSNumber *) returnAmount;
   - (transactionType) returnType;
   ```

   The first method simply initializes the object with a type and amount. (I explain more about initialization in Chapter 12.) The second and third methods return the amount of the transaction and type of transaction (cash or charge), respectively. As you probably know by now, you shouldn't access an object's instance variables directly, and these two methods allow `main` to get the data it needs. In Chapter 14, I show you a way to have Objective-C create these kinds of methods for you (using declared properties).

Adding the Transaction class implementation

Now that you have created the class interface, you need to implement it.

In the `Transaction.m` file, add the code in bold, as shown in Listing 9-2.

Listing 9-2:   The New Transaction Class Implementation

```
#import "Transaction.h"

@implementation Transaction
- (void) createTransaction: (double) theAmount ofType:
          (transactionType) aType{
```

(continued)

Listing 9-2 *(continued)*

```
  type = aType;
  amount = @( theAmount );
}

- (NSNumber *) returnAmount{

  return amount;
}

- (transactionType) returnType {

  return type;
};

@end
```

This implements the methods I declared in the interface.

Now that I have created the transaction object that has an amount and know what kind of transaction it is, I can put both cash and charge transactions in the same array and use a `switch` statement to ensure that the right message is sent to the `Budget` object.

Using switch Statements

A `switch` statement is a kind of *control statement*. Control statements are used to determine what to do when a certain condition arises. I introduce one of those, the `if` statement, in Chapter 4. Later in this chapter, in the section "Taking the Leap: Jump Statements," I introduce you to the balance of those C statements. Although these kinds of statements can be useful in object-oriented programming, you need to be especially careful about how you use them.

For now however, you'll work with the `switch` statement.

I want to review the code that you will add that will implement the `switch` statement:

```
    switch ([aTransaction returnType]) {
      case cash:
        [europeBudget spendDollars:
            [aTransaction returnAmount]];
        break;
      case charge:
```

```
        [europeBudget chargeForeignCurrency:
            [[aTransaction returnAmount] doubleValue]];
     break;
   default:
     break;
   }
}
```

Let me explain how this works.

A `switch` statement is a type of control statement that allows the value of a variable or expression to control the flow of program execution. In this case, you are using the `transactionType`.

As you can see in Listing 9-2, for a `transactionType` `cash` (remember, you declared `transactionType` and the values it can take on in the `typedef` in Listing 9-1), you send the `spendDollars:` message to the `europeBudget` object with the amount returned to you by the `returnAmount` method as the argument.

Similarly, for a `transactionType` `charge`, you send the `chargeForeign-Currency:` message to the `europeBudget` object.

The general form of a `switch` statement is as follows:

```
switch (expression) {
  case constant1:
    Statement(s) to execute for case 1;
  break;
case constant2:
    Statement(s) to execute for case 2;
  break,
  .
  .
  .
default:
  Default statement(s);
}
```

Here is the sequence:

1. Evaluate `expression`.

2. If `expression` is equal to `constant1`:

    a. Execute `Statement(s) to execute for case 1` until it reaches a `break` statement.

    b. Execute the `break` statement, which causes a jump to the end of the `switch` structure.

3. If `expression` is not equal to `constant1`, see whether `expression` is equal to `constant2`. If it is:

    a. Execute `Statement(s) to execute for case 2` until it reaches a `break` statement.

    b. Execute the `break` statement, which causes a jump to the end of the `switch` structure.

4. If `expression` does not match any of the constants (you can include as many case labels as values you want to check), the program will execute `Default statement(s)` if a `default` exists (which is optional).

In this case, the expression used by the `switch` statement is the `transactionType` (the constant used to "do the switch") returned by the `returnType` method. `transactionType` is the `enum` you defined in `Transaction.h` (in Listing 9-1):

```
typedef enum {cash, charge} transactionType;
```

If the transaction type returned is `cash`, the `switch` statement executes the instructions under the `cash` case:

```
case cash:
   [europeBudget spendDollars:[aTransaction returnAmount]];
   break;
```

The `break` statement causes execution to transfer to the end of the `switch` structure. But because the `switch` statement is in the array enumerator block

```
for (Transaction * aTransaction in transactions) {
```

the next `Transaction` object in the array is fetched, and the `switch` statement is executed again. This goes on until all the `Transaction` objects in the `transactions` array are processed.

As you can see, the `switch` statement uses *labels* (`case cash:`, for example). A label is made up of a valid identifier followed by a colon (`:`). This is why you need the `break` statement. If no `break`s exist, all the statements following the label (`case cash:`) will be executed until the end of the `switch` block or a break `statement` is reached.

This is actually a feature, because you can do something like the following:

```
typedef enum {cash, charge, atm} transactionType;
switch ([aTransaction returnType]) {
  case atm:
  case cash:
    [europeBudget spendDollars:
            [aTransaction returnAmount]];
    break;
  case charge:
    [europeBudget chargeForeignCurrency:
            [[aTransaction returnAmount] doubleValue]];
    break;
  default:
    break;
  }
}
```

In this case, I decide I want a new transactionType of atm, but (for the time being at least) I want to treat it in the same way as transactionType of cash. This switch structure would end up executing the same block of code for both cash and atm and a different block for charge.

Nothing is special about a switch statement — actually, it performs in the same way as several if and else instructions:

```
if ([aTransaction returnType] == cash) {
  [europeBudget spendDollars:[aTransaction returnAmount]];
}
else {
  if ([aTransaction returnType] == charge) {
  [europeBudget chargeForeignCurrency:
        [[aTransaction returnAmount] doubleValue]];
  }
  else {
    //equivalent of default
    }
}
```

If you don't want default behavior, you could even use a series of if statements, as shown here:

```
if ([aTransaction returnType] == cash) {
  [europeBudget spendDollars:[aTransaction returnAmount]];
  }
if ([aTransaction returnType] == charge) {
  [europeBudget chargeForeignCurrency:
        [[aTransaction returnAmount] doubleValue]];
  }
```

The switch statement is really useful when you have many conditions and when using the if else construct becomes too complicated to figure out or follow.

Do you have a way to simplify all of this? Yes, and in fact object-oriented programming deals specifically with making this kind of complex logic uncomplicated. I show you that in the next chapter.

You can use a switch only to compare an expression to a constant. If you need to compare an expression to something other than a constant, you are stuck with the if else construct.

Now that you have your Transaction class and your switch statement, you need to create some Transactions and add them to the array to test it.

You could, for example, code the following:

```
aTransaction1 = [Transaction new];
[aTransaction1 createTransaction: n*100 ofType: cash];
[transactions addObject:aTransaction1];
...

aTransactionN = [Transaction new];
[aTransactionN createTransaction: n*100 ofType: credit];
[transactions addObject:aTransactionN];
```

This is what you've been doing until now, and you could copy and paste to create more transactions to test the functionality that you are building. In the next section, however, I show you an easier way to create transactions by using loop statements.

Using Loop Statements to Repeat Instructions

Loop statements allow you to have the same set of instructions repeated over and over and over again — at least until some criterion is met. You actually do that in Chapter 8, using the enumerator for in statement. In this chapter, I expand upon that. Loops are the kinds of things you'll continue to use as you discover more about Objective-C and programming in general.

Remember, using loops here is only a convenience in your program to create transactions. In the real world (and in Chapters 17 and 18), you allow the users to enter transactions through a user interface. But even so, loops, as you will find out, are fundamental to programming — so fundamental that you find them in most computer languages.

So, it's time to find out more about loops. You'll use three kinds of loops:

- ✔ The `for` loop
- ✔ The `while` loop
- ✔ The `do while` loop

The for loop

In Chapter 7, I introduce you to loops with the `for in` loop, which enables you to take each entry in an array and do something with it until you run out of entries in the array:

```
for (NSNumber * aTransaction in europeTransactions) {
    [europeBudget spendDollars: aTransaction];
}
```

The `for in` loop is a special case of something more general called a *for loop*.

A very simple `for` loop looks like this:

```
for (int i = 1; i <  4; i++) {

  NSLog(@"i = %i", i );
}
```

This results in

```
i = 1
i = 2
i = 3
```

The `for` loop repeats a set of statements for a specific number of times. In the example, you have only one statement:

```
NSLog(@"i = %i", i );
```

But you can have as many as you want.

`for` loops use a variable as a counter to determine how many times to repeat the loop. In this case, the counter is `i`.

The easiest way to think of the `for` loop is that when it reaches the brace at the end, it jumps back up to the beginning of the loop, which checks the condition again and decides whether to repeat the block one more time or stop repeating it and move on to the next statement after the block.

The execution flow for a `for` loop is as follows:

1. The counter is initialized (only once):

   ```
   int i = 1
   ```

2. The counter is evaluated. If it is `true`, execution within the block continues; otherwise, the loop ends, and the next statement after the block is executed:

   ```
   i < 4
   ```

3. The loop statement(s) that appear in a block enclosed in braces, { }, or a single statement is executed:

   ```
   NSLog(@"i = %i", i );
   ```

4. The counter is incremented:

   ```
   i++
   ```

5. Steps 2 through 4 are repeated until the condition for terminating the loop is met. When it is, execution continues with the next statement after the `for` loop statements.

You add the following `for` loop to your program to add some transactions to the array you just created:

```
Transaction *aTransaction ;
for (int n = 1; n <  2; n++) {
  aTransaction = [Transaction new];
  [aTransaction createTransaction:n*100 ofType:cash];
  [transactions addObject:aTransaction];
}
```

Can you determine how many times this loop will be executed?

That's right, once. You are creating one transaction of `transactionType` cash for 100 (`n*100`, where n=1) and adding it to the `transactions` array.

Although normally you wouldn't use a loop to execute a statement only once, I use it here because it's simple enough that you can really see how the counter is evaluated and how the condition is met.

Again putting on my tie, the formal description is

```
for ( counter; condition; update counter) {
  Statement(s) to execute while the condition is true
}
```

As you can see, three sections follow the first parenthesis, each terminated by a semicolon:

- ✔ **Counter:** The counter can be declared here, or you can use some other variable that you've already declared and initialized. In this case, it is declared and initialized:

  ```
  int n = 1
  ```

- ✔ **Condition:** The condition is some expression that returns YES or NO and contains one of the logical or relational operators explained in Chapter 4 (you know, like ==, < , | |, and so on). The statements in the loop will be executed as long as the condition remains YES. In this case, it is as long as *n* is less than 2:

  ```
  n < 2
  ```

- ✔ **Expression to update counter:** The update counter can be any expression — ++n or even n + a where a is a variable that may be updated in the code block. In this case, the counter is incremented by 1 each time through the loop:

  ```
  n++
  ```

The initialization and increase fields are optional, but the semicolon must still be there. For example, for (; n<10 ;) specifies no initialization and no increase because the variable was initialized previously and you were incrementing it in one of the Statement(s) to execute while the condition is true.

You can also use the comma operator (,) to specify some pretty complex initialization and counter updates. For example:

```
for (int n = 0, y = 10; n <= y; ++n, y-=2) {
...
}
```

The while loop

The for loop is typically used when the number of iterations is known before entering the loop, whereas the while and do while loops repeat until a certain condition is met.

for or for in?

for loops are used when you know what the number of iterations is going to be. Because [europeTransactions count] determines how many times you need to iterate through the array, you could have used a for loop instead of using the for in array iterator described in Chapter 7.

The iterator you used was

```
for (NSNumber * aTransaction
    in europeTransactions) {
  [europeBudget spendDollars:
    aTransaction];
}
```

To accomplish the same thing with a for loop, you use the array's count method, which tells you the number of elements it has. (As I mention in Chapter 7, this is one of the key methods you will use.)

```
for (int n = 1; n <=
    [europeTransactions
    count]; n++) {

    [europeBudget
    spendDollars:

    [europeTransactions
    objectAtIndex:n]];
}
```

The iterator is just faster and more convenient than coding your own for loop.

To add transactions to your array by using a while loop, you code the following:

```
int n = 1;
while (n < 3) {
  aTransaction = [Transaction new];
  [aTransaction createTransaction:n*100 ofType:charge];
  [transactions addObject:aTransaction];
  n++;
}
```

A while loop is similar to a for loop. As you can see, all you have to do to turn a for loop into a while loop is the following:

1. Initialize the counter:

   ```
   int n = 1;
   ```

2. Increment the counter in the code block:

   ```
   n++;
   ```

The formal while loop is

```
while ( condition ) { Statement(s) to execute while the
          condition is true }
```

The sequence is as follows:

1. `condition` is evaluated. If it is true, execution within the block continues; otherwise, the loop ends and the next statement after the block is executed.

2. The `Statement(s) to execute while the condition is true` block is executed — it can be either a single statement or a block enclosed in braces { }.

3. The loop goes back to Step 1.

Notice that the `Statement(s) to execute while the condition is true` might never be executed.

Obviously, the value of the condition will have to change for the loop to end. In this case, you are changing the value of the condition in the loop, so this acts, for all practical purposes, like a `for` loop. In general, however, you will more likely test an outside condition in the `while` loop. For example, you might repeatedly update the position of a ball in a maze as a user is moving his or her iPhone. `while` loops are used when you don't know precisely how many times the loop needs to repeat.

The do while loop

The `do while` loop works the same way as the `while` loop with one exception. The `condition` is evaluated *after* the execution of `Statement(s) to execute while the condition is true` instead of before, meaning that you will always have at least one execution of `Statement(s) to execute while the condition is true` even if the condition is never fulfilled:

```
do {
   aTransaction = [Transaction new];
   [aTransaction createTransaction: n*100 ofType:
                                          charge];
   [transactions addObject:aTransaction];
   n++;
} while (n <= 3);
```

The `do while` loop is usually used when the condition that determines the end of the loop is a result of actions taken within the loop. For example, you could use a `do while` to prompt the user to enter data; the user could then enter some data, press Enter, or do something else to terminate the loop.

The formal `do while` loop is

```
do { Statement(s) to execute while the condition is true }
        while ( condition );
```

The sequence is as follows:

1. `Statement(s) to execute while the condition is true` is executed.

2. `condition` is evaluated. If it is true, the loop goes back to Step 1.

You wouldn't want to use a `do while` loop if there were a possibility that you might not want to execute the code. In this example, if an array could be empty, you wouldn't want to use a `do while` loop to iterate through it.

Keep in mind that you must include a trailing semicolon after the `do while` loop in the preceding example, but the other loops should not be terminated with a semicolon, adding to the confusion.

Although the preceding code is a pretty lame example of a `do while` loop — you'll never use it in this way — the example does illustrate the mechanics of using a `do while` loop.

Adding Loops to Your Program

To add the `switch` statement and loops to `main` in the `main.m` file, delete the bold, italic, underlined code and add the code in bold, as shown in Listing 9-3.

Listing 9-3:   Adding switch Statements and Loops to the main Function

```
#import <Foundation/Foundation.h>
#import "Budget.h"
#import "Transaction.h"

int main (int argc, const char * argv[]) {

//double numberEuros = 100;
//double numberDollarsInPoundland = 100;
  double numberPounds = 100;

//NSNumber *europeDollarTransaction = @100.00;
//NSNumber *europeDollarTransaction2 = @200.00;
  NSNumber *englandDollarTransaction = @100.00;
//NSMutableArray *europeTransactions = [[NSMutableArray
          alloc] initWithCapacity:1];
//[europeTransactions addObject:europeDollarTransaction];
//[europeTransactions addObject:europeDollarTransaction2];

  NSMutableArray *transactions =
```

```
[[NSMutableArray alloc] initWithCapacity:10];
Transaction *aTransaction ;
for (int n = 1; n <  2; n++) {
  aTransaction = [Transaction new];
  [aTransaction createTransaction:n*100 ofType:cash];
  [transactions addObject:aTransaction];
}

int n =1;
while (n < 3) {
  aTransaction = [Transaction new];
  [aTransaction createTransaction:n*100 ofType:charge];
  [transactions addObject:aTransaction];
  n++;
}

do {
  aTransaction = [Transaction new];
  [aTransaction createTransaction:n*100 ofType:charge];
  [transactions addObject:aTransaction];
  n++;
} while (n <= 3);

Budget *europeBudget = [Budget new];
[europeBudget createBudget:1000.00
                            withExchangeRate:1.2500];

//for (NSNumber *aTransaction in europeTransactions) {
  //[europeBudget spendDollars:aTransaction];
for (Transaction * aTransaction in transactions) {

    switch ([aTransaction returnType]) {
      case cash:
        [europeBudget spendDollars:
                [aTransaction returnAmount]];
        break;
      case charge:
        [europeBudget chargeForeignCurrency:
                [[aTransaction returnAmount] doubleValue]];
        break;
      default:
        break;
    }
}
//   [europeBudget chargeForeignCurrency:numberEuros];

Budget *englandBudget = [Budget new];
[englandBudget createBudget:2000.00
        withExchangeRate:1.5000];
[englandBudget spendDollars:englandDollarTransaction];
[englandBudget chargeForeignCurrency:numberPounds];

return 0;
}
```

Here are the steps you took to add the `switch` statement and loops:

1. So that the compiler knows what a `Transaction` is, you added

```
#import "Transaction.h"
```

2. You deleted the following line of code because you don't need it anymore. (You no longer need to set the number of euros. You do that when you create the `Transaction`.)

```
double numberEuros = 100;
```

3. You deleted the old `NSNumber` transactions and the old `europe Transactions` array:

```
NSNumber *europeDollarTransaction = @100.00;
NSNumber *europeDollarTransaction2 = @200.00;

NSMutableArray *europeTransactions = [[NSMutableArray
        alloc] initWithCapacity:1];
[europeTransactions addObject:
                            europeDollarTransaction];
[europeTransactions addObject:
                            europeDollarTransaction2];
```

4. You declared the `transactions` array (notice that you changed the initial specification of the number of entries from 1 to 10) and created and added the transactions in three different kinds of loops. You cleverly used the counter (n) to vary the transaction amount (n*100):

```
NSMutableArray *transactions =
[[NSMutableArray alloc] initWithCapacity:10];
Transaction *aTransaction ;
for (int n = 1; n <  2; n++) {
  aTransaction = [Transaction new];
  [aTransaction createTransaction:
                          n*100 ofType:cash];
  [transactions addObject:aTransaction];
}

int n =1;
while (n < 3) {
  aTransaction = [Transaction new];
  [aTransaction createTransaction:
                          n*100 ofType:charge];
  [transactions addObject:aTransaction];
  n++;
}

do {
  aTransaction = [Transaction new];
  [aTransaction createTransaction:
```

```
                              n*100 ofType:charge];
    [transactions addObject:aTransaction];
    n++;
} while (n <= 3);
```

Changing the name prepares you for Chapter 10, where you manage all transactions in a single array, regardless of transaction type or destination — which will significantly reduce the complexity of the program. You created a transactions array with the new transactions.

5. You changed the type in the enumerator from NSNumber to Transaction to reflect the new object type that is now in the array.

6. You replaced

```
[europeBudget spendDollars:aTransaction];
```

with the new switch structure:

```
switch ([aTransaction returnType]) {
  case cash:
    [europeBudget spendDollars:
          [aTransaction returnAmount]];
    break;
  case charge:
    [europeBudget chargeForeignCurrency:
          [[aTransaction returnAmount] doubleValue]];
    break;
  default:
    break;
}
```

7. You deleted the following line of code because you don't need it anymore (the chargeForeignCurrency is now in the switch statement):

```
//[europeBudget chargeForeignCurrency:numberEuros];
```

Building the New Application

So that you can admire all the work you've done, it is time to build the application.

Click the Run button on the Project Window toolbar to build and run the application.

You should see the following in the Debugger Console:

```
Converting 100.00 US dollars into foreign currency leaves
     $900.00
Charging 100.00 in foreign currency leaves $775.00
Charging 200.00 in foreign currency leaves $525.00
Charging 300.00 in foreign currency leaves $150.00
Converting 100.00 US dollars into foreign currency leaves
      $1900.00
Charging 100.00 in foreign currency leaves $1750.00
```

You can find the completed project at the website in the Example 9 folder, which is in the Chapter 9 folder.

Taking the Leap: Jump Statements

To finish your tour of C coding, I provide the rest of the control statements that are available in Objective-C. You'll use a few of them, such as `break` (which you used in `switch` statements) and `return`, in your code. You'll use the rest occasionally (with the exception of the `goto` statement, which should never use). The rest of the control statements are as follows:

- ✔ `break`: Using `break`, you can leave a loop even if the condition for its end is not fulfilled. It can be used to end an infinite loop or to force it to end before its natural end. Recall that this is how you terminate instruction execution after it starts executing instructions for a given `case`.

- ✔ `continue`: The `continue` statement causes the program to skip the rest of the loop in the current iteration and jump to the start of the next iteration.

- ✔ `return`: The `return` statement ends a method or function. You used a `return` statement in `main`, as well as in your methods. It is included here to remind you that you can include a `return` statement anywhere in a method or function, bypassing any subsequent instructions in the function (as well as being able to depart in the middle of a loop) to return control to the caller.

- ✔ `goto`: The `goto` statement allows you to make an absolute jump to another point in the program. It is considered evil incarnate by virtually all object-oriented programmers, and more than a few procedural ones. As an object-oriented applications programmer, you should never use it.

- ✔ `exit`: The `exit` statement terminates your program with an exit code. Its prototype is

  ```
  void exit (int exitcode);
  ```

  `exit` is used by some operating systems and may be used by calling programs. By convention, an exit code of 0 means that the program finished normally, and any other value means that some error or unexpected results happened.

Knowing the Problems with switch Statements

Although I have achieved my goal of creating a single array of transaction objects for a given country, I still have a way to go if I want to make it possible to have a single array that handles all transaction types for all countries.

For example, if I were to add a country and a returnCountry: method to the transaction, I'd have to add an additional switch structure within each existing case to use the right budget object — makes my head hurt to think about it. And as you can see, my program would become much more complicated as I add more transactions and countries. Whereas this is only one place in this program (so far) that I need to use that kind of logic, in a real program, you could find it all over the place.

In the following code example, I implemented a switch structure to handle different countries, within the switch structure to handle the type of transaction. You can see how easily this will get out of hand:

```
for (Transaction * aTransaction in transactions) {
    switch ([aTransaction returnType]) {
      case cash:
        switch ([aTransaction returnCountry]) {
          case Europe:
            [europeBudget spendDollars:
                            [aTransaction returnAmount]];
            break;
          case England:
            [englandBudget spendDollars:
                            [aTransaction returnAmount]];
            break;
          }
        break;
      case charge:
        switch ([aTransaction returnCountry]) {
          case Europe:
            [europeBudget chargeForeignCurrency:
                            [aTransaction returnAmount]];
            break;
          case England:
            [englandBudget chargeForeignCurrency:
                            [aTransaction returnAmount]];
            break;
          }
        break;
      default:
        break;
      }
}
```

You can get a much more elegant solution than the `switch` statement by taking advantage of inheritance and polymorphism. I cover both in Chapter 10.

Part III

Walking the Object-Oriented Walk

The 5th Wave   By Rich Tennant

"They're moving on to the memory management section. That should daze and confuse them enough for us to finish changing the tire."

In this part . . .

You've mastered the instruction set and language features that you need, and now you're ready to start building a real object-oriented program — one whose code you wouldn't be embarrassed to show to your developer friends.

In this part, you focus on what is known as the program architecture. Think of it as analogous to the way an architect designs a building to meet the needs of its occupants. In this case, however, you create something that not only works but also can be extended to easily add new functionality.

I also show you the fundamental application functionality that every program needs to implement — memory management and object initialization. Apple has added a new memory management feature to Objective-C: Automatic Reference Counting. In this part I tell you what you need to know to use this feature in your applications so you devote less work on your app's memory and more time making your app work.

Chapter 10

Basic Inheritance

· ·

In This Chapter

▶ Understanding inheritance

▶ Implementing inheritance

▶ Understanding the connection between inheritance and polymorphism

· ·

*I*n Chapter 9, you create a `Transaction` object and use a `switch` statement to manage more than one kind of transaction in a single array. The
problem with that approach is that the `switch` statements can rapidly get
very complicated, and a program with `switch` statements scattered throughout becomes difficult to extend and enhance.

Quite frankly, this kind of complex control structure is characteristic of the
procedural program paradigm that I speak of in Chapter 3. Object-oriented
programming and Objective-C do not "improve" this control structure as
much as eliminate it as much as possible. The way this is done is by using
one of those Objective-C's extensions to C — *inheritance* — to take advantage
of *polymorphism* (which I explain in Chapter 3). As you find out as I lead you
through implementing an inheritance-based class structure in this chapter,
this greatly simplifies things, and you end up with a program that is a great
deal easier to understand and extend (the two actually go hand in hand).

After you get into the rhythm of thinking this way, programming and making
changes become more fun and less dreary. You introduce fewer bugs as you
add functionality to your program, and your coding becomes completely
focused on the new functionality instead of requiring that you go back through
everything you have done to see whether you are about to break something
that now works just fine.

Replacing a Control Structure with Polymorphism

Right now, you iterate through an array, and your logic in `main` (the `switch` statement) decides whether to send the `spendDollars:` or `chargeForeign Currency:` message to a `Budget` for that kind of transaction, passing the transaction as an argument.

Here's the current code showing the use of the `switch` statement:

```
for (Transaction * aTransaction in transactions) {
  switch ([aTransaction returnType]) {
   case cash:
     [europeBudget spendDollars:
             [aTransaction returnAmount]];
     break;
   case charge:
     [europeBudget chargeForeignCurrency:
             [[aTransaction returnAmount] doubleValue]];
     break;
   default:
     break;
   }
 }
```

In the object-oriented universe, you have two kinds of transaction objects — cash and credit card. Both kinds respond to a `spend` message, and every transaction has a pointer to the budget it is associated with. You iterate through the array and send the `spend` message to each transaction. If it is a cash transaction in Europe, for example, it has a reference to the `europe Budget` object and sends the `europeBudget` object the `spendDollars:` message. If it is a credit card transaction in England, it sends the `charge ForeignCurrency:` message to `englandBudget`. No fuss, no bother, and no control structure. This means that you have one array that holds every transaction for every country you visit — much better. This enables you to replace that entire `switch` structure with

```
for (Transaction*  aTransaction in transactions) {
  [aTransaction spend];
 }
```

If you want a new transaction, all you need to do is code it up and add it to the array, and if you want to visit a new country, all you have do is create a budget for that country and attach it to the transactions that occurred in that country.

You can see that illustrated in Figure 10-1.

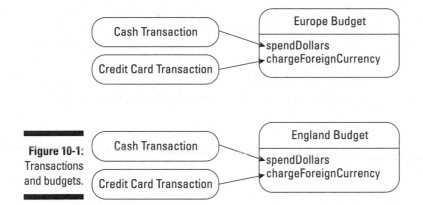

Figure 10-1:
Transactions
and budgets.

I start with what a transaction object looks like.

You need two instance variables:

```
Budget *budget;
NSNumber *amount;
```

You need two methods:

```
- (void) createTransaction: (double) theAmount
                        forBudget: (Budget*) aBudget;
- (void) spend;
```

As you can see, besides a method to provide values to initialize the instance variables, you have a method named spend. You also have an instance variable, budget, that enables the Transaction object to send a message to its budget, and another instance variable, amount, that holds the amount of this transaction. Because every type of transaction has a spend method, you can enumerate through the array and send each object a spend message, and each object, depending on its type, turns around and sends the right message to its budget.

So far, both cash and credit card transactions look the same; the only difference is in the implementation of spend.

The cash transaction implements spend as

```
- (void) spend {

  [budget spendDollars:amount];
  }
```

The credit card looks like

```
- (void) spend {

  [budget chargeForeignCurrency:[amount doubleValue]];
  }
```

This ability for different objects to respond to the same message each in its own way is an example of polymorphism, which I cover in Chapter 3, and is one of the cornerstones of enhanceable and extensible programs.

How inheritance works

You may notice a bit of a problem here. You got rid of the complicated switch, but now you have to maintain all those transactions. If want to make a change or add to generic transaction functionality, you have to go back and modify both the cash and credit card transactions. In Chapter 5, when I discuss adding a separate struct for New Zealand to track wool purchases, I say specifically that this is something you want to avoid (you may want to refer to Chapter 5).

What I say at the end of Chapter 5 is still true, but fortunately, I don't have to worry about maintaining a host of similar classes. Objective-C, like other object-oriented programming languages, permits you to base a new class definition on a class that's already defined. The base class is called a *super-class;* the new class is its *subclass.* The subclass is defined only by its differences from its superclass; everything else remains the same. All I need to do is create a transaction base superclass that encapsulates what is the same between a cash and credit card transaction, and then create cash and credit card transaction subclasses that implement the differences.

The terms *superclass* and *subclass* can be confusing. When most people think of *super,* they think of something with more functionality, not less. In some languages, the term used is *base class,* which I think does a better job of conveying meaning. But it is what it is, so keep this in mind.

In Figure 10-2, you see an example of a *class diagram* that uses the UML (Unified Modeling Language) notation (the superclass and subclass arrows and terms are not part of the notation; they are there to illustrate the hierarchy of the Transaction classes in the program) — one often used by programmers to describe their classes. The name of the class is at the top of the box, the middle section describes the instance variables, and the bottom box shows you the methods of that (sub) class.

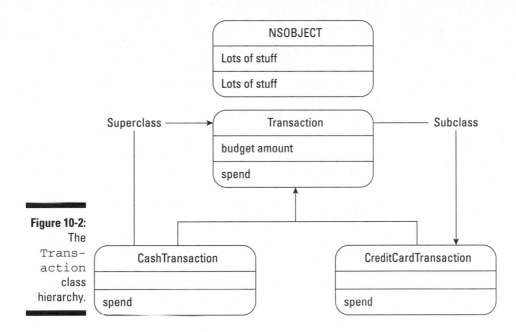

Figure 10-2:
The
Trans-
action
class
hierarchy.

Figure 10-2 shows that both CashTransaction and CreditCard-Transaction classes are subclasses of Transaction. Each inherits all the methods and all the instance variables of its superclass.

Every class but NSObject (the root of all your classes, as I explain in Chapter 5) can thus be seen as another stop on the road to increasing specialization. As you add subclasses, you are adding to the cumulative total of what's inherited. The CashTransaction class defines only what is needed to turn a Transaction into a CashTransaction.

Class definitions are cumulative; each new class that you define *inherits* methods and instance variables of all its base classes. I do not have to include the fact that I am going to "reimplement" spend in the interfaces for CashTransaction and CreditCardTransaction. All I have to do is implement spend in the @implementation. But as I mention the section "Scoping instance variables" in Chapter 6, a subclass can be prevented from accessing instance variables marked as @private.

Incidentally, if you think about it, inheritance also implements a kind of encapsulation. You can extend the behavior of an existing object without affecting the existing code that already works — remember, it's all about enhanceability and extensibility.

In Objective-C, every class has only one superclass but can have an unlimited number of subclasses. In some languages, however, a class can have multiple superclasses. This is known as *multiple inheritance.* Although Objective-C does not support multiple inheritance, it does provide some features not found in those languages that enable you to get many of the benefits of multiple inheritance, without the accompanying disadvantages. These include categories and protocols, both of which I cover in Chapter 16.

The new class is not a copy of the methods and instance variables of its root class, which contains all the methods and instance variables of its root class and so on. The new class is a *child class* of its superclass.

Knowing what inheritance enables you to do

Inheritance enables you to do a number of things that make your programs more extensible and enhanceable. In a subclass, you can make the following three kinds of changes to what you inherit from a superclass. Think of this section as describing the mechanics of creating a subclass.

- ✔ **You can add new methods and instance variables.** Although you haven't done that yet, this is the one of the most common reasons for defining a subclass in general.

- ✔ **You can refine or extend the behavior of a method.** You do this by adding a new version of the same method while still continuing to use the code in the old method. To add a new version, you implement a new method with the same name as one that's inherited. The new version *overrides* the inherited version. In the body of the new method, you send a message to execute the inherited version. I illustrate this later in this chapter, in Listing 10-6, and explain it in Step 3 following the listing (and again when I explain initialization in Chapter 12). Implementing a new method with the same name as one that's inherited is referred to as *overriding* a method.

- ✔ **You can change the behavior of a method you inherit.** You do this by replacing an existing method with a new version. Overriding the old method does this. In this case, however, you do not send a message to execute the inherited version. The old implementation is still used for the class that defined it and other classes that inherit it, although classes that inherit from the new class use your implementation. Changing behavior is not unusual, although it does make your code harder to follow. If you find yourself frequently overriding a method to completely change its behavior, you should question your design.

Even though you may override a method in a class, subclasses of the class still do have access to the original. For obvious reasons, this is generally not a good idea, and again should have you questioning your design.

Although a subclass can override inherited methods, it can't override inherited instance variables. If you try to declare a new one with the same name as an inherited one, the compiler complains.

Using inheritance effectively

Given the preceding possibilities, here are some ways that you can use inheritance in your programs:

✔ **Create a contract.** You are actually creating a contract with the `Transaction` class. A contract in this sense is a list of method(s) that subclasses are expected to implement. The superclass might have empty versions of the methods, or it might implement partial versions that you use in the subclass methods. In either case, the superclass's declaration (its list of methods) defines a structure of methods that all its subclasses must follow if they implement their own particular versions of the same methods.

When different classes implement similarly named methods, a program is better able to make use of polymorphism (see the discussion of the more-of-the-same approach in Chapter 3). Actually one of the things I really like about Objective-C is that it provides additional ways to do this, as you see when I explain delegation in Chapter 16. Both inheritance and delegation are extensively used in Cocoa.

This use of inheritance is exemplified by the concept of an *abstract* class — often called an *abstract superclass* (or *abstract base class*). This is a class designed to have classes inherit from it. An abstract class brings together the methods and instance variables that are to be used by subclasses. In doing that, abstract classes define the structure of an application, and when you create your subclasses, they fit effortlessly into the application structure and work seamlessly with other objects.

You usually do not create an instance of an abstract class, because it really can't do anything, being dependent on its subclasses to implement the key functionality. It does, however, contain code that each of its subclasses normally has to create on its own. In this case, `Transaction` is an abstract class.

Unlike some other languages, in Objective-C, you have no way to specify a class as abstract, therefore making it possible to create an instance of an abstract class.

✔ **Reuse code.** Reusing code has traditionally been a poster child for inheritance use. You find three approaches:

- *Increasing specialization.* If classes have some things in common, but also differ in key ways, the common functionality can be put in a superclass that all classes can inherit. `Transaction` is a good example of that.

- *Implementing generic functionality,* which is often coupled with the protocol approach. In the `AppKit` and `UIKit`, user interface objects have been created for your using pleasure. They implement as much generic functionality as they can, but it is up to you to add the specific functionality to make it so that they do something useful in your application. For example, a view can display itself on the screen, scroll, and so on, but you need to implement methods that display what you want to be displayed.

- *Modifying a class that more or less does what you want it to do.* You may have a class that does most of what you want it to, but you need to change some things about how it works. You can make the changes in a subclass.

In programming, as in life, however, not much is either/or. You use inheritance to do all those things, and often you create new subclasses to implement one or more than one of the approaches I just described.

Implementing Inheritance in a Program

Now it's time to put everything you know about inheritance and polymorphism together and add it to your program. You have to start by making some changes to the `Transaction` class.

Creating the Transaction superclass

If you have been following along with me, I extend what you do in Chapter 9. If you prefer to start with a clean copy of the project from where you left off, you can use the project found in the Chapter 10 Start Here folder, which can be found in the Chapter 10 folder.

Go into the Xcode Project navigator and click `Transaction.h` to edit it. Then delete the bold. italic, underlined code in Listing 10-1 and add the code in bold. After that, select `Transaction.m` in the Project navigator, delete the bold. italic, underlined code in Listing 10-2, and add the code in bold.

Listing 10-1: Transaction.h

```
#import <Foundation/Foundation.h>
@class Budget;
//typedef enum {cash, charge} transactionType;

@interface Transaction : NSObject {

//transactionType type;
  Budget *budget;
  NSNumber *amount;
}

// - (void) createTransaction: (double) theAmount ofType:
          (transactionType) aType;
- (void) createTransaction: (double) theAmount forBudget:
          (Budget*) aBudget;
- (void) spend;
- (void) trackSpending: (double) theAmount;
//- (double) returnAmount;
// - transactionType) returnType;
@end
```

Listing 10-2: Transaction.m

```
#import "Transaction.h"
#import "Budget.h"
@implementation Transaction
//- (void) createTransaction: (double) theAmount ofType:
          (transactionType) aType{
- (void) createTransaction: (double) theAmount forBudget:
          (Budget*) aBudget {

  //type = aType;
  budget = aBudget;
  amount = @( theAmount );
}
- (void) spend {

// Fill in the method in subclasses
}

- (void) trackSpending: (double) theAmount {

  NSLog (@"You are about to spend another %.2f",
          theAmount);
}

//- (NSNumber *) returnAmount{
//
```

(continued)

Listing 10-2 *(continued)*

```
//  return amount;
//}

//- (transactionType) returnType {
//
//  return type;
//};
@end
```

Here are the steps you took to create the `Transaction` superclass:

1. Added `#import "Budget.h"` so that the `Transaction` class can access the methods of `Budget`.

2. Changed the method `createTransaction:ofType:` to `createTransaction:forBudget:`, allowing your code to pass in `aBudget` rather than `aType`.

   As I mention earlier, each transaction sends the right message to the `Budget` object, and it has to know what `Budget` it needs to spend against.

3. Created an empty `spend` method to be implemented in the subclasses.

4. Deleted `returnAmount` and `returnType` because you won't need them anymore — that information was needed by the `switch` statement.

5. Added a new method, `trackSpending:`, that shows you how to send messages to inherited methods. (I do that in the `spend:` methods of `CashTransaction` and `CreditCardTransaction`.)

   ```
   - (void) trackSpending: (double) theAmount;
   ```

6. Made the necessary changes (in Listing 10-1) to the interface to support the implementation changes.

   You also included an `@class` statement. Earlier, I explained that the compiler needed to know certain things about classes that you were using, such as what methods you defined and so on, and the `#import` statement in the implementation (.m) file solved that problem. But when you get into objects that point at other objects, you also need to provide that information in the interface file, which can cause a problem if you have circular dependencies (sounds cool, but it is beyond the scope of this book). To solve that problem, Objective-C introduces the `@class` keyword as a way to tell the compiler that the instance variable `budget`, whose type `Budget` the compiler knows nothing about (yet), is a pointer to that class. Knowing that is enough for the compiler, at least in the interface files. You still have to do the `#import` in the implementation file when you refer to methods of that class, however.

If you examine what you have done so far, you realize that you have really created an abstract superclass that creates a protocol for subsequent subclasses.

Adding the files for the new subclasses

Next, you take advantage of what you just did and create two subclasses of `Transaction`, `CashTransaction`, and `CreditCardTransaction`. They inherit all the methods and instance variables of the `Transaction` class, but each implements its own `spend:` method. I also have both methods send a message to their superclass's `trackSpending:` method to show you how to send messages to your superclass.

Object-oriented programmers like to think of subclasses like `CashTransaction` as having an "is a" relationship to their superclasses. A cash transaction "is a" transaction — a `CashTransaction` "is a" `Transaction`.

Now, look at how to create the two new subclasses.

First, you need to create four new files, as you do in Chapter 6. Follow these steps:

1. **Select the `Classes` folder in the Project navigator list.**

   This tells Xcode to place the new file in the `Classes` folder.

2. **Choose File⇨New File (or press ⌘+N) to get the New File dialog.**

3. **In the leftmost column of the dialog, first select Cocoa under OS X; then select the Objective-C class template in the upper-right pane. Click Next.**

   You see a new dialog asking for some more information.

4. **Enter** CashTransaction **in the Class field and enter** Transaction **in the Subclass Of drop-down menu; then click Next.**

   Choose a location to save the new class files (the default location works just fine) and click Create.

5. **Choose File⇨New File again (or press ⌘+N) to get the New File dialog.**

6. **In the leftmost column of the dialog, first select Cocoa under OS X; then select the Objective-C class template in the upper-right pane. Click Next.**

   You see a new dialog asking for some more information.

7. **This time enter** CreditCardTransaction **in the Class field and enter** Transaction **in the Subclass Of drop-down menu; then click Next.**

Choose a location to save the new class files, and click Create.

You should now have four new files under the classes folder: Cash Transaction.h and .m and CreditCardTransaction.h and .m.

Implementing the new subclasses

Now that you have the files for the new subclasses in place, it's time to get to work filling those files with code. You do that by adding and deleting the code in Listings 10-3 and 10-4 to the CashTransaction.m and CreditCard Transaction.m files. The CashTransaction.h and CreditCard Transaction.h files don't require any modification.

Listing 10-3:   CashTransaction.m

```
#import "CashTransaction.h"
#import "Budget.h"

@implementation CashTransaction
- (void) spend {

  [self trackSpending:[amount doubleValue]];
  [budget spendDollars:amount];
}

@end
```

Listing 10-4:   CreditCardTransaction.m

```
#import "CreditCardTransaction.h"
#import "Budget.h"


@implementation CreditCardTransaction
- (void) spend {

  [super trackSpending:[amount doubleValue]];
  [budget chargeForeignCurrency:[amount doubleValue]];
}

@end
```

To add the two new subclasses, you only had to declare the unique behavior in each class. Here are the steps you took to implement these two classes:

1. You left the CashTransaction.h and CreditCardTransaction.h files alone, because Xcode did everything necessary to make them subclasses of Transaction. By entering Transaction in the Subclass Of drop-down menu field, you told Xcode that these two classes would have Transaction as their superclass. Xcode created the correct #import statement and @interface statement to ensure this.

   Your new subclasses inherit all the methods and instance variables of the Transaction class, which includes all the instance variables and methods it inherits from its superclass and so on up the inheritance hierarchy. (In this case, as you can see, the Transaction superclass is NSObject, so it ends there.) So you're cool when it comes to being able to behave like a good Objective-C object.

   Although you didn't do it here, you can also add instance variables to a subclass as well, and as many methods as you need.

2. You added the #import for the Budget interface file to the new classes' implementation files because the Budget class is used by the methods in CashTransaction and CreditCardTransaction.

   As I explain in Chapter 6, you need to import both interface files so that the compiler can understand what Transaction and Budget are.

3. You had CashTransaction and CreditCardTransaction send a message to their superclass's method, trackSpending:.

   trackSpending: displays that you are about to spend some money (a feature my wife, for one, thinks is a good idea to remind me that even though the money looks funny, ordering another bottle of wine does cost something). Notice that I had you do this in two different ways:

   ```
   [self trackSpending:[amount doubleValue]];
   [super trackSpending:[amount doubleValue]];
   ```

   The first statement shows you how to send messages to methods that are part of your class, which includes those that you inherit. As you can see, even though trackSpending: is defined only in the superclass Transaction, you have inherited trackSpending: and the message to self works fine, although unless you have overridden it, you should really use [super trackSpending: amount]. In this case, self and super are interchangeable, but as you see in the Chapter 12 section "Initializing Objects," that isn't always the case.

Modifying main to use the new classes

Now that you have done all the spadework, you can take the final step in making your program much more extensible and enhanceable. You use that new inheritance-based `Transaction` class design in `main`.

To do that, add the code in bold and delete the bold, italic, underlined code in Listing 10-5 to `main` in the `main.m` file.

Listing 10-5:   main in main.m

```
#import <Foundation/Foundation.h>
#import "Budget.h"
#import "Transaction.h"

#import "CashTransaction.h"
#import "CreditCardTransaction.h"

int main (int argc, const char * argv[]) {

//double numberPounds = 100;
//NSNumber *englandDollarTransaction = @100.00;

  Budget  *europeBudget = [Budget new];
  [europeBudget createBudget:1000.00
                                withExchangeRate:1.2500];
  Budget  *englandBudget = [Budget new];
  [englandBudget createBudget:2000.00
                                withExchangeRate:1.5000];

  NSMutableArray *transactions = [[NSMutableArray alloc]
          initWithCapacity:10];
  Transaction *aTransaction ;
  for (int n = 1; n <  2; n++) {
//   aTransaction = [Transaction new];
     aTransaction = [CashTransaction new];
//   [aTransaction createTransaction:n*100 ofType:cash];
     [aTransaction createTransaction:n*100
                                forBudget:europeBudget];
     [transactions addObject:aTransaction];
     aTransaction = [CashTransaction new];
     [aTransaction createTransaction:n*100
                                forBudget:englandBudget];
     [transactions addObject:aTransaction];
  }

  int n =1;
//while (n < 3) {
```

```
   while (n < 4) { //** now 4
//   aTransaction = [Transaction new];

   aTransaction = [CreditCardTransaction new];
//   [aTransaction createTransaction:n*100 ofType:charge];
     [aTransaction createTransaction:n*100
                                   forBudget:europeBudget];
     [transactions addObject:aTransaction];
     aTransaction = [CreditCardTransaction new];
     [aTransaction createTransaction:n*100
                                   forBudget:englandBudget];
     [transactions addObject:aTransaction];
     n++;
   }


//do {
//   aTransaction = [Transaction new];
//   [aTransaction createTransaction:n*100 ofType:charge];
//   [transactions addObject:aTransaction];
//   n++;
//} while (n <= 3);


//Budget  *europeBudget = [Budget new];
//[europeBudget  createBudget:1000.00
                               withExchangeRate:1.2500];

   for (Transaction*  aTransaction in transactions) {
//switch ((int)[aTransaction returnType]) {
//   case cash:
//     [europeBudget spendDollars:[aTransaction
             returnAmount]];
//     break;

//   case charge:
//     [europeBudget chargeForeignCurrency:[aTransaction
             returnAmount]];
//     break;
//   default:
//     break;
     [aTransaction spend];
   }

//Budget *englandBudget = [Budget new];
//[englandBudget createBudget:2000.00
                               withExchangeRate:1.5000];
//[englandBudget spendDollars:englandDollarTransaction];
//[englandBudget chargeForeignCurrency:numberPounds];

   return 0;
}
```

This is what you did in Listing 10-5:

1. You added the necessary #import statements so that the compiler knows what to do with the new classes:

```
#import "CashTransaction.h"
#import "CreditCardTransaction.h"
```

2. You moved up the code that created the Budget objects because you need to use the Budget as an argument when you initialize each Transaction:

```
Budget *europeBudget = [Budget new];
[europeBudget createBudget:1000.00
                withExchangeRate:1.2500];

Budget  *englandBudget = [Budget new];
[englandBudget createBudget:2000.00
                withExchangeRate:1.5000];
```

3. You created cash and credit card transactions for both Europe *and* England in both the for and while loops (to which one more iteration is added — from n = 3 to n = 4):

```
aTransaction = [CreditCardTransaction new];
[aTransaction createTransaction:n*100
                        forBudget:europeBudget];
[transactions addObject:aTransaction];
aTransaction = [CreditCardTransaction new];
[aTransaction createTransaction:n*100
                        forBudget:englandBudget];
[transactions addObject:aTransaction];
```

4. You changed the enumerator to send the spend message to each Transaction object in the transactions array. You deleted

```
[europeBudget spend:aTransaction];
```

and replaced it with

```
[aTransaction spend];
```

This is something you find in many applications — a set of instructions that send the same message to a list of objects. *This is what polymorphism is all about* — a program architecture that makes your program easier to extend. This is because as long as it is a subclass of Transaction, any new transactions immediately can be used in your program without any changes to the rest of your program (except, of course, to create and implement the transaction itself!).

5. You deleted all the stuff that's no longer needed, including the gratuitous do while loop.

After you are done with all that deleting and adding, main looks like what is shown in Listing 10-6. You can see how much "cleaner" it looks. More important, you can see how easy it is to add a new kind of transaction to the mix. All you have to do is create the new transaction type and add it to the array, and it makes itself at home with the rest of the transactions.

Listing 10-6:   main.m

```objc
#import <Foundation/Foundation.h>
#import "Budget.h"

#import "Transaction.h"
#import "CashTransaction.h"
#import "CreditCardTransaction.h"

int main (int argc, const char * argv[]) {

  Budget *europeBudget = [Budget new];
  [europeBudget createBudget:1000.00
                              withExchangeRate:1.2500];
  Budget *englandBudget = [Budget new];
  [englandBudget createBudget:2000.00
                              withExchangeRate:1.5000];


  NSMutableArray *transactions = [[NSMutableArray alloc]
          initWithCapacity:10];
  Transaction *aTransaction ;
for (int n = 1; n < 2; n++) {
    aTransaction = [CashTransaction new];
    [aTransaction createTransaction:n*100
                              forBudget:europeBudget];
    [transactions addObject:aTransaction];
    aTransaction = [CashTransaction new];
    [aTransaction createTransaction:n*100
                              forBudget:englandBudget];
    [transactions addObject:aTransaction];
  }

  int n =1;
  while (n < 4) {
    aTransaction = [CreditCardTransaction new];
    [aTransaction createTransaction:n*100
                              forBudget:europeBudget];
    [transactions addObject:aTransaction];
     aTransaction = [CreditCardTransaction new];
    [aTransaction createTransaction:n*100
                              forBudget:englandBudget];
    [transactions addObject:aTransaction];
    n++;
  }

  for (Transaction* aTransaction in transactions) {
    [aTransaction spend];
  }

  return 0;
}
```

The for and while loops are there only to generate transactions — think of them as simulating a user interface.

Now click the Run button on the Project Window toolbar to build and run the application.

You should see the following in the Debugger Console:

```
You are about to spend another 100.00
Converting 100.00 US dollars into foreign currency leaves
        $900.00
You are about to spend another 100.00
Converting 100.00 US dollars into foreign currency leaves
        $1900.00
You are about to spend another 100.00
Charging 100.00 in foreign currency leaves $775.00
You are about to spend another 100.00
Charging 100.00 in foreign currency leaves $1750.00
You are about to spend another 200.00
Charging 200.00 in foreign currency leaves $525.00
You are about to spend another 200.00
Charging 200.00 in foreign currency leaves $1450.00
You are about to spend another 300.00
Charging 300.00 in foreign currency leaves $150.00
You are about to spend another 300.00
Charging 300.00 in foreign currency leaves $1000.00
```

As expected, the output is the same, except for the additional transactions I added for the England part of my trip (shown in bold), as well as the output from trackSpending:.

You can find the completed project at the website in the Example 10 folder, which can be found in the Chapter 10 folder.

Considering Polymorphism and Inheritance

You have just used one of the Objective-C extensions to C — inheritance — to implement polymorphism (or as I like to think of it, more-of-the-same). As you have seen, polymorphism is the ability of different object types to respond to the same message, each one in its own way. Because each object can have its own version of a method, a program becomes easier to extend and enhance because you don't have to change the message to add functionality. All you have to do is create a new subclass, and it responds to the same messages in its own way.

This enables you to isolate code in the methods of different objects instead of gathering them in a single function that has to know all the possible cases and in control structures such as `if` and `switch` statements. As you have seen, this makes the code you write more extensible and enhanceable, because when a new case comes along, you won't have to recode all those `if` and `switch` statements — you need only add a new class with a new method, leaving well enough alone as far as the code that you've already written, tested, and debugged is concerned.

Using inheritance with polymorphism is one of the extensions to C that is hard to implement without language support. For this to really work, the exact behavior can be determined only at runtime (this is called *late binding* or *dynamic binding*).

When a message is sent, the Objective-C runtime I talk about in Chapter 1 looks at the object you are sending the message to, finds the implementation of the method matching the name, and then invokes that method.

Chapter 11

Encapsulating Objects

● ●

In This Chapter

▶ Understanding the Model-View-Controller pattern

▶ Knowing the role of interfaces

▶ Seeing how composite objects work

▶ Factoring your code to implement Model-View-Controller

● ●

*U*sing encapsulation enables you to safely tuck data behind an object's walls. You can keep the data safe and reduce the dependencies of other parts of your app on what the data is and how it is structured.

Encapsulation is also useful when you apply it to application functionality. When you limit what your objects know about other objects in your application, changing objects or their functionality becomes much easier because it reduces the effect of those changes on the rest of your application.

In this chapter, I show you a way to design, or architect, your application that limits the knowledge that objects have of other objects.

Getting to Know the Model-View-Controller (MVC) Pattern

The Cocoa framework you use on the Mac is designed around certain programming paradigms, known as *design patterns* — a commonly used template that gives you a consistent way to get a particular task done.

Although you need to be comfortable with several design patterns in Cocoa, one of them implements the kind of object encapsulation that reduces the effect of changes to an application — the Model-View-Controller (MVC) design pattern. This design pattern is not unique to Cocoa — a version of it has been in use since the early days of Smalltalk (which the Objective-C extensions to the C language were based on). It goes a long way back, and the fact that it is still being used tells you something about its value.

MVC divides your application into three groups of objects and encourages you to limit the interaction between objects to others in its own group as much as possible. It creates, in effect, a world for the application, placing objects in one of three categories — *model, view,* and *controller,* described in the following list — and specifies roles and responsibilities for all three kinds of objects, as well as the way they're supposed to interact with each other. Model, view, and controller objects are explained in the following list, using an example of a 60-inch flat screen TV:

- **Model objects:** Model objects make up what I call *the content engine* of your application. This is where all the objects (as opposed to the code in the `main` function) you have been developing so far fit in. They process transactions and compute what you have left in your budget. If you were to add things such as hotel objects, train objects, and so on, this is where they belong. They are very generous with what they can do and are happy to share what they know with the rest of your application. But not only do they not care about what other objects use them, or what these other objects do with the information they provide, being good objects, they also really don't want to know.

  You can think of the *model* (which may be one object or several objects that interact) as a particular television program — one that does not give a hoot about what TV set it is being shown on.

- **View objects:** These objects display things on the screen and respond to user actions. This is what is generally thought of as the user interface, and pretty much anything you see on the screen is part of the view group of objects. View objects are pros at formatting and displaying data, as well as handing user interactions, such as allowing the user to enter a credit card transaction, make a new hotel reservation, and add a destination or even create a new trip. But they don't care about where that data comes from and are unaware of the model.

  You can think of the *view* as a television screen that doesn't care about what program it is showing or what channel you just selected.

  If you create an ideal world where the view knows nothing about the model and the model knows nothing about the view, you need to add one more set of objects. These objects connect the model and view — making requests for data from the model and sending that data back for the view to display. This is the collective responsibility of controller objects, described next.

- **Controller objects:** These objects connect the application's view objects to its model objects. They deliver to the view the data that needs to be displayed — getting it from the model. They deliver user requests for current data (how much money do I have left in my budget?) to the model, as well as new data (I just spent 300 euros) to the model as well.

  You can think of the *controller* as the circuitry that pulls the show off the cable and sends it to the screen or that can request a particular pay-per-view show.

One of the advantages of using this application model is that it enables you to separate these three parts of your application and work on them separately. You just need to make sure that each group has a well-defined interface. When the time is right, you just connect the parts — and you have an application.

A category of functionality that is not handled by the MVC pattern exists at the *application level,* or all the nuts and bolts and plumbing needed to run an application. These objects are responsible for startup, shutdown, file management, event handling, and everything else that is not M, V, or C.

Implementing the MVC Pattern

Because you will eventually be providing user-interface functionality, it is time to make sure that you have only model functionality (managing data, for example) in the model objects, and similarly that all the model functionality is in model objects and not scattered in main. That way, you can easily slide the model into place after you define the views and controllers necessary for your application.

Earlier, I said what made the separation between models, views, and controllers possible is a well-defined interface, which I show you how to develop in this chapter. You create an interface between the model and the sometime-in-the-future-to-be-developed controller by using a technique called *composition,* which is a useful way to create interfaces. A composite object is like a toolbox containing different objects, each of which delivers different features and functionality.

I'm a big fan of composition because it's another way to hide what is really going on behind the curtains. It keeps the objects that use the composite object ignorant of the objects that the composite object uses and actually makes the components ignorant of each other, allowing you to switch components in and out at will.

As it stands now, some user-interface type functionality is scattered throughout our model, and a lot of model knowledge is in main, so I start by having you take all the user-interface functionality and putting it in main. You'll also take model functionality out of main and create a new composite object — Destination — that will be the interface to main. You will use main as a surrogate for both the views and controllers that you will be adding in Chapters 17 and 18. Practically speaking, as you'll see, controllers need to be more intimate with views than with models, so I'm comfortable having you place all that functionality in main and then separate it when you develop the user interface.

Now, take a look at the application so far and think about how functionality is currently distributed and what you would have to do to make it consistent with the MVC pattern.

Get out of main

In Listing 11-1, you can look at what goes on in `main` and begin to think about what needs to be moved into the new `Destination` object.

Listing 11-1:   The Current main Function

```
int main (int argc, const char * argv[]) {

   Budget *europeBudget = [Budget new];
   [europeBudget   createBudget:1000.00
                                    withExchangeRate:1.2500];
   Budget *englandBudget = [Budget new];
   [englandBudget createBudget:2000.00
                                    withExchangeRate:1.5000];

   NSMutableArray *transactions =
                [[NSMutableArray alloc] initWithCapacity:10];
   Transaction *aTransaction ;
   for (int n = 1; n <  2; n++) {
      aTransaction = [CashTransaction new];
      [aTransaction createTransaction:n*100
                                    forBudget:europeBudget];
      [transactions addObject:aTransaction];
      aTransaction = [CashTransaction new];
      [aTransaction createTransaction:n*100
                                    forBudget:englandBudget];
      [transactions addObject:aTransaction];
   }

   int n =1;
   while (n < 4) {
      aTransaction = [CreditCardTransaction new];
      [aTransaction createTransaction:n*100
                                    forBudget:europeBudget];
      [transactions addObject:aTransaction];
      aTransaction = [CreditCardTransaction new];
      [aTransaction createTransaction:n*100
                                    forBudget:englandBudget];
      [transactions addObject:aTransaction];
      n++;
   }

   for (Transaction *aTransaction in transactions) {
      [aTransaction spend];
   }

   return 0;
}
```

REMEMBER

Oh no, not factoring again!

While it may appear to you that you have spent a lot of time writing code, only to discard it, that is in fact true.

As I mention earlier, I need to show you both the mechanics of programming in Objective-C and how to use those mechanics to create an application. This means that as you find out more, you need to refine the application to use what you have discovered.

In this chapter especially, you do a major factoring of your code, which you will find, when developing your own applications, is an integral part of the development process.

What comes to my mind is the following:

1. Take the creation of the Budgets for each leg of my trip out of main. While the request for a budget for a new leg of my trip comes from the user interface — hey, I want to go someplace new — it shouldn't be the user interface or controller that creates those Budget objects. It's not in their respective job descriptions.

2. Similarly, take the creation and management of the Transactions for each part of my trip out of main. Although a user interface is definitely responsible for delivering transactions to the model, managing the list of transaction objects is not something that should be in a controller or view.

3. If you do Steps 1 and 2, you also need to take sending the message to each Transaction to apply itself to its Budget out of main.

Get into main

While you're at it, remember that views are responsible for supplying information to the user. Currently, Budget has NSLog statements that will evolve into user-interface functionality. That functionality should be moved into main and later into a view.

Creating a New Project

Now that you have some idea of what you need to move out of `main`, I want you to create a new object — `Destination` — that acts as the interface to `main` and that becomes the composite object for each part of my trip.

Up to now, you've been experimenting with the various features of Objective-C as you built this program. Now that you know quite a bit, it is time to take a more professional attitude toward this project. From this chapter on, you move away from finding out about Objective-C as a *language* and toward how to use the language you mastered to build useful *applications*. I concentrate on architecture and the functionality you need to make your application commercial quality.

I show you how to design this as you would a "real" application and create a structure that will actually be the basis for an application of this type, in case you want to move forward with it.

You start by creating a new project that will be the basis for your commercial-quality application (and also because the name *Budget Object* no longer describes what the application is about). I also want you to go through creating a new project so that I can show you the mechanics for reusing the classes you've developed thus far in a new project — something you'll likely be doing regularly.

You create a new project here. You can do that, or you can skip Steps 1 through 9 (I know it's tedious, but it's for your own good) and start with the Project in Example 11A, in the Chapter 11 folder at the website. Or, if prefer to start from a clean copy of the project from where you left off, you can use the project found at the website in the Chapter 11 Start Here folder, which is in the Chapter 11 folder.

You follow these steps to get started with the Vacation project:

1. **Launch Xcode.**

2. **Start the New Project Assistant by Choosing File⇨New⇨Project to create a new project.**

3. **In the New Project window, click Application under the OS X heading.**

4. **Select Command Line Tool from the choices displayed and then click Next.**

Enter Vacation **in the Product Name field and select Foundation from the Type drop menu. Make sure that the Use Automatic Reference Counting check box is selected. Click Next.**

Xcode then displays a standard save sheet.

5. **Click Create.**

   After you click Save, Xcode creates the project and opens the project window.

6. **Go back to Xcode, open the previous version of the Budget Object project (or the project found in the Chapter 11 Start Here folder, which is in the Chapter 11 folder at the website), and place it next to your new project, as shown in Figure 11-1.**

7. **Create a new group in** Vacation **and name it** Classes.

   Drag the files in the Classes **group from the Budget Object project to the new one, as shown in Figure 11-1.**

   An alternative is to click the Classes group in the new project and choose Project⇨Add to Project. Then navigate to the files you want to add (I show you how to do that in more detail in Chapter 18).

Figure 11-1:
Drag the
Classes
folder to the
new project.

The Copy dialog shown in Figure 11-2 appears.

8. **Be sure to select the Copy Items check box (if needed) to copy items into the destination group's folder, as shown in Figure 11-2. Make sure that the** Vacation **target is checked in the Add to Targets list. Click Finish.**

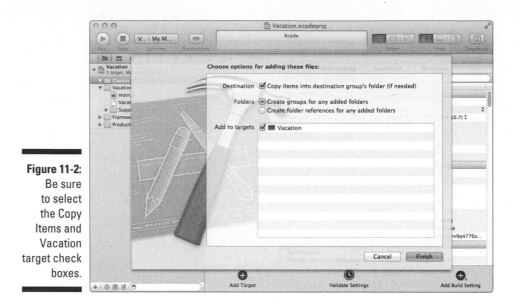

Figure 11-2:
Be sure
to select
the Copy
Items and
Vacation
target check
boxes.

9. **Select and copy all the code in `main.m` in the Budget Object Xcode project. Then delete everything in `main.m` in the new project and paste what was in `main.m` of the Budget Object Xcode project into `main.m` of the Vacation Xcode project (see Figure 11-3).**

Figure 11-3:
Copy
`main.m`
from Budget
Object and
paste it into
`main.m` in
Vacation.

10. **To make sure that the preceding steps worked, click the Run button on the Project Window toolbar to build and run the application.**

You should see the following in the Debugger Console:

```
You are about to spend another 100.00
Converting 100.00 US dollars into foreign currency
        leaves $900.00
You are about to spend another 100.00
Converting 100.00 US dollars into foreign currency
        leaves $1900.00
You are about to spend another 100.00
Charging 100.00 in foreign currency leaves $775.00
You are about to spend another 100.00
Charging 100.00 in foreign currency leaves $1750.00
You are about to spend another 200.00
Charging 200.00 in foreign currency leaves $525.00
You are about to spend another 200.00
Charging 200.00 in foreign currency leaves $1450.00
You are about to spend another 300.00
Charging 300.00 in foreign currency leaves $150.00
You are about to spend another 300.00
Charging 300.00 in foreign currency leaves $1000.00
```

Nice to see that the application still works. Now, it's time to get down to work.

You can find the completed project at the website in the Example 11A folder, which is in the Chapter 11 folder.

Creating the Destination Class

If you have been following along with me, I extend what you just did in the first exercise. If you prefer to start from a clean copy of the project from where you left off, you can use the project found in the Example 11A folder, which is in the Chapter 11 folder.

The next thing I want you to do is to add the new `Destination` object, as follows:

1. **Select the `Classes` group in the Project navigator.**

   This tells Xcode to place the new file in the `Classes` group.

2. **Choose File⇨New⇨File (or press ⌘+N) to get the New File dialog.**

3. **In the leftmost column of the dialog, select Cocoa under OS X and then select the Objective-C class template in the upper-right pane. Click Next.**

   You see a new screen asking for some more information.

4. **Enter** Destination **in the Class field and make sure that NSObject is selected in the Subclass Of drop menu. Click Next.**

5. **Save the new class files in the default location and click Create.**

Now, take a look at designing and implementing this new Destination class. The @interface file — Destination.h — is where the design of the class resides, and this is where other classes that use the Destination class will find what the Destination class provides for other classes to use.

To act as an interface to be used by a controller, the Destination class needs to declare methods that do the following:

✔ Create Transaction objects from the transaction amounts that will be sent from the user interface.

✔ Return the data that the user interface needs to display.

In Listing 11-2, in the following section, you can see that the Destination class interface accomplishes both of the preceding tasks.

Designing the destination

Enter the bold code in Listing 11-2 into the Destination.h file.

Listing 11-2:   Destination.h — the Destination Design

```
#import <Foundation/Foundation.h>
@class Budget;
@interface Destination : NSObject
{

  NSString       *country;
  NSMutableArray *transactions;
  Budget         *theBudget;
}

- (void) createWithCountry: (NSString*) theCountry
          andBudget: (double) budgetAmount
          withExchangeRate: (double) theExchangeRate;
- (void) spendCash: (double) amount;
- (void) chargeCreditCard: (double) amount;
- (double) leftToSpend;

@end
```

The methods and instance variables you declared in this class will enable you to do the following:

1. `createWithCountry:andBudget:withExchangeRate:`'s arguments will enable you to initialize a new `Destination` with the country you are headed to (as you can see, as you factor the code, I have you add additional functionality that you can use), the amount you want to budget, and the current exchange rate.

2. Create the `Budget` object previously created in `main`. This was the first goal in the section "Get out of/into main."

3. Create and manage a `Transaction` array. This supports the second goal in the section "Get out of/into main," earlier in this chapter.

4. Enable `main` (the controller surrogate) to send transaction amounts to the `Destination` object (by sending the `spendCash:` and `charge CreditCard:` messages). The `Destination` object can then, in turn, create and manage the appropriate `Transaction` objects and send them the `spend:` message. This was the balance of the second goal in the section "Get out of/into main."

5. Enable the `main` (by sending the `leftToSpend`) method to ask the model for the information it needs to deliver to the surrogate user interface. This displays how much money remains in the budget.

   Notice the instance variables that reference other objects — the `transactions` array and `theBudget`. This is a model for what makes a composite object and how it gets its work done — using other objects to distribute the work.

   Object-oriented programmers like to think of composite objects like `Destination` as having a "has a" relationship to their parts. The destination "has a" budget, for example.

Now, it's time to take a look at how to implement these methods.

Implementing the methods

Enter the bold code in Listing 11-3 into the `Destination.m` file.

Listing 11-3:   Destination.m

```objc
#import "Destination.h"
#import "CashTransaction.h"
#import "CreditCardTransaction.h"
#import "Budget.h"
#import "Transaction.h"

@implementation Destination

- (void) createWithCountry: (NSString*) theCountry
          andBudget: (double) budgetAmount
          withExchangeRate: (double) theExchangeRate{

  transactions = [[NSMutableArray alloc]
                                     initWithCapacity:10];
  theBudget = [Budget new];
  [theBudget createBudget:budgetAmount
                      withExchangeRate:theExchangeRate];
  country = theCountry;
  NSLog (@"I'm off to %@", theCountry);
}


-(void) spendCash: (double) amount {

  Transaction *aTransaction = [CashTransaction new];
  [aTransaction createTransaction:amount
                                   forBudget:theBudget];
  [transactions addObject:aTransaction];
  [aTransaction spend];
}

-(void) chargeCreditCard: (double) amount {

  Transaction *aTransaction = [CreditCardTransaction new];
  [aTransaction createTransaction:amount
                                   forBudget:theBudget];
  [transactions addObject:aTransaction];
  [aTransaction spend];
}

- (double) leftToSpend {

  return [theBudget returnBalance];
}

@end
```

All of this is pretty straightforward. It is either what was being done in main before or new code to implement the new functionality.

This new functionality is as follows:

- ✔ A new method leftToSpend: It is there, as I said, to provide the user interface with the data it needs to display. (This also requires adding a new method to Budget, as you see next.)

- ✔ A new NSLog statement:

```
NSLog (@"I'm off to %@", theCountry);
```

This statement in Destination is not intended to be part of the user interface — you are just including it to trace program execution (I also use it to illustrate some points about memory management in Chapter 13). It uses my newly minted country instance variable.

You may notice that Xcode flags the one line of code in the method leftToSpend as an error. Xcode is correct: The statement return [theBudget returnBalance] is trying to send the message returnBalance to the Budget object, only you haven't modified the Budget.h or Budget.m file yet. Xcode is your loyal servant, pointing out that what it sees is a mistake. You can safely ignore this because I have you enter the modifications to Budget next.

Modifying the Budget class

Finishing the implementation of the Destination object's functionality as the interface to the model requires that you make changes to the Budget class. Because the Destination object is responsible for reporting to the controller the amount left to spend, it needs to get the amount from the Budget object, requiring you to add a new method, returnBalance, to Budget. And in line with factoring all your code to move all user-interface functionality out of the model objects, you also need to remove the "user interface" from Budget — that is, the NSLog statements. You do all of this by following these steps:

1. **Delete the bold, italic, underlined code in Listing 11-4 in the** Budget.m **file. Then add the code in bold.**

Listing 11-4: Budget.m

```objc
#import "Budget.h"

@implementation Budget

- (void) createBudget: (double) aBudget
            withExchangeRate: (float) anExchangeRate {

  exchangeRate = anExchangeRate;
  budget = aBudget;
}

- (void) spendDollars: (double) dollars {

  budget -= dollars;
//NSLog(@"Converting %.2f US dollars into foreign currency
         leaves $%.2f", dollars, budget);
}

- (void) chargeForeignCurrency: (double) foreignCurrency {

  exchangeTransaction = foreignCurrency*exchangeRate;
  budget -= exchangeTransaction;
//NSLog(@"Charging %.2f in foreign currency leaves $%.2f",
         foreignCurrency, budget);
}

- (double) returnBalance {

  return budget;
}

@end
```

2. **Add the code in bold in Listing 11-5 to the** Budget.h **file.**

Listing 11-5: Budget.h

```objc
#import <Foundation/Foundation.h>

@interface Budget : NSObject {

  float  exchangeRate;
  double budget;
  double exchangeTransaction;
}

- (void) createBudget: (double) aBudget
            withExchangeRate: (float) anExchangeRate;
```

```
- (void) spendDollars: (double) dollars ;

- (void) chargeForeignCurrency: (double) foreignCurrency;
- (double) returnBalance;
@end
```

Removing UI type functionality from the Transaction objects

Because you are moving all the user-interface functionality out of the model, you can delete the Transaction's trackSpending message used by CashTransaction and CreditCardTransaction. You implement comparable functionality in main.

Delete the bold, italic, underlined code in Listings 11-6 through 11-9.

Listing 11-6:   Transaction.h

```
#import <Foundation/Foundation.h>
@class Budget;
@interface Transaction : NSObject {

  Budget *budget;
  NSNumber *amount;
}

- (void) createTransaction: (double) theAmount forBudget:
        (Budget*) aBudget;
- (void) spend;
//- (void) trackSpending: (double) theAmount;

@end
```

Listing 11-7:   Transaction.m

```
#import "Transaction.h"
#import "Budget.h"

@implementation Transaction

- (void) createTransaction: (double) theAmount forBudget:
        (Budget*) aBudget {
```

(continued)

Listing 11-7 *(continued)*

```
  budget = aBudget;
  amount = @( theAmount );
}

- (void) spend {

}

//- (void) trackSpending: (double) theAmount {
//    NSLog (@"You are about to spend another %.2f",
          theAmount);
//}

@end
```

Listing 11-8:   CashTransaction.m

```
#import "CashTransaction.h"
#import "Budget.h"

@implementation CashTransaction

- (void) spend {

//[self trackSpending:[amount doubleValue]];
  [budget spendDollars:[amount doubleValue]];
}

@end
```

Listing 11-9:   CreditCardTransaction.m

```
#import "CreditCardTransaction.h"
#import "Budget.h"

@implementation CreditCardTransaction

- (void) spend {

//[super trackSpending:[amount doubleValue]];
  [budget chargeForeignCurrency:[amount doubleValue]];
}

@end
```

Coding the New main

That leaves only `main`. As I said, the functionality that remains there acts as a surrogate for the user interface and controller.

Because the changes you need to make to `main` are so significant, it's easier to delete everything in `main` and start from scratch. So, in the `main.m` file, replace `main` with Listing 11-10. (Notice that you no longer need that long list of `#import`s in `main`, shown in the following code, because now its sole interface to the model is through `Destination`.)

```
#import "Budget.h"
#import "Transaction.h"
#import "CashTransaction.h"
#import "CreditCardTransaction.h"
```

Listing 11-10: The New main Function in Vacation.m

```
#import <Foundation/Foundation.h>
#import "Destination.h"

int main (int argc, const char * argv[]) {

  Destination* europe = [Destination new] ;
  NSString* europeText = [[NSString alloc]
                      initWithFormat:@"%@", @"Europe"];
  [europe createWithCountry:europeText andBudget:1000.00
                              withExchangeRate:1.25];
  Destination* england = [Destination new] ;
  NSString* englandText = [[NSString alloc]
                      initWithFormat:@"%@", @"England"];
  [england createWithCountry:englandText andBudget:2000.00
                              withExchangeRate:1.50];

  for (int n = 1; n < 2; n++) {
    double transaction = n*100.00;
    NSLog(@"Sending a %.2f cash transaction",
                                    transaction);
    [europe spendCash:transaction];
    NSLog(@"Remaining budget %.2f", [europe leftToSpend]);
    NSLog(@"Sending a %.2f cash transaction",
                                    transaction);
    [england spendCash:transaction];
    NSLog(@"Remaining budget %.2f",
                              [england leftToSpend]);
  }

  int n = 1;
```

(continued)

Listing 11-10 *(continued)*

```
while (n < 4) {
  double transaction = n*100.00;
  NSLog(@"Sending a %.2f credit card transaction",
                                    transaction);
  [europe chargeCreditCard:transaction];
  NSLog(@"Remaining budget %.2f", [europe leftToSpend]);
  NSLog(@"Sending a %.2f credit card transaction",
                                    transaction);
  [england chargeCreditCard:transaction];
  NSLog(@"Remaining budget %.2f",
                              [england leftToSpend]);

  n++;
}

return 0;
}
```

I want to review exactly what you did when you added the new code to main:

1. You started by creating the destination objects:

   ```
   Destination* europe = [Destination new];
   ```

   One interesting thing is the way that you created the country string to use as an argument:

   ```
   NSString* europeText = [[NSString alloc]
                 initWithFormat:@"%@", @"Europe"];
   ```

   This initializes a new string as the result of a formatting operation, just like you've been doing within the NSLog statements, except here I'm creating an honest-to-goodness NSString object to use as the country argument in createWithCountry:andBudget:withExchangeRate:. You have alternative ways to create a string, but you will use initWith Format: fairly often when you're writing code to display information your program may not know before it's executing.

2. You then initialized the Destination object for Europe and created and initialized the Destination object for England:

   ```
   [europe createWithCountry:europeText
           andBudget:1000.00 withExchangeRate:1.25];
   Destination* england = [Destination new];
   NSString* englandText = [[NSString alloc]
                 initWithFormat:@"%@", @"England"];
   [england createWithCountry:englandText
           andBudget:2000.00 withExchangeRate:1.50];
   ```

3. Then you sent some transaction *amounts* to the `Destination` objects. Notice that you are no longer creating `Transaction` objects, but simply sending transaction amounts:

```
[europe spendCash:transaction];
...
[england chargeCreditCard:transaction];
```

4. You added `NSLog` statements to "simulate" user-interface behavior. The first `NSLog` lets you know that the user will be entering a transaction. The second `NSLog` acts as a surrogate for displaying the updated budget information to the user. It uses the new `leftToSpend` method. As you will see when you create your controllers, `spendCash:` and `charge CreditCard:` will be the methods the controllers use to send data to the model, and the `leftToSpend` method will be used to request data from the model.

To make sure that this worked, click the Run button on the Project Window toolbar to build and run the application.

You should see the following in the Debugger Console:

```
I'm off to Europe
I'm off to England
Sending a 100.00 cash transaction
Remaining budget 900.00
Sending a 100.00 cash transaction
Remaining budget 1900.00
Sending a 100.00 credit card transaction
Remaining budget 775.00
Sending a 100.00 credit card transaction
Remaining budget 1750.00
Sending a 200.00 credit card transaction
Remaining budget 525.00
Sending a 200.00 credit card transaction
Remaining budget 1450.00
Sending a 300.00 credit card transaction
Remaining budget 150.00
Sending a 300.00 credit card transaction
Remaining budget 1000.00
```

You can find the completed project at the website in the Example 11B folder, which is in the Chapter 11 folder.

If I were designing this application from scratch, rather than using it as a way to show you how to program in Objective-C, I'd actually end up in the same place. The difference is that I would have started with this `Destination` object in the beginning. Then I would have created the `Budget` and `Transaction` objects that the `Destination` needs, instead of taking the `Budget` and `Transaction` objects that already exist and making them part of `Destination`.

Yes, Another Two Steps Forward and One Step Back

What you've accomplished in this chapter is significant. You have factored your code in a way that will make adding an iPhone user interface in Chapter 17 and a Mac user interface in Chapter 18 as easy as pie.

You have achieved this at a cost, however — the time and effort needed to factor your code.

As I mention earlier, I need to show you both the mechanics of programming in Objective-C and how to use those mechanics to create an application. This means that as you find out more, you need to refine the application to use what you have discovered.

Although, to be fair, if I were talking only about application design, I would have started with a `Destination` object from the beginning — and I expect in the future, based on what you have discovered in this chapter, you will, too.

Chapter 12

The Birth of an Object

U p until now, you have been doing initialization on an ad hoc basis, using initialization methods such as these:

```
- (void) createTransaction: (double) theAmount
                           forBudget: (Budget*) aBudget;
- (void) createBudget: (double) aBudget
                 withExchangeRate: (float) anExchangeRate;
```

A standard way exists to do initialization, however — one designed to work in a class hierarchy that ensures that all the superclasses and subclasses are initialized properly.

In this chapter, I show you how to implement these standard initialization methods. First, though, you must allocate memory for the new object, as described in the first section of this chapter.

Allocating Objects

To create an object in Objective-C, you must do the following:

1. **Allocate memory for the new object.**

2. **Initialize the newly allocated memory, as described in the next section.**

Allocation (`alloc`) starts the process of creating a new object by getting the amount of memory it needs from the operating system to hold all the object's instance variables. The `alloc` message is sent to the `NSObject` class, from which all the classes you are using are derived. But not only does the `alloc` method allocate the memory for the object. It also initializes all the memory it allocates to 0 — all the `int`s are 0, all the `float`s become 0.0, all the pointers are `nil`, and the object's `isa` instance variable points to the object's class (this tells an object of what class it is an instance).

Well, at least that was easy.

Initializing Objects

Initialization is not required. And if you can live with all the instance variables initialized to 0 and `nil`, you don't need to do anything. But if your class (or your superclass) has instance variables that you need to initialize to anything other than 0 or `nil`, you are going to have to code some kind of initialization method.

The initialization method does not have to include an argument for every instance variable because some will only become relevant during the course of your object's existence. You must make sure, however, that all the instance variables your object needs, including objects it needs to do its work, are in a state that enables your object to respond to the messages it is sent.

For example, right after

```
Destination *europe = [Destination new]
```

I had you code a method

```
- (void) createWithCountry: (NSString*) theCountry
            andBudget: (double) budgetAmount
            withExchangeRate: (double) theExchangeRate;
```

in which you created a budget, created a transactions array, and set the exchange rate.

In fact, the `Destination` object you created was unusable until you did that.

You may think that the main job in initialization is to, well, initialize your objects (hence, the name), but more is involved when you have a superclass and a subclass chain.

Start by looking at the new initializer that I have you code for the CashTransaction class in Listing 12-1.

Listing 12-1:   CashTransaction Initializer

```
- (id) initWithAmount: (double) theAmount forBudget:
          (Budget*) aBudget {

  if (self = [super initWithAmount:theAmount
                              forBudget:aBudget]) {

    name = @"Cash";
  }
  return self;
}
```

By convention, initialization methods begin with the abbreviation init. (This is true, however, only for instance — as opposed to class — methods.) If the method takes no arguments, the method name is just init. If it takes arguments, labels for the arguments follow the *init* prefix. For example, you have been initializing NSMutableArrays with the initWithCapacity: method. As you can see, the initializer has to have a return type of id. You discover the reason for that in the next section.

The CashTransaction initializer calls its superclass's initializer like this:

```
  if (self = [super initWithAmount:theAmount
                              forBudget:aBudget]) {
```

I named my new initializer initWithAmount: plus another argument (for Budget) that completely describes what I am going to initialize. It should be no surprise that both of these are initialized in the createTransaction: forBudget: method you have been using to initialize a transaction.

Initialization involves these three steps:

1. Invoke the superclass's init method.

2. Initialize instance variables.

3. Return self.

The following sections explain each step.

Invoking the superclass's init method

This is the general form you use:

```
self = [super initWithAmount:theAmount
                                   forBudget:aBudget]
```

If you are having a little problem figuring this out, you might like to know that it took me more than a few minutes to get my arms around this statement, so don't feel bad. Fortunately, I do understand it now, and I explain it to you very slowly (which is what I wish that someone had done for me).

I start with the easy part of the compound statement, where all I do is invoke the superclass's init method:

```
[super initWithAmount:theAmount forBudget:aBudget]
```

In Chapter 10, you see that this is how you send a message to your superclass.

In Chapter 10, you also see that you can use self to send a message to your superclass, and I also say that self and super are not always interchangeable. In this case, you need to be careful to use super because the method that's sending the message has the same name as the method you want to invoke in your superclass. If you were to use self here, you would just send a message to yourself, the initWithAmount:forBudget: method in CashTransaction, which would turn around and send the same message to itself again, which would then send the same message to itself again. . . . You get the picture. Fortunately, the OS will put up with this for only a limited amount of time before it gets really annoyed and terminates the program.

Notice that the superclass's initialization method is always invoked before the subclass does any initialization. Your superclass is equally as respectful of its superclass and does the same thing. And up, up, and away you go from superclass to superclass until you reach NSObject's init method. NSObject's init method doesn't do anything; it just returns self. It's there to establish the naming convention described earlier, and all it does is return to its invoker, which does its thing and then returns to its invoker, until it gets back to you.

In this case, the CashTransaction's superclass is Transaction, and you invoke its initialization method initWithAmount:forBudget:. As you can see in Listing 12-2, Transaction invokes its superclass's init method as well. But in this case, it simply calls init (as per convention) because its superclass is NSObject.

Listing 12-2:   Transaction Initializer

```
- (id) initWithAmount: (double) theAmount forBudget:
          (Budget*) aBudget {

 if (self = [super init]) {

   budget = aBudget;
   amount = @( theAmount );
   }
  return self;
}
```

Next, examine this unusual-looking statement:

```
if (self = [super initWithAmount:theAmount
          forBudget:aBudget]) {
```

Ignore the `if` for the moment (I promise I'll get back to it). What you are doing is assigning what you got back from your superclass's `init` method to `self`. As you remember, `self` is the "hidden" variable accessible to methods in an object that points to its instance variables (if you're unclear on this, refer to the discussion in Chapter 6). So, it would seem that `self` should be whatever you got back from your allocation step. Well, yes and no. Most of the time, the answer is yes; but sometimes the answer is no, which may or may not be a big deal. So, examine the possibilities.

When you invoke a superclass's initialization method, one of three things can happen:

- **You get back the object you expect.** Most of the time, this is precisely what happens, and you go on your merry way. This will be true all the time for the classes you are working on in this part of the book — those where you have control over the entire hierarchy — such as the `Transaction` class you are working on now.

- **You get back a different object type.** Getting back a different object type is something that can happen with some of the framework classes, but it's not an issue here. Even when it happens, if you are playing by the rules (a good idea if you're not the one who gets to make them), you don't even care.

  Why, you might ask? Well, some of the framework classes such as `NSString` are really class clusters. When you create an object of one of these classes, its initialization method looks at the arguments you are passing and returns the object it thinks you need (big brotherish to say the least, but effective nonetheless). Anything more about getting back different object types is way beyond the scope of this book.

But as I said, if you follow the rules, not only will you not notice getting back a different object type, but you also won't care. It is in these cases that the compound statement format I've been showing you is important:

```
SomeClass *aPointerToSomeClass =
                        [[SomeClass alloc] init];
```

If you had done the following

```
SomeClass *aPointerToSomeClass = [SomeClass alloc];
[aPointerToSomeClass init];
```

`init` could return a different pointer, which you haven't assigned to `aPointerToSomeClass`. If you then send that object a message, you are in for a big surprise. This is also why the return type for an initializer needs to be `id` (a pointer to an object) and not the specific class you are dealing with.

✔ **You get `nil` back.**

One possibility, of course, is that you simply run out of memory or some catastrophe befalls the system, in which case you are in deep trouble. While you might be able to do some things, they aren't for the faint-hearted or beginners, so I skip them for now.

Getting back `nil` actually explains the statement that seems so puzzling:

```
if (self = [super initWithAmount:theAmount
        forBudget:aBudget]) {
```

When `nil` is returned, two things happen: `self` is *assigned* to `nil`, which as a side effect causes the `if` statement to be evaluated as NO. As a result, the code block that contains the statements you would have used to initialize your subclass is never executed.

Initializing instance variables

Initializing instance variables, including creating the objects you need, is what you probably thought initialization is about. Notice that you are initializing your instance variable after your superclass's initialization, which you can see in Listings 12-1 and 12-2. Waiting until after your superclass does its initialization gives you the opportunity to actually change something that your superclass may have in initialization, but more important, it enables you to perform initialization knowing that what you have inherited is initialized and ready to be used.

In the `CashTransaction initWithAmount:forBudget:` initializer, all that is done is the initialization of the `name` instance variable of the superclass (`Transaction`) with the kind of transaction it is:

```
name = @"Cash";
```

Returning self

In the section "Invoking the superclass's init method," earlier in this chapter, the `self =` statement ensures that `self` is set to whatever object you get back from the superclass initializer. After the code block that initializes the variables, you find

```
return self;
```

No matter what you get back from invoking the superclass initializer, in the initialization method, you need to set `self` to that value and then return it to the invoking method. The method that invokes your class's initializer could be a method in another part of your code that is creating an instance of your class. Or it could be a subclass that is itself being initialized and is invoking its superclass's initializer to ensure that its data is ready to go when the subclass object needs it.

When you are instantiating a new object, it behooves you to determine whether a return of `nil` is a nonfatal response to your request (and if so, coding for it). In this book, the answer is always no, and that will generally be the case with framework objects as well. In this example

```
theBudget = [[Budget alloc] initWithAmount:budgetAmount
            withExchangeRate:theExchangeRate];
```

getting `nil` back is more than my poor app can handle and signals that I am in very deep trouble.

Listings 12-3 through 12-11 show the modifications that you need to make to finally implement initializers in the conventional way. You'll be deleting the initializers you had been using and creating the correct `init...` structure that will enable you to more easily initialize new instance variables that you may add to existing classes, as well as ensuring that you can do initialization correctly when you add new superclasses or subclasses.

If you have been following along with me, I extend what you do in Chapter 11. If you prefer to start from a clean copy of the project from where you left off, you can use the project at the website found in the Chapter 12 Start Here folder, which is in the Chapter 12 folder.

Because the changes you need to make are quite specific, I just indicate what needs to be deleted with bold, italic, and underline and what needs to be added in bold in each file in Listings 12-3 through 12-8. (Be sure to note the new name instance variable in Transaction.h.)

Listing 12-3:   Budget.h

```
//- (void) createBudget: (double) aBudget
                withExchangeRate: (float) anExchangeRate;
- (id) initWithAmount: (double) aBudget
           withExchangeRate: (double) anExchangeRate ;
```

Listing 12-4:   Budget.m

```
//- (void) createBudget: (double) aBudget
                withExchangeRate: (float) anExchangeRate{
//  exchangeRate = anExchangeRate;
//  budget = aBudget;
//}
- (id) initWithAmount: (double) aBudget
              withExchangeRate: (double) anExchangeRate {

  if (self = [super init]) {
    exchangeRate = anExchangeRate;
    budget = aBudget;
  }
  return self;
}
```

Listing 12-5:   Transaction.h

```
@interface Transaction : NSObject
{
  NSString *name;
  Budget *budget;
  NSNumber *amount;
}
//- void) createTransaction: (double) theAmount
                         forBudget: (Budget*) aBudget;
- (id) initWithAmount: (double) theAmount
                    forBudget: (Budget*) aBudget;
```

Listing 12-6:   Transaction.m

```
//- (void) createTransaction: (double) theAmount
          forBudget: (Budget*) aBudget {
//   budget = aBudget;
//   amount = theAmount;
// }

- (id) initWithAmount: (double) theAmount
                         forBudget: (Budget*) aBudget {

  if (self = [super init]) {

    budget = aBudget;
    amount = @( theAmount );
  }
  return self;
}
```

Listing 12-7:   CashTransaction.m

```
- (id) initWithAmount: (double) theAmount
                         forBudget: (Budget*) aBudget {

  if (self = [super initWithAmount:theAmount
                                forBudget:aBudget]) {
    name = @"Cash";
  }
  return self;
}
```

Listing 12-8:   CreditCardTransaction.m

```
- (id) initWithAmount: (double) theAmount
                         forBudget: (Budget*) aBudget {

  if (self = [super initWithAmount:theAmount
                                forBudget:aBudget]) {
    name = @"Credit card";
  }
  return self;
}
```

You probably notice that I didn't have you add a method declaration in the @interface file for the initializer method for either CashTransaction or CreditCardTransaction. That's because the initializer method — initWithAmount:forBudget: — is identical to that declared in the superclass, Transaction. Objective-C knows about the method declared in the superclass, and so when you implement an identical method in the subclass — possibly to do some additional initialization — Objective-C does the right thing.

Because the changes to the Destination class and main are a bit more involved, I include all the code in Listings 12-9 through 12-11.

Listing 12-9:   Destination.h

```
#import <Foundation/Foundation.h>
@class Budget;

@interface Destination : NSObject {

  NSString        *country;
NSMutableArray *transactions;
  Budget          *theBudget;

}
//(void) createWithCountry: (NSString*) theCountry
         andBudget: (double) budgetAmount
            withExchangeRate: (double) theExchangeRate;
- (id) initWithCountry: (NSString*) theCountry
         andBudget: (double) budgetAmount
            withExchangeRate:(double) theExchangeRate;
- (void) spendCash: (double) aTransaction;
- (void) chargeCreditCard:(double) aTransaction;
- (double) leftToSpend;

@end
```

Listing 12-10:   Destination.m

```
#import "Destination.h"
#import "CashTransaction.h"
#import "CreditCardTransaction.h"
#import "Budget.h"
#import "Transaction.h"
@implementation Destination

//- (void) createWithCountry: (NSString*) theCountry
         andBudget: (double) budgetAmount
            withExchangeRate: (double) theExchangeRate{

//   transactions = [[NSMutableArray alloc]
         initWithCapacity:10];
//   theBudget = [Budget new];
//   [theBudget  createBudget:budgetAmount withExchangeRate
            :theExchangeRate];
//   exchangeRate = theExchangeRate;
//   country = theCountry;
//   NSLog (@"I'm off to %@", theCountry);
//}
```

```
- (id) initWithCountry: (NSString*) theCountry andBudget:
        (double) budgetAmount withExchangeRate:
        (double) theExchangeRate{
  if (self = [super init]) {
    transactions = [[NSMutableArray alloc]
          initWithCapacity:10];
    theBudget = [[Budget alloc]
          initWithAmount:budgetAmount withExchangeRate:
          theExchangeRate];
    country = theCountry;
    NSLog (@"I'm off to %@", theCountry);
  }

  return self;
}


-(void) spendCash:(double)amount{

//Transaction *aTransaction = [CashTransaction new];
//aTransaction createTransaction:amount
                              forBudget:theBudget];
  Transaction *aTransaction = [[CashTransaction alloc]
        initWithAmount:amount forBudget:theBudget];
  [transactions addObject:aTransaction];
  [aTransaction spend];
}

-(void) chargeCreditCard: (double) amount{

//Transaction *aTransaction = [CreditCardTransaction new];
//[aTransaction createTransaction:amount
                              forBudget:theBudget];
  Transaction *aTransaction =
        [[CreditCardTransaction alloc]
        initWithAmount:amount forBudget:theBudget];
  [transactions addObject:aTransaction];
  [aTransaction spend];
}

- (double ) leftToSpend {

  return [theBudget returnBalance];
}

@end
```

Listing 12-11:   main in main.m

```objc
#import <Foundation/Foundation.h>
#import "Destination.h"

int main (int argc, const char * argv[]) {

//Destination* europe = [Destination new] ;
  NSString* europeText = [[NSString alloc]
        initWithFormat:@"%@", @"Europe"];
//[europe createWithCountry:europeText andBudget:1000.00
        withExchangeRate:1.25];
  Destination* europe = [[Destination alloc]
        initWithCountry:europeText andBudget:1000.00
        withExchangeRate:1.25];
//Destination* england = [Destination new] ;
  NSString* englandText = [[NSString alloc]
                    initWithFormat:@"%@", @"England"];
//[england createWithCountry:englandText andBudget:2000.00
        withExchangeRate:1.50];
  Destination* england = [[Destination alloc]
        initWithCountry:englandText andBudget:2000.00
        withExchangeRate:1.50];

  for (int n = 1; n < 2; n++) {
    double transaction = n*100.00;
    NSLog (@"Sending a %.2f cash transaction",
        transaction);
    [europe spendCash:transaction];
    NSLog(@"Remaining budget %.2f", [europe leftToSpend]);
    NSLog (@"Sending a %.2f cash transaction",
        transaction);
    [england spendCash:transaction];
    NSLog(@"Remaining budget %.2f", [england
        leftToSpend]);
  }

  int n = 1;
  while (n < 4) {
    double transaction = n*100.00;
    NSLog(@"Sending a %.2f credit card transaction",
        transaction);
    [europe chargeCreditCard:transaction];
    NSLog(@"Remaining budget %.2f", [europe leftToSpend]);
    NSLog(@"Sending a %.2f credit card transaction",
        transaction);
    [england chargeCreditCard:transaction];
    NSLog(@"Remaining budget %.2f", [england
        leftToSpend]);
    n++;
  }
  return 0;
}
```

To make sure that this worked, click the Run button on the Project Window toolbar to build and run the application.

You should see the following in the Debugger Console. This output should be identical to the output in the previous example:

```
I'm off to Europe
I'm off to England
Sending a 100.00 cash transaction
Remaining budget 900.00
Sending a 100.00 cash transaction
Remaining budget 1900.00
Sending a 100.00 credit card transaction
Remaining budget 775.00
Sending a 100.00 credit card transaction
Remaining budget 1750.00
Sending a 200.00 credit card transaction
Remaining budget 525.00
Sending a 200.00 credit card transaction
Remaining budget 1450.00
Sending a 300.00 credit card transaction
Remaining budget 150.00
Sending a 300.00 credit card transaction
Remaining budget 1000.00
```

The Designated Initializer

You can have more than one initializer per class. After you have more than one initializer in a class, according to Cocoa convention, you are expected to designate one as the *designated initializer*. This designated initializer is usually the one that does the most initialization, and *it is the one responsible for invoking the superclass's initializer*. Because this initializer is the one that does the most work, again by convention, the other initializers are expected to invoke it with appropriate default values as needed.

While at some point you will need to explore this topic further, it is really a framework and therefore beyond the scope of this book.

Chapter 13

Getting a Handle on Memory Management

*I*n Chapter 12, I explain object allocation and initialization. You start with `alloc` and `init`. It is `alloc`, if you remember, that sets aside some memory for the object and returns a *pointer* to that memory. This is important to keep in mind because the memory used by this object cannot be used for any other purpose while that object is still in use by some part of your program. If your computer had an infinite amount of memory available for your program to use, this wouldn't be a problem. But it doesn't, and so your program needs to manage the memory it allocates — and your program must free up that memory when it's no longer needed.

Managing the memory allocated for your objects used to be one of the few real hassles in programming with Objective-C. But now there's a new feature available that removes all the problems that your code could encounter by managing memory in code. Both iOS and Mac OS X applications can take advantage of *Automatic Reference Counting (ARC)*. But a word to the wise: Even if you want to program using ARC, read through this chapter anyway because it really will help solidify your understanding of pointers and objects and what gets passed when you include objects as arguments in messages.

Memory management is not glamorous, but it trumps cool in an application. In fact, memory management is probably the single most vexing thing about iOS and Mac OS X programming. It has made countless programmers crazy, and I can't stress enough how important it is to build memory management into your code from the start. Take it from me, retrofitting can be a nightmare, and I still have dreams where "Hell" is having to go back through an infinite number of lines of code and retrofit memory management code. And if you want to survive Apple's App Store reviewers, your apps need to manage their memory responsibly.

Xcode comes with a feature that makes converting older code to use ARC much easier than walking through each line of code, and I show you how to do that later in this chapter.

Raising and Terminating Responsible Objects

What with everything else going on, managing memory can be a real challenge, not only to someone new to programming but also to those of us with many lines of code under our belts. Allocating memory when you need it isn't that hard. It is realizing that you don't need an object anymore and then releasing the memory back to the operating system that can be a challenge. If you don't do that, and your program runs long enough, eventually you run out of memory (sooner on an iOS device than a Mac for a variety of reasons — see the upcoming sidebar, "The iOS challenge") and your program will come crashing down. Long before that you may even notice system performance approaching "molasses in February — outdoors in Hibbing, Minnesota." Oh, and by the way, if you do free an object (memory) and that object is still being used, you have "London Bridge Is Falling Down" as well. Now, if you created a giant application and run out of memory while all the objects you created are being used, that's one issue, and one I'm not going to deal with here. But if you run out of memory because you have all these objects floating around that no one is using, that's another thing, and it's known as a *memory leak*.

Now that you've heard about the bad things that can happen with poor memory management, it's time to talk about the things you can do to make managing your app's memory easy. Living the good life with your objects means enabling ARC for your project. ARC makes memory management so easy there's almost nothing more you need to do. There are some rules you will have to follow to make sure that your code is correctly taking advantage of ARC. But they're pretty easy, and obeying them makes it easier for you to focus on the features of your applications without spending time making sure that all your objects are being managed properly.

The iOS challenge

Although iOS devices and the Mac both use what is known as virtual memory, unlike the Mac, virtual memory in an iOS device is limited to the actual amount of physical memory. This is because when it begins to run low on memory, iOS frees memory pages that contain read-only content (such as code), where all it has to do is load the "originals" into memory when they're needed. It doesn't, like the Mac OS, temporarily store "changeable" memory (such as object data) to the disk to free up space and then read the data back later when it's needed. This state of affairs limits the amount of memory available.

Understanding the object life cycle

In the preceding chapter, you find out how to allocate and initialize objects by using a combination of `alloc` and `init`. Many objects that you allocate stay around for the duration of your program, and for those objects, all you have to do is, well, nothing really. When your program terminates, they are deallocated, and the memory is returned to the operating system.

But some objects you use for a while to get your money's worth, and then you're done with them. When you are done with them, you should return the memory allocated to them back to the OS so that it can allocate that memory for new objects. This is the scenario that can cause problems.

Start by looking at how memory management works.

In Objective-C 2.0 (as opposed to earlier versions), you can manage memory in two ways:

- ✔ **Reference counting:** You are the one responsible for doing your part in keeping the system up-to-date on whether an object is currently being used.
- ✔ **Automatic Reference Counting:** The compiler takes all the responsibility and does all the work to free up memory when it's no longer needed.

I cover reference counting first so that you understand what's actually happening behind the scenes. However, by using ARC, you'll find almost no need to use reference counting in your projects, unless you're using code from a project that didn't or couldn't take advantage of ARC when it was first created. I cover how to convert older projects to use ARC in the section "Converting Non-ARC Code to ARC."

Understanding Reference Counting

Using ARC for all the projects you start from scratch makes managing your objects' memory very easy. However, there may come a time when you encounter legacy code — Objective-C modules that were originally crafted before ARC. You'll even find some of this code at the Apple developer website in the Sample Code. Apple does a great job of trying to keep its examples up-to-date, but you may come across that one example that your application just cannot do without, and it's the one for which Apple hasn't provided an ARC version. In this section, I give you instruction about *manual* memory management so you understand exactly what the retain, release, and autorelease methods are all about. This section is all about reference counting, which is how an Objective-C application keeps track of whether an object is still being used by some code, somewhere in your application.

Managing memory, retro-style

In many ways, Objective-C is like the coolest guy in your school, who now makes a seven-figure income bungee jumping and skateboarding during the summers while snowboarding around the world in the winter.

In other ways, though, Objective-C is like the nerd in your class who grew up to be an accountant and reads the *Financial Times* for fun. Memory management falls into this category.

In fact, manual memory management is simply an exercise in counting. To manage its memory, Objective-C (actually Cocoa) uses a technique known as *reference counting.* Every object has its own reference count, or *retain count.* When an object is created via alloc or new — or through a copy message, which creates a copy of an object, but has some subtleties beyond the scope of this book — the object's retain count is set to 1. As long as the retain count is greater than 0, the memory manager assumes that someone cares about that object and leaves it alone. It is your responsibility to maintain that reference count by directly or indirectly increasing the retain count when you are using an object, and then decreasing it when you are finished with it. When the retain count goes to 0, Cocoa assumes that no one needs it anymore. Cocoa automatically sends the object a dealloc message, and after that, its memory is returned to the system to be reused. As part of your responsibility for manual memory management, you may need to override dealloc to release any related resources that the object being deallocated might have allocated.

Never invoke dealloc directly — Cocoa sends the dealloc message to your object at the right time.

Take a look at an example now. In the Vacation project's `main.m`, you create
a string object and then pass that as an argument into the `init` method
when you create the `destination` object, as shown here:

```
NSString* englandText = [[NSString alloc]
                    initWithFormat:@"%@", @"England"];
Destination* england = [[Destination alloc]
        initWithCountry:englandText andBudget:2000.00
        withExchangeRate:1.50];
```

I explain why I need to create the `englandText` by using `alloc` and `init`
later in this section, as I promised to do in Chapter 11.

The `Destination` object remains around until the program is terminated. At
that point, everything gets deallocated, so no problem and no real (although
some potential) memory management issues exist.

But what happens if I decide sometime along the way on my trip not to go
to England after all. I really have always wanted to go to Antarctica, and an
opportunity to hitch a ride on a rock star's private jet presents itself, so
bye-bye England, and hello Ushuaia, Tierra del Fuego, Argentina.

Before I take off, however, I want to do one thing, besides send for my long
underwear, which I left safely packed away at a friend's house in Minneapolis.
I need to delete England as a destination, freeing that budget money, and
create a new destination — Antarctica.

As I said earlier, when you are doing memory management, it is your responsibility to keep Cocoa informed about your use of objects, so if you don't
need an object any longer, you send it a `release` message:

```
[england release];
```

`release` does not deallocate the object!

Let me say that again — `release` does not deallocate the object!

All `release` does is decrement the retain count by 1. This is very important
to keep in mind because although one method or object in your application
may no longer need an object, it still may be needed by another method or
object in your program. That's why you don't `dealloc` it yourself, trusting
Cocoa to manage the retain count for you. But it is your job (and I repeat
myself a lot here to make sure that you understand this) to keep Cocoa
informed of your object by using the `release` message.

Well that's cool, and being a good citizen, the `england` object wants to
release all its objects in its `dealloc` method. No problem here, one would
think. `Destination` has instance variables pointing to the objects it uses:

```
NSString* country;
double exchangeRate;
NSMutableArray *transactions;
Budget* theBudget;
```

So in the `dealloc` method that is invoked before the OS deallocates the `Destination` object, those other objects can be released:

```
- (void) dealloc {

  [transactions release];
  [country release];
  [theBudget release];
  [super dealloc];
}
```

Although you don't have to release the `exchangeRate` because it is not an object, do you really want to release all those other objects? What if other objects in your program still need to use those objects? Actually, taking that into account is very easy, as long as you follow the rules.

As I said earlier, when you create an object by using `alloc` or `new`, or through a `copy` message, the object's retain count is set to 1. So you are cool. In fact, whenever you create an object like that, your solemn responsibility is to release it when you are done. There is a flip side to this coin, however: If you are using an object, a pointer to it is sent to you as an argument in a message, as is the case for the `NSString` object in the following code:

```
Destination* england = [[Destination alloc]
        initWithCountry:englandText andBudget:2000.00
        withExchangeRate:1.50];
```

Then it is also your responsibility to increment the retain count by sending it the `retain` message, as you can see in bold code in the following implementation of the `initWithCountry:andBudget:withExchangeRate:` method:

```
- (id) initWithCountry: (NSString*) theCountry andBudget:
        (double) budgetAmount withExchangeRate:
        (double) theExchangeRate{
  if (self = [super init]) {
    transactions = [[NSMutableArray alloc]
                                    initWithCapacity:10];
    theBudget = [[Budget alloc]
                    initWithAmount:budgetAmount
                    withExchangeRate:theExchangeRate];
    exchangeRate = theExchangeRate;
    country = theCountry;
    [country retain];
  }
  return self;
}
```

In this method, the Destination object creates two objects on its own, theBudget and transactions. As a result, the retain count for each is set to 1. It also gets passed a pointer to an NSString object that was created at another time and place. If Destination plans to use that object, it needs to send it the retain message. That way, the retain count is increased by 1. If the creator of that object decides that it no longer needs the object and sends it the release message, the retain count is decremented by 1. But because the Destination object sent it a retain message, the release count is still greater than 0 — the object lives! The creator of the NSString is freed from the responsibility of having to know anything about what other object is still using the NSString it created and of worrying about when it has to free it.

What really does confuse some developers is the concept of retain and release. They worry that releasing an object will deallocate that object. (Note that all release does is tell the memory manager that you are no longer interested in it. The memory manager is the one that makes the life-and-death decision.) New developers sometimes worry that as a creator, they have to be concerned about others using their objects. In reality, it is your job to simply follow the memory management rules.

Here's the fundamental rule of manual memory management:

> You are responsible for releasing any object that you create when using a method whose name begins with alloc or new or contains copy, or if you send it a retain message. You can do that by sending it a release or autorelease message (which I explain shortly). In Applespeak, if you create an object by using any of these four messages, you are said to *own* the object (objects are allowed to have more than one owner — talk about how to use terminology to really make things confusing).

That's it, with corollaries of course:

> If you want to continue to use an object outside the method it was received in, save a pointer to it as an instance variable, as you just did with the NSString object. Then you must send the object the retain message. In Applespeak, this means that you are now an owner of the object.

In general, somewhere in your code, you should have a release for every statement that creates an object by using alloc or new, or contains copy or sends a retain message.

I now explain why I have you create a string object in the Chapter 11 section "Coding the New main" when you initialize a Destination object. I could have had you code it this way:

```
Destination* england = [[Destination alloc]
        initWithCountry:@"England" andBudget:2000.00
        withExchangeRate:1.50];
```

If you had done so, the compiler would have created a string constant that existed for the life of the program. In this case, sending it a `retain` or `release` message has no effect (try it yourself). If you only have a couple of these string constants, the effect is insignificant, but a lot of them could have an effect on your memory footprint — although creating and then deallocating lots of small objects have their own cost in CPU use as well.

Using ARC

You create a project to use ARC when you tell Xcode to create a new project for you. You can see this in Figure 13-1, which is similar to Figure 2-20 in Chapter 2.

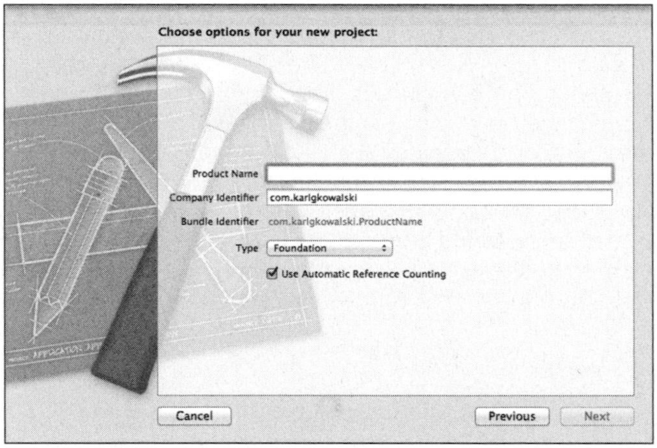

Figure 13-1: ARC enabled for a new Xcode project.

Every new project you create with ARC enabled takes advantage of ARC's ability to manage the memory your code allocates. As I mention previously in this chapter, there are some rules you need to obey while writing code when using ARC. These rules are

✔ Do not send `retain`, `release`, or `autorelease` messages to your objects.

✔ Do not store pointers to Objective-C objects in C structures (`structs`).

✔ Inform the compiler about ownership when using Core Foundation-style objects.

✔ Use the `@autoreleasepool` keyword to mark the start of an autorelease block.

✔ Follow the naming conventions.

I cover each of these rules next.

Rule 1: Do not send retain, release, or autorelease messages to your objects

These three messages are used when applications managed reference counting on their own, as described in the section "Understanding Reference Counting". You're really only likely to run into an issue with this rule when you use code written for a pre-ARC application. But this is the most important rule of the set: It's the easiest one to follow, and it's also the one you're most likely to come across. Each of these messages, which are inherited from `NSObject`, performs a function that manages memory of objects. If your project was not using ARC, you would create code that would send these messages to your objects during your application's lifetime. This form of programming requires you to manage your memory manually, rather than automatically with ARC. With ARC, using these messages is not permitted — the compiler marks them as errors, as you can see in Figure 13-2.

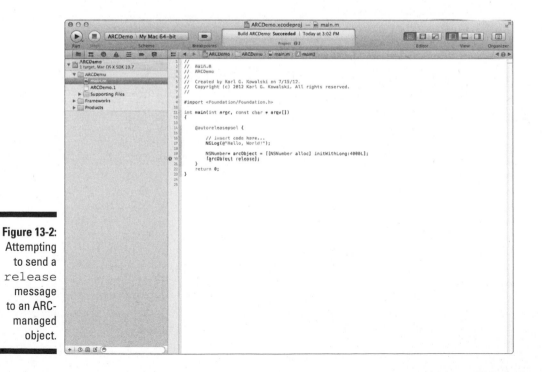

Figure 13-2: Attempting to send a `release` message to an ARC-managed object.

In Chapter 10 I introduce you to inheritance, which enables you to create a subclass that inherits functionality from its superclass. One of the features of inheritance enables you to create methods that override the superclass' method of the same name. Although this feature is useful for creating and extending the functionality of your classes and their subclasses, you must not attempt to create methods named `retain`, `release`, or `autorelease` in any of your subclasses in a project using ARC. The compiler marks them as errors.

Rule 2: Do not store pointers to Objective-C objects in C structures (structs)

When your code creates an object, the compiler returns a pointer to that object in memory. You can use this pointer just like any other, including storing it as part of a C `struct` that contains a member element of the pointer's type. However, doing this when ARC is enabled would make ARC's job impossible because ARC would lose track of where the pointer is. The compiler marks code that tries to do this as an error, as you can see in Figure 13-3.

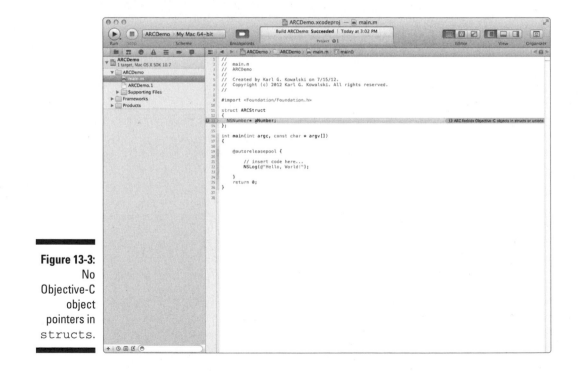

Figure 13-3:
No Objective-C object pointers in `structs`.

Rule 3: Inform the compiler about ownership when using Core Foundation-type objects

ARC does not automatically manage the memory for objects created by using the *Core Foundation framework*. These objects have their own memory management rules and functions. I don't demonstrate any examples of these in the code I have you write in this book, but you should be aware that ARC is not managing the memory of these objects if your applications create them and that you have to manage these yourself, using the appropriate Core Foundation functions.

Rule 4: Use the @autoreleasepool keyword

The `@autoreleasepool` keyword is a compiler directive that sets up code to handle situations where memory is automatically released. In your command tool projects, Xcode created initial code in `main.m` that looks like this:

```
int main( int argc, const char * argv[] )
{
  @autoreleasepool {
    // insert code here...
    NSLog(@"Hello, World!");

  }
  return 0;
}
```

You should leave the `@autoreleasepool { ... }` construct in place from now on. The use of `@autoreleasepool` in your own code is beyond the scope of this book.

Rule 5: Follow the naming conventions

When ARC is enabled, the compiler examines your code and applies some rules to determine whether an object returned by a method has been retained. In order for you to tell the compiler whether a returned object has been retained, there are several method-naming conventions that the compiler understands and reviews to indicate the status of the returned object. The compiler assumes that a method whose name starts with one of the following words is returning a retained object:

✔ alloc

✔ copy

✔ init

✔ mutableCopy

✔ new

So just avoid using any of these words as the first word in your methods' names, and you won't break Rule 5. Okay, that won't work all the time — you will undoubtedly create methods that begin with the word init. Just be sure that the object returned by an init method has been retained — and you can be sure of this because your code should execute [super init] within your init method implementation, which should eventually lead to the init method in the NSObject ancestor class.

Last, you cannot use new as the beginning of a name of an Objective-C *property*. I discuss properties in Chapter 14, but as an example, the following code causes an error when you try to build a project using it when ARC is enabled:

```
@interface Budget : NSObject
@property NSDate* newYear;
@end
```

The error you see from the compiler contains text like this:

```
property's synthesized getter follows Cocoa naming
        convention for returning 'owned' objects
```

If you encounter this error during your application development, somewhere there's a property that's incorrectly named.

That's all there is to using ARC and avoiding some of its quirks. You should definitely enable it for all your new projects, and you'll find it makes coding much easier because you don't have to worry about whether the object you've created is going to get freed up when your code no longer needs it — the compiler makes sure that the right instructions are added to your code to make the right things happen.

Converting Non-ARC Code to ARC

Now you're ready to convert a module built to do manual memory management to work with a project where ARC is enabled. You'll come across code built like this in older sample code and other examples online or in print. Luckily, Xcode makes it fairly easy to find and fix all the manual memory management issues so that your non-ARC modules can work in an ARC project.

If you want to avoid all the typing below, you can find this project at the website in the Start Here folder of the Chapter 13 folder.

To see how this works, follow these steps:

1. **Launch Xcode.**

2. **Create a new project by selecting New➪Project from the File menu.**

3. **Select Application under OS X in the left pane and Command Line Tool in the right pane. Click Next.**

4. **Enter a name for the project — I chose NonARCDemo — and deselect the Use Automatic Reference Counting check box, as shown in Figure 13-4. Click Next.**

Figure 13-4:
Turning
off ARC.

5. **Pick a convenient location to save the project and click Create.**

   You've now created an Xcode project that is not subject to ARC rules.

6. **Add a new class to the project by selecting New➪File from the File menu. Select Cocoa under OS X and Objective-C class in the right pane. Click Next.**

7. **Choose a name for your class — I picked NonARCClass to stay in keeping with the project name — and make sure that NSObject is selected in the Subclass Of drop-down menu. Click Next.**

8. **Pick a convenient location to save the new class files and click Create.**

   You should now have the NonARCClass.h and NonARCClass.m files in your project.

9. **Add the code shown in bold in Listing 13-1 to NonARCClass.h.**

10. **Add the code shown in bold in Listing 13-2 to NonARCClass.m.**

   The NSDate class used in this example is a Cocoa class for date and time handling.

Listing 13-1:   NonARCClass.h

```
#import <Foundation/Foundation.h>

@interface NonARCClass : NSObject
{
  NSMutableArray *userUrls;
  NSString *userFavoriteUrl;
  NSDate *lastModified;
}

- (void) addUrl: (NSString *) aUrl;
- (void) setFavoriteUrl: (NSString *) favoriteUrl;
- (NSString *) getFavoriteUrl;
- (NSDate *) getDateLastModified;

@end
```

Listing 13-2:   NonARCClass.m

```
#import "NonARCClass.h"

@implementation NonARCClass

- (id) init
{
  if (self = [super init])
  {
    userUrls = [[NSMutableArray alloc] init];
  }
  return (self);
}

- (void) addUrl: (NSString *) aUrl
{
  // no need to retain aUrl
  // the array takes care of it
  [userUrls addObject: aUrl];
}

- (void) setFavoriteUrl: (NSString *) favoriteUrl;
{
  // only proceed if favoriteUrl is real
  if (nil != favoriteUrl)
  {
    // first, make sure we keep a copy alive
    [favoriteUrl retain];
    // if we already have a favorite
    if (nil != userFavoriteUrl)
    {
```

```
            // make sure we release it
            [userFavoriteUrl release];
        }
        // second, make sure we keep the new one
        userFavoriteUrl = favoriteUrl;
        if (nil != lastModified)
        {
            // make sure we release any previous NSDate
            [lastModified release];
        }
        // finally, set lastModified to be now
        lastModified = [[NSDate date] retain];
    }
}

- (NSString *) getFavoriteUrl;
{
    return (userFavoriteUrl);
}

- (NSDate *) getDateLastModified;
{
    return (lastModified);
}

- (void) dealloc
{
    // if we have a favorite,
    // release it
    if (nil != userFavoriteUrl)
    {
        [userFavoriteUrl release];
    }
    // if we're keeping a lastModified
    // release it
    if (nil != lastModified)
    {
        [lastModified release];
    }
    // release the array and it will
    // release all its contents
    [userUrls release];
    // tell our superclass to dealloc
    [super dealloc];
}

@end
```

11. Build the project by selecting Build from the Product menu.

You should encounter no errors, because the code doesn't do anything. But now you convert it to use ARC.

12. Select Refactor⇨Convert to Objective-C ARC from the Edit menu. Click the triangle next to NonARCDemo.

You should see a panel that looks like Figure 13-5. Xcode is requesting your assistance in determining which modules to convert.

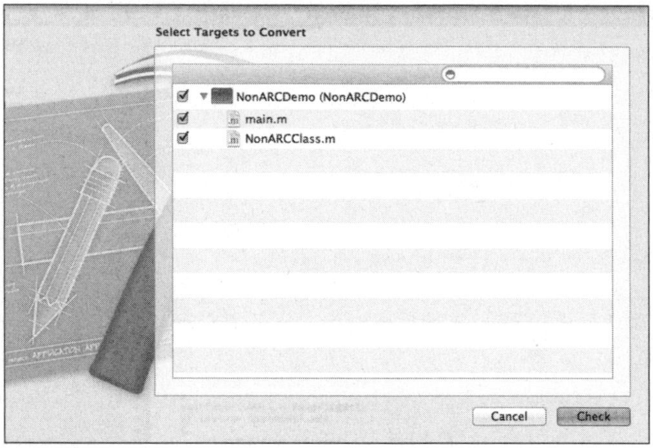

Figure 13-5:
Selecting
the code
you want to
convert
to ARC.

13. Click the Check button.

Xcode does some processing and then displays the Convert to Automatic Reference Counting panel, as shown in Figure 13-6.

Figure 13-6:
Xcode
explain-
ing the
conversion
process.

14. Click Next to let Xcode generate a preview of changes.

Xcode then displays a panel for you to review the pieces of your code —
in this case, within `NonARCClass.m` — that Xcode needs to change to
bring your code into harmony with ARC. Figure 13-7 shows the changes —
with the After Conversion view on the left, and the Before Conversion
view on the right — and you can see that Xcode is going to remove all
the code that uses `release` or `retain`, as well as the entire `dealloc`
method.

15. Click Save to have Xcode make the changes.

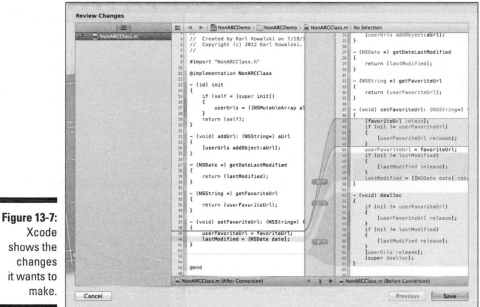

Figure 13-7:
Xcode
shows the
changes
it wants to
make.

Xcode may ask whether you want to take a "snapshot" of your project
before it performs the conversion, which can be useful to ensure that
you have a backup before making a major change. For now, just click the
Disable button if Xcode does ask.

Those are the steps you follow to convert older, non-ARC code to use ARC.
Of course, this was a simple project with only a few `retain`s and `release`s;
a larger project with more modules may prove more challenging to resolve.
But you now know that Xcode can handle taking older projects and moving
them to use the more-reliable and easier-to-understand Automatic Reference
Counting.

Part IV
Moving from Language to Application

The 5th Wave   By Rich Tennant

HORNER BROS.
MAKERS OF PREMIUM
BELLS & WHISTLES

"As an application developer, I never thought
I'd say this, but your app needs more
bells and whistles."

In this part . . .

In this part, you begin to add more functionality to your program. I introduce you to how to work with data as well as more advanced ways to extend your program.

After you get all the application functionality up and running, you will probably be eager to make it available to the user. In this part, you fit your application into the user interface frameworks on the Mac and iOS devices that make developing applications for them so easy (well, okay, relatively easy). What will be really exciting (for me at least) is when you experience how easy it is to take the application you develop and just slide it into a user interface. Of course, you have to create the user interface, and I give you a crash course in Interface Builder, a tool that comes with Xcode. After you've built an interface, just add a few lines of code, and presto change-o, you're running iOS and then Mac applications (the same application code, I might add, with some minor user interface differences).

The technical term for this accomplished feat is "way cool."

Chapter 14

Getting Data from Other Objects

*I*n Chapter 11, you factor your code to create a `Destination` object that manages the other objects you need in your model. You see how the `Destination` object can use other objects by sending them messages. Although most of those messages are to get an object to do something (`spendDollars:`, for example), as you see when you implement `return Balance` in `Budget` and `leftToSpend` in `Destination`, some of these messages are about data.

That data returned by those methods is stored as instance variables, but as you know, one object can't and shouldn't access another object's instance variables directly (hence, the need for those two methods). In this chapter, I show you another way to get data from an object — *declared properties* — and I also tell you about some things you need to handle with care.

Getting Data from Objects

As I refine the Vacation application, I need to start thinking more about the practical aspects of using this application, especially as I march down the road toward putting on a user interface.

One thing that strikes me is that this whole exchange rate thing is not very robust. After all, the currency exchange rate changes often during the day, so I do need a way to update it. Right now at least, Budget owns the exchange rate, but I have no way to communicate with the Budget, other than through a Destination. So, before deciding how I want to update the exchange rate, I really need to consider which object should own the exchange rate. Currently, both Budget and Destination have instance variables storing it.

Peering into my crystal ball, I see in the future an exchange rate object that will be able to get exchange rates in real time. When this happens, you'll create an exchange rate object that will be used by the Destination object. To prepare for the eventuality, it makes sense for the Destination object to own the exchange rate now. Then when you implement an exchange rate object, you will have to make only a few changes to the Destination object's code, and none to the other objects that need to know the exchange rate. They'll still use Destination to get it, and Destination will simply turn around and ask the exchange rate object to do its bidding (no pun intended). It makes sense then for Destination to own the exchange rate for now, keeping the exchange rate a Destination instance variable and creating a method that can be invoked from main to update the exchange rate (and later by a controller).

Having its exchange rate instance variable taken away creates a problem for Budget. How will Budget get the exchange rate it needs to compute the budget impact of a credit card transaction?

By now, you know of course that Budget can't, and shouldn't be able to, access the exchangeRate instance variable in Destination. In object-oriented programming, a class's instance variables are safely protected behind the object's walls and can't be accessed directly. The only way to access them is by creating *accessor methods,* which allow the specific instance variable of an object to be read and (if you want) updated. But even if you were tempted to access them directly, the compiler wouldn't let you because, as I discuss in Chapter 6, its scope is defined as @protected (the default) in the class. I dare you — go try it on your own.

I also want access to the country name of a Destination. When I delete a destination, I will give users a chance to change their minds — I want to be able to display Are you sure you want to delete *country* from your trip? For now, however, I just display that the destination country was deleted.

Well, I could write methods to return the exchange rate and the country name as I have been doing with returnBalance in Budget and leftToSpend, or I could use a feature of Objective-C 2.0 called *declared properties.* When you use declared properties, the compiler will create the accessor methods for you.

Working with Declared Properties

As you soon discover, you will use declared properties a lot (most people just call them *properties*). If you need to have an instance variable accessible by other objects in your program, you need to create accessor methods for that particular instance variable.

Accessor methods effectively get (using a *getter method*) and set (using a *setter method*) the values for an instance variable. For many years, programmers had to code these methods themselves or buy add-on tools that would do it for them (usually advertised late at night on the Programmers Channel). The nice folks in charge of Objective-C came to our collective rescue when they released Objective-C 2.0 with its *declared properties* feature. Now the compiler can write access methods for you, according to the direction you give it in the *property declaration*. Kind of like getting the smartest kid in your class to do your homework while you hang out with your friends at the malt shoppe.

Objective-C creates the getter and setter methods for you by using a @property declaration in the interface file. The default names for the getter and setter methods associated with a property are *whateverThePropertyNameIs* for the getter (yes, the default getter method name is the same as the property's name) and set*WhateverThePropertyNameIs*: for the setter. (You replace what is in italic with the actual property name or identifier.) For example, the accessors that are generated for the exchangeRate instance variable are exchangeRate as the getter and setExchangeRate: as the setter.

Adding properties

If you have been following along with me, I extend what you did in Chapter 12. If you prefer to start from a clean copy of the project from where you left off, you can use the project found in the Chapter 14 Start Here folder, which is in the Chapter 14 folder.

To declare some properties for the Destination class, add the code in bold, and remove the bold, italic, underlined code in Listing 14-1 to Destination.h.

Listing 14-1:   Adding Properties to the Destination Class

```
#import <Foundation/Foundation.h>
@class Budget;

@interface Destination : NSObject {

  NSString* country;
  NSMutableArray *transactions;
  Budget* theBudget;
}

@property (nonatomic, strong) NSString* country;
@property (readwrite) double exchangeRate;

- (id) initWithCountry: (NSString*) theCountry
          andBudget: (double) budgetAmount
          withExchangeRate: (double) theExchangeRate;
- (void) spendCash: (double) aTransaction;
- (void) chargeCreditCard: (double) aTransaction;
- (double) leftToSpend;
@end
```

Creating accessor methods is a simple process that is achieved with the `@property` declaration, which tells the compiler to create accessor methods for these variables.

That is what you just did — coded the corresponding `@property` declarations for `country` and `exchangeRate`. These specify how the accessor methods are to behave. I explain exactly what that means in the next section.

This is all you need to do to make use of properties in your classes. For every `@property` you declare in your `@interface` file, Objective-C creates all the accessor methods for you when you build your code.

Implementing declared properties

At the end of the day, you need to do only one thing in your code for the compiler to create accessors: Declare an instance variable in the interface file as an `@property`.

This is straightforward, but there are a couple of interesting parts to the `@property` declaration, and so I explain them here.

The declaration specifies the name and type of the property and some *attributes* that provide the compiler with information about exactly how you want the accessor methods to be implemented.

Strong and weak properties

One memory management challenge happens when each of two objects contains a reference to the other. ARC runs into difficulty when it comes time to free up the memory of these two objects because trying to free up the memory for object A causes it to check whether any other object still has a reference to it — which will be object B. And when ARC tries to free up the memory of object B, it finds that object A still has a reference to it. Each object can be recycled only when the other is. So ARC depends on you to give it a hint about which reference is more important than the other by using the attributes strong and weak for your properties (strong is used by default). If object A maintains a strong reference to object B, then the application does not free up the memory for object B as long as object A is still in use. To prevent the aforementioned challenge, object B should mark its reference to object A as weak, so that the application knows it can free up the memory for object A without causing problems for object B. Generally, you don't need to worry about using these property attributes, but you may someday find a need to create a mutually referencing relationship between objects — one example is a container object maintaining references to the objects it contains and its relationship to the contained objects maintaining a reference back to their container. The container should maintain its references to the contained objects as strong; the contained objects should maintain their reference to the container as weak.

For example, the declaration

```
@property (readwrite) double exchangeRate;
```

declares a property named exchangeRate, which is a double. The property attribute (readwrite) tells the compiler that this property can be both read and updated outside the object.

You also could have specified readonly, in which case, only a getter method is implemented in the @implementation. This means that if you attempt to assign a value by using the accessor (I explain how to do that later for variables you can update), you get a compiler error.

Now take a look at the following declaration:

```
@property (nonatomic, strong) NSString* country;
```

It declares a property named country, which is a pointer to an NSString object. Enclosed in parentheses are two attributes: nonatomic and strong.

nonatomic addresses an important technical consideration for multi-threaded systems, which is beyond the scope of this book. nonatomic works fine for applications like this one.

`strong` directs the compiler to refrain from recycling the referenced object's memory until the owning object — in this case, a `Destination` — has been recycled. Because the `NSString` assigned to a `Destination` could be referenced from other objects, `strong` prevents the application from giving up the memory occupied by the `NSString` when some other object that references itself is being recycled.

And, oh yes, `nonatomic` and `strong` apply only to pointers to objects.

In Chapter 13, I go over Automatic Reference Counting (ARC), an important feature of Objective-C that makes managing your application's memory simple and easy.

Accessing the instance variables from within the class

After you declare the properties, you can access them from other objects or from `main`. But before I show you that, I want to show you about accessing them within the class.

You can use the getter and setter accessors within your code. Objective-C follows a simple pattern for naming the accessors it creates for your properties. For instance, for the property named `country`, the getter is

```
NSString* myCountry = [self country];
```

For the same property, the setter is

```
[self setCountry:aCountry];
```

You also can use the dot notation (which refugees from other object-oriented languages will recognize):

```
NSString* aCountry = self.country;
self.country = aCountry;
```

Now, I want you to update `Destination.m` to use properties by deleting the bold, italic, underlined code in Listing 14-2 and adding the code in bold.

Listing 14-2:   Using Accessors within the Destination Class

```
#import "Destination.h"
#import "CashTransaction.h"
#import "CreditCardTransaction.h"
#import "Budget.h"
```

```
#import "Transaction.h"


@implementation Destination


- (id) initWithCountry: (NSString*) theCountry andBudget:
          (double) budgetAmount withExchangeRate:
          (double) theExchangeRate{
  if (self = [super init]) {
    transactions = [[NSMutableArray alloc]
          initWithCapacity:10];

  // theBudget = [[Budget alloc]  initWithAmount:
     budgetAmount withExchangeRate: theExchangeRate];
     theBudget = [[Budget alloc]
          initWithAmount:budgetAmount forDestination:self];
  // exchangeRate = theExchangeRate;
     self.exchangeRate = theExchangeRate;
  // country = theCountry;
     [self setCountry: theCountry];
     NSLog (@"I'm off to %@", theCountry);
  }
  return self;
}


- (void) spendCash: (double)amount{

  Transaction *aTransaction = [[CashTransaction alloc]
          initWithAmount: amount forBudget: theBudget];
  [transactions addObject:aTransaction];
  [aTransaction spend];

}

- (void) chargeCreditCard: (double) amount{

  Transaction *aTransaction = [[CreditCardTransaction
          alloc] initWithAmount: amount forBudget:
          theBudget];
  [transactions addObject:aTransaction];
  [aTransaction spend];
}

- (double) leftToSpend {

  return [theBudget returnBalance];
}

@end
```

You did the following to `Destination`:

1. You changed the `Budget init` method, which is explained in the next section.

   You had to change the `Budget init` method to pass in a reference to the `Destination` object. `Budget` will need that to send a message to get the `exchangeRate`.

2. You used an accessor to assign the `theExchangeRate` argument in the `initWithAmount:andBudget:withExchangeRate:` method to the `exchangeRate` instance variable by using the dot notation:

   ```
   self.exchangeRate = theExchangeRate;
   ```

3. You used an accessor to assign the `theCountry` argument in the `init WithAmount:andBudget:withExchangeRate:` method to the `country` instance variable by using an Objective-C message:

   ```
   [self setCountry:theCountry];
   ```

Using Accessors to Get Data from Objects

Now that you have created these accessors, you can use them. You will have to make some changes to `Budget.m` and `Budget.h`. These are shown in Listings 14-3 and 14-4. Use the following steps to make the `Budget` class meet the expectations of the `Destination` class:

1. **Start by deleting the bold, italic, underlined code in Listing 14-3 and adding the code in bold to `Budget.m`.**

Listing 14-3:   Budget.m

```
#import "Budget.h"
#import "Destination.h"


@implementation Budget

//- (id) initWithAmount: (double) aBudget
//        withExchangeRate: (double) anExchangeRate {
//
//   if (self = [super init]) {
//     exchangeRate = anExchangeRate;
//     budget = aBudget;
//   }
```

```
//   return self;
//}

- (id) initWithAmount: (double) aBudget forDestination:
            (Destination*) aDestination {
  if (self = [super init]) {
    self.destination = aDestination;
    budget = aBudget;
  }
  return self;
}


- (void) spendDollars: (double) dollars {

  budget -= dollars;
}

- (void) chargeForeignCurrency: (double) foreignCurrency {
//exchangeTransaction = foreignCurrency*exchangeRate;
  exchangeTransaction = foreignCurrency*
                    [self.destination exchangeRate];
  budget -= transaction;
}

- (double) returnBalance {

  return budget;
}

@end
```

You added the `#import "Destination.h"` to make the compiler happy when it sees a message to the `Destination` object. You also did the following:

a. Modified the `init` method to add a pointer to the `Destination` object as an argument and removed the `anExchangeRate` argument. You also stored the pointer to the `Destination` object in a new property — `destination` — which you will next add to `Budget.h`.

b. Changed `chargeForeignCurrency:` to use the getter accessor `exchangeRate` to get the exchange rate from the `Destination` object.

What you also may have noticed is that you left the `returnBalance`, which you coded earlier, instead of replacing it with an accessor. Why didn't I have you make that a property as well?

I have (as you might expect) some definite opinions and really mixed feelings about properties, which I explain in the next section. For now, though, you finish the changes to Budget.h.

2. **Delete the bold, italic, underlined code in Listing 14-4 and add the code in bold to** Budget.h.

Listing 14-4: Budget.h

```
#import <Foundation/Foundation.h>
@class Destination;

@interface Budget : NSObject {
  float         exchangeRate;
  double        budget;
  double        exchangeTransaction;
}

@property (nonatomic) Destination *destination;

//(id) initWithAmount: (double) aBudget withExchangeRate:
          (double) anExchangeRate ;
- (id) initWithAmount: (double) aBudget
             forDestination: (Destination*) aDestination;

- (void) spendDollars: (double) dollars ;
- (void) chargeForeignCurrency: (double) euros;
- (double) returnBalance;
@end
```

You find no surprises here. You added the @class statement to make the compiler happy; added the new property, destination; and made the changes to the init method declaration that you did in the implementation.

Now, look at Listing 14-5, which shows the changes to main.m that allow you to change the exchange rate as needed.

3. **Add the code in bold in Listing 14-5 to** main **(in the file** main.m**).**

Listing 14-5: Modifying main in main.m

```
#import <Foundation/Foundation.h>
#import "Destination.h"

int main (int argc, const char * argv[]) {

  @autoreleasepool {

    NSString* europeText = [[NSString alloc]
```

```
                              initWithFormat:@"%@", @"Europe"];
Destination* europe = [[Destination alloc]
      initWithCountry:europeText andBudget:1000.00
      withExchangeRate:1.25];
[europeText release];
NSString* englandText = [[NSString alloc]
                    initWithFormat:@"%@", @"England"];
Destination* england = [[Destination alloc]
      initWithCountry:englandText andBudget:2000.00
      withExchangeRate:1.50];
[englandText release];

for (int n = 1; n < 2; n++) {
  double transaction = n*100.00;
  NSLog (@"Sending a %.2f cash transaction",
      transaction);
  [europe spendCash:transaction];

  NSLog(@"Remaining budget %.2f", [europe
      leftToSpend]);
  NSLog (@"Sending a %.2f cash transaction",
      transaction);
  [england spendCash:transaction];
  NSLog(@"Remaining budget %.2f",
                          [england leftToSpend]);
}

[europe setExchangeRate:1.30];
[england setExchangeRate:1.40];

int n = 1;
while (n < 4) {
  double transaction = n*100.00;
  NSLog(@"Sending a %.2f credit card transaction",
      transaction);
  [europe chargeCreditCard:transaction];
  NSLog(@"Remaining budget %.2f", [europe
      leftToSpend]);
  NSLog(@"Sending a %.2f credit card transaction",
      transaction);
  [england chargeCreditCard:transaction];
  NSLog(@"Remaining budget %.2f", [england
      leftToSpend]);
  n++;
}

}
return 0;
}
```

All you did in main was add back the @autorelease pool block, which helps ARC to manage some of the memory allocations your program will go through. You also added sending a setExchangeRate: message to both the europe and england objects, which updates the exchange rate for each, replacing the value for exchangeRate that you originally initialized them with.

Notice how easy all this is.

4. **Click the Run button on the Project Window toolbar to build and run the application.**

   You should see the following in the Debugger Console:

```
I'm off to Europe
I'm off to England
Sending a 100.00 cash transaction
Remaining budget 900.00
Sending a 100.00 cash transaction
Remaining budget 1900.00
Sending a 100.00 credit card transaction
Remaining budget 770.00
Sending a 100.00 credit card transaction
Remaining budget 1760.00
Sending a 200.00 credit card transaction
Remaining budget 510.00
Sending a 200.00 credit card transaction
Remaining budget 1480.00
Sending a 300.00 credit card transaction
Remaining budget 120.00
Sending a 300.00 credit card transaction
Remaining budget 1060.00
```

You can find the completed project at the website in the Example 14 folder, which is in the Chapter 14 folder.

Properly Using Properties

What you just did with the exchange rate and country data in the Destination object may seem, well, a bit pointless to you. If the point of object-oriented programming is to encapsulate data, what difference does it really make whether you allow direct data access or whether you force the user of the data to send a message and the supplier to code the @property statements? It really seems like gratuitous code, and that this whole data encapsulation thing is a sham.

For example, what happens when I change how I get the exchange rate from being set by the user and store it in a `Destination` instance variable, to access it from another object — my plan as I mention in the beginning of this chapter? It seems that would break the clients of `Destination` that use the `exchangeRate` property.

I actually agree with that criticism of properties to an extent, although as you will see, you have ways to deal with this issue.

Putting on my methodologist hat for a second (well, only a few seconds, I promise), let me explain this issue.

First, look at when accessing the object's data through accessors is really the way to do things:

- **Customizing user-interface objects:** In a framework, the user-interface object, a window or view, for example, really needs to have certain parameters set to make it function in the way the user needs. Instead of forcing the user to subclass it, properties allow it to be tailored to a particular user's (the developer's) needs. In this case, properties are being used to set parameters, like color, rather than to implement a class's responsibility to accept data.

- **Accessing instance variables:** Again, in a framework, the same argument applies to accessing the instance variables. The instance variables should become properties when they hold information about the state of the object — is the window opened or closed, where did the user just drag this object to on the screen, and so on.

It's my opinion, however, that except for those and similar circumstances in your own classes, you are much better off from an enhanceability perspective to avoid using properties to implement an object's responsibility to accept data from and supply data to other objects. You should define methods that accept or supply data and not use a property that implies structural information about the data.

That being said, some features about properties also enable you to do some interesting things to mitigate the effect if you later decide to change an instance variable you have made available as a property. For example:

- **To deal with changes, you can implement the accessor (instead of having it generated by the complier) to access the property.** For example, if you moved the exchange rate to an exchange rate object, you could implement your own `exchangeRate` method currently synthesized by the compiler (it will only synthesize those methods if you have not implemented them in your implementation file). The method you implemented sends a message to the new exchange rate object to get, and then return, the exchange rate (you probably wouldn't need a setter in this case). If you do that, though, be sure to implement the accessor in a way that is consistent with the property's attributes. Creating your own accessors for properties is another topic that is beyond the scope of this book.

✔ **The accessor does not have to be named the same as the instance variable.** If you want to hide the name of the instance variable, you can use

```
@property (readwrite, getter=myExchangeRate)
            double exchangeRate;
```

Chapter 15

Show Me the Data

In Chapter 1, I explain that a computer program is a set of instructions that perform operations on data. Although this is what you have been steadily doing since Chapter 1 — coding statements that operate on data — all the data you have been working with so far has been "hard-coded" into the program.

After you put on the user interface, of course, that will change. The user will be entering transactions, and you will be processing them, and probably storing both the transactions and the results as well. For example, you'll want to save all the credit card transactions to reconcile them against your statement when you get home, and you definitely want the ability to store what's left of your budget after a series of transactions so that every time you restart the program, you don't start with your original budget (well, it would be nice if you could do that, but I guess that's not realistic).

In this chapter, I show you how to store what's left of your budget after a series of transactions to a file, and then read that file when the application starts up again. This illustrates some of the ways you can save data. But before I show you that, I want to make you aware of another kind of data that you need for your program: *application-based data*.

Understanding Application-Based Data

As I look at my program, I think it would be nice to be able to display the euro symbol (€) when I display a euro-based credit card transaction and the pound symbol (£) when I display a pound-based one.

Although I could "hard-code" those symbols in my program, doing so doesn't give me much flexibility. Either I have to build some kind of array into my program for the currency symbols of the places I might go (and "waste" the CPU cycles and memory to build it every time I run the program), or I can store all the currency symbols in a file, and based on the country I am processing transactions for, look up the currency symbols in that file.

When that kind of data is in a file, I won't have to rebuild my program every time I add or change a country, currency, or currency symbol — all I have to do is change the file, which as you'll see, is pretty easy.

Fortunately, Cocoa supports an easy-to-use mechanism called a *property list* to manage this kind of data. The next section covers property lists.

Defining property lists

Applications and other system software on OS X and iOS use property lists extensively. For example, the Mac OS X Finder stores file and directory attributes in a property list, and iOS uses them for user defaults. You also get a property list editor with Xcode, which makes property list files (or *plists* as they are referred to) easy to create and maintain in your own programs.

Figure 15-1 shows the property list I show you how to build, one that will enable you to add the euro and pound symbols to your application.

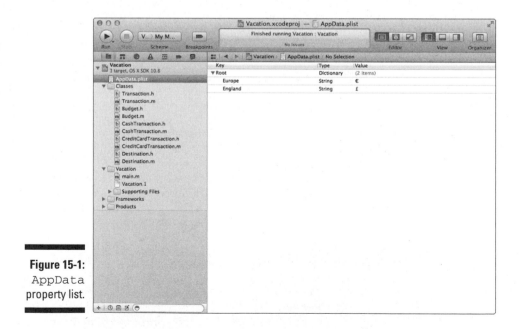

Figure 15-1:
`AppData`
property list.

After you know how to work with property lists, it's actually easy, but like most things, getting there is half the fun.

Working with property lists

Property lists are perfect for storing small amounts of data that consist primarily of strings and numbers. What adds to their appeal is the ability to easily read them into your programs, use or even modify the data, and then write them back out again. That's because Cocoa provides a small set of objects that have that behavior built in.

The technical term for these objects is *serializable.* A serializable object can convert itself into a stream of bytes so that it can be stored in a file and can then reconstitute itself into the object it once was when it is read back in — yes "beam me up, Scotty" does exist, at least on your computer.

These objects, called *property list objects,* that you have to work with are as follows:

- ✔ `NSData` and `NSMutableData`
- ✔ `NSDate`
- ✔ `NSNumber`
- ✔ `NSString` and `NSMutableString`
- ✔ `NSArray` and `NSMutableArray`
- ✔ `NSDictionary` and `NSMutableDictionary`

As you can see in the plist in Figure 15-1, the property list contains two strings, one each for the Europe and England currency symbols. The property list itself is a dictionary created for you automatically by Xcode.

Property lists contain two kinds of property list objects:

- ✔ **Primitives:** The term *primitives* is not a reflection on how civilized these property objects are, but it is a word used to describe the simplest kind of object. They are what they are.
- ✔ **Containers:** Containers can hold primitives as well as other containers.

One thing that differentiates property list object containers (`NSArray`, `NSDictionary`), besides their ability to hold other objects, is that they both have methods called `writeToFile:atomically:`, which write the property list to a file, and a corresponding `initWithContentsOfFile:`, which initializes the object with the content of a file. So, if I create an array or dictionary and fill it chock-full of objects of the property list type, all I have to do to save it to a file is tell it to go save itself or create an array or dictionary and then tell it to initialize itself from a file.

You have already worked with arrays, and I introduce you to dictionaries in the next section. The containers can contain other containers, as well as the primitive types. Thus, you might have an array of dictionaries, and each dictionary might contain other arrays and dictionaries, as well as the primitive types.

But before I tell you any more about property lists, let me explain one of the more important property list objects — the dictionary.

NSData and NSMutableData are wrappers (an object that is there mostly to turn something into an object) in which you can dump any kind of data and then have that data act as an object. They are used extensively to store and manipulate blocks of data.

Using Dictionaries

Dictionaries are like the city cousins of arrays. They both pretty much do the same things, but dictionaries add a new level of sophistication.

I love dictionaries, now. But I have to admit that when I started programming with Objective-C and Cocoa, trying to get my head around the idea of dictionaries was a real challenge — not because dictionaries are hard; they really aren't. The "problem" was because of what you can do with them. Not only will you use them to hold property list objects, but you'll also use them to hold application objects — just as you did with the array that holds Transaction objects.

So, now, I take you through them slowly and with lots of illustrations.

Understanding a dictionary's keys and values

As I said, in many ways, dictionaries are like the arrays that you used earlier — they are a container for other objects. Dictionaries are made up of pairs of *keys* and *values*. A key-value pair within a dictionary is called an *entry*. Both the key and the value must be *objects,* so each entry consists of one *object* that is the key (usually an NSString) and a second object that is that key's value (which can be anything, but in a property list must be a property list object). Within a dictionary, the keys are unique.

You use a key to look up the corresponding value. This works like your real-world dictionary, where the word is the key and its definition is the value. (Do you suppose that's why they are called dictionaries?)

So, for example, if you have an NSDictionary that stores the currency symbol for each currency, you can ask that dictionary for the currency symbol (value) for the euro (key).

Although you can use any kind of object as a key in an NSDictionary, keys in property list dictionaries have to be strings, and I'm sticking to that here. You can also have any kind of object for a value, but again if you are using them in a property list, they all have to be property list objects as well.

The same rules hold for arrays. Now you are using one to hold Transaction objects, but if you want to write and read an array as a plist file (and you will), they can hold only property list objects.

NSDictionary has a couple of basic methods that you will be using:

- ✔ count: The count method gives you the number of entries in the dictionary.
- ✔ objectForKey:: The objectForKey: method gives the value for a given key.

In addition, the methods writeToFile:atomically: and initWith ContentsOfFile: cause a dictionary to write a representation of itself to a file and to read itself in from a file, respectively.

If an array or dictionary contains objects that are not property list objects, you can't save and then restore them by using the built-in methods for doing so.

Just as with an array, a dictionary can be _static_ (NSDictionary) or _mutable_ (NSMutableDictionary). NSMutableDictionary adds a couple of additional basic methods — setObjectForKey: and removeObjectForKey:, which enable you to add and remove entries, respectively.

Creating a dictionary

Enough talk; it's time to code.

To create a dictionary in my program that will enable me to look up the currency symbol for a given country, I must add the following lines of code:

```
NSDictionary *appDictionary = [[NSDictionary alloc]
        initWithObjectsAndKeys:
        @"€", @"Europe", @"£", @"England", nil];
```

This creates a dictionary for me with two keys, `Europe` and `England`. (To get the currency symbols as I did, in Xcode choose Edit⇨Special Characters or press ⌘+Option+T.)

`initWithObjectsAndKeys:` takes an alternating sequence of *objects* and *keys*, terminated by a `nil` value (as you can probably guess, just as with an array, you can't store a `nil` value in an `NSDictionary`).

I want to point out that the order is *objects* and *keys*. I can't begin to tell you how often I get that backward.

This step creates the dictionary that you see in Figure 15-2.

Figure 15-2:
The
`appDic-`
`tionary`.

appDictionary	
Key	**Value**
Europe	€
England	£

To look up the value for a key in a dictionary, you send the `objectForKey:` message:

```
NSLog(@"The currency symbol for the euro is %@",
        [appDictionary objectForKey:@"Europe"]);
```

In this case, I am using the key `Europe` to look up the currency symbol in the `appDictionary`. Lo and behold, what I get is this:

```
The currency symbol for the euro is €
```

You can imagine using this quite a bit in applications like this one, as well as for other things. By the way, if no key exists, for Antarctica for example, `objectForKey:` returns `nil`, which gives me the opportunity to respond to the user or do whatever I might want to about it.

On Mac OS X 10.5 and later, `NSDictionary` supports fast enumeration just like its cousin `NSArray`. As I point out, a dictionary is very similar to an array with obviously some extra stuff. You can, for example, iterate through a dictionary by using the `for in` construct to go through the keys of a dictionary:

```
for (id key in appDictionary) {
  NSLog(@"key: %@, value: %@", key,
                    [appDictionary objectForKey:key]);
}
```

The previous lines of code will go through every key in the dictionary, returning the key in the `key` variable, allowing you to look up that entry by using the `objectForKey:` method. You can also use the following, more compact form:

```
for (id key in appDictionary) {
  NSLog(@"key: %@, value: %@", key, appDictionary[key] );
}
key: Europe, value: €
key: England, value: £
```

Adding a plist to Your Project

Although I'm sure you found that explanation of dictionaries fascinating, I still haven't shown you how to use a file instead of having to create the dictionary in your program. If you use a file, you can use Xcode's handy editor (which I show you in a moment) to add new currencies and countries as you develop your program.

If you have been following along with me, note that I extend what you did in Chapter 14. If you want to start from a clean copy of the project, you can use the project found in the Chapter 15 Start Here folder at the website.

Create a plist for your program by following these steps:

1. **In the Project navigator (at the left in the Xcode Project window), select Vacation (at the top of the pane) and then choose File⇨New File or press ⌘+N.**

   The New File dialog appears.

2. **Choose Resource under the OS X heading in the left pane and then select Property List, as shown in Figure 15-3.**

3. **Click the Next button.**

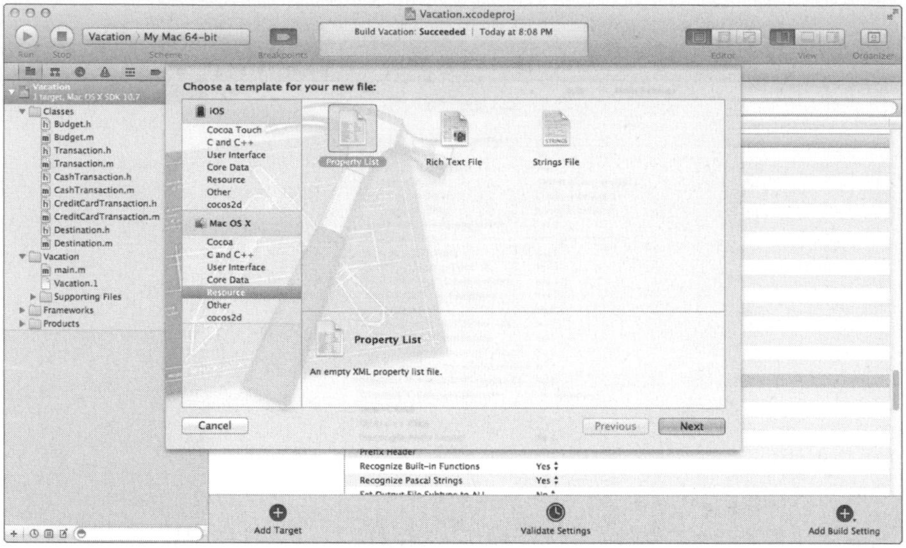

Figure 15-3:
Creating
the plist.

4. **Enter the filename** AppData.plist. **Navigate to your computer's Desktop and create a new folder named Example 15A as the location to create this file. Then press Return (Enter) or click Create.**

You should now see a new item called AppData.plist under Vacation, in the Project navigator files list shown in Figure 15-4. It is very important that you save this file to a specific location; I chose to create a folder called Example 15A because it's easy to remember and it's simple to specify that location programmatically when your code is executing, as you see later.

In the Editor pane, you can see Xcode's property list editor — empty, waiting for you to add entries to it.

5. **Select the Root item and choose Editor⇨Add Item.**

A new entry appears, as you can see in Figure 15-5.

6. **Click the pop-up menu arrows to choose the type of entry and select String.**

It can be any of the property list objects I talked about at the beginning of this chapter, but String, which should already be selected, is the one you want here.

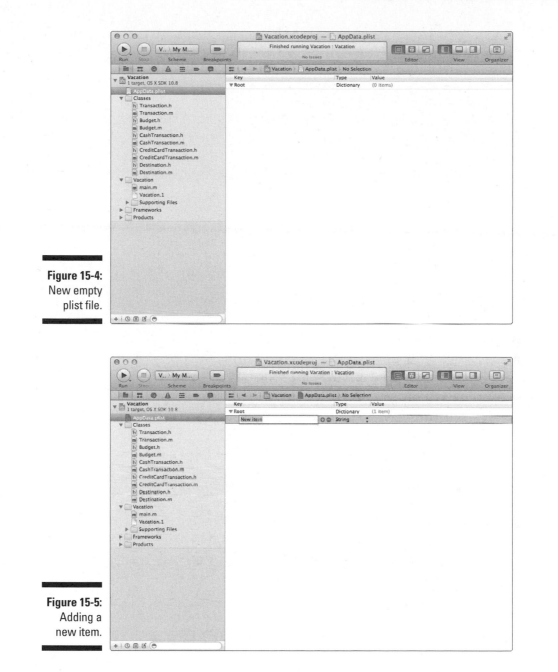

Figure 15-4:
New empty
plist file.

Figure 15-5:
Adding a
new item.

7. **In the Key field, enter** Europe, **and then double-click (or tab to) the Value field and enter** €, **as shown in Figure 15-6.**

Figure 15-6:
Enter
Europe
and €.

TIP

To get the currency symbols, choose Edit⇨Special Characters or press ⌘+Option+T.

8. **Click the + icon in the middle of the entry (row) you just added, and you get a new entry. This time enter** England **and** £.

When you are done, your plist should look like the one shown earlier in Figure 15-1.

Using plists

The only file you work with in this chapter is main.m. So start by making the following changes to use the plist.

In main in main.m, add the code to main in bold and delete the bold, italic, underlined code in Listing 15-1.

Listing 15-1:   Using plists

```objc
#import <Foundation/Foundation.h>
#import "Destination.h"

int main (int argc, const char * argv[]) {
  @autoreleasepool {

    NSString* appDataPath  =
        @"/Users/Karl/Desktop/Example 15A/AppData.plist";
    NSMutableDictionary *appDictionary =
            [[NSMutableDictionary alloc] initWithContentsOf
            File:appDataPath];
    NSString* europeSymbol = [[NSString alloc]
            initWithFormat:@"%@",
            [appDictionary valueForKey:@"Europe"]];
    NSString* englandSymbol = [[NSString alloc]
            initWithFormat:@"%@",
            [appDictionary valueForKey:@"England"]];

    NSString* europeText = [[NSString alloc]
                        initWithFormat:@"%@", @"Europe"];
    Destination* europe = [[Destination alloc]
            initWithCountry:europeText andBudget:1000.00
            withExchangeRate:1.25];
    NSString* englandText = [[NSString alloc]
            initWithFormat:@"%@", @"England"];
    Destination* england = [[Destination alloc]
            initWithCountry:englandText andBudget:2000.00
            withExchangeRate:1.50];


    for (int n = 1; n < 2; n++) {
      double transaction = n*100.00;
//    NSLog (@"Sending a %.2f cash transaction",
            transaction);
      NSLog (@"Sending a $%.2f cash transaction",
            transaction);
      [europe spendCash:transaction];

//    NSLog(@"Remaining budget %.2f", [europe leftToSpend]);
      NSLog(@"Remaining budget $%.2f", [europe
            leftToSpend]);
//    NSLog (@"Sending a %.2f cash transaction",
            transaction);
      NSLog (@"Sending a $%.2f cash transaction",
            transaction);
      [england spendCash:transaction];
```

(continued)

Listing 15-1 *(continued)*

```
//   NSLog(@"Remaining budget %.2f", [england
         leftToSpend]);
       NSLog(@"Remaining budget $%.2f", [england
         leftToSpend]);
  }

  [europe setExchangeRate:1.30];
  [england setExchangeRate:1.40];

  int n =1;
  while (n < 4) {
     double transaction = n*100.00;
//   NSLog (@"Sending a %.2f credit card transaction",
         transaction);
       NSLog (@"Sending a %@%.2f credit card transaction",
         europeSymbol, transaction);
     [europe chargeCreditCard:transaction];
//  NSLog(@"Remaining budget %.2f", [europe leftToSpend]);
       NSLog(@"Remaining budget $%.2f", [europe
         leftToSpend]);
//   NSLog (@"Sending a %.2f credit card transaction",
         transaction);
       NSLog (@"Sending a %@%.2f credit card transaction",
         englandSymbol , transaction);
     [england chargeCreditCard:transaction];
//   NSLog(@"Remaining budget %.2f", [england
         leftToSpend]);
       NSLog(@"Remaining budget $%.2f", [england
         leftToSpend]);

     n++;
  }


  }
  return 0;
}
```

The first thing you did here was tell the file system where the AppData. plist file is

```
NSString* appDataPath =
    @"/Users/Karl/Desktop/Example 15A/AppData.plist";
```

As you can see, mine is on the desktop (/Users/Karl/Desktop/Example 15A), and the name of the file is AppData.plist (/AppData.plist), which is what I name it in Step 4. This is known as a *path*. A path is a string that contains the location and name of a file.

Your new plist file is placed in a folder on the Desktop of your machine, which means that the path describing the location of your AppData.plist file is different (unless your name is also Karl), so you have to change the path in `main.m` to reflect your unique configuration.

You change the path every time you change the location or name of a folder your AppData.plist file is in.

When you start programming with either the `AppKit` (for the Mac) or the `UIKit` (for the iPhone), you won't have to specify the path so precisely. You will generally have your plist files in what's called a *bundle* or in your home directory. An application bundle contains the application executable and any resources used by the application. It includes, for example, the application icon, other images, localized content, *and plist files.* You also will store your files in your home directory — generally of the form `/Users/your_account_name` — or in some other place where you will be able to find them by using Cocoa functionality available in your program — you won't have to "hard-code" the location as I have here. In the case of a Foundation Command Line Tool, however, you need to specify exactly where the plist file is.

This is a great opportunity to introduce bugs, as you move this code from project to project. So, if something doesn't seem to be working right, the location of the plist file is one of the first places to check to see whether it's the cause of the problem.

Creating a mutable dictionary

Next you create a mutable dictionary and read the file into it, using the `initWithContentsOfFile:` method (it needs to be mutable because I show you how to modify it in the section "Updating the dictionary," later in this chapter):

```
NSMutableDictionary *appDictionary =
        [[NSMutableDictionary alloc]
         initWithContentsOfFile:appDataPath];
```

You specified where the file was located (`appDataPath`) and then sent a message to the `NSMutableDictionary` to initialize itself with that file.

`NSDictionary`, `NSMutableDictionary`, `NSArray`, and `NSMutable Array` all have the methods `initWithContentsOfFile:` and `writeToFile:atomically:` that read themselves in from a file and write themselves out to a file, respectively. This is one of the things that makes property list objects so useful.

As I mention earlier, property list containers, and only property list containers, can read themselves in from and write themselves out to a file. The other property list objects can only store themselves, without any effort on your part, as part of a file.

Creating, initializing, and using the symbol string

The next thing you do is access the key Europe and create and initialize a string `europeSymbol` with its value. I do the same thing for England and `englandSymbol`:

```
NSString* europeSymbol = [[NSString alloc] initWithFormat:
        @"%@", appDictionary[@"Europe"]];
NSString* englandSymbol = [[NSString alloc]
        initWithFormat:@"%@",
        appDictionary[@"England"]];
```

`NSDictionary` and `NSMutableDictionary` objects allow your code to use the bracket notation (`[]`) to access objects via their keys. You can also use the following code to do the same thing:

```
NSString* europeSymbol = [[NSString alloc] initWithFormat:
        @"%@", [appDictionary valueForKey:@"Europe"]];
NSString* englandSymbol = [[NSString alloc]
        initWithFormat:@"%@",
        [appDictionary valueForKey:@"England"]];
```

Either approach causes the dictionary to look for the key you give it (`@"England"`). If it finds the key, the corresponding value is returned (in this case £); if it can't find the key, it returns `nil`.

`NSArray` and `NSMutableArray` objects also allow your code to use bracket notation to access their contents; the only difference is that your code must use integer values between the brackets, just as you would if you were calling the method `objectAtIndex:`.

The rest of the changes just add the right currency symbol to the `NSLog` statements for the currency you are using — $ for your dollar-based transactions and the amount of your budget remaining, and `europeSymbol` (€) and `englandSymbol` (£) for credit card transactions in euros and pounds, respectively.

Now that you have updated the file, click the Run button on the Project Window toolbar to build and run the application.

You should see the following in the Debugger Console:

```
I'm off to Europe
I'm off to England
Sending a $100.00 cash transaction
Remaining budget $900.00
Sending a $100.00 cash transaction
Remaining budget $1900.00
Sending a €100.00 credit card transaction
Remaining budget $770.00
Sending a £100.00 credit card transaction
Remaining budget $1760.00
Sending a €200.00 credit card transaction
Remaining budget $510.00
Sending a £200.00 credit card transaction
Remaining budget $1480.00
Sending a €300.00 credit card transaction
Remaining budget $120.00
Sending a £300.00 credit card transaction
Remaining budget $1060.00
```

You can find the completed project at the website in the Example 15A folder, which is in the Chapter 15 folder.

Dictionaries of Dictionaries

Although using a plist and dictionary this way is very clever (at least I think so), it just barely shows what you can do with dictionaries — especially considering what you see as you look at some of the code in the frameworks. In that spirit, I make things a little more interesting.

Creating a more complex plist

You can continue working based on what you have done or use the project at the website in the Example 15A folder, which is in the Chapter 15 folder, as your base.

Follow these steps to delete all the entries in the plist and create a more interesting plist:

1. **Delete the Europe and England entries from your plist.**

   That takes you back to what was shown earlier in Figure 15-4. You have no entries.

2. **In the Editor window, select the Root item and choose Editor⇨Add Item (or Control-click in the window and select Add Row), as you did in Step 5 in the earlier section, "Adding a plist to Your Project" (refer to Figure 15-4).**

   A new entry appears.

3. **Click the pop-up menu arrows to select Dictionary for the type of entry you want instead of String, again, as you did in Step 6 in the section "Adding a plist to Your Project."**

4. **Type in** Europe **as the key.**

5. **Click the triangle next to Europe and make sure that it is pointing down, as shown in Figure 15-7. Then click the + icon (make sure that the triangle is pointing down; if not, you'll be adding a new item at the same level as the dictionary, rather than inside the dictionary).**

These disclosure triangles work the same way as those in the Finder and the Xcode editor. The Property List editor interprets what you want to add based on the triangle. So, if the items are revealed (that is, the triangle is pointing down), it assumes that you want to add a subitem. If the subitems are not revealed (that is, the triangle is pointing sideways), it assumes that you want to add an item at that level. In this case, with the arrow pointing down, you are adding a new entry to the Europe dictionary. If the triangle is pointing sideways, you are entering a new entry under the root. A + tells you that you are going to be creating a new item at the selected level.

6. **Enter a String, with a key of** Currency **and a value of** euro, **as shown in Figure 15-8.**

   This dictionary has two entries. One is the name of the currency, in this case euro, with the key of Currency, and the other is the currency symbol with the key of Symbol. (You won't need the currency name until you add more functionality — on your own — but you will have it here for future use.)

7. **Add the second entry to the Europe dictionary, this time with the key of** Symbol **and the value of** €, **as shown in Figure 15-9.**

8. **Click the disclosure triangle to hide the Europe dictionary entries, as shown in Figure 15-10.**

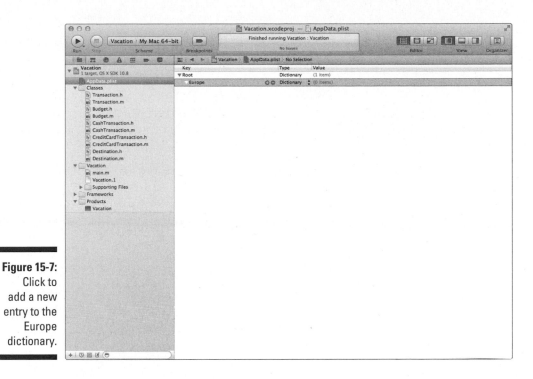

Figure 15-7:
Click to
add a new
entry to the
Europe
dictionary.

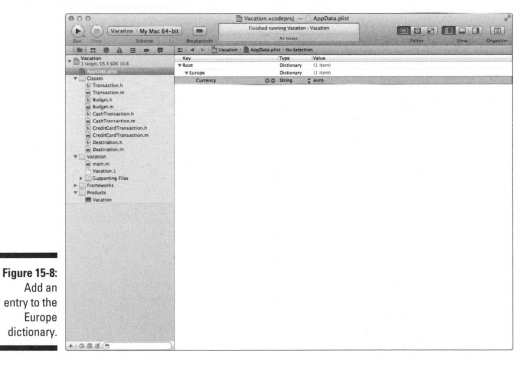

Figure 15-8:
Add an
entry to the
Europe
dictionary.

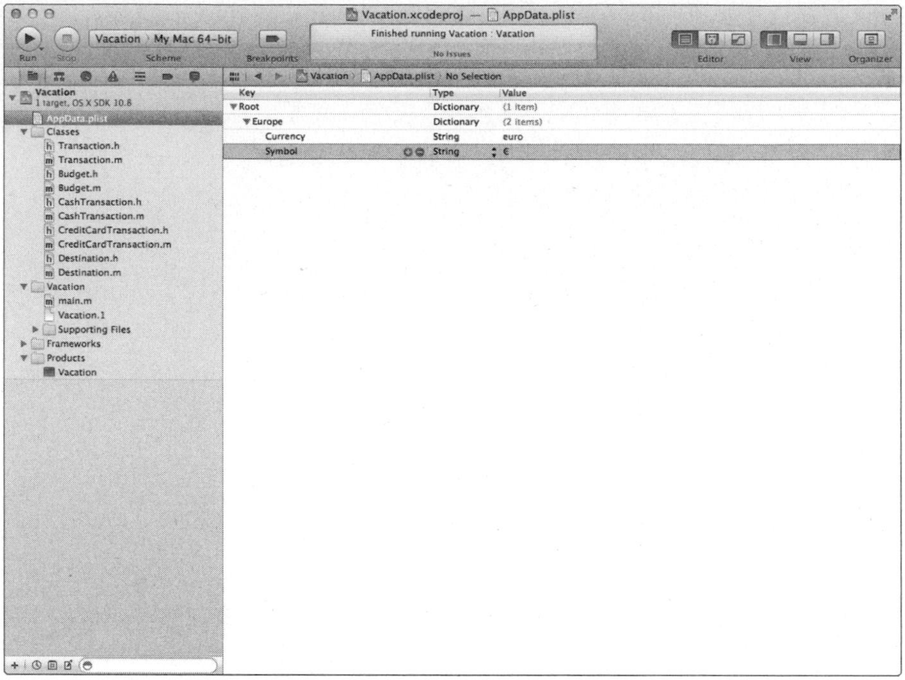

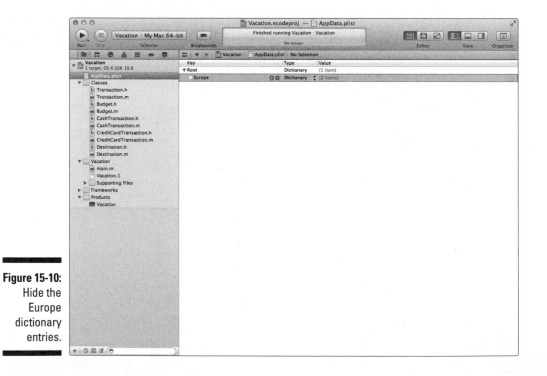

Figure 15-9:
One more
entry.

Figure 15-10:
Hide the
Europe
dictionary
entries.

9. **Click the + icon next to the Europe dictionary and add the England dictionary, as shown in Figure 15-11.**

   As I mention, because the Europe dictionary subitems are hidden, clicking the + icon adds a new entry to the Root.

10. **Repeat Steps 6 and 7 for the England dictionary. This time use the key** `Currency` **and the value** `pound`**, as well as the key** `Symbol` **and the value** `£`**.**

   When you are done, it should look like what is shown in Figure 15-12. (Make sure that you click all the disclosure triangles to expand it all so that you can see it all.)

Earlier I said that the entries in a dictionary can be any property list object. What you have just done is create a dictionary of dictionaries. You have a dictionary for each country that enables you to find the currency (`Currency`) for each country you are visiting and its associated currency symbol (`Symbol`). Again, although you won't be using the currency name, you will need in it the future as you turn this into a "real" application.

The first time I saw the use of a dictionary of dictionaries in code, I had trouble figuring it out, but you will see things like this, as well as arrays of dictionaries, dictionaries of arrays, and so on throughout Cocoa and sample apps.

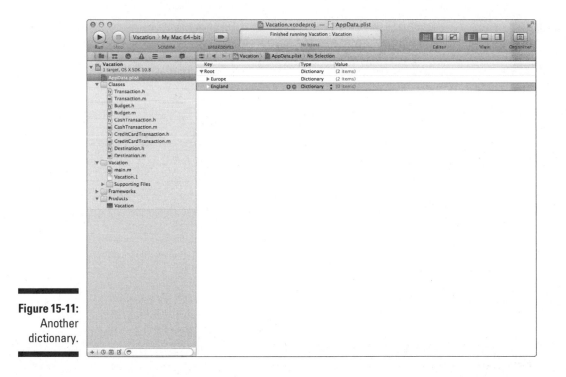

Figure 15-11:
Another dictionary.

And because a picture is worth many hours of contemplation, Figure 15-13 shows how everything fits together.

Using this new "dictionary of a dictionary" is a little more complex than before, but not much, as you see when you write the code.

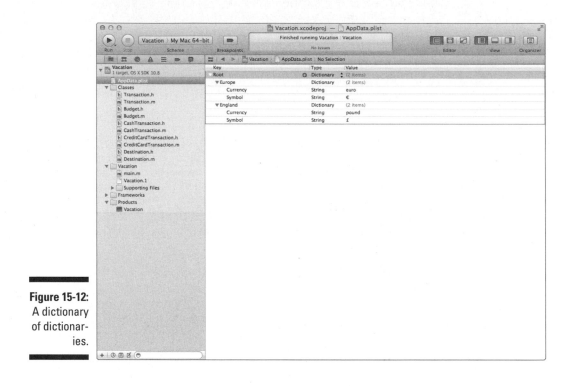

Figure 15-12:
A dictionary of dictionaries.

Figure 15-13:
Visualizing
a dictionary
containing
dictionaries.

Managing a dictionary of dictionaries

Just as you did with the simple dictionary in the last version, you read in the plist and create a dictionary:

```
NSMutableDictionary* appDictionary = [[NSMutableDictionary
        alloc] initWithContentsOfFile:appDataPath];
```

This time, however, the Europe and England keys have a value of another dictionary instead of a currency symbol. So what you need to do is treat them as NSDictionary objects. The following code takes the value for both the Europe and England keys and assigns it to pointers to those dictionaries:

```
NSDictionary* europeDictionary =
        appDictionary[@"Europe"];
NSDictionary* englandDictionary =
        appDictionary[@"England"];
```

Now, you can access the dictionary just as you did before using the key Symbol to get the currency symbol and store it in the variables europe Symbol and englandSymbol:

```
NSString* europeSymbol = [[NSString alloc]
        initWithFormat:@"%@",
        europeDictionary[@"Symbol"]];
NSString* englandSymbol = [[NSString alloc]
        initWithFormat:@"%@",
        englandDictionary[@"Symbol"]];
```

The methods that add entries to dictionaries (as well as arrays) make *copies* of each key argument and add the copy to the dictionary. The value object, on the other hand, receives a retain message to ensure that it won't be deallocated before the dictionary is finished with it.

To create a dictionary of dictionaries in main, follow these steps:

1. **In main in main.m, shown in Listing 15-2, delete the bold, italic, underlined code and add the code in bold.**

   I didn't put in the whole listing for main because I made changes only to the first few lines of code.

2. **Be sure to change the** appDataPath **to whatever your folder name is for this project. I duplicated my project and gave the folder a new name — Example 15B — but use your own project folder name here.**

Listing 15-2:   New, Improved plist

```
//NSString* appDataPath = @"/Users/Karl/Desktop/Example
      15A/AppData.plist";
NSString* appDataPath = @"/Users/Karl/Desktop/Example 15B/
      AppData.plist";
NSMutableDictionary* appDictionary=[[NSMutableDictionary
      alloc]initWithContentsOfFile:appDataPath];
NSDictionary* europeDictionary = appDictionary[@"Europe"];
NSDictionary* englandDictionary =
      appDictionary[@"England"];
//NSString* europeSymbol = [[NSString alloc]
      initWithFormat:@"%@",
      [appDictionary valueForKey:@"Europe"]];
NSString* europeSymbol = [[NSString alloc] initWithFormat:
      @"%@", europeDictionary[@"Symbol"]];
//NSString* englandSymbol = [[NSString alloc]
      initWithFormat: @"%@",
      [appDictionary valueForKey:@"England"]];
NSString* englandSymbol = [[NSString alloc]
      initWithFormat: @"%@",
      englandDictionary[@"Symbol"]];
```

3. **Click the Run button on the Project Window toolbar to build and run the application.**

    You should see the following in the Debugger Console:

```
I'm off to Europe
I'm off to England
Sending a $100.00 cash transaction
Remaining budget $900.00
Sending a $100.00 cash transaction
Remaining budget $1900.00
Sending a €100.00 credit card transaction
Remaining budget $770.00
Sending a £100.00 credit card transaction
Remaining budget $1760.00
Sending a €200.00 credit card transaction
Remaining budget $510.00
Sending a £200.00 credit card transaction
Remaining budget $1480.00
Sending a €300.00 credit card transaction
Remaining budget $120.00
Sending a £300.00 credit card transaction
Remaining budget $1060.00
```

You can find the completed project at the website in the Example 15B folder, which is in the Chapter 15 folder.

Modifying the plist

One thing about plists is that they can be modified. Although you don't want to directly modify the system-level files that you will be using (like preferences — you should use the API provided instead), it's open season on your own files.

As I said, one of the limitations of this application is that each time you run it, you start with a clean budget. Although this is fun from a fantasy viewpoint, it doesn't help you manage your money. So, because all good things must come to an end, you start keeping track of the remaining budget. Each time you run the program, you start where you left off the last time.

You can do this a couple of ways. You can add a new entry to the existing container you created earlier (AppData), or you can create a new file to store what remains in your budget. I show you both ways.

You start by adding a new entry to the AppData plist list, a Budgets dictionary. This dictionary will have keys for Europe and England. The value for each key will be the amount of the remaining budget.

Of course, you could have used Xcode's Property List editor to add the new entry, but I want to show you how to do this kind of thing in your program.

Adding a new entry to the plist

To save the budget data, you start by declaring two variables to hold the budget balances for Europe and England:

```
double europeBudget = 1000;
double englandBudget = 2000;
```

Checking to see whether the dictionary is there

You have to initialize these variables because the first time you run the program, you will have no Budgets key and corresponding dictionary in the AppData plist. This gives you a place to start.

Just as I did with the value for the Europe and England keys, I take the value of the Budgets key and assign it to a pointer to that dictionary:

```
NSMutableDictionary* budgetsDictionary =
        appDictionary[@"Budgets"];
```

This dictionary has to be mutable because I update the values later with the new balances.

Because the `Budgets` dictionary isn't in the plist the first time you run the application, you need to create it. You can determine whether it's already there by checking whether the assignment statement returns `nil` when you look up the `Budgets` key value:

```
if (budgetsDictionary) {
  // dictionary is there
  ...
}
else {
  // dictionary is not there
  ...
}
```

Creating the new entry if it's not there

If `appDictionary[@"Budgets"]` returns `nil`, you create the new diction-ary with the default values and add it to the plist:

```
NSNumber* europeBalance = @( europeBudget );
NSNumber* englandBalance = @( englandBudget );
budgetsDictionary = [[NSMutableDictionary alloc] initW
        ithObjectsAndKeys:europeBalance, @"Europe",
        englandBalance, @"England", nil];
```

If you remember, this is exactly what you did earlier in this chapter when I first show you how to create a dictionary programmatically. In this case, you create a `budgetsDictionary` and initialize it with the `europeBalance` object (our old friend `NSNumber`) and the `Europe` key, and the `england-Balance` objects and the `England` key.

Because dictionaries require each entry to be an object, you are going to create `NSNumber` objects for each of those balances — this is covered in Chapter 7. (Yes, sometimes programming has a strong resemblance to the movie *Groundhog Day.*)

Getting the data stored in the dictionary if it's there

If the dictionary is there, however, you look up the remaining balances for Europe and England by using those keys and assign those values to the two variables you declared earlier:

```
if (budgetsDictionary) {
  europeBudget = [budgetsDictionary[@"Europe"]
        doubleValue];
  englandBudget = [budgetsDictionary[@"England"]
        doubleValue];
  }
```

Then to keep everyone informed, you display the amount left to spend:

```
NSLog(@"You have $%.2f to spend in Europe",
        europeBudget);
NSLog(@"You have $%.2f to spend in England",
        englandBudget);
```

You also now use these balances when you create the destination objects:

```
Destination* europe = [[Destination alloc]
        initWithCountry: europeText
        andBudget:europeBudget withExchangeRate:1.25];
Destination* england = [[Destination alloc]
        initWithCountry:englandText
        andBudget:englandBudget withExchangeRate:1.50];
```

Updating the dictionary

Every time you run your program, you save what's left of your budget by using setObject:forKey:. If you use setObject:forKey: on a key that's already there, it replaces the old value with the new one. (If you want to take a key out of a mutable dictionary, use the removeObjectForKey: method.) Remember, these methods work only for NSMutableDictionary objects.

First you create the europeBalance and englandBalance as objects:

```
NSNumber* europeBalance = @( [europe leftToSpend] );
NSNumber* englandBalance = @( [england leftToSpend] );
```

Now that you have europeBalance and englandBalance as objects, you update the dictionary you created earlier when you read in the plist:

```
budgetsDictionary[@"Europe"] = europeBalance;
budgetsDictionary[@"England"] = englandBalance;
```

You use the bracket notation ([]) once again, only this time in reverse: You are assigning europeBalance as an object in the budgetsDictionary with the key @"Europe". You could also write the same code as follows:

```
[budgetsDictionary setObject:europeBalance forKey:
        @"Europe"];
[budgetsDictionary setObject:englandBalance forKey:
        @"England"];
```

Now for the exciting part. After you update the `Budgets` dictionary, you write the whole file back to the plist file by using the path you defined earlier (`appDataPath`):

```
[appDictionary writeToFile:appDataPath atomically:YES];
```

Well, actually you don't write it; in fact, you don't do any work. `writeToFile:atomically:` is an `NSDictionary` method and does what it implies. You are actually directing the dictionary to write itself to a file. The `atomically` parameter tells it to first write the data to an auxiliary file and, after that is successful, rename it to the path you specified. This guarantees that the file won't be corrupted even if the system crashes during the write operation.

Now that I have written it out, I will be using the new updated dictionary when I read it back in.

You can continue working based on what you have done or use the project at the website in the Example 15B folder, which is in the Chapter 15 folder, as your base.

To add the code that keeps a running balance and saves it in a new dictionary in the plist, make the following changes in Listing 15-3 to `main` in the `main.m` file:

1. **In Listing 15-3, delete the bold, italic, underlined code in** `main` **in** `main.m` **and add the code in bold.**

2. **Be sure to change the** `appDataPath` **to whatever your folder name is for this project. I duplicated my project and put it in a new folder, Example 15C, but use your own project folder name here.**

Listing 15-3: Modifying the Dictionary and plist

```
#import <Foundation/Foundation.h>
#import "Destination.h"

int main (int argc, const char * argv[]) {
  @autoreleasepool {


//NSString* appDataPath  = @"/Users/Karl/Desktop/Example
        15B/AppData.plist";
    NSString* appDataPath  = @"/Users/Karl/Desktop/Example
        15C/AppData.plist";
    NSMutableDictionary*
        appDictionary=[[NSMutableDictionary
        alloc]initWithContentsOfFile:appDataPath];
```

```
    NSDictionary* europeDictionary =
        appDictionary[@"Europe"];
    NSDictionary* englandDictionary =
        appDictionary[@"England"];
    NSString* europeSymbol = [[NSString
        alloc] initWithFormat:@"%@",
        europeDictionary[@"Symbol"]];
    NSString* englandSymbol = [[NSString alloc]
        initWithFormat:@"%@",
        englandDictionary[@"Symbol"]];

    double europeBudget = 1000;
    double englandBudget = 2000;
    NSMutableDictionary* budgetsDictionary =
        appDictionary[@"Budgets"] ;
    if (budgetsDictionary) {
      europeBudget = [budgetsDictionary[@"Europe"]
        doubleValue];
      englandBudget = [budgetsDictionary [@"England"]
        doubleValue];
    }
    else {
      NSNumber* europeBalance = @( europeBudget );
      NSNumber* englandBalance = @( englandBudget );
      budgetsDictionary = [[NSMutableDictionary alloc]
        initWithObjectsAndKeys:
          europeBalance,@"Europe",
          englandBalance,@"England", nil];
      appDictionary[@"Budgets"] = budgetsDictionary;
    }
      NSLog(@"You have $%.2f to spend in Europe",
        europeBudget );
      NSLog(@"You have $%.2f to spend in England",
        englandBudget );


    NSString* europeText = [[NSString alloc]
        initWithFormat: @"%@", @"Europe"];
//Destination* europe = [[Destination alloc]
        initWithCountry: europeText andBudget:1000.00
        withExchangeRate: 1.25];
    Destination* europe = [[Destination
        alloc] initWithCountry:europeText
        andBudget:europeBudget withExchangeRate:1.25];
NSString* englandText = [[NSString alloc]
        initWithFormat:@"%@", @"England"];
//Destination* england = [[Destination alloc]
        initWithCountry:englandText andBudget:2000.00
        withExchangeRate:1.50];
    Destination* england = [[Destination alloc]
```

(continued)

Listing 15-3 *(continued)*

```
        initWithCountry:englandText
        andBudget:englandBudget withExchangeRate: 1.50];

  for (int n = 1; n <  2; n++) {
    double transaction = n*100.00;
    NSLog (@"Sending a $%.2f cash transaction",
        transaction);
    [europe spendCash:transaction];
    NSLog(@"Remaining budget $%.2f", [europe
        leftToSpend]);
    NSLog(@"Sending a $%.2f cash transaction",
        transaction);
    [england spendCash:transaction];
    NSLog(@"Remaining budget $%.2f", [england
        leftToSpend]);
  }

  [europe setExchangeRate:1.30];
  [england setExchangeRate:1.40];

  int n =1;
  while (n < 4) {
    double transaction = n*100.00;
    NSLog (@"Sending a %@%.2f credit card transaction",
        europeSymbol, transaction);
    [europe chargeCreditCard:transaction];
    NSLog(@"Remaining budget $%.2f", [europe
        leftToSpend]);
    NSLog (@"Sending a %@%.2f credit card transaction",
        englandSymbol, transaction);
    [england chargeCreditCard:transaction];
    NSLog(@"Remaining budget $%.2f", [england
        leftToSpend]);
    n++;
  }

  NSNumber* europeBalance = @( [europe leftToSpend] );
  NSNumber* englandBalance = @( [england leftToSpend] );
  budgetsDictionary[@"Europe"] = europeBalance;
  budgetsDictionary[@"England"] = englandBalance;
  [appDictionary writeToFile:appDataPath
        atomically:YES];


  }
  return 0;
}
```

3. **Click the Run button on the Project Window toolbar to build and run the application.**

You should see the following in the Debugger Console:

```
You have $1000.00 to spend in Europe
You have $2000.00 to spend in England
I'm off to Europe
I'm off to England
Sending a $100.00 cash transaction
Remaining budget $900.00
Sending a $100.00 cash transaction
Remaining budget $1900.00
Sending a €100.00 credit card transaction
Remaining budget $770.00
Sending a £100.00 credit card transaction
Remaining budget $1760.00
Sending a €200.00 credit card transaction
Remaining budget $510.00
Sending a £200.00 credit card transaction
Remaining budget $1480.00
Sending a €300.00 credit card transaction
Remaining budget $120.00
Sending a £300.00 credit card transaction
Remaining budget $1060.00
```

You need to run this again to appreciate your handiwork. Before you do, notice the amounts in the last two "Remaining budget" statements — $120.00 and $1060.00, respectively (they are shown in bold).

4. **Click the Run button on the Project Window toolbar to build and run the application.**

As you can see, the starting budgets (in bold) are the same as the ending ones I had you notice in Step 3 (as you would expect).

```
You have $120.00 to spend in Europe
You have $1060.00 to spend in England
I'm off to Europe
I'm off to England
Sending a $100.00 cash transaction
Remaining budget $20.00
Sending a $100.00 cash transaction
Remaining budget $960.00
Sending a €100.00 credit card transaction
Remaining budget $-110.00
Sending a £100.00 credit card transaction
Remaining budget $820.00
```

```
Sending a €200.00 credit card transaction
Remaining budget $-370.00
Sending a £200.00 credit card transaction
Remaining budget $540.00
Sending a €300.00 credit card transaction
Remaining budget $-760.00
Sending a £300.00 credit card transaction
Remaining budget $120.00
```

Of course, after you run this a few times, you find yourself deeply in debt. If you close and then reopen the project, you actually see the new entry in the AppData plist. Delete it in the dictionary, using the Xcode plist editor by selecting the Budgets dictionary entry and pressing Delete, and then selecting File⇨Save (or press ⌘+S).

If you don't see the Budgets dictionary in the plist, and you don't want to go to the trouble of closing and then opening the project, click in any Key or Value field in the AppData plist and add and then delete a space (I know you really haven't changed anything, but that's the point). Then choose File⇨Save or press ⌘+S. You get a message saying This document's file has been changed by another application since you opened or saved it; click Save and you go back to your original budget.

You can find the completed project at the website in the Example 15C folder, which is in the Chapter 15 folder.

Saving Data in a Separate File

Of course, a dictionary is just another property list object, and so is an array. So instead of adding the new Budgets dictionary to the AppData plist, I show you how to save the budget data in an array.

You declare the array you are going to save and initialize it to nil:

```
NSArray* tripBalance = nil;
```

You add a new file here, so you need to create a new path for the file you want to save:

```
NSString* balancePath =@"/Users/Karl/Desktop/Example 15D/
        BalanceData.txt";
```

Notice that the filename will be `BalanceData.txt`, and it will be in the Example 15D folder. As with `appData`, you will change the path every time you change the location or the name of the folder your project is in.

You start again by reading in the data. Reading in the array you saved is similar to reading in the plist:

```
if ([[NSFileManager defaultManager] fileExistsAtPath:
        balancePath]) {
```

First, you ask the file manager (`[NSFileManager defaultManager]`) to check whether the file is there. Previously, you knew the plist was there; you just weren't sure that the `Budgets` entry had been added. If this is the first time you are running the program, the file won't be there. Alternatively, you could have just read in the file and checked for `nil`.

If the file is there, you read in the array by using its `initWithContentsOf-File:` (just as I did with the plist) and copying the values in the array to the `europeBudget` and `englandBudget` variables as you did before:

```
tripBalance = [[NSArray alloc]
                        initWithContentsOfFile:balancePath];
europeBudget = [tripBalance[0] doubleValue];
englandBudget = [tripBalance[1] doubleValue];
    }
```

If the file isn't there, you just continue to use the default values that you initialized `europeBudget` and `englandBudget` with earlier.

The following is an alternative method for reading in files:

```
initWithContentsOfFile:options:error:
```

The `options:` argument gives you control over file system caching and is way, way beyond the scope of this book. The `error:` argument returns a pointer to an `NSError` object. I leave the exploration of this topic to you as a "personal" exercise.

Again, after sleeping, eating, and drinking your way through Europe and England, you need to save what little you have left:

```
tripBalance= [[NSArray alloc] initWithObjects:
            europeBalance, englandBalance, nil];
[tripBalance writeToFile:balancePath atomically:YES];
```

You check to see whether you have an array that you created when you read in the data — that is why you have to be sure to initialize it to `nil` when you declare it. If you do, release it and create a new one. This is an alternative to replacing each object in the array and means that you don't need a mutable array. Then just as you did with the dictionary, you tell the array to write itself as a file.

You can continue working based on what you have done or use the project at the website in the Example 15C folder, which is in the Chapter 15 folder, as your base.

Follow these steps to use a file for saving and retrieving your program's Europe and England budgets:

1. **In Listing 15-4, delete the bold, italic, underlined code in** `main` **in** `main.m` **and add the code in bold.**

   I didn't include the whole listing for `main` because you will delete only the code you added in the earlier section, "Modifying the plist."

   Instead of doing the delete-and-add thing, you can start again with the Example 15B project at the website and add the new code in the same places that you added the code in the previous section.

2. **Be sure to change the** `appDataPath` **to whatever your folder name is for this project. I duplicated my project and put it in a new folder, Example 15D, but use your own project folder name here.**

3. **Notice that you have a new** `NSString` `balancePath` **holding the path to the new file. Be sure to change the** `balancePath` **to whatever your folder name is for this project.**

Listing 15-4:   Saving Balance Data to an Array

```
//NSString* appDataPath  = @"/Users/Karl/Desktop/Example
        15C/AppData.plist";
  NSString* appDataPath  = @"/Users/Karl/Desktop/Example
        15D/AppData.plist";
. . .
  double europeBudget = 1000;
  double englandBudget = 2000;;
//NSMutableDictionary* budgetsDictionary = [appDictionary
        valueForKey:@"Budgets"] ;
//if (budgetsDictionary) {
//   europeBudget = [budgetsDictionary[@"Europe"]
        doubleValue];
//   englandBudget = [budgetsDictionary[@"England"]
        doubleValue];
```

```
//}
//}
//else {
//   NSNumber* europeBalance = @( europeBudget );
//   NSNumber* englandBalance = @( englandBudget );
//   budgetsDictionary = [[NSMutableDictionary alloc] ini
              tWithObjectsAndKeys:europeBalance, @"Europe",
              englandBalance, @"England", nil];
//   appDictionary[@"Budgets"] = budgetsDictionary;
//}

  NSArray* tripBalance = nil;
  NSString* balancePath =@"/Users/Karl/Desktop/Example
          15D/BalanceData.txt";

  if ([[NSFileManager defaultManager]
                  fileExistsAtPath: balancePath]) {
    tripBalance = [[NSArray alloc]
                  initWithContentsOfFile:balancePath];
    europeBudget = [tripBalance[0] doubleValue];
    englandBudget = [tripBalance[1] doubleValue];
}
  NSLog(@"You have $%.2f to spend in Europe",
                                  europeBudget );
  NSLog(@"You have $%.2f to spend in England",
                                  englandBudget );
...

  NSNumber* europeBalance = @( [curope leftToSpend] );
  NSNumber* englandBalance = @( [england leftToSpend] );

//budgetsDictionary[@"Europe"] = europeBalance;
//budgetsDictionary[@"England"] = englandBalance;
//[appDictionary writeToFile:appDataPath
                                  atomically:YES];

  tripBalance = [[NSArray alloc] initWithObjects:
          europeBalance, englandBalance, nil];
  [tripBalance writeToFile:balancePath atomically:YES];
```

4. **Click the Run button on the Project Window toolbar to build and run the application.**

    You should see the same result that you saw previously.

This time, to start over, you need to delete the new file that you created — `BalanceData.txt`, which you find at the path you specified in `balancePath`.

You can find the completed project at the website in the Example 15D folder, which is in the Chapter 15 folder.

Saving Objects as Objects

This chapter shows you a great way to start saving your data, but you have other ways as well.

As you develop applications, you will find that not all your objects are made up of property list objects. Even in this simple application, your `Destination` object has an array of `Transaction` objects.

Although most objects can eventually be deconstructed into property list objects, this can take a lot of work and requires changing the logic you use if you add or remove something from an object — not very extensible is it?

Cocoa does, however, provide several ways to save objects as objects. I leave this, too, as an exercise for you to do on your own.

Chapter 16

Extending the Behavior of Objects

· ·

In This Chapter

▶ Using delegation to implement a new transaction

▶ Defining formal and informal protocols

▶ Using categories to extend a class

· ·

1 n your application so far, you have two kinds of transaction objects, a `CashTransaction` and a `CreditCardTransaction`. As I was field-testing the application, sitting in a bar (bars in Italy serve coffee, so don't get too excited) on the Grand Canal in Venice, I needed some euros, so I went to the ATM.

It dawned on me that because this was not my own bank's ATM, I might have to pay a $2 transaction fee. I realized I need to add a new type of transaction — ATM.

In Chapter 10, you find out how to use inheritance to create subclasses such as `CashTransaction` and `CreditCardTransaction` to *implement subclass–specific functionality*, whose default implementation was defined by a superclass, such as the spend functionality in the `Transaction` class. I also mention that you could also use inheritance to add new functionality, new methods, and new instance variables to a subclass.

So it makes sense to use inheritance to create a new subclass. If I did that it would also mean, thanks to polymorphism, that the only changes I would have to make to my program, besides defining the new class, would be to add a new method to `Destination` (in addition to the existing `spendCash:` and `chargeCreditCard:` methods) — `useATM:` to create the new ATM transaction.

As you start to work with the `UIKit` and `AppKit` frameworks, you will be using inheritance to extend the behavior of framework classes and to add your own unique application behavior. But sometimes, for some technical or architectural reason, inheritance will not be an option. But all is not lost.

Objective-C allows you to accomplish virtually the same thing by using *delegation,* which enables you to implement methods defined by other classes, and *categories,* which enable you to extend the behavior of a class without subclassing.

Although you are probably not going to use delegation and categories in your programs (yet), they are used a lot in the frameworks. So, to make using the frameworks as transparent as possible, I explain them before you stumble across them on your own. As I mention, frameworks provide a good model for how to create extensible and enhanceable applications, and in this chapter, you see an example of that in action.

To show you how to do that, instead of using inheritance and modifying the code in `Destination` (or creating a `Destination` subclass) to implement `useATM:`, I show you how to accomplish the same thing by using delegation and categories.

I am not suggesting that you implement a new `Transaction` type this way. On the contrary; creating a new `Transaction` subclass is the best way to do that. I show you how to use delegation and categories in this way only to illustrate how delegation and categories work because it is often one of the more difficult concepts for programmers new to Cocoa and Objective-C to understand.

Understanding Delegation

I start by showing you how to use delegation to create a class that implements the `spend` method of the `Transaction` (the *delegator*) class, one that behaves in the same way as a subclass.

Delegation is a pattern (I explain patterns in Chapter 11) used extensively in the `UIKit` and `AppKit` frameworks to customize the behavior of an object without subclassing. Instead, one object (a framework object) delegates the task of implementing one of its methods to another object.

To implement a delegated method, you put the code for the behavior your application requires into a separate (*delegate*) object. When a request is made of the delegator, the delegate's method that implements the application-specific behavior is invoked by the delegator.

The methods a class delegates are defined in a *protocol* — similar to the "`spend:` protocol" that you define in the `Transaction` class in Chapter 10. Protocols can be *formal* or *informal.* I start with formal protocols and then work my way into informal ones.

Using Protocols

The Objective-C language provides a way to formally declare a list of methods (including declared properties) as a protocol. The language and the runtime system support formal protocols. For example, the compiler can check for types based on protocols they adopt, and objects can report whether they conform to a protocol.

Declaring a protocol

You declare formal protocols with the `@protocol` directive. If you want to create a `TransactionDelegate` protocol that required that its delegates implement a `spend` message (like its subclasses), you code the following:

```
@protocol TransactionDelegate
@required

- (void) spend: (Transaction *) aTransaction;

@optional

- (void) transaction: (Transaction *) transaction spend:
        (double) amount;

@end
```

Methods can be optional or required. If you do not mark a method as optional, it is assumed to be required; but you can make that designation specific via the use of the `@required` keyword.

I declared the `TransactionDelegate` protocol with a required method — `spend:` — and an optional method, `transaction:spend:`.

The more formal representation is

```
@protocol ProtocolName

  method declarations
@end
```

The method `transaction: (Transaction*) transaction spend: (double) amount` may look a little weird. The method name is `transaction:spend:`, and you see examples of this in some of the framework protocols where a pointer to the delegating object is the first argument in the method.

In Chapter 17, you see that you can use Interface Builder to connect objects to their delegates. Or, you can set the connection programmatically through the delegating object's `setDelegate:` method or `delegate` property. In this chapter, I show you how to set the connection programmatically.

Generally, protocol declarations are in the file of the class that defines it. So you will create the `TransactionDelegate` protocol declaration in its own file, `TransactionDelegate.h`.

Creating a protocol

You start with defining the protocol because that's the easiest step. You won't affect the classes currently in your project; you're just adding something that will be used farther ahead.

If you have been following along with me, I now extend what you did in Chapter 15. If you want to start from a clean copy, you can use the project at the website in the Chapter 16 Start Here folder.

To create the `TransactionDelegate` protocol, here's what you do:

1. **Select the** `Classes` **group in the Project navigator and then choose File**➪**New File (or press ⌘+N) to get the New File dialog.**

2. **In the leftmost column of the dialog, first select Cocoa under Mac OS X; then select the Objective-C protocol in the upper-right pane, as shown in Figure 16-1. Click Next.**

Figure 16-1:
The Objective-C protocol template.

Choose a template for your new file:

- **iOS**
  - Cocoa Touch
  - C and C++
  - User Interface
  - Core Data
  - Resource
  - Other

- **OS X**
  - Cocoa
  - C and C++
  - User Interface
  - Core Data
  - Resource
  - Other

Objective-C class   Objective-C category   Objective-C class extension   Objective-C protocol

Objective-C test case class

Objective-C protocol

An Objective-C protocol which conforms to the <NSObject> protocol, and includes the <Foundation/Foundation.h> header.

Cancel   Previous   Next

3. **Enter** TransactionDelegate **in the Protocol field and click Next.**

4. **Click Create to add the file to the project and save it in the default location.**

   You've now added a single file, `TransactionDelegate.h`, to your project. Anytime you want to create a class that can act as a delegate for a `Transaction` object, you use this protocol as a starting point.

5. **Add the code in bold in Listing 16-1 to** `TransactionDelegate.h`**.**

Listing 16-1:   The TransactionDelegate Protocol

```
#import <Foundation/Foundation.h>
@class Transaction;

@protocol TransactionDelegate <NSObject>

@required

- (void) spend: (Transaction*) aTransaction;

@optional

- (void) transaction: (Transaction*) aTransaction
          spend: (double) anAmount;

@end
```

You've created the delegate protocol — the set of methods that a delegate object must implement, and which a class making use of that delegate can execute. Next you add code to the `Transaction` class to enable it to call upon a `TransactionDelegate` objcct, if one is assigned to it.

Adding delegation to Transaction

So far, you have created a protocol that defines how a protocol for the `Transaction` class should act to handle the `spend:` method. It now becomes the responsibility of the delegator, `Transaction`, to invoke the `spend:` method in its delegate. Here's how you do that in `Transaction`:

1. **Remove the bold, italic, underlined code and add the code in bold to the** `Transaction.h` **file.**

   ```
   #import <Foundation/Foundation.h>
   #import "TransactionDelegate.h"
   @class Budget;

   @interface Transaction : NSObject {
   ```

```
   //Budget *budget;
   //NSNumber *amount;
   NSString *name;
}

- (id) initWithAmount: (double) theAmount forBudget:
         (Budget*) aBudget;
- (void) spend;
@property (nonatomic) Budget *budget;
@property (nonatomic) id<TransactionDelegate>
         delegate;
@property (nonatomic,readwrite) NSNumber *amount;

@end
```

You did several things here:

   a. Added the instance variable `delegate`. This is the object that implements the behavior you specified in the protocol. This object is declared as `id<TransactionDelegate>` so that the compiler knows to expect that the object implements the `TransactionDelegate` protocol and so that Xcode can let you know when you try to assign an object that doesn't implement it.

   b. Removed the budget and amount instance variables. These are being re-created as properties.

   c. Added three properties: one to be able to set the `delegate` and two others to allow the delegate access to the `amount` and `budget` instance variables. Doing this means that you have to change the code in `CashTransaction.m` and `CreditCardTransaction.m`, but the change is pretty easy and you can take care of that after you change `Transaction.m`.

2. **Remove the bold, italic, underlined code and add the code in bold to the** `Transaction.m` **file.**

```
#import "Transaction.h"
#import "Budget.h"

@implementation Transaction

- (void) spend {
  if (self.delegate)
  {
    [self.delegate spend:self];
  }
}

- (id) initWithAmount: (double) theAmount forBudget:
         (Budget*) aBudget {
```

```
    if (self = [super init]) {
      //budget = aBudget;
      //amount = @( theAmount );
      self.budget = aBudget;
      self.amount = @( theAmount );
    }
      return self;
  }


@end
```

You modified the assignment statements for the budget and amount values because you changed them to properties, so now your code must use them as properties. Changing budget and amount to properties enables other classes — such as ATMTransactionDelegate — to access them directly.

To make sure that the subclasses of Transaction respect the implementation of budget and amount as properties, you need to modify both CashTransaction.m and CreditCardTransaction.m as follows:

1. **Remove the bold, italic, underlined code and add the code in bold to the CashTransaction.m file.**

   ```
   - (void) spend {
     //[budget spendDollars: amount];
     [self.budget spendDollars: self.amount];
   }
   ```

2. **Remove the bold, italic, underlined code and add the code in bold to the CreditCardTransaction.m file.**

   ```
   - (void) spend {
     //[budget chargeForeignCurrency: [amount
         doubleValue]];
     [self.budget chargeForeignCurrency: [self.amount
         doubleValue]];
   }
   ```

The changes to CashTransaction.m and CreditCardTransaction.m simply make sure that your code formally obeys the implementation of budget and amount as properties within the superclass.

Thus far, Destination has never created a Transaction object, and its spend: method has never been invoked. Using delegation, however, requires creating Transaction objects that invoke the delegate's spend: method in the Transaction object's spend: method.

Because this is a formal protocol, I can assume that because `spend:` is `@required`, the delegate object will have implemented it — the compiler refuses to build your program if a class that declares it adopts the protocol that does not implement the required methods. For optional methods, I need to determine whether the message is implemented before I execute it. To find out whether the optional `transaction:spend:` method has been implemented by `delegate`, I can send the delegate this message:

```
if ([delegate respondsToSelector:
                    @selector(transaction:spend:)])
```

`respondsToSelector:` is an `NSObject` method that tells you whether a method has been implemented. Because I made the `spend:` method `@required` and because the delegate object must adopt the protocol `TransactionDelegate`, I don't have to determine that. However, I wanted to show you how much information is available at runtime in Objective-C, and how to implement delegation for the optional methods of formal protocols and for all methods of informal protocols.

Adopting a protocol

Adopting a protocol is similar in some ways to declaring a superclass. In both cases, you are adding methods to your class. When you use a superclass, you are adding inherited methods; when you use a protocol, you are adding methods declared in the protocol list. A class adopts a formal protocol by listing the protocol within angle brackets after the superclass name:

```
@interface ClassName : ItsSuperclass < protocol list >
```

A class can adopt more than one protocol, and if so, names in the protocol list are separated by commas:

```
@interface Translator : NSObject < English, Italian >
```

Just as with any other class, you can add instance variables, properties, and even nonprotocol methods to a class that adopts a protocol.

In the code that follows, you create a new class, `ATMTransactionDelegate`, that adopts the `TransactionDelegate` protocol, which you created a few moments ago.

Use the following steps to add a class — `ATMTransactionDelegate` — that will adopt the `TransactionDelegate` protocol to your project:

1. **Select the** `Classes` **folder in the Project navigator and then select File⇨New File (or press ⌘+N) to get the New File dialog.**

   This tells Xcode to place the new file in the `Classes` group.

2. **In the leftmost column of the dialog, first select Cocoa under OS X; then select the Objective-C class in the upper-right pane. Click Next.**

   You see a new screen asking for some more information.

3. **Enter ATMTransactionDelegate in the Class field and make sure that NSObject is selected in the Subclass Of drop-down menu. Then click Next.**

   This is the new class that will process the ATM transactions.

4. **Choose a location to save the class files, and click Create.**

5. **Add the code in bold to the** `ATMTransactionDelegate.h` **file.**

```
#import <Foundation/Foundation.h>
#import "TransactionDelegate.h"

@interface ATMTransactionDelegate : NSObject
        <TransactionDelegate> {


}

@end
```

   You need to import the header file where the protocol is declared because the methods declared in the protocol you adopted are not declared elsewhere — in this case, as I said, you will be declaring the protocol in the `TransactionDelegate.h` file.

6. **Add the code in bold to the** `ATMTransactionDelegate.m` **file.**

```
#import "ATMTransactionDelegate.h"
#import "Transaction.h"
#import "Budget.h"

@implementation ATMTransactionDelegate

- (void) spend: (Transaction *) aTransaction {

  NSNumber *atmAmount = @( [aTransaction.amount
                doubleValue] + 2.00 );
  [aTransaction.budget spendDollars: atmAmount];
}

@end
```

When you adopt a protocol, you must implement all the required methods that the protocol declares; otherwise, the compiler issues a warning. As you can see, the ATMTransactionDelegate class does define all the required methods declared in the TransactionDelegate protocol. As I said, you can add instance variables, properties, and even nonprotocol methods to a class that adopts a protocol, although your ATMTransactionDelegate is a class that simply implements the required protocol methods.

As you can see, this new transaction is at heart a dollar transaction that adds a $2.00 "convenience" fee charged by the ATM. Because Transaction stores its amount as an NSNumber, your code must first get the value it contains, add 2.00 to it, and then convert it back to an NSNumber.

Even though ATMTransactionDelegate implements a protocol that is used by the Transaction object, it does not automatically have access to the instance variables of the Transaction object. This is why you made amount and budget Transaction class properties and pass a pointer to the Transaction object so that ATMTransactionDelegate can access those instance variables.

I am not going to implement the optional method; I just wanted to show you how to declare one.

You will encounter classes — and likely make some yourself — that adopt protocols *and* handle other responsibilities. For instance, the Destination class maintains an NSMutableArray that contains all the transactions; if you were to write an iOS or OS X app to show that list of transactions, you might use an Apple user interface class that displays a scrolling table which requires a delegate to provide each row of the table with the amount of each transaction. You would then have Destination adopt and implement the needed delegate protocol of the user-interface class, to supply the scrolling table.

Categories

To complete the implementation of the ATM transaction, you need to add a method to Destination to process an ATM transaction just as it does cash and credit cards. The preferred approach is to add the new method to the Destination class or add a new method to a subclass (you'd have to add a subclass if you did have the source code, as is the case with a framework), but instead I want to show you another Objective-C feature.

One of the features of the dynamic runtime dispatch mechanism used by Objective-C is that you can add methods to existing classes without subclassing. The Objective-C term for these new methods is *categories*. A *category* enables you to add methods to an existing class — even to one to which you do not have the source. This is a powerful feature that enables you to extend the functionality of existing classes.

Using categories, you can also split the implementation of your own classes between several files.

How would I use categories to add the `useATM:` method to my `Destination` class? I would start by creating a new category — `ATM`:

```
@interface Destination (ATM)
```

This looks a lot like class interface declaration — except that the category name is listed within parentheses after the class name, and you have no superclass (or colon for that matter). Unlike protocols, categories *do* have access to all the instance variables and methods of a class. And I do mean all, even ones declared `@private`, but you need to import the interface file for the class it extends. You can also add as many categories as you want.

You can add methods to a class by declaring them in an interface file under a category name and defining them in an implementation file under the same name. What you can't do is add additional instance variables.

The methods that the category adds become honestly and truly part of the class type; they aren't treated as "step methods." The methods you add to `Destination` by using the `ATM` category become part of the `Destination` class and are inherited by all the class's subclasses, just like other methods. The category methods can do anything that methods defined in the class proper can do. At runtime, there's no difference.

So, to add this new method, `useATM:`, to `Destination`, you create a category, as follows:

1. **Select the `Classes` group in the Project navigator and then select File⇨New File (or press ⌘+N) to get the New File dialog.**

   This tells Xcode to place the new file in the `Classes` group.

2. **In the leftmost column of the dialog, first select Cocoa under OS X; then select the Objective-C category in the upper-right pane. Then click Next.**

   You see a new screen asking for some more information.

3. **Enter ATM in the Category field and make sure that Destination is selected in the Category on drop-down menu; then click Next.**

4. **Click Create to save the file in the default location.**

   Xcode has named these files `Destination+ATM.h` and `Destination+ATM.m`, as shown in Figure 16-2. This means that you know at a glance that this is a category named ATM for the `Destination` class.

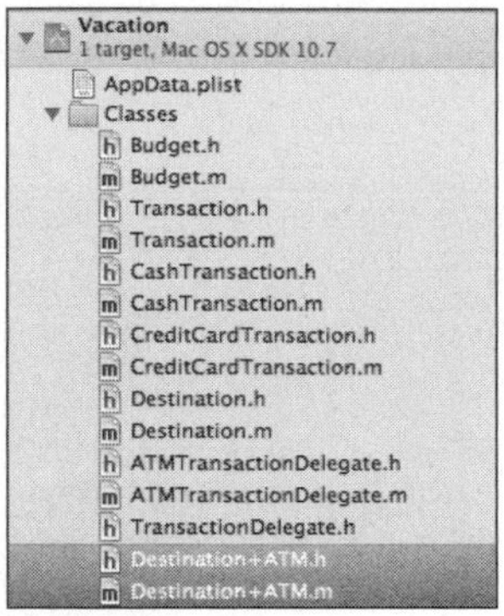

Figure 16-2:
The `Destina-tion+ATM` categories added to Xcode.

5. Create a folder on your desktop to store the data files your project uses — AppData.plist **and** BalanceData.txt. **Be sure to change the** appDataPath **and** balanceDataPath **in** main **in** main.m **to whatever your folder name is for this project.**

I duplicated my project and gave it a new name, Example 16, but use your own project name and user account name here. Make sure that AppData.plist is present in the new folder you create for this project. The program checks for the existence of BalanceData.txt, but it expects to find AppData.plist already at the path you specify.

```
//NSString* appDataPath =@"/Users/Karl/Desktop/Example
      15D/AppData.plist";
NSString* appDataPath = @"/Users/Karl/Desktop/Example
      16/AppData.plist";
//NSString* balancePath =@"/Users/Karl/Desktop/Example
      15D/BalanceData.txt";
NSString* balancePath = @"/Users/Karl/Desktop/Example
      16/BalanceData.txt";
```

6. Add the code in bold to the Destination+ATM.h **file.**

```
#import "Destination.h"


@interface Destination (ATM)

   - (void) useATM: (double) amount;


@end
```

7. **Delete the commented-out bold, italic, underlined code and add the code in bold to the** `Destination+ATM.m` **file.**

```
#import "Destination+ATM.h"
#import "Transaction.h"
#import "ATMTransactionDelegate.h"


@implementation Destination (ATM)

- (void) useATM: (double) amount {

  ATMTransactionDelegate *aTransactionDelegate =
        [[ATMTransactionDelegate alloc] init];

  Transaction *aTransaction = [[Transaction alloc]
        initWithAmount: amount forBudget: theBudget];
  aTransaction.delegate = aTransactionDelegate;
  [transactions addObject:aTransaction];
  [aTransaction spend];
}

@end
```

The new `useATM:` method is almost the same as the previous destination methods; you even added the transaction to the `transactions` array. The only difference here is that you are creating both a `Transaction` object and a delegate that will implement the `spend:` message and updating the transaction object with its delegate in the `useATM:` method.

Figure 16-3 shows the relationship among the `Destination+ATM`'s `useATM:`, the `Transaction`'s `spend:`, and the `ATMTransaction Delegate`'s `spend:` methods.

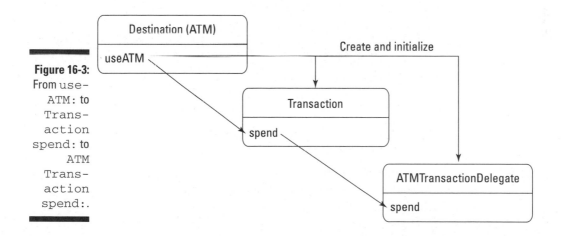

Figure 16-3:
From `use-ATM:` to `Trans-action spend:` to `ATM Trans-action spend:`.

It would have been a lot easier not to create all these new files and just stuff the implementations and interfaces in existing files. I chose to do it the "hard way" because I want you to understand how to structure a real application. You'll thank me later.

8. **Somewhere in the group of** `#imports` **in** main **in** main.m, **add**

```
#import "Destination+ATM.h"
```

9. **Scroll down and after the** while **loop in** main **in** main.m, **add the following lines of code — this will be your only ATM transaction:**

```
NSLog (@"Sending a $50.00 ATM transaction");
[europe useATM: 50];
NSLog(@"Remaining budget $%.2f",
                    [europe leftToSpend]);
```

10. **Delete any previous** balanceData.txt **file — which makes it easier to see that your updated application works correctly.**

11. **Click the Run button on the Project Window toolbar to build and run the application.**

You should see the following in the Debugger Console. I highlighted the new transaction in bold.

```
You have $1000.00 to spend in Europe
You have $2000.00 to spend in England
I'm off to Europe
I'm off to England
Sending a $100.00 cash transaction
Remaining budget $900.00
Sending a $100.00 cash transaction
Remaining budget $1900.00
Sending a €100.00 credit card transaction
Remaining budget $770.00
Sending a £100.00 credit card transaction
Remaining budget $1760.00
Sending a €200.00 credit card transaction
Remaining budget $510.00
Sending a £200.00 credit card transaction
Remaining budget $1480.00
Sending a €300.00 credit card transaction
Remaining budget $120.00
Sending a £300.00 credit card transaction
Remaining budget $1060.00
Sending a $50.00 ATM transaction
Remaining budget $68.00
```

Make sure to delete the file, BalanceData.txt, so that your budget balances are initialized in the code, and not from any previous run.

You can find the completed project on the website in the Chapter 16 folder.

Using categories

You can use categories in the following ways:

- ✔ To extend classes defined by other implementers (instead of subclassing — this is what you just did for `Destination`).
- ✔ To declare informal protocols — I told you I'd get back to this. You have come full circle here, so I examine informal protocols.

Defining informal protocols

In addition to formal protocols, you can also define an informal protocol by grouping the methods in a category declaration:

```
@interface Transaction (TransactionDelegate)

- (void) spend;

@end
```

In fact, if you added the preceding code to the `Transaction.h` file and changed the `ATMTransactionDelegate.h` as follows

```
@interface ATMTransactionDelegate : NSObject/*
          <TransactionDelegate> */
```

your program would work the same way.

Being informal, protocols declared in categories don't receive much language support. You get no type checking at compile time, for example.

An informal protocol may be useful when all the methods are optional, such as for a delegate, but it is typically better to use a formal protocol with optional methods.

I include informal protocols here because they are used by Cocoa, especially in the `AppKit` on the Mac.

Chapter 17

Adding an iPhone User Interface

. . . .

. . . .

I've been promising you all along, at least since Chapter 11, that if you create the right class structure, putting on a user interface will be easy. As you see, I wasn't exaggerating when I said that. The only challenge will be actually finding out how to create a user interface on the iPhone in this chapter and on the Mac in Chapter 18. To do that, you need to know the basics of a program called Interface Builder (part of Xcode), which you use to build the user interface.

Along the way, I also tie together a number of the concepts I talk about that relate to creating enhanceable and extensible applications. Frameworks, as I say again and again, are the poster children for enhanceability and extensibility, and now you finally get to see why. They are created to be reused, so you can integrate techniques that the framework builders use into your own programs. The frameworks are also created to be extended, so that you can go beyond what the framework builders intended and add in your own creative enhancements to make your applications different from every other app by using the frameworks.

When you are done with this chapter and Chapter 18, though, you will have discovered something about developing iPhone and Mac OS X applications: You need to find out more about both. So, I suggest you get copies of *iPhone Application Development For Dummies,* 4th Edition, by Neal Goldstein, and *Mac Application Development For Dummies,* by Karl Kowalski (both published by John Wiley & Sons, Inc.).

I start with the iPhone and then move on to the Mac in the next chapter. Even if you are interested in only one of these platforms, I encourage you to read both chapters because I discuss different aspects of extensibility in each.

This chapter will focus on iPhone development, but you can take the lessons you learn here and use them to develop for the iPad as well.

Creating Your Project

To develop an iPhone application, you work in an Xcode project — just as you have done so far. The only difference is that this time you are creating an iPhone project.

So let's get started. Follow these instructions to create an iPhone application Xcode project:

1. **Launch Xcode if it is not already running.**

2. **Choose File⇨New Project to create a new project, or press Shift+⌘+N.**

3. **In the New Project window (see Figure 17-1), click Application under the iOS heading.**

   Just as before, when you select a template, a brief description of the template is displayed underneath the main pane. As you know, each of these choices is actually a template that generates some code. In the past, when you were using the Foundation Command Line Tool, that code was minimal. Now, however, you are going to see a lot more.

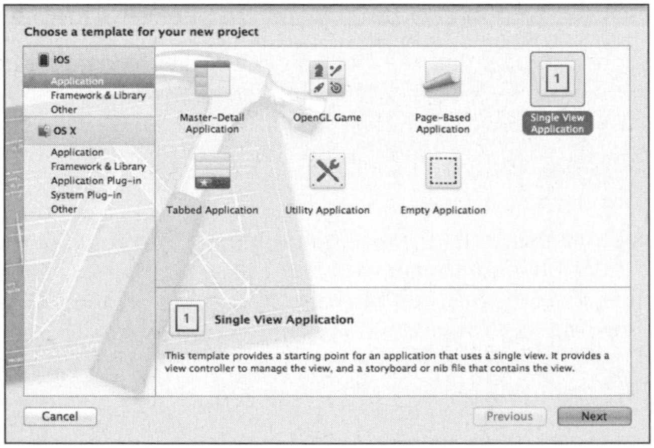

Figure 17-1:
The New Project Assistant.

4. Select Single View Application from the choices displayed and then click Next.

Xcode displays a screen asking you for more information.

Enter the name iVacation in the Product Name field. Enter an identifier in the Company Identifier field, select iPhone in the Devices pop-up menu, and enter iVacation as the Class Prefix. Make sure that the Use Automatic Reference Counting check box is selected and the others are deselected, and click Next.

The Company Identifier can be anything you choose, but Apple recommends using a reverse domain name, as I do in Figure 17-2. The Class Prefix is used by Xcode to name the classes that Xcode will automatically create for you when it creates the project. I don't explain storyboards or unit tests here. I go over Automatic Reference Counting in Chapter 13, and to keep things simple, I enable it in this project.

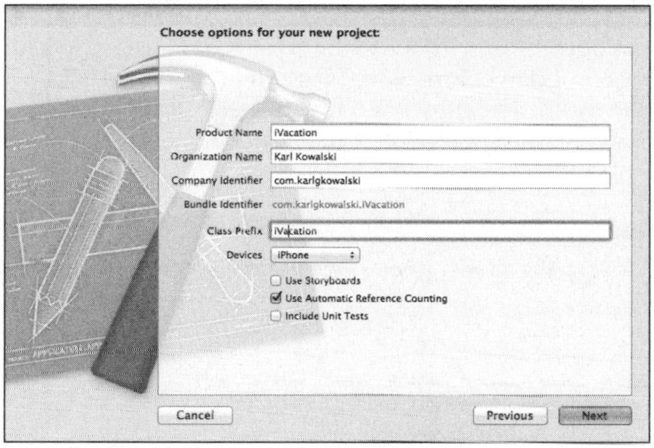

Figure 17-2:
Choosing options for your iPhone project.

5. Choose a Save location, and then click Create.

After you click Create, Xcode creates the project and opens it in the Workspace window.

If you explore the project at this point, you see code generated for you that does many of the things you need to do to initialize an application. You also see some code commented out. I get to what's relevant to this application later.

Note that the Scheme pop-up menu on the Workspace window toolbar shows iPhone 5.1 Simulator (or whatever the latest release of the iOS is). If not, select it from the pop-up menu.

With your project set up, you are now ready to use Interface Builder — the part of Xcode that you use to design and build the user interface. Interface Builder uses .xib files, which Xcode conveniently created for you when you chose the project template to create a Single View Application.

Using Interface Builder to Create a User Interface

Here's how to use Interface Builder to create a user interface:

1. **In the Project navigator (on the left side of the Workspace window), click the triangle next to the** iVacation **folder to expand it if it's not already open, as shown in Figure 17-3.**

2. **Click the** iVacationViewController.xib **file.**

   Doing so opens the .xib file using Interface Builder. If you've never used this program before, you'll see something that looks like what is shown in Figure 17-4. (If you've already been using Interface Builder, you'll see the windows as you last left them.)

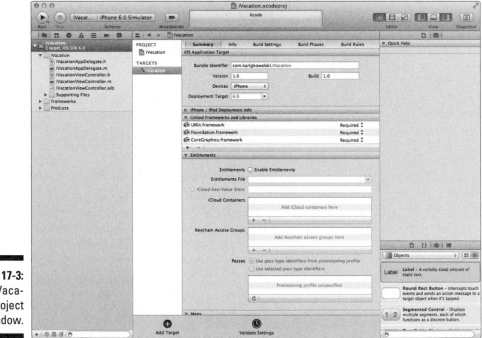

Figure 17-3: The iVacation Project window.

Hide or show
the utilities

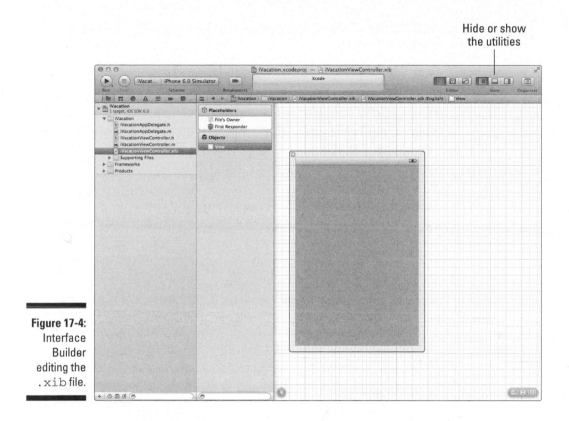

Figure 17-4:
Interface
Builder
editing the
.xib file.

Interface Builder is not merely a program that builds graphical user interfaces. As you'll see, it works with Objective-C to let you build (and automatically create at runtime) both objects for the user interface and the objects that provide the infrastructure for your application.

XIB Files

Interface Builder was originally developed at NeXT Computer, and the files it created were called *nib* files, from NeXT Interface Builder. A nib file is a special type of resource file that you use to store the iOS user interface you create with the Interface Builder editor. Originally, a nib file contained binary data — all 1s and 0s — which was rather difficult to read (for humans).

xib files are XML versions of the original nib files, and these are the user-interface resource files that the Interface Builder editor uses to store all the information about the user interfaces you create for your applications. However, stored deep inside your finished application is a nib file, a compiled version of the xib file you create and edit with Interface Builder.

3. **Click the Hide or show the Utilities button or press ⌘+Option+0 (zero).**

   Your Project window should now look like what is shown in Figure 17-5. Make sure that Show the Object Library is selected in the Library selector bar at the top of the Library pane, and that Objects is selected in the Category menu below the mode selector.

   I resized the Project window to show both the full iPhone screen in the Editor and the contents of the Utilities pane. The Library has all the components you can use to build a user interface. These include the things you see on the iPhone screen — such as labels, buttons, and text fields — and those you need to create the "plumbing" to support the views (and your model), such as the controller I explain in Chapter 11. You won't need to add any objects in this chapter, but you do in Chapter 18.

   As you see, Xcode created `iVacationViewController.xib` when you created the project from the template. In the Interface Builder editor canvas, as you can see in Figure 17-4, a *view* is already there, which is what you will see on the iPhone screen. Now you add some text fields, buttons, and labels so that you can enter a transaction and have the remaining budget displayed. When your application is launched, those items are created for you and displayed on the screen.

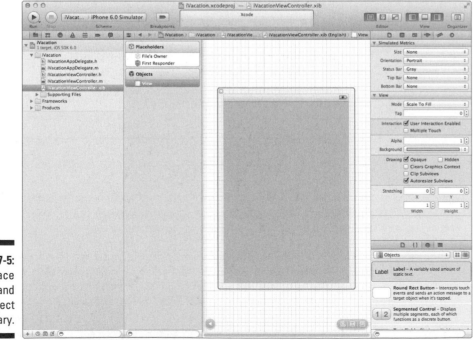

Figure 17-5:
Interface Builder and the Object Library.

4. **Drag a Text Field item from the Library into the View window to add a text entry field, as shown in Figure 17-6.**

Notice the blue lines (at the border) displayed by Interface Builder. They're there to help you conform to the Apple User Interface Guidelines. (You can see the lines best onscreen.)

A Text Field enables you to enter data, and this is where you will be able to enter a transaction amount (yes, no more automatically generated transactions in the `for` and `while` loops — I bet you thought that would never end).

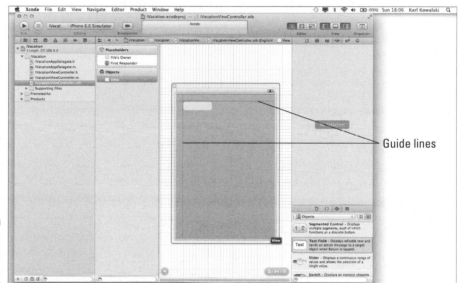

Guide lines

5. **Drag a Label item from the Library window to the View window, as shown in Figure 17-7.**

You see the blue lines again to help you align the items.

Labels display static text in the view (*static text* can't be edited by the user).

6. **Double-click in the Label to enter** 100,000.00 **(the default budget — don't I wish), as shown in Figure 17-8.**

This displays momentarily when the application launches and before the application has a chance to fill in the real budget. I did that to provide enough room in the label to display the budget.

Alternatively, you can widen the label by selecting it and using the selection points you see. Then double-click the Label text and delete the text, "Label" — that way nothing will be displayed in the Label when you launch the application.

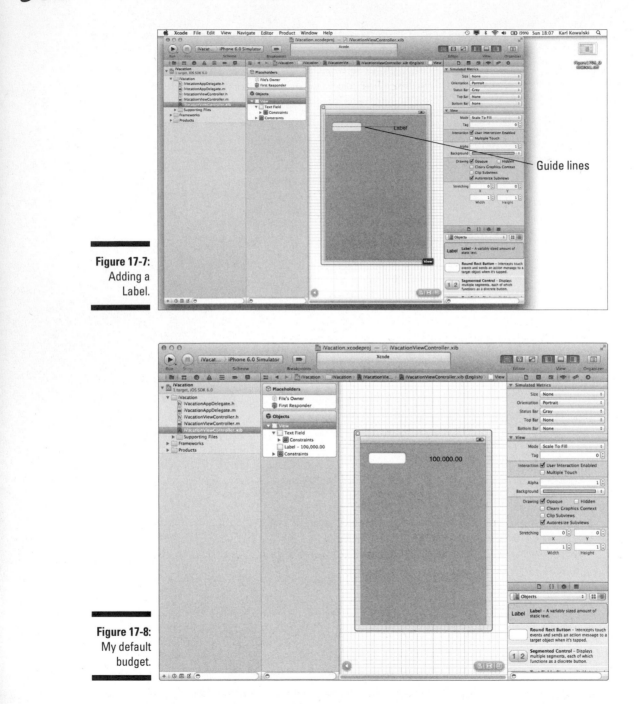

Figure 17-7:
Adding a
Label.

Guide lines

Figure 17-8:
My default
budget.

7. **Drag in two more Labels. Double-click each and enter** Transaction **and** Balance, **respectively.**

8. **Drag in two Round Rect buttons (located between the Label and Text items), double-click each, and enter** Cash **and** Charge, **respectively.**

When you are done, your window should look like what is shown in Figure 17-9.

This is pretty ugly, but it shows you a lot. Although I said this is a crash course, I think you ought to do something about the window color.

9. **Click the background of the View to select the View itself (rather than any of the Labels or the Text Field) in the View window. Click the Show the Attributes Inspector button on the Inspector selector bar, or press ⌘+Option+4.**

The Attributes Inspector appears in the Inspector pane, as shown in Figure 17-10. I resized the Project window to show all the items in the Attributes Inspector.

Note the six icons shown on the Inspector selector bar. They correspond to the File, Quick Help, Identity, Attributes, Size, and Connections Inspectors, respectively, and you can select them here or from the View⇨Utilities menu.

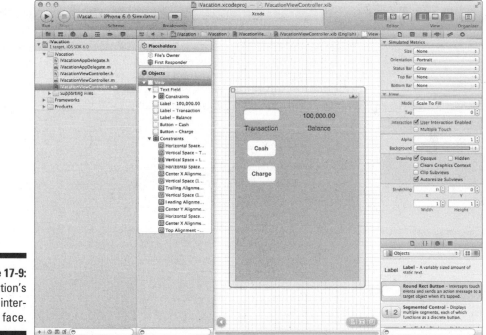

Figure 17-9: iVacation's user interface.

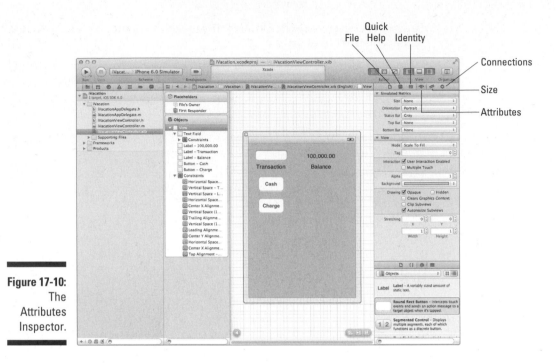

Quick
File Help Identity

Connections

Size

Attributes

Figure 17-10:
The
Attributes
Inspector.

10. Click the left side of the Background drop menu in the Attributes Inspector.

A color picker appears — if you clicked the right side of the Background button, you see a drop menu instead, and you need to select Other from the menu to display the color picker. If it is not the crayon box, click the Crayon Box button at the top of the Colors window, as shown in Figure 17-11.

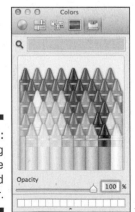

Figure 17-11:
Changing
the
background
color.

11. **Choose the Lime crayon in the color picker to change the background color selection from gray to green.**

    You should see the results of your color selection on your screen. Feel free to try out different colors to find the one that best suits your style.

    Now, I want to show you how to do a couple more things to make the user interface a little more like an iPhone-like.

12. **Click the Label that is displaying** `100,000.00`.

    Note that selecting the View rather than the Label changes what you see in the Attributes Inspector.

13. **Next to Layout in the Inspector window, select Center in the Alignment control, as shown in Figure 17-12.**

    This keeps the amount left in your budget centered over the Balance Label.

    Finally, if you touch in a Text Field on an iPhone or click in one by using the simulator, a keyboard is automatically displayed. The default keyboard has both text and numbers, but you can customize the keyboard by using the Inspector.

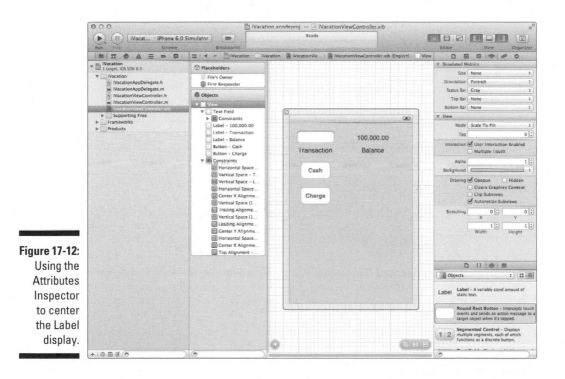

Figure 17-12:
Using the Attributes Inspector to center the Label display.

14. **Click Text Field in the View window, click the Keyboard drop menu, and select Numbers and Punctuation, as shown in Figure 17-13.**

15. **To see what your user interface will look like on the iPhone, click the Run button. Figure 17-14 shows the final result.**

16. **Make your Xcode window the active window again.**

If you can't find it or you minimized it, just click the Xcode icon in the Dock. The iVacation project should still be the active project. (You can always tell the active project by looking at the project name at the top of the Workspace window.)

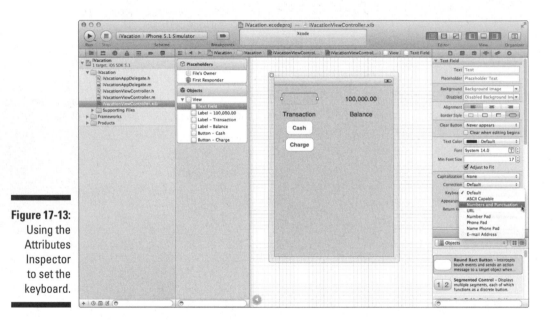

Figure 17-13:
Using the Attributes Inspector to set the keyboard.

When you click the Run button, Xcode installs your app on the iPhone Simulator and launches the Simulator, displaying the user interface.

The Simulator enables you to debug your application and do some other testing on your Mac by simulating the iPhone. Rather than touches, though, you need to use your mouse. You can also use the keyboard you see on the iPhone, clicking one key at a time with your mouse, or the "real" keyboard on the Mac that you're running the Simulator on.

This is only a fraction, and a small one at that, of what you can do with Interface Builder. Now it's time to go back to Xcode and do what little coding you need to run your application on the iPhone. Then you come back to Interface Builder, and I show you how to hook everything up so that when the application is launched, you're ready to go.

Figure 17-14:
The user
interface in
all its glory.

Implementing the User Interface

As I promise earlier, the coding you have to do to hook up the user interface is minimal.

In this section, I extend what you did in Chapter 16. If you want to start from a clean copy of the project from where you left off, you can use the project found at the website in the Chapter 17 Start Here folder, which is in the Chapter 17 folder.

The first thing you have to do is copy all the classes in the Classes folder in the Groups & Files list in the Vacation project (from Chapter 16) into the iVacation project. I show you how to do that in Chapter 11 — you can see how to do that in Figure 17-15.

Figure 17-15:
Copy the classes to the new project.

WARNING!

Be sure to select the Copy Items into Destination Group's Folder check box, and make certain that the check box for iVacation is selected in the Add to Targets section when the Copy dialog pops up.

I also could have chosen Project⇨Add to Project or pressed ⌘+Option+A, navigated to the Vacation project folder, and selected the classes I wanted to add.

Although developing for the iPhone and Mac OS are amazingly similar, a few differences exist.

So far, you have used Foundation headers. But for iPhone development, you have to change that. You need to replace #import <Foundation/ Foundation.h> in the .h files of your classes with #import <UIKit/ UIKit.h>. You can do that in one of two ways.

You can go through all your .h files and replace the statements one by one. Or, you can do a global search and replace. Because I am basically lazy, I prefer the latter.

To perform a global search and replace, follow these steps:

1. **Press ⌘+Option+Shift+F or choose Edit⇨Find⇨Find and Replace in Workspace. This changes the Project navigator pane to what you see in Figure 17-16.**

2. **Enter** #import <Foundation/Foundation.h> **in the Replace field (if it's not already there) and press Return. This gives you a list of all the occurrences. You should see six, as shown in Figure 17-17.**

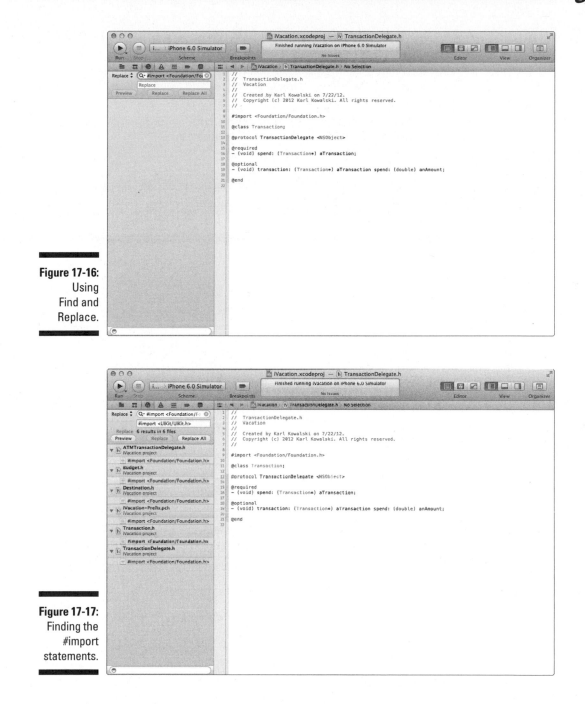

Figure 17-16:
Using
Find and
Replace.

Figure 17-17:
Finding the
#import
statements.

3. **Enter** #import <UIKit/UIKit.h> **in the text field below the Replace field, and click Replace All.**

   You see a dialog asking whether you'd like Xcode to create a snapshot of your project. Xcode is trying to keep you and your work safe, but you don't need this feature right now.

4. **Click Disable to dismiss the dialog, and Xcode performs the global search and replace. Figure 17-18 shows the results.**

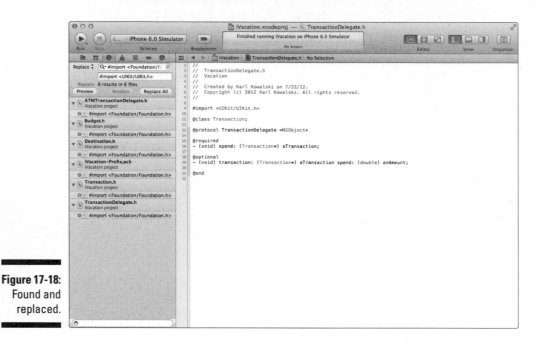

Figure 17-18:
Found and
replaced.

When you create the project, Xcode gives you two classes to start with. The first is the `iVacationAppDelegate` class. This is a *delegate* that is implemented by using a formal protocol of the kind I talk about in Chapter 16. If you click the `iVacationAppDelegate.h` file, you can see the following:

```
@interface iVacationAppDelegate :
                NSObject <UIApplicationDelegate>
```

If you look in the `iVacationAppDelegate.m` file, you see that `application:didFinishLaunchingWithOptions:` was implemented automatically by the template. Adding code here gives you an opportunity to do application-level initialization. You may want to restore the balance data that you have been saving here, for example. You can see that the code here does some fancy footwork with the `viewController` and `window`. You'll also often implement `applicationWillTerminate:`, which gives you an opportunity to do what is necessary before your application shuts down. It is here that you will likely save the balance data. I don't get into that in this book, but you are welcome to play around with it yourself.

This is a great example of how to create extensible applications, using the Objective-C features I explain in Chapter 16. The framework knows how to do everything to create and run a "generic" iPhone application, but it can't know what you need to do for your particular application. To solve that problem, the framework designers created a (formal) UIApplicationDelegate Protocol for you to adopt, with a number of methods that you can implement to give you a say in the application-running process. As I explain in Chapter 16, this is a situation where the framework has to count on your code because it doesn't know what you want to do to initialize or shut down an application. Subclassing is not an option here (the application object is created at startup, before your individual application is even a glimmer in anyone's eye).

What you now focus on is the `iVacationViewController`. In Chapter 11, I explain the Model-View-Controller (MVC) pattern. Understanding it is critical if you are going to develop iOS apps, so if you are a little foggy on that topic, please refer to Chapter 11. The `iVacationViewController` plays the role of the controller in the MVC pattern. In fact, the view you created in Interface Builder is the view part of the pattern, and all those classes you just added are the model, with the `Destination` object acting as the interface for the controller to the model. See, it does all finally fit together.

The `iVacationViewController` is responsible for getting data from the model to the view (which you created in Interface Builder) to display (that `Balance` label, for example) and for sending messages to the model to update itself with new information (transactions, for example). `iVacation-ViewController` is also responsible for view control actions (Text Field input and the Cash and Charge buttons).

You start by entering the pieces necessary to implement these view controller responsibilities. You add some things by editing the Objective-C files and some things by using Interface Builder.

I start with some things you need to add to the `iVacationView Controller.h` file:

1. **Go to the Xcode project window and in the Project navigator pane, click the triangle next to** `iVacation` **to expand the folder.**

2. **From the** `iVacation` **folder, select iVacationViewController.h — the header file for** `iVacationViewController`.

3. **Look for the following lines of code in the header:**

```
#import <UIKit/UIKit.h>

@interface iVacationViewController : UIViewController


@end
```

4. **Type the following four lines of code, indicated in bold, into the**
   iVacationViewController.h **file:**

```
#import <UIKit/UIKit.h>
@class Destination;

@interface iVacationViewController : UIViewController
{

   Destination              *europe;

}


@end
```

@class Destination declares the Destination class, just as before.
The iVacationViewController creates the Destination object, and
Destination *europe is an instance variable that the iVacationView-
Controller uses to send messages to Destination (the model interface).
I show you how to implement only a single destination in this example. In a
real application, you would probably have an array of destinations instead.

Adding outlets

Here is how you connect your visual interface with the ViewController code:

1. **In the Project navigator pane, select iVacationViewController.xib to
   open Interface Builder.**

2. **Click the Show the Assistant Editor button and resize the Project
   window so that you can see the full iPhone screen, as shown in
   Figure 17-19.**

   The Assistant Editor is going to help you make connections between
   elements in your user interface — the .xib file — and the Objective-C

header and source files for the `iVacationViewController`. The Assistant Editor has opened the `iVacationViewController.h` file in a separate editor.

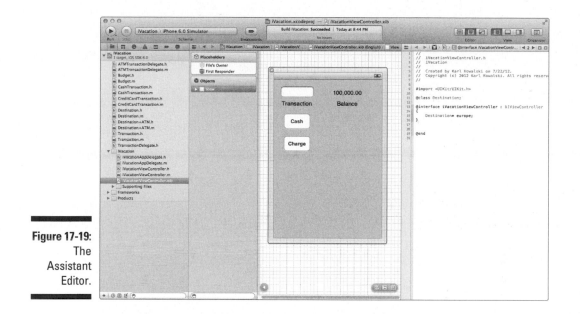

Figure 17-19:
The
Assistant
Editor.

3. **Click and hold the Text Field, press the Control key, and drag from the Text Field into the** `iVacationViewController.h` **file displayed in the Assistant Editor, just above the** `@end` **statement in the file, as shown in Figure 17-20.**

   You are adding an *outlet* to your app that connects the code in your Objective-C files with the user interface item in the `.xib` file. The `iVacationViewController` class can now refer to the Text Field on the iPhone screen by using this outlet. Xcode displays a small dialog that you fill out to identify the components of this connection, which you can see in Figure 17-21.

4. **Enter** transactionField **as the connection's name and click the Connect button.**

5. **Repeat the last two steps for the 100,000.00 Label and enter** balanceField **for the name of the connection.**

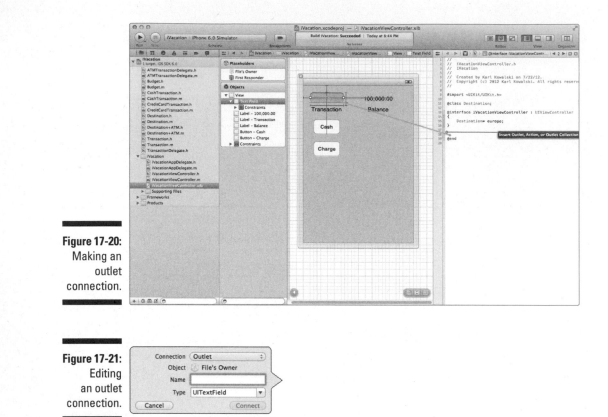

Figure 17-20:
Making an
outlet
connection.

Figure 17-21:
Editing
an outlet
connection.

As I say, the view controller connects the view to the model. In the view, the user will enter the amount of a transaction in the UITextField (the object that implements a Text Field) that you just added to the view, and you display the balance in the UILabel (the object that implements the Label). But to get information from the Text Field and update the Label text, you need to know where those objects are. Fortunately, the framework is designed to enable you to do this easily and gracefully. The view controller can refer to objects in the nib (as the .xib file is called) by using a special kind of instance variable referred to as an *outlet*. Using the Assistant Editor, you have accomplished two things:

1. Declared an outlet in your code
2. Told Interface Builder to point the outlet to the Text field in the view that you just created

Then when your application is initialized, the Text Field and Label outlets are automatically initialized with a pointer to the UITextField and UILabel objects, respectively. You can then use those outlets from within your code to get the text the user entered in the Text Field and display the balance in the Label. Pretty cool, isn't it?

@synthesize

In iVacationViewController.m, you will notice that the Assistant Editor has also added two directives that look like this:

```
@synthesize transactionField;
@synthesize balanceField;
```

These directives tell the compiler to *synthesize* the getter and setter methods for the two properties that were added to iVacationViewController.h. Xcode no longer requires the presence of the @synthesize directive, but the Assistant Editor still puts these into the implementation file. Your code will still build and run correctly, with or without them.

The Assistant Editor has added two @property instance variables to iVacationViewController.h, one for each of the outlets you just connected. The outlets are automatically initialized with a pointer to the text field (transactionField) and label (balanceField) objects when the application is launched and the view is displayed. The Assistant Editor added these two outlets to your code like this:

```
@property (strong, nonatomic) IBOutlet UITextField
          *transactionField;
@property (strong, nonatomic) IBOutlet UILabel
          *balanceField;
```

IBOutlet is a keyword that is recognized by Interface Builder when it comes time to connect the user interface elements added to the .xib with the code elements that your app's code needs to work with. If you continue to use the Assistant Editor when connecting your user interface to your code, you don't need to think about IBOutlets.

Next, you're going to connect the buttons to methods in iVacationView-Controller so that the methods are executed when the user clicks the buttons.

Connecting Targets with Actions

If you have a button in your interface, you need to add a method to your code to handle those times when somebody decides to actually tap the button. You do this much like you did when you added the Text Field and Label as outlets, using the Assistant Editor:

1. **Select** iVacationViewController.xib **to open the Interface Builder if it's not already on display. Click the Show the Assistant Editor button.**

2. **Click and Control-drag from the Cash button into the Assistant Editor, right above the** `@end` **statement, as shown in Figure 17-22.**

Xcode displays the connection dialog again, this time for the Cash button.

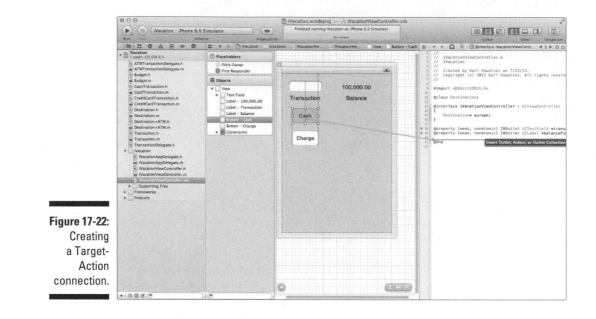

Figure 17-22:
Creating
a Target-
Action
connection.

3. **Select Action from the Connection drop menu, and enter** spendDollars **in the Name field, as shown in Figure 17-23. Then click Connect.**

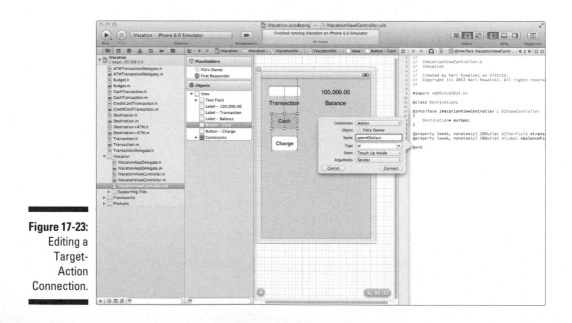

Figure 17-23:
Editing a
Target-
Action
Connection.

4. **Repeat the preceding two steps for the Charge button, and name its method** chargeCreditCard. **Your Project window should now look like mine does in Figure 17-24.**

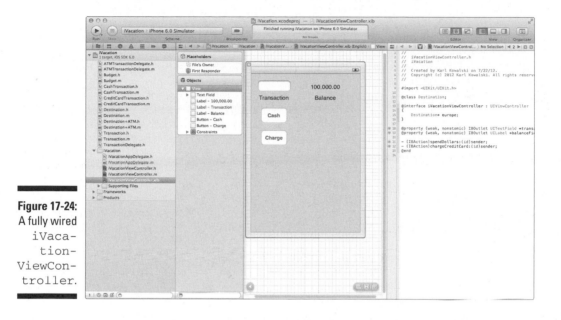

Figure 17-24:
A fully wired
iVaca-
tion-
ViewCon-
troller.

The Target-Action connections you just created link events that happen to UI components with actions that are executed on target objects within your application. The Touch Up Inside event is the event that is generated by iOS when inside the button is the last place the user touched before lifting his or her finger. This setting is more or less the standard for an iPhone button control like this.

You just wired up your iPhone screen's buttons to the code that will execute when the buttons are pressed. You told the Assistant Editor to do the following:

1. Declare two methods — spendDollars: and chargeCreditCard: — in iVacationViewController.h and implement them in iVacationViewController.m.

2. Connect the two buttons — Cash and Charge — to execute their respective methods when the user taps them while the app is running.

The two methods you created are called *actions,* because they are the actions that will take place — the messages that will be sent to an object in your application — when a user taps the buttons. The iVacationView Controller is referred to as the *target.*

Xcode declares the two methods as follows:

```
- (IBAction)spendDollars:(id)sender;
- (IBAction)chargeCreditCard:(id)sender;
```

While declaring methods is not new, what is new is the keyword — IBAction.

IBAction is one of those cool little techniques, like IBOutlet, that does nothing in the code but provide a way to inform Interface Builder (hence, the IB in both of them) that this method can be used as an action for Target-Action connections. All IBAction does is act as a tag for Interface Builder — identifying this method (action) as one that you can connect to an object (namely the button) in a .xib file. In this respect, the IBAction mechanism is similar to the IBOutlet mechanism I discuss earlier. In that case, however, you were tagging instance variables; in this case, you are tagging methods. Same difference.

IBAction is actually defined as a void, so if you think about it, all you've done is declare a new method with a return type of void.

```
(IBAction) buttonPressed: (id) sender;
```

is functionally equivalent to

```
(void) buttonPressed: (id) sender;
```

You can give the method any name you want, but it must have a return type of IBAction. Usually, the action method takes one argument — typically defined as id, a pointer to the instance variables of an object — which is given the name sender. The control that triggers your action uses the sender argument to pass a reference to itself. So, for example, if your action method is called as the result of a button tap, the argument sender contains a reference to the specific button that was tapped.

If you want to see all the connections you created between iVacationView-Controller and the iPhone UI, just do the following:

1. **Select** iVacationViewController.xib **in the Project navigator.**

2. **Resize the window to create some space between the iPhone screen and the list of objects.**

3. **Press and hold the Control key while clicking the File's Owner item in the Placeholders list. You can also right-click the File's Owner item. Xcode displays a floating window like that shown in Figure 17-25.**

Figure 17-25:
All the con-
nections.

You can see that the connections you made for the Label, the Text Field, and the two buttons are all highlighted. The Text Field is connected to the `transactionField` outlet and the Label, while the text 100,000.00 is connected to the `balanceField` outlet. The Charge button executes the `chargeCreditCard:` method, and the Cash button executes the `spend-Dollars:` method. If you click the *x* marks next to these items on the right side of the window, you disconnect the outlets and actions from their user-interface counterparts.

The Target-Action mechanism enables you to create a control object and tell it not only what object you want to handle the event but also the message to send. For example, if the user touches the Cash button onscreen, you want to send a "spendDollars" message to the view controller. But if the Charge button on the screen is touched, you want to be able to send the same view controller the "chargeCreditCard" message. If you couldn't do that and every button had to send the same message, the coding would be more complex. You would have to determine which button had sent the message and then what to do in response (likely using a `switch` statement). That would make changing the user interface more work and more error prone.

What you are doing here is implementing the third of the three major design patterns for applications. The first was *Model-View-Controller,* the second was *Delegation,* and this third one is *Target-Action.*

The Target-Action pattern is used to let your application know that a user has done something. For example, he or she may have tapped a button or entered some text. The control — a button, say — sends a message (the action message) that you specify to the target you selected to handle that particular action. The receiving object, or the target, is usually a view controller object.

Adding the methods

Now that you are finished with the interface specifications, it is time to implement the code.

Okay, you declared the method. The next thing for you to do is actually add the `spendDollars:` and `chargeCreditCard:` methods to the implementation file, `iVacationViewController.m`. Follow these steps:

1. **Go back to the** `Classes` **folder in the Project navigator and select iVacationViewController.m — the implementation file for** `iVacation ViewController`**.**

   You can also hide the Assistant Editor by clicking the Show the Standard Editor button, to give you more space.

2. **Look for the following lines of code in the implementation file:**

   ```
   #import "iVacationViewController.h"

   @implementation iVacationViewController
   ```

3. **Add the following after** `#import "iVacationViewController.h"`**:**

   ```
   #import "Destination.h"
   ```

4. **Add the following bold lines to the** `spendDollars:` **method:**

   ```
   - (IBAction)spendDollars:(id)sender{

     NSLog (@"Sending a %.2f cash transaction",
                          [transactionField.text
         floatValue]);
     [europe spendCash:[transactionField.text
         doubleValue]];
     balanceField.text = [[NSString alloc] initWithFormat:
                          @"%.2f",[europe
         leftToSpend]];
   }
   ```

5. **Add the following bold lines to the** `chargeCreditCard:` **method:**

   ```
   - (IBAction)chargeCreditCard:(id)sender {
     NSLog (@"Sending a %.2f credit card transaction",
         [transactionField.text floatValue]);
     [europe chargeCreditCard:[transactionField.text
         doubleValue]];
     balanceField.text = [[NSString alloc] initWithFormat:
                          @"%.2f",[europe
         leftToSpend]];
   }
   ```

Note that I am still tracking what my program is doing in the Debugger Console.

balanceField.text is a property in the UILabel object that points to the text the label is supposed to display. What you are having it display, in this case, is a string that you created to display the balance:

```
[[NSString alloc]initWithFormat:
                     @"%.2f",[europe leftToSpend]];
```

I want to remind you that when you assign to a property in this way (using the dot syntax), you are actually calling the setter method. You could have coded that statement as

```
[balanceField setText:[[NSString alloc]initWithFormat:
                     @"%.2f", [europe leftToSpend]]];
```

The same thing is also true of transactionField.text. This could have been coded as

```
[europe spendCash:[[transactionField text] floatValue]];
```

This code should look familiar because it is basically what you have been using for the last several chapters to send transactions to the Destination object. The only difference here is the transaction amount. Instead of the fixed values you have been using, now you are getting the transaction amount the user has entered. You get that by sending a message to the transactionField object in your view, using the outlet you declared in the interface file to retrieve the text the user enters. (Notice how easy it is to turn a string into a float by using an NSString method.)

Similarly, instead of the NSLog statement you used to use to display the remaining balance, you are sending a message to the UILabel through the balanceField outlet to update its text and display it in the view.

This is all the logic you need to connect the model and user interface — of course, there is some plumbing left to do, so I'll get started. Follow these steps to implement the remaining code that will make your iVacation app run on the iPhone simulator:

1. **Scroll down through the code for** iVacationViewController.m **until you reach the following lines:**

```
- (void)viewDidLoad
{
    [super viewDidLoad];
    // Do any additional setup after loading the view,
        typically from a nib.
}
```

2. **Add the following lines of code in bold:**

```
- (void)viewDidLoad {

    [super viewDidLoad];
        // Do any additional setup after loading the view,
            typically from a nib.
    NSString* europeText = [[NSString alloc]
                           initWithFormat: @"%@", @"Europe"];
    europe = [[Destination alloc]
            initWithCountry:europeText andBudget:10000.00
                               withExchangeRate:1.25];
    NSString* balanceFieldText = [[NSString alloc]
            initWithFormat:@"%.2f", [europe leftToSpend]];
    balanceField.text = balanceFieldText;
}
```

viewDidLoad is a view controller method that you are *overriding*.
Again, you find no surprises here in the code. The only difference is that
I added a message to the balanceField to initialize it with the starting budget, which, you may have noticed, I bumped up to $10,000. Of
course, in a "real" application, you would provide a way for the user to
enter the starting budget in a view.

3. **Choose File⇨Save or press ⌘+S to save what you have done.**

Running iVacation in the Simulator

Your iVacation app is now ready to run. You created the user interface, connected the buttons and the Label and the Text Field with the view controller
that manages everything, and added the code from all the previous chapters
to support creating and executing transactions on your vacation budget with
your iPhone.

Go back to the Xcode project window and click the Run button on the Project
Window toolbar.

This launches the iPhone simulator. Figure 17-26 shows what happens if you
click in the Text Field, enter **100** (either clicking on the simulator keyboard or
using your Mac keyboard), and then click the Cash button.

You can find the completed project at the website in the Example 17 folder,
which is in the Chapter 17 folder.

Frankly, I could have done a lot better job with the aesthetics of this user
interface, and before showing it to a user, I would.

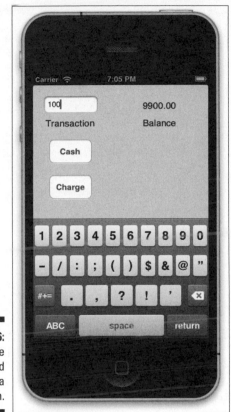

Figure 17-26:
Click in the
Text Field
to enter a
transaction.

A Final Note

This is it! For those of you who haven't programmed before, you may be thinking that just as you expected (and I promised), the programming described in this book is pretty easy. But for those of you with programming experience, the ease with which you can accomplish things by using object-oriented programming can be truly breathtaking. I still feel like a kid in a candy store when I code this way.

Although you have a lot more to do to turn `iVacation` into a useful application, including saving data, you now have the knowledge and skill to explore extending this application on your own — so go for it!

Chapter 18

Adding a Mac User Interface

● ●

In This Chapter

▶ Painlessly putting a user interface on the model

▶ Create a user interface with Interface Builder

▶ Adding controls to the view

▶ Creating a view controller

▶ Running the application on the Mac

● ●

*I*n this chapter, I keep the second part of the promise I've been talking about since Chapter 11 — if you create the right class structure, putting on a user interface will be easy.

Now that you have seen how easy it is to take your application's components and add an iPhone user interface, I show you how to do the same thing for the Mac OS. Although the basic idea is the same, you find a few differences in detail that I explain in this chapter.

Creating Your Project

As with the iPhone, you will be working in an Xcode project. Create a Mac application project by following these steps:

1. **Launch Xcode if it is not already running.**

2. **Choose File⇨New⇨Project to create a new project. You can also press Shift+⌘+N.**

3. **In the New Project window (see Figure 18-1), click Application under the OS X heading.**

   Just as before, when you select a template, a brief description of the template is displayed underneath the main pane. As you know, each of these choices is actually a template that generates some code. In the past, when you were using the Command Line Tool, that code was minimal. Now, however, you are going to see a lot more.

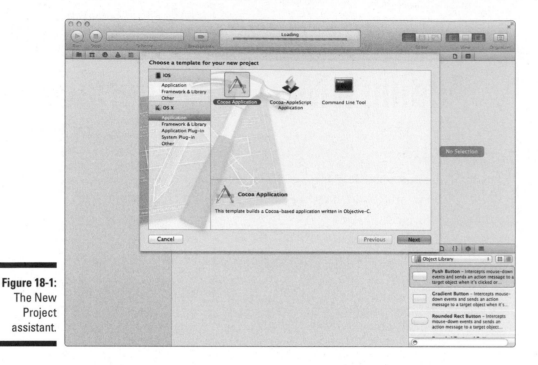

Figure 18-1:
The New
Project
assistant.

4. **Select Cocoa Application from the choices displayed and then click Next.**

   Xcode then asks for more information.

5. **Enter the name** mVacation **in the Product Name field and** mVacation **as the Class Prefix. Leave the App Store Category at None, make sure that the Use Automatic Reference Counting check box is selected, and all the other check boxes should be deselected, as shown in Figure 18-2. Then click Next.**

   Xcode asks you where to save the project.

6. **Click Create to save the project in the default location.**

7. **In the Project Navigator pane (on the left side of the Project window), click the triangles next to the** mVacation **and** Supporting Files **folders to expand them.**

Figure 18-3 shows you the Project window that Xcode opens after you create your OS X project. You notice only an mVacationAppDelegate class, but nothing corresponding to the iVacationViewController. That's one difference between the iPhone and OS X templates. You create a class to accomplish the same things that iVacationViewController did in the last chapter, but for now, you add your user interface with Interface Builder.

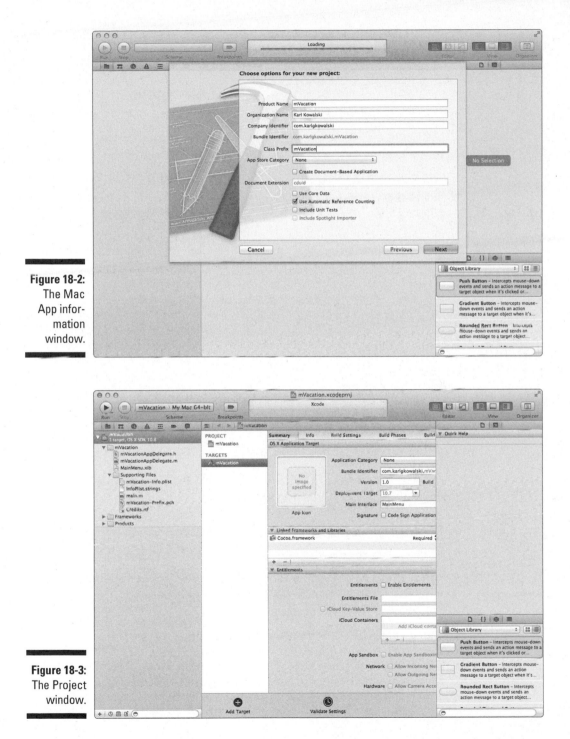

Figure 18-2:
The Mac App infor-mation window.

Figure 18-3:
The Project window.

Using Interface Builder to Create a User Interface

Just as you do in Chapter 17, you use Interface Builder to create your user interface. Follow these steps:

1. **In the Project navigator, click the `MainMenu.xib` file.**

   The Interface Builder editor displays the contents of `MainMenu.xib`.

2. **Select the Window – mVacation item in the Objects list, as shown in Figure 18-4.**

   If Interface Builder shows a set of icons instead of text to the left of the editor area, click the Show Document Outline button in the bottom left corner of the editor area.

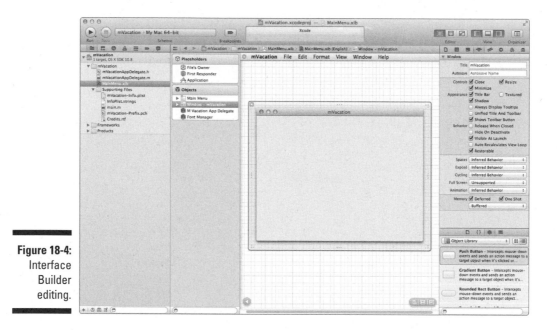

Figure 18-4:
Interface
Builder
editing.

3. **Check to see whether the Object Library pane (at the lower right in Figure 18-4) is open. If it isn't, open it by choosing View➪Utilities➪Show Object Library, or press Control+Option+⌘+3. Select Controls in the drop menu below the mode selector.**

As you see in Chapter 17, the Library has many of the components you can use to build a user interface. This one looks a little different than the one in iPhone, though.

`MainMenu.xib` was created by Xcode when you created the project from the template. In Figure 18-4, as you can see, a *window* is already there, and that's what you see on the Mac when you launch the application. A menu object is also in the Document Outline, but I won't get into that, and you can close it if you like.

Next, you need to add the Mac version of the text field, buttons, and labels that you can use to enter a transaction and have the remaining budget displayed. When your application is launched, those items are created automatically, just as they were on the iPhone.

4. **Scroll down in the Controls list to find the Text Field. Drag a Text Field item from the Library into the View window to add a text entry field (see Figure 18-5).**

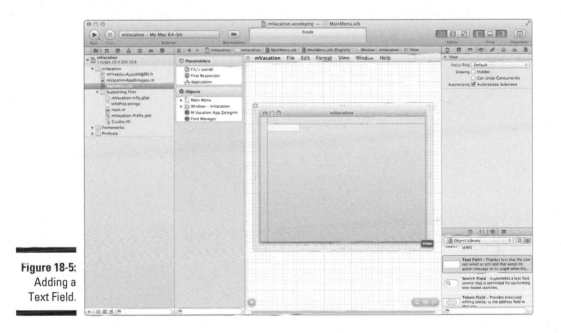

Figure 18-5:
Adding a
Text Field.

A Text Field item is just like the Text Field for the iPhone, although it is a different class.

5. **Drag a Label item from the Library window over to the View window, as you do in Chapter 17**.

6. **Double-click the Label field to enter** 100,000.00 **(still my default budget; talk about wishful thinking).**

As I explain in Chapter 17, this makes the label wide enough to display the budget.

7. **Drag in two more Labels, double-click each one, and enter** Transaction **and** Balance, **respectively.**

8. **Scroll back up to the top of the list of Controls and drag in two Push Buttons.**

9. **Double-click the first button and type** Cash. **Do the same thing for the second button, but this time type** Charge.

When you are done, your window should look like what is shown in Figure 18-6.

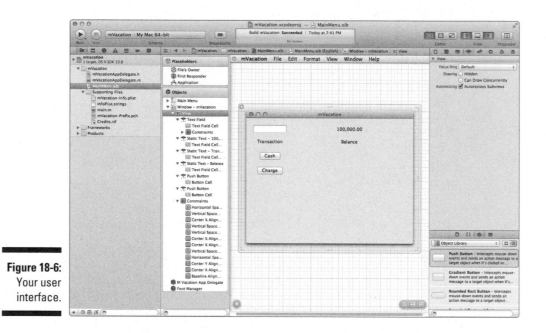

Figure 18-6:
Your user interface.

10. **Select the 100,000.00 Label and click the Show the Attributes Inspector button, as you do in Chapter 17. Alternatively, you can press ⌘+Option+4.**

11. **Select center alignment in Alignment control to center the text in the Label.**

I am leaving the window's background color just as it is for this application.

Implementing the User Interface

Just as on the iPhone, the coding required to hook the user interface to the model is minimal.

If you have been following along with me, I extend what you did in Chapter 16. If you prefer to start from a clean copy of the project from where you left off, you can use the project found at the website in the Chapter 18 Start Here folder, which can be found in the Chapter 18 folder.

As with the iPhone application, you have to copy all the classes from Chapter 16 into your new project. In Chapter 17, I have you drag them in. You can do it that way or you can use Project⊅Add To Project.

You need to add the following files — .h and .m — to the mVacation project:

- ⊾ ATMTransactionDelegate
- ⊾ Budget
- ⊾ CashTransaction
- ⊾ CreditCardTransaction
- ⊾ Destination
- ⊾ Destination+ATM
- ⊾ Transaction
- ⊾ TransactionDelegate (only .h)

To add all the classes' implementation and header files to your OS X project, here's what you do:

1. **Select the** mVacation **folder in the Project navigator, and choose File⊅Add Files to "mVacation," or press ⌘+Option+A. Navigate to the Vacation project from Chapter 16 (or whichever project you are using) and select all the files to be added, as I did in Figure 18-7.**

2. **Again, be sure to select the Copy Items into Destination Group's Folder (If Needed) check box, and make sure that** mVacation **is selected in the Add to Targets list when the dialog pops up.**

3. **Click Add.**

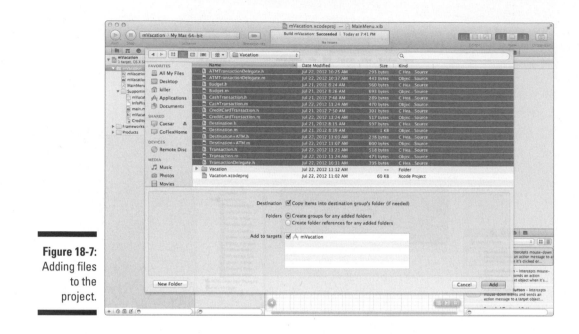

Figure 18-7:
Adding files
to the
project.

Although developing for iOS and OS X are amazingly similar, you find a few differences.

In your iPhone project, you deleted `#import <Foundation/Foundation.h>` in header files. This time, you leave them unchanged.

Whereas the iPhone Xcode template you used added a view controller class to your project, in the case of the Mac, you have to do that yourself. Here's how:

1. **Select the** `mVacation` **folder in the Project navigator.**

   This tells Xcode to place the new file in the `mVacation` folder.

2. **Choose File⇨New⇨File or press ⌘+N to get the New File dialog.**

3. **In the leftmost column of the dialog, first select Cocoa under OS X; then select the Objective-C class in the upper-right pane. Click Next.**

   You see a new screen asking for some more information.

4. **Enter** `mVacationController` **in the Class field and select NSObject from the Subclass of drop menu; then click Next.**

5. **Make sure that** `mVacation` **is selected as the Target and save the** `mVacationController` **class files in the default location by clicking Create.**

I start with some things that you need to add to the mVacationController.h file:

1. **Select** mVacationController.h — **the header file for** mVacation-Controller — **in the Project navigator.**

2. **Look for the following lines of code in the header:**

   ```
   #import <Foundation/Foundation.h>
   @interface mVacationController : NSObject


   @end
   ```

3. **Add the following four lines of code, indicated in bold, to the** mVacationController.h **file:**

   ```
   #import <Foundation/Foundation.h>
   @class Destination;


   @interface mVacationController : NSObject
   {
      Destination *europe;
   }

   @end
   ```

The first line (@class Destination) declares the Destination class, just as you have been doing so far. The mVacationController creates the Destination object, and Destination *europe; is an instance variable that the mVacationController uses to send messages to Destination (the model interface).

Using the Assistant Editor to add outlets and Targets-Actions

The only differences between what you have to do here and what you do in Chapter 17 are that the classes of the Label and the Text Field have changed in the IBOutlet declarations. On the iPhone, you use a UITextField and UILabel; with OS X, you use NSTextField for both.

The two IBAction method declarations — spendDollars: and charge CreditCard: — are the same.

You're going to add the IBOutlets and the IBActions just as you do in Chapter 17, using the Assistant Editor. But you first need to tell Xcode that the mVacationController class you just created will be used with the app's interface.

You do this because when your application is launched, the runtime goes out and loads and creates the objects in your .xib file (there's actually more to it, but this is more or less what happens). Adding an mVacation Controller object here means that in addition to the window and menu you see on the screen, your mVacationController object is created automatically as well. That also means that the awakeFromNib message is automatically sent to the object that you just implemented (because it is sent to all objects created from the .xib) — this tells the mVacationController object that all's right with the world and that all the outlets and Targets-Actions are connected.

To connect your user interface to the code in your mVacationController class, follow these steps:

1. **In the Project Navigator pane, select MainMenu.xib to open Interface Builder.**

2. **Select Objects & Controllers from the drop menu in the Library. Drag an Object from the Library into the list of Objects, as shown in Figure 18-8.**

   The Object you just added is an NSObject, and now you need to tell Interface Builder that it's really an mVacationController object.

3. **Select the Object you just added in Step 2, and click the Show the Identity Inspector button on the selector bar for the Utility pane. In the menu for the Class in the Custom Class section, select** mVacation-Controller, **as shown in Figure 18-9.**

   You may have to scroll all the way to the bottom of the menu to find mVacationController — the menu is arranged alphabetically, but lowercase letters are alphabetically *after* uppercase letters.

   You can now use Interface Builder and the Assistant Editor to add the IBOutlets and IBActions to mVacationController and connect them to their UI counterparts in MainMenu.xib.

4. **Select Window – mVacation to show the window with the user interface components you added earlier. Then click the Show the Assistant Editor button.**

   You see the Assistant Editor displayed to the right of the Interface Builder editor, as shown in Figure 18-10. You can hide the Utility pane because you won't need to use it. The Assistant Editor shows the contents of mVacationController, which is where you now add the IBOutlets and IBActions.

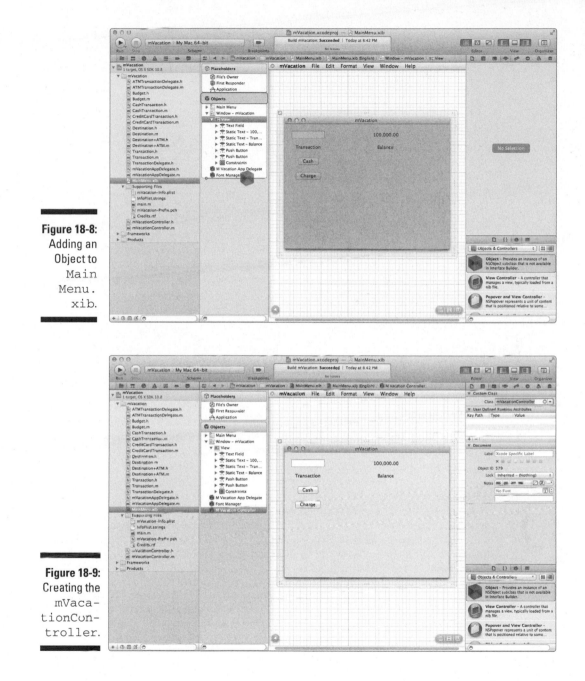

Figure 18-8:
Adding an
Object to
`Main
Menu.
xib.`

Figure 18-9:
Creating the
`mVaca-
tionCon-
troller.`

You can configure the Assistant Editor by selecting View⇨Assistant Editor and selecting how you want the Assistant Editor to display on the screen. I prefer having the Assistant Editor on the right, which is what you see in Figure 18-10.

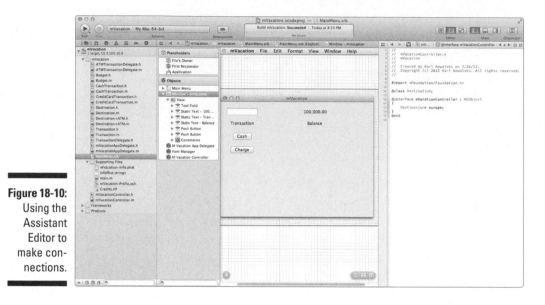

Figure 18-10:
Using the Assistant Editor to make connections.

5. **Control-drag from the Text Field into the Assistant Editor, just above the** @end **statement. Make sure that the Type drop menu shows NSTextField, and set the Name to** transactionField. **Leave the Storage set to weak and click Connect.**

It took me a couple of tries to get this right. Interface Builder automatically adds some layout objects for each UI component in the window, and I kept selecting those instead of the Text Field. One way to make sure that you are clicking the correct item is to Control-drag from the item in the Document outline pane — on the left side of the Interface Builder editor — to the Assistant Editor pane.

You connect the remaining UI components to the mVacationController class as follows:

1. **Control-drag from the 100,000.00 Label into the Assistant Editor, above the** @end **statement. Make sure that the Type drop menu shows NSTextField and set the Name to** balanceField. **Leave the Storage set to weak and click Connect.**

2. **Control-drag from the Cash button into the Assistant Editor, above the** @end **statement. Change the Connection drop-down menu to Action and enter** spendDollars **into the Name field. Click Connect.**

3. **Control-drag from the Charge button into the Assistant Editor above the** @end **statement. Change the Connection drop-down menu to Action and enter** chargeCreditCard **into the Name field. Click Connect.**

Implementing the methods

Okay, you now created the methods and the outlets within the header and implementation files for mVacationController. The next thing you need to do is to add the code to the spendDollars: and chargeCreditCard: methods in the implementation file, mVacationController.m. Follow these steps:

1. **Go back to the** mVacation **folder in the Project navigator and select mVacationController.m — the implementation file for** mVacation-Controller.

2. **Look for the following lines of code in the implementation file:**

```
#import "mVacationController.h"@implementation
    mVacationController
```

3. **Add the following after** #import "mVacationController.h":

```
#import "Destination.h"
```

4. **Add the code in bold to the two action methods:**

```
- (IBAction)spendDollars:(id)sender{

  NSLog (@"Sending a %.2f cash transaction",
        [transactionField.stringValue floatValue]);
  [europe spendCash:
        [transactionField.stringValue doubleValue]];
  [balanceField setStringValue:
      [[NSString alloc]initWithFormat:@"%.2f",
      [europe leftToSpend]]];
}

- (IBAction)chargeCreditCard:(id)sender {

  NSLog (@"Sending a %.2f credit card transaction",
        [transactionField.stringValue floatValue]);
  [europe chargeCreditCard:
        [transactionField.stringValue floatValue]];
  [balanceField setStringValue:
      [[NSString alloc] initWithFormat:@"%.2f",
      [europe leftToSpend]]];
}
```

This is essentially the same thing that you do for the iPhone implementation in Chapter 17 (you can refer to it if you are a little hazy on the topic). The differences are that instead of `balanceField.text` and `transactionField.text` that you used on the iPhone, you use `balanceField.stringValue` and `transactionField.stringValue`. Also notice that this time, rather than the dot notation, you are sending a message to the getters and setters in the "conventional way."

This is all the logic that you need to connect the model and user interface. Of course, just as with the iPhone, some plumbing is left to do here. You need to create the `Destination` object, when the program is at the point where all the UI components have been created. You do this by adding the following code to `mVacationController.m`, just before the `@end` statement:

```
- (void)awakeFromNib {

  [super awakeFromNib];
  NSString* europeText = [[NSString alloc]
            initWithFormat:@"%@", @"Europe"];
  europe = [[Destination alloc]
        initWithCountry:europeText andBudget:10000.00
        withExchangeRate:1.25];
[balanceField setStringValue:[[NSString alloc]
            initWithFormat:@"%.2f",
            [europe leftToSpend]]];
}
```

This is virtually the same code you add to the `viewDidLoad:` method in Chapter 17. Instead of using `viewDidLoad`, which you *override,* you use `awakeFromNib`. This is actually an *informal* protocol method, and classes implement this method to initialize application information after objects have been loaded from the Interface Builder `.nib` file. An `awakeFromNib` message is sent to each object loaded from the `.nib` file after all the objects in the archive have been loaded and initialized. This is one of the reasons I explain informal protocols in Chapter 16.

Running mVacation on the Mac

Your OS X application is now ready to go.

Click the Run button to compile and build the application.

You can click in the Transaction field to enter a transaction and then click one of the buttons. In Figure 18-11, you see that I entered 100 and then clicked the Cash button — and lo and behold, the math works.

Figure 18-11:
The Mac
version
of the
application.

You can find the completed project at the website in the Example 18 folder,
which is in the Chapter 18 folder.

Knowing What's Left to Do

Just like with the iPhone application, you have a little more to do besides
the cosmetics and additional application functionality — for example, the
menu and other user-interface functionality expected by the user of a Mac
application.

The End of the Beginning

Now that you finished *Objective-C For Dummies,* your adventure really starts.

Go out there and write programs, and let me know how you are doing. You'll
find information and ideas about programming and design on Neal's website,
www.nealgoldstein.com. And you can contact Karl at kgkfordummies@
gmail.com.

Until then — happy programming until we meet again.

Part V
The Part of Tens

"I've tried every other way of debugging it. Let's just throw the chicken bones and see what happens."

In this part . . .

Along the way, I have been sprinkling words of wisdom based on not just my own but also other developers' collective experience. In this part, I codify some of them.

First, I talk a bit about debugging and give you some tips on both avoiding bugs and where and how to look for them. Bugs are inevitable, so it's better to take a Zen-like approach and "be at one" with the debugging process.

Finally, I close by giving you some ideas about how to avoid the kinds of problems most new developers encounter in their first few applications. Think of this as a map of places to avoid when you are alone at night in a strange city.

Chapter 19

Ten Debugging Tips

*W*hen you're developing an application, you'll find that a few things don't work out quite the way you planned. That means you will have to go through your code and determine what happened, and more important, what to do about it.

Check for Semicolons

Semicolons are the heart and soul of Objective-C statements, and leaving one out can cause incredible havoc. For some reason, forgetting to end a statement with one is something I'm pretty good at. So, when I see a lot of errors and warnings, especially if I've just added a few lines of code, semicolons are one of the first things I check. And Xcode will assist you with this, if you use Fix-It.

"Right" Is Not Always "right"

Remember, Objective-C is case sensitive, and For is not the same thing as for. Using the wrong case can send the complier into a tizzy, and although you will get warnings and errors, what you have done may not always be obvious.

When You've Blown It, You've Blown It

It's generally better to ignore the subsequent errors after the first syntax error because they may be the result of that first error. This is especially true when you leave out #import statements (or spell them wrong) or forget a semicolon or comma, or colon, or anything else that the complier uses to make sense of your statements.

Compiler Warnings Are for Your Own Good

You may get only one chance to pay attention to a compiler warning. If you don't make any changes to the file that generated the warning, you won't see the warning the next time you build your program, but you can always see them again by clicking Show Issue on the Navigator selector bar.

You can also choose Product⇨Clean to remove all the files the compiler creates — so your next build starts from a clean state — and you probably should on a regular basis.

Get Friendly with Your Debugger

The debugger has a lot of features that can really help you. Breakpoints are especially helpful. Take the compiler out for a date some time and really get to know it.

It may seem intuitively obvious (although in the heat of the moment after a program crash, you may forget), but make sure to read what the Debugger Console says. For example

```
2012-05-28 10:18:07.148 Vacation[26213:a0f] ***
          Terminating app due to uncaught exception
          NSInvalidArgumentException', reason: '-[__
          NSCFNumber doublValue]: unrecognized selector
          sent to instance 0x7fdb02c017f0'
```

makes things pretty clear. Although not covered here, you should also get to know the commands that you can type into the Debugger Console.

Messages to nil

In Objective-C, you can send messages to a nil object. Although this does not crash your program, in some cases, it will make you crazy trying to figure out why something doesn't work the way it should.

Dialing a Wrong Number

One of the great features of Objective-C is its implementation of polymorphism. As long as the object has implemented the method you are sending the message to, Objective-C will let you send the object that message. Sometimes, however, that object may not be the one you wanted to send the message to, so be careful of that concern.

Create a "Paper" Trail

I am a big fan of NSLog. Sure, the debugger gives you a stack trace, and you can use breakpoints, but NSLog can create a narrative of what is going on. Use it to display where you are in your code and the value of variables. Using all the tools available gives you the best chance of fixing that bug before the next SDK and all those new devices are released.

Just be careful, though, because NSLog can also be a source of bugs — ironic but true. If you try to use a C String as in NSLog("I'm here"), you will get complier warnings. If you try to display a nonobject by using the %@ string formatter, you may cause a program crash. What is more insidious, though, is when you use the wrong formatter, and you don't get what you expect, and you spend hours tracking it down, only to find that you were trying to display an int as a float.

Incrementally Test

Most software developers quickly figure out that incremental development is the way to go. Write a method and try to test it immediately if you can, even if it means just putting in NSLog statements to examine the output. It is a lot easier to debug 15 lines of code than to try to figure out why the 200 lines of code you've been working on for two days don't work the way you expect.

Use Your Brain

I do use all the tools and tips I just gave you to track down bugs, but for logic errors, which are by far the hardest, I actually find thinking about it first is the fastest way to a solution. I find two approaches useful. First, start by trying to figure out what would have to be true for this to happen, and then see if that's the fact. A second way is to ask, "How could I have made this happen if I'd wanted it to." And then go look to see whether that's what you did.

Chapter 20

Ten Ways to Be a Happy Developer

I really like writing software. When I first started, I couldn't believe that I was actually paid to do something that was so much fun (believe me, I quickly got over that). Along the way, I've discovered a few ways to make my life as a developer easier.

Keep Everyone in the Dark

One of the things that can really cause you problems as you develop your application is building into your code "detailed" knowledge about how things in your program work. This ranges from data structures, to instance variable visibility (to other objects), to how methods work, to the basic structure of the program. As I speak about more than once, you want to make sure that you keep your objects as ignorant as you can about their environment. Although you will always have some dependency whenever one object uses another, limit those dependencies to what other objects do rather than to how they do it, and limit the number of objects each one uses.

Similarly, avoid the compulsion to create switch statement–like control structures that determine the order in which objects get called and that dole out instructions to them. The best object-oriented programs have their objects work like a team, with every one playing its role and doing its part instead of the traditional hierarchical command-and-control structure, where someone is in charge and tells everyone else what to do.

Sergeant Schultz of *Hogan's Heroes* captured the spirit of object-oriented programming with his trademark line:

"I hear nothing, I see nothing, I know nothing!"

Make Your Code Easy to Understand

Often developers think that comments are for other people who are reading your code. In reality, think about them as being for yourself when you are picking up some code that you wrote six months ago. It will amaze you how foreign it can appear. I suggest the following:

- ✔ Use comments often, but especially when you are doing something clever — especially if it took you a while to figure out how to do that thing in the first place.
- ✔ Give your classes descriptive names.
- ✔ Do the same thing with method names.
- ✔ Do the same thing with both local and instance variables.
- ✔ Take advantage of argument names in method declarations so that you know what each argument is for.

Remember Memory

With Automatic Reference Counting — ARC — you can now develop iOS and OS X apps without using `retain`, `release`, or `autorelease`. But you should still keep in mind what you read about memory management in

Chapter 13 because it's important to understand exactly what's going on behind the scenes. And although you may write your own code by using ARC, you likely will encounter example code that still has `retains` and `releases`.

Start by Initializing the Right Way

Even though it is just about as unglamorous as things get, initialization is extremely important. Don't try to backfit later in your development cycle; do it correctly from the start. Always use the following form:

```
- (id) init...: {

  if (self = [super ...]) {
    your initialization goes here
  }
  return self;
}
```

Take Advantage of the Documentation

This may sound silly, but it's a good idea to actually read the documentation if you want to know how something works. What I find myself doing when I am learning something new, Control-right-click a symbol and then select Find Text in Documentation — I use this all the time.

Of course you can find search in the Help menu and Option-double-click a symbol to bring up Quick Help. Also, these two Apple Dev Center sites have a plethora of reference material:

```
http://developer.apple.com/ios
http://developer.apple.com/mac
```

Code, Code, Code

Every book I write has a few themes running through it, and one of those in this book is code, code, code. My experience, both personally and in teaching, is that the more you type — that is, the more code you actually write — the more you understand and the faster you understand it.

You should try things out to see how they work. For example, experiment with similar methods to see how they work differently. Try everything out to make sure that when you invoke a method, you can predict what the result will be. Let your curiosity run free, and if something intrigues you, go explore it. And don't worry, you can't do anything in an Xcode application that will break anything in Xcode, much less take down your entire system. This isn't Windows, after all.

Understand That Development Is Not Linear

Development is not linear. In this book, I talked about showing you how to do something, and then having you delete the code and try it a different or better way. If I'm trying something new, I often just code a rough version of it to make sure that I understand the basics before things get complicated.

You'll find yourself creating a rough application structure, implementing a few classes, seeing whether the idea works, and then going back and refining it, especially when it comes to using inheritance and polymorphism. Personally, even if I know I will have class hierarchy, like I did with `Transaction`, I'll build out one concrete example of it — say `CashTransaction` — and make sure that it works. Then I create the superclass and the first subclass and make sure that I get the same results, and then go on to create other subclasses. This is known as *factoring* your code, and it's all in a day's work.

Do It Right from the Start If You Need to Do It Right from the Start

I just talked about the nonlinear approach to development: building something to see how it works and then doing it the right way. Although that works for some things, it doesn't work for a few other things over the long term. You have to start doing some things the right way from day one of development, including the following:

- Building your application, using the Model-View-Controller pattern
- Initialization
- Memory management

✔ Localization (I don't cover this, but you can find lots of information in other texts and online)

✔ Error handling

Although you might not always do the listed things exactly right from the get-go, you better go back and do them properly before you get very far — it becomes an enormously error-prone task to backfit these. I still have nightmares about going back and retrofitting my first iPhone program to correctly manage memory.

Avoid the Code Slinger Mentality

Some programmers get so carried away with the purity of the language and programming that they spend days arguing about a point that, in the long run, makes no difference to how well your program actually works.

Also avoid cleverness as much as you can, as well as excessive nesting of statements. If clarity requires a few more lines of code, you are always better off in the long run.

This is a good time to point out that your main interest should be in developing great applications, while quickly working through issues (often style issues) that make no difference. Usually, if equal passion exists on both sides, each side has its pros and cons, and no one is really "right."

I like to keep in mind a quotation from Voltaire:

> *The perfect is the enemy of the good.*

The Software Isn't Finished Until the Last User Is Dead

If I can guarantee one thing about app development, it's that Nobody Gets It Right the First Time. The design for all applications evolves over time, as you discover the capabilities and intricacies of the platform, as user behavior changes in response to your application, and as the users, based on usage, get a better idea of what they can do with technology.

Object orientation makes extending your application (not to mention fixing bugs) easier, so pay attention to the principles.

Keep It Fun

This is another one of those ongoing themes in this and my other books (and in my personal life as well). Programming is inherently fun (at least after you get going), and the point is to keep it that way.

It's important to remember this when you have spent hours trying to debug your program, and you think all is lost. Don't worry; you'll eventually figure it out. You wrote it, after all.

Take a break, play a game, go for a walk, or e-mail me ruing the day you started programming. Do whatever works — and then go back, and (perhaps) miraculously what you need to do will become obvious.

Index

Math & Science

Algebra I For Dummies,
2nd Edition
978-0-470-55964-2

Biology For Dummies,
2nd Edition
978-0-470-59875-7

Chemistry For Dummies,
2nd Edition
978-1-1180-0730-3

Geometry For Dummies,
2nd Edition
978-0-470-08946-0

Pre-Algebra Essentials
For Dummies
978-0-470-61838-7

Microsoft Office

Excel 2010 For Dummies
978-0-470-48953-6

Office 2010 All-in-One
For Dummies
978-0-470-49748-7

Office 2011 for Mac
For Dummies
978-0-470-87869-9

Word 2010
For Dummies
978-0-470-48772-3

Music

Guitar For Dummies,
2nd Edition
978-0-7645-9904-0

Clarinet For Dummies
978-0-470-58477-4

iPod & iTunes
For Dummies,
9th Edition
978-1-118-13060-5

Pets

Cats For Dummies,
2nd Edition
978-0-7645-5275-5

Dogs All-in One
For Dummies
978-0470-52978-2

Saltwater Aquariums
For Dummies
978-0-470-06805-2

Religion & Inspiration

The Bible For Dummies
978-0-7645-5296-0

Catholicism For Dummies,
2nd Edition
978-1-118-07778-8

Spirituality For Dummies,
2nd Edition
978-0-470-19142-2

Self-Help & Relationships

Happiness For Dummies
978-0-470-28171-0

Overcoming Anxiety
For Dummies,
2nd Edition
978-0-470-57441-6

Seniors

Crosswords For Seniors
For Dummies
978-0-470-49157-7

iPad 2 For Seniors
For Dummies, 3rd Edition
978-1-118-17678-8

Laptops & Tablets
For Seniors For Dummies,
2nd Edition
978-1-118-09596-6

Smartphones & Tablets

BlackBerry For Dummies,
5th Edition
978-1-118-10035-6

Droid X2 For Dummies
978-1-118-14864-8

HTC ThunderBolt
For Dummies
978-1-118-07601-9

MOTOROLA XOOM
For Dummies
978-1-118-08835-7

Sports

Basketball For Dummies,
3rd Edition
978-1-118-07374-2

Football For Dummies,
2nd Edition
978-1-118-01261-1

Golf For Dummies,
4th Edition
978-0-470-88279-5

Test Prep

ACT For Dummies,
5th Edition
978-1-118-01259-8

ASVAB For Dummies,
3rd Edition
978-0-470-63760-9

The GRE Test For
Dummies, 7th Edition
978-0-470-00919-2

Police Officer Exam
For Dummies
978-0-470-88724-0

Series 7 Exam
For Dummies
978-0-470-09932-2

Web Development

HTML, CSS, & XHTML
For Dummies, 7th Edition
978-0-470-91659-9

Drupal For Dummies,
2nd Edition
978-1-118-08348-2

Windows 7

Windows 7
For Dummies
978-0-470-49743-2

Windows 7
For Dummies,
Book + DVD Bundle
978-0-470-52398-8

Windows 7 All-in-One
For Dummies
978-0-470-48763-1